Jonathan Scott

**Ferishta's History of Dekkan from the first Mahummedan Conquests**

Vol. 1

Jonathan Scott

**Ferishta's History of Dekkan from the first Mahummedan Conquests**
*Vol. 1*

ISBN/EAN: 9783743414709

Manufactured in Europe, USA, Canada, Australia, Japa

Cover: Foto ©ninafisch / pixelio.de

Manufactured and distributed by brebook publishing software (www.brebook.com)

Jonathan Scott

**Ferishta's History of Dekkan from the first Mahummedan Conquests**

*FERISHTA's*

# HISTORY OF DEKKAN,

FROM

THE FIRST MAHUMMEDAN CONQUESTS:

WITH

A CONTINUATION FROM OTHER NATIVE WRITERS, OF THE EVENTS IN THAT PART OF INDIA, TO THE REDUCTION OF ITS LAST MONARCHS BY THE EMPEROR AULUMGEER AURUNGZEBE:

ALSO,

THE REIGNS OF HIS SUCCESSORS IN THE EMPIRE OF HINDOSTAN TO THE PRESENT DAY:

AND

## *THE HISTORY OF BENGAL,*

FROM THE ACCESSION OF ALIVERDEE KHAN TO THE YEAR 1780.

*COMPRISED IN SIX PARTS.*

———

BY JONATHAN SCOTT,

CAPTAIN IN THE EAST INDIA COMPANY'S SERVICE, PERSIAN SECRETARY TO THE LATE GOVERNOR GENERAL, WARREN HASTINGS, ESQ. AND MEMBER OF THE ASIATIC SOCIETY IN CALCUTTA.

———

TWO VOLUMES.
VOL. I.

———

SHREWSBURY:
PRINTED BY J. AND W. EDDOWES,
FOR JOHN STOCKDALE, PICCADILLY, LONDON,
1794.

TO THE HONOURABLE
## THE CHAIRMAN AND COURT OF DIRECTORS
## OF THE EAST INDIA COMPANY,

THIS ATTEMPT

TO ADD TO THE PUBLICK STOCK OF HINDOOSTAN HISTORY,

IS, BY THEIR PERMISSION, MOST HUMBLY DEDICATED;

IN GRATITUDE FOR THAT LIBERAL PATRONAGE,

WHICH THE TRANSLATOR HAS RECEIVED

FROM THAT HONOURABLE BODY,

EVER FORWARD TO REWARD

ANY EFFORTS OF THEIR SERVANTS TO MERIT

THE ENCOURAGEMENT OF

THE HONOURABLE COMPANY,

BY

THEIR FAITHFUL AND

MOST OBEDIENT HUMBLE SERVANT,

JONATHAN SCOTT.

SHREWSBURY,
1st JAN. 1794.

# PREFACE.

IT is hoped that this attempt to make known the native history of a country, which was the first scene of our consequence in India, of the gallant exploits of General LAWRENCE, Lord CLIVE, Sir EYRE COOTE, and, very lately, the field of most important and successful operation to Britain under Marquis CORNWALLIS, will not be wholly unacceptable. The earlier transactions of our countrymen in Dekkan have already been amply detailed, by the elegant pens of a CAMBRIDGE and an ORME. Dr. THOMSON, in his Memoirs of the War in Asia, has done justice to the skill and gallantry of Sir EYRE COOTE and his deserving followers, who, supported by the active zeal of the virtuous but yet suffering HASTINGS, (posterity will most certainly venerate his character, for prejudice will in time give place to judgment) saved our part of Dekkan to the British empire.

Our late successes have been shortly narrated by Major DIROM, who had a share in the toils of the two campaigns; and,

PREFACE.

and, I have heard, that his and other able pens are employed in preparing a fuller detail of British transactions in Dekkan. Of that country I only profess to give the native accounts from its own writers; which will, I hope, at least gratify the curiosity of those who wish to learn the former state of this part of India, and fill up a chasm in history.

FERISHTA, author of the history now offered to the public in an English dress, is one of the most esteemed writers of Hindooftan, and was of noble rank, and high in office at the court of Ibrahim Adil Shaw, of Beejapore, one of the sultans of Dekkan.

Besides the \*History of the Dhely emperors, and this of Dekkan, FERISHTA compiled one of every province in India, and many complete copies of his works have been brought home by English gentlemen.

My first intention was to have published a literal translation; but, on revision, I thought it would be more pleasing to an English ear, deprived of some of the numerous hyperbolical epithets and too frequent conjunctions, which drew out the periods to a distracting length, hurtful to the sense in our language. This alone has been done; yet perhaps, some readers may still think the stile too oriental; but to have deviated farther from the original, would have been imposing a compilation for a translation.

To

\* Translated and published many years since by colonel Dow.

# PREFACE.

To thofe who have been in India, and are converfant with the hiftory and manners of the natives, fome of the notes may appear trivial: but every explanation is neceffary to render fatisfactory, to moft readers, the perufal of foreign idiom, cuftoms, and uncommon names. The laft I have endeavoured to write as pronounced in the country.

It is neceffary to mention, that from page 400 to the end of the Nizam Shawee dynafty, is not taken from FERISHTA, his work concluding with the fall of Ahmednuggur. What follows, was from a work written by Shaw-nowauz Khan, a nobleman of Dekkan, entitled, Maffer al Amra, or Biography of Nobles.

In his account of the Golconda Princes, FERISHTA was fo very brief, that, as he mentioned no more than what was contained in the Lub al Towareekh, an abbreviated hiftory of Hindooftan, I had recourfe only to the latter work; but it was thought inconvenient for fo few pages to alter the running title of the volume. Had the moft earneft fearch after fuller materials for the hiftory of Golconda been fuccefsful, my readers fhould have had a fuller account of the princes of that fovereignty.

# INTRODUCTION.

DEKKAN, or the southern division of [a] Hindooftan, called by European geographers, The Peninfula, has varied in boundary, at different periods, with the poffeffions of its rulers in adjacent provinces. Khandefhe, and part of Malwa, now comprized in it by the natives, feem not to have been fo, till the late conquefts of the Mharattas; fince which, Dekkan has been confidered by them to, comprehend all the countries from the fouthern banks of the river Nerbudda to Guzarat, which province is alfo chiefly dependant upon it.

---

[a] I have called Dekkan the fouthern divifion of Hindooftan, becaufe I believe the natives underftand it in that fenfe; and when it is confidered, that the Hindoo religion is that of the Aborigines, and has been fo, as far as tradition can carry us, and that the natives with little (if any to common vifitors) variation, are the fame in modes and character throughout the vaft tract to which the term Hindooftan has been applied; alfo, that the moft early accounts of the Hindoos mention all the provinces which European geographers include in the maps of Hindooftan, as being under the fovereignty of one Hindoo Maharaja; the term, I think, cannot be improper. Hindooftan, or Country of Hindoos, is a Perfian appellation, but adopted for ages back by the natives themfelves. Formerly, according to Mr. Wilkins, the firft proficient in the Sanfcrit, or moft ancient language of India, it was called Bharata, which term is now difufed, except in the facred books of the bramins.

INTRODUCTION.

When the Bhamenee fultans, whofe hiftory is the fubject of the following pages, ruled Dekkan, it was underftood to confift of that tract bounded from North Weft to North Eaft by Guzarat, Khandefhe, that part of Berar called Nagpore, and the province of Oriffa; on the South and Eaft by the Bay of Bengal; and on the Weft by the Indian ocean; a region, according to the computation of Major RENNELL, in his lately publifhed and very valuable Map and Memoir of Hindooftan, equal to the Britifh iflands, Spain, and Turky in Europe.

Prior to the Mahummedan conquefts of Dekkan, we have little information refpecting its hiftory. FERISHTA traditionally (and we have unfortunately no better authority) writes, that Dekkan took its prefent name from ᵃ Dekkan, the fon of Hind, fon of Ham, the fon of Noah. ᵇ Mheerut, ᶜ Kuzz, and ᵈ Telinga, his fons, gave their names to three divifions of Dekkan. With any Hindooeh accounts of Dekkan I am unacquainted.

According to FERISHTA's tradition, Kifhen, fon of Poorub, fon of Hind, ruled the whole of the countries now called by Europeans The Eaft Indies, China excepted. In the reign of Maharauje, his fucceffor, the zemindars of Carnatic and Ceylon rebelled, and difplaced his governor

---

ᵃ The Hindoos claim a much higher antiquity than Ferifhta allows them. Their origin, like that of all nations, is involved in obfcurity; to clear up which is vain, and can only reward fearch by materials for conjecture, which, however ingenious, can never fatisfy the enquirer. From what authority Ferifhta gives his tradition of the peopling of Dekkan, I know not.

ᵇ Modern Mheerut is a diftrict of the province of Dowlutabad, to which it probably gave the name fome ages back, if not to a larger divifion of Dekkan and the original country of the Mharattas.

ᶜ Called now Carnatic.

ᵈ Now the province of Golconda, but formerly an extenfive kingdom, firft under Hindoo princes, and afterwards a principal divifion of the Bhamenee fovereignty, upon the fall of which it became again a monarchy, under the dynafty of Koottub Shawee, whofe hiftory will be given in the proper place.

# INTRODUCTION.

governor of Dekkan, but were reduced by his general Baul Chund. On the death of Maharauje they again revolted from his succeffor Keelorauje, who compelled them to fubmiffion, with the affiftance of an army fent to his fupport by Manochere, emperor of Perfia, under Saum Nereeman, grandfather to the celebrated Rooftum, the hero of Ferdofi's Shaw Nammeh, or Hiftory of ancient Perfia.

Dekkan was afterwards divided into feveral ftates: Kool Chund founded the city and government of ᵃ Koolburga; Raja Mere Chund that of ᵇ Meruch; and Beejah Chund the kingdom of Beejanuggur, the moft celebrated in ᶜ Dekkan. Raja Bieder, the founder of a ᵈ city of that name, reigned over part of Dekkan when Alexander invaded

---

ᵃ Called by Europeans Calburga, now of little note.

ᵇ Now the capital of a Mharatta jaghiredar, fituated, according to Rennell, about one hundred and thirty miles South Weft from Poonah, the metropolis of the Mharatta ftates.

ᶜ Called in moft maps Bifnagar and Nerfinga. This kingdom, before the conquefts of the muffulmauns, comprehended the whole of Carnatic, which then extended over the greateft part of the peninfula from coaft to coaft (Coromandel and Malabar) as will be feen in the progrefs of the Bhamenꞌe fovereigns. According to Ferihhta, the city of Beejanuggur, the capital of this ancient monarchy, in the early days of muffulmaun invafion, was founded by Raja Bellaul Deo, A. D. 1344, and named after his fon Beejah Roy. He does not mention the more ancient metropolis of Carnatic. Major Rennell in his Memoir fays, Beejanuggur is fituated near the weftern bank of the Tummedra or Tungebadra river, about thirty miles fouth-eaft or fouth-fouth eaft from Bancapore, and one hundred and thirty German miles from Goa. It was a large city when vifited by Cæfar Frederick, A. D. 1567. The fall of this kingdom will be feen in its proper place.

ᵈ Called by moft Europeans Beder. According to Rennell, it is about eighty miles to the north-weft of Hyderabad, the capital of the Nizam, who poffeffes it at prefent. Near the ruins of Bieder, Ahmed Shaw Bhamenꞌe founded the city of Ahmedabad, which he made his capital in place of Koolburga, and this is the modern Bieder or Beder. There is another Ahmedabad, called moft commonly Ahmednuggur, and founded by Ahmed Shaw, the firft of the Nizam Shawee fovereigns, of whom a hiftory will be given. There is alfo a third Ahmedabad, the capital of the province of Guzarat.

## INTRODUCTION.

invaded India, and sent him presents to obtain his favour. Saulbahun, a raja of Dekkan, slew in action the prince of Malwa, Bickermajeet, recorded by the Hindoo tradition as an example for sovereigns, and whose reign forms the æra of the modern Hindoo computation.

Nothing more respecting Dekkan is mentioned by FERISHTA, till, in his account of the reign of the Patan emperor of Dhely, Jellaul ad Dien Firose Shaw, he says, that monarch sent his son in law Alla ad Dien to reduce it to his authority.

In the year 1295 of our æra, Alla ad Dien marched through Berar to Deoghur, now called Dowlutabad, from the raja of which he gained an immense plunder. Ramdeo, it appears, was only sovereign of a part of Dekkan, as the rajas of Koolburga and Raujemundree, (the latter district at present forming only one of our nothern sirkaurs, dependant on Madrass) are stiled by FERISHTA, Independant Princes.

Alla ad Dien on his accession to the throne of Dhely, which he acquired by the assassination of Firose Shaw, in the year 1306 sent an army to demand tribute from the raja of Deoghur. His general Mallek Naib, after reducing that fortress and the territory of Meerhut, carried the raja Ramdeo prisoner to Dhely; from whence he obtained leave to return to Dekkan and had a jaghire conferred on him by the emperor.

In 1309, Alla ad Dien sent an army by way of Bengal to reduce Warunkul, the capital of Telingana, but without success; upon which he dispatched a reinforcement under Mallek Naib, who obliged the raja Ludderdeo to become tributary to the sultan, and exacted from him a contribution of money and jewels to a vast amount, besides three hundred elephants and seven hundred horses.

The

## INTRODUCTION.

The year following, Mallek Naib invaded Carnatic, took the [a] raja Bellaul Deo prisoner, and pushed his depredations as far as [b] Seet Bunder Rameſſar, where he erected a moſque. The booty acquired in this expedition was immenſe, and next to incredible. He invaded Dekkan again in 1312, put to death the ſon of the raja of Deoghur, and obliged Telingana and Carnatic to become tributary to the throne of Dhely.

In 1316, Herpaul Deo, ſon to the raja of Deoghur, rebelled, and forced the muſſulmauns to relinquiſh ſeveral diſtricts in Meerhut; but was afterwards reduced, taken priſoner, and flayed alive by the Dhely emperor, Mubaric Shaw, who made conſiderable conqueſts in Dekkan.

In the ſucceeding reign, Ludder Deo, raja of Warunkul, and the raja of Deoghur, rebelled, but were ſubdued by Aligh Khan, who took the fortreſſes of Bieder and Warunkul, with the families of the rebels. In 1324, Aligh Khan ſucceeded his father Gheauſe ad Dien as emperor of Dhely, and aſſumed the title of Mahummud Tughluk Shaw. He fixed on Deoghur, which he renamed Dowlutabad, as his capital, and obliged the inhabitants of Dhely to remove to it; but afterwards relinquiſhed it. His reign proved unfortunate, ſeveral provinces being wreſted from him by rebellious nobles, who aſſumed royalty; and Dekkan was then formed into the ſovereignty, the hiſtory of which is the ſubject of the following pages.

[a] Probably the ſame who afterwards founded Beejanuggur.
[b] A port on the Coromandel coaſt, oppoſite to the iſland of Ceylon, and a celebrated place of Hindoo pilgrimage.

# TRANSLATION

OF

# *FERISHTA*'s
## HISTORY OF DEKKAN.

# SULTAN 'ALLA AD DIEN

# HOUSSUN KANGOH BHAMENEE,

FOUNDER OF

## THE BHAMENEE DYNASTY

OF

## *DEKKAN SOVEREIGNS.*

L ET it not remain concealed from the explorers of antiquity, that hiſtorians, in their accounts of the origin and progreſs of ſultan Alla ad Dien, are varying and contradictory. The moſt probable and generally believed, I have, avoiding prolixity, drawn as briefly as poſſible into the circle of narration.

Houſſun was an inhabitant of Dhely, and dependant on Kangoh, a bramin and aſtrologer, high in the favour of the [b] prince Mahummud Tughluk Shaw. It is ſaid, that he laboured under the greateſt poverty. Upon his requeſting ſome employment from the bramin, he gave him a pair of oxen, with two labourers, to cultivate a piece of

---

[a] The exalter of the faith of Mahummud.
[b] Son of the emperor Gheauſe ad Dien, whom he ſucceeded on the throne of Dhely, A. D. 1321.

of waste ground near the city, the produce of which he added to his former allowance.

As the labourers were one day at work, the plough stuck in some hard body, and Houssun, upon examination, found it was entangled in a chain round the neck of an earthen vessel, which proved to be full of antique gold coins. He immediately carried them to the bramin, who commended his honesty, and informed the prince of the discovered treasure. The circumstance being communicated to the emperor Gheause ad Dien, he ordered Houssun to the presence, and conferred upon him the command of one hundred horse.

It is also related, that the bramin assured Houssun, he saw from his stars that he would rise to exalted fortune, and be eminently favoured by providence. He therefore requested, when the Almighty should have bestowed royalty upon him, that he would add the name of Kangoh to his own, and appoint him his minister of finance, in order that he might share with him in immortal fame. Houssun readily complied with the requests of his kind patron. It is said also, that his future dignity was prophesied by the venerable [a] Shekh Nizam ad Dien Oulea. From these assurances, the ambition of reigning in Dekkan, the promised land of empire, possessed the mind of Houssun, and he ardently sought for some establishment in that country, that he might gradually attain the jewel of his desires.

When sultan Mahummud Tughluk had acceded to the throne of Dhely, he, in one of his expeditions to Dekkan, appointed his tutor Kuttullugh Khan governor of Dowlutabad, and gave permission to such officers as were under his patronage to serve with him. Houssun, thinking this an opportunity favourable to his views, embraced

---

[a] A celebrated Mahummedan saint, whose tomb near Dhely is still much venerated, and resorted to in pilgrimage by the mussulmauns of Hindoostan. The translator has not given the circumstances of the saint's prophecy at large, thinking they would be tedious to the reader.

braced the service of Kuttullugh Khan, and obtained from him in jaghire the town of Konechee, with lands dependant on the district of \* Roy-Baugh.

Some years after this, sultan Mahummud Tughluk drew his armies against the refractory nobles of Guzarat, who were defeated, and many of them took refuge in Dekkan; where Kuttullugh Khan, contrary to his duty and the royal commands, entertained them in his service: upon which, the sultan determined to remove him, and all the nobility, to other provinces. With this view, he dispatched a firmaun by Ahmed Lacheen and other officers to Allum al Moolk, commanding him to send the Dekkan officers to Guzarat.

Allum al Moolk, in obedience to the royal orders, sent messengers to summon the persons mentioned in the firmaun from the several stations; but some months elapsed before they were all collected at Dowlutabad. At length they arrived, and having received their dismission, departed with Ahmed Lacheen for Guzarat. Ahmed had entertained hopes of obtaining from them valuable presents, for his interest in their favour with the sultan; but being disappointed, treated them haughtily; and remarked to his attendants, that the Dekkan officers deserved death, for harbouring the rebellious nobility of Guzarat, and neglecting so long the royal summons to the presence. The amras, hearing of his opinions, were alarmed for their safety; and, upon their arrival on the frontiers of Dekkan, held a council among themselves how to act. It was remarked, that the sultan frequently punished with death the slightest offences, and often without examining an accusation; so that it would be safer for them to remain by force in Dekkan, than give themselves up tamely like sheep to the slaughterer.

Their resolve being taken, they began their retreat from the frontiers; and Ahmed Lacheen, attempting to oppose them, was defeated,

\* Now belonging to the Nizam.

defeated, and slain with many of his followers. They were now joined daily by numbers of the disaffected, and repaired towards Dowlutabad in great force. The native princes of Dekkan, injured and disgusted by the tyranny of the sultan, rejoiced at this revolt; in which some of them personally joined, and others, more circumspect, privately assisted with money and supplies. An insurrection arose, which the hand of conciliation could not quell. Justly does a celebrated poet observe, "The subject, when oppressed by injustice, "turns from his prince in the crisis of danger; for, when a ruler is "tyrannical, his government cannot continue to flourish." Ummaud al Moolk, son in law to the sultan, governor of Berar and Khandeshe, who resided at ᵃ Elichpore, finding himself daily deserted by numbers of his troops, and fearing his officers would finally deliver him to the rebels, left the city with his family, under pretence of hunting, and retired into ᵇ Nudderbar; upon which the nobles of Berar, having plundered the royal treasury, proceeded to join the malecontents near Dowlutabad. The garrison of this fortress, observing the gathering force of the rebels, thought proper to seek their friendship: they seized their governor, and delivered up the place. Thus, in a few months, departed from the yoke of the Dhely emperors their dominion in Dekkan, which had been conquered in a long series of war, and at a vast expense of blood and treasure.

Upon the acquisition of Dowlutabad, the allied amras agreed to elect from among themselves a sovereign, that their operations might receive dignity and order, when the lot of empire fell on Ismaeel, an Afghaun ameer of ᶜ one thousand, whose brother, Mallek

---

ᵃ The ancient capital of Berar, now subject to the Nizam, who pays a tribute from the revenues to the Mharatta state.

ᵇ A small district between Khandeshe and Guzarat, now in possession of the Mharattas.

ᶜ In Hindoostan the rank of nobility is estimated according to military command, and the number of cavalry mentioned in the patent of creation; as, "We have "exalted

Mallek Moogh, commanded the imperial army in the province of Malwa. In the hopes that he would assist his brother, the amras of Dekkan elected Ismaeel their sultan, by the title of ' Nasir ad Dien. Honours were bestowed, and each ameer gratified with a portion of the lands of the new sovereignty; when Houssun received the title of ᵇ Zuffir Khan, and some districts in jaghire for the support of his dignity and troops.

Sultan Mahummud Tughluk Shaw, on this alarming crisis of his affairs, hastened with an army from Guzarat to Dekkan, and was joined by ᶜ Ummaud al Moolk Tibreezee, and Mallek Moogh governor of Malwa. On his arrival near Dowlutabad, the newly elected sultan quitted the fortress, and encamped with thirty thousand horse, on the same plain where Alla ad Dien had defeated the son of Ramdeo, raja of Deoghur. The rebels charged vigorously, and routed the two wings of the imperialists; so that sultan Mahummud was even preparing to fly, when suddenly the curse of disloyalty fell upon them. Khan Jehaun, one of the principal rebel chiefs, being wounded by an arrow, fell from his horse, upon which his followers, about six thousand, turned their faces to flight; and at the same instant, the standard bearer of Nasir ad Dien, being struck with a panic, let the colours fall from his hands. The rebels, supposing their chief had forsaken them, desisted from the fight; and night falling, retired to their camp. Sultan Mahummud did the same, and both armies observed the strictest vigilance. Nasir ad Dien, and Zuffir Khan, with the principal rebel chiefs, held a council, in which it was agreed, as it was not safe for the present to hazard another contest in the field, that the new sultan should retire to Dowlutabad

" exalted such a person to such titles, and the command of so many thousand horse, " with the privilege of using such and such insignia and ornaments to his palanquin."
ᵃ Promoter of the faith.
ᵇ Victorious.
ᶜ Pillar of the state.

Dowlutabad with a proper garrifon; while the amras fhould protect their own diftricts, harafs the enemy's convoys, and cut off fupplies. This being concluded on, the rebels filently decamped to their feveral ftations, fo that at daylight fultan Mahummud faw not a veftige of his late oppofers. Upon this, he difpatched a force under Ummaud al Moolk Tibreezee, to purfue Zuffir Khan, and prepared to befiege Dowlutabad. The garrifon was nearly reduced to defpair, when intelligence arrived of the infurrection of the Dhellians, under a flave named Tughee; who, with a body of difaffected rabble, was committing great enormities in the capital, and threatened the provinces, efpecially Guzarat. Sultan Mahummud upon this quitted the camp to the care of his generals, and haftened to quell the infurgents. The Dekkan amras, encouraged by his abfence, collected from all parts; and the befiegers being alarmed, retreated foon after their fovereign. They were clofely preffed by the Dekkanees as far as the banks of the Nirbudda, and loft much baggage, with feveral of the imperial elephants laden with gold.

Zuffir Khan, emboldened by this fuccefs, marched with twenty thoufand horfe to [a] Bieder, where Ummaud al Moolk Tibreezee was ftationed; but did not for fome time venture to engage him, as the latter was much fuperior in the number of his troops, and ftrongly pofted. At length Zuffir Khan, being joined by fifteen thoufand men, fent by the raja of Telingana, and five thoufand horfe, detached to his affiftance by Nafir ad Dien from Dowlutabad, attacked the imperial general. The action lafted from daylight till the fun began to decline, with the greateft obftinacy on both fides. At length, the Almighty difpofer of kingdoms having decreed that Zuffir Khan fhould be exalted to the dominion of Dekkan, and the ring of empire grace his hand, Ummaud al Moolk was flain, and his army

---

[a] Formerly the capital of a raja of this name, and afterwards of the Bhamenee fovereigns; now in poffeffion of the Nizam and Mharattas jointly.

army routed. Many of the fugitives took shelter in Bieder, others in ᵃ Candahar, and some few retired with difficulty to Malwa.

Zuffir Khan, immediately on his victory, detached Mallek ᵇ Syef ad Dien Ghoree to reduce Bieder and Candahar, while he marched himself with the trophies and plunder gained from the enemy to Dowlutabad; at some distance from which he was met by Nasir ad Dien, who, observing that greater attention was paid by the nobility and army to the general than himself, and that they wished him for their sovereign, judged it prudent to retire to a more private station. Calling an assembly of the amras, he declared himself from his great age incapable of governing, and requested they would elect a new sultan; observing, that Zuffir Khan, on whose aspect shone the rays of dignity and valour, seemed to him most worthy of the throne. The assembly with one voice applauded his remark, and the astrologers were directed to explore a fortunate instant for the inauguration of Zuffir Khan. Accordingly, in a chosen hour on Friday, the 24th of Rubbee al Akhir, they placed the crown of empire on his head, and spread over his throne a black umbrella, the colour of the Abasside caliphs, as auspicious. The ᶜ Khootbah, was read in his name, and coins struck, impressed with his titles of Sultan Alla ad Dien Houssun Kangoh Bhamenee. ᵈ Koolburga, his residence, was newly named ᵉ Ahssunabad, and chosen for the capital of the mussulmauns in Dekkan.

A. H. 748.
A. D. 1347.

C          Sultan

---

ᵃ A fortress not far distant from Bieder. There is another so called on the northern frontier of Hindoostan.

ᵇ The Sword of the Faith.

ᶜ A form of prayer, or benediction, used by the Mahummedans on Fridays and festivals, for the souls of all deceased prophets and kings, and for the welfare of their reigning sovereign.

ᵈ Now belonging to the Nizam, under a tribute to the Mharattas, called by European geographers Calberga.

ᵉ Most excellent abode. It is the superlative of the sultan's appellation of Houssun.

Sultan Alla ad Dien, having engaged in the charge of government, neglected none of the duties of royalty, so that the tract of his dominions was daily extended. The countries from the ᵃ river Beemrah to the vicinity of the fortress of ᵇ Roodnee, and from the port of ᶜ Choule to the city of Bieder, were brought within the circle of his possession. It is related, that his first royal act was the distribution of four hundred pounds weight of gold, and one thousand of silver, in charitable donations, in memory of Nizam ad Dien Oulea, who had predicted his rising fortunes. Mallek Syef ad Dien Ghoree, distinguished for his integrity, judgment, and policy, was appointed prime minister, and the resigned sovereign, who had reassumed his original name of Ismaeel, honoured with the title of ᵈ ameer al amra. Mindful of his promise to his former patron, the sultan entrusted the care of his treasury to the bramin Kangoh, who had quitted the service of the emperor Mahummud Tughluk Shaw, and repaired to Dekkan. His name was also affixed to all royal edicts, and joined to that of the sultan.

It is universally allowed, that Kangoh was the first bramin who accepted an office in the service of a mussulmaun prince. Before him, the bramins never condescended to engage in publick affairs, but passed their lives in the duties of religion, and study of the sciences; indifferent to fortune, and esteeming the service of princes as hurtful to virtue, and hazardous to their eternal welfare. If, as physicians, astronomers, moralists, or historians, they sometimes associated with the rich or powerful, they yet would never wear the chain of servitude on their necks, though courted by gifts and high favours. However, since Kangoh's acceptance of employment, the

direction

---

ᵃ A principal branch of the Kistnah river. According to Ferishta, it is also called Bewrah. Rennell writes it Beernah.
ᵇ I do not find this place in any map under this name.
ᶜ On the Malabar coast, not very far south of Bombay.
ᵈ Chief of the nobles.

direction of finance has been committed generally to bramins, by all the princes of Dekkan.

Sultan Alla ad Dien, as well by wise policy as force of arms, towards the end of the reign of Mahummud Tughluk Shaw, subdued every part of Dekkan which had been subject to the throne of Dhely, and gained over by conciliating measures the Afghaun, Mogul, and Raajepoote chiefs, stationed by the emperor at Bieder and Candahar, which were delivered up. He took ᵃKolaufs with its dependancies from the roy of ᵇWarunkul, and formed with him a treaty of alliance. The death of the emperor Mahummud Tughluk Shaw in 752, removing all apprehensions of attack from Dhely, the sultan engaged earnestly in the internal regulation and security of his dominions, and celebrated the marriage of his eldest son Mahummud with the daughter of Mallek Syef ad Dien Ghoree. On this occasion he distributed ten thousand robes of cloth of gold, velvet and sattin among the nobility and others. One thousand Arab and Persian horses, and two hundred sabres set with jewels, were also divided. The populace were entertained with various amusements, and engines were erected in the streets of Koolburga, which cast forth showers of confectionary among the crowd. The rejoicings lasted a whole year; on the last day of which, the nobility and officers presented offerings of jewels, money, and the rarest productions of all countries, to the sultan.

A.D. 1351.

As Mallek Syef ad Dien Ghoree was honoured by the royal alliance, his place in publick assemblies was allotted above those of all the nobility, which gave offence to the ameer al amra, who complained of the precedence to the sultan, and was answered, that in every government the pen took rank of the sword. He became seemingly

---

ᵃ A town in Telingana.
ᵇ The ancient capital of Telingana. The province is now called Golconda.

seemingly satisfied with the royal orders; but secretly conspired with some disaffected nobles to assassinate the sultan, and resume the throne he had given up. As his designs were not favoured by providence, the sultan had timely information of them, from persons who had joined in the plot, but had repented. Having convened all the nobles and eminent officers of the court, he, in their presence, accused the ameer al amra of treachery, which he denied by a solemn oath. The sultan then called forth the informers, and offered pardon to all the conspirators who would reveal the crimes of the ameer al amra; upon which most of his associates testified against him, so that no doubt remained of his guilt, and he was immediately put to death. His relations and adherents were pardoned, nor was the smallest confiscation made of their property; but \* Bahadur Khan, son to the deceased, was appointed ameer al amra, and the royal favour extended, as before, on the family.

From this, and other instances of justice tempered with mercy, loyalty to the sultan became fixed in every breast, and his power daily encreased. The roy of Telingana, who had become disobedient, but was treated with generous forbearance on account of former assistance to the sultan, was overcome by the sense of his virtues, submitted to his authority, and agreed to pay the tribute he had heretofore remitted to the sovereign of Dhely.

Sultan Alla ad Dien, by advice of Mallek Syef ad Dien Ghoree, dispatched a considerable force against the country of Carnatic, from whence his general returned successful, with valuable contributions from several roies in money and jewels, besides two hundred elephants, and one thousand female singers. Having received an invitation from roy Perrun, the representative of the ancient rajas of Guzarat, to invade that country, (which owing to the weakness of the Dhely emperors, was become a prey to rebellious jaghiredars,) sultan

\* Valiant.

sultan Alla ad Dien, in the month of Shauban, 758, took the field A.D. 1356. in person. The prince Mahummud was advanced in front with twenty thousand horse, while the sultan followed, by easier marches, with the main army. The prince arriving at [a] Nosaree, found the country abounding in game, of which he sent an account to his father, who was eagerly fond of the chase and falconry. The sultan advanced with expedition, and spent nearly a month in the pleasures of the field; at the end of which he was attacked by an intermitting fever; and, not using proper caution in refraining from violent exercise and high living, his disorder encreased to an alarming illness, which obliged him to return hastily to Koolburga. Upon his arrival at the capital, he convened the divines and holy men, in whose presence he vowed to abstain in future from all things forbidden by the law of the Koraun. Arranging his dominions in four principal governments, he conferred that of the capital and its dependancies, to [b] Dabul, Beejore, and Mudkul, on Mallek Syef ad Dien Ghoree; Choule, Khiber, Dowlutabad, and Mheeroputtun, with the territory of Mheerut, he committed to Mahummud, son of his brother Ali Shaw; Mahoor, Ramgeer, and his division of Berar, were entrusted to Kusder Khan Syestaunee; and Bieder, Indour, with Kolauss, and the possessions in Telingana, to Azim Humaioon, son of Mallek Syef ad Dien Ghoree.

The sultan remained six months in a declining state; during which he gave publick audience twice a day, and transacted business; assiduously engaging in administering justice to the poor and friendless. He gave orders to release all prisoners throughout his dominions, except

[a] A town and district on the the banks of the Teena. Rennell calls it Bhousenee. It belongs now to the Nizam.
[b] All the places mentioned in this disposition are now in possession of the Nizam, subject to a contribution of a fourth part of the revenues to the Mharatta state; Dabul excepted, a small port near Bombay and Choule, which are held wholly by the latter. From the division of his kingdom it appears, that Alla ad Dien possessed what is now called the Nizam's country, and a considerable part of Kokun.

except those accused of capital offences, whom he commanded to Koolburga; and having himself examined them, set at liberty all but seven, whom he delivered to his son Mahummud, that, after his death he might act towards them as he should judge proper. At length, finding no benefit from medicine, and feeling nature exhausted, he discharged his physicians, and waited patiently the final cure of human ills. In this state, enquiring of his youngest son, Mhamood, who had been reading with his tutor, what book he had that day perused, the prince replied, the ᵃ Bosetaun of ᵇ Saadee, and the following passage:

" I have heard, that ᶜ Jumshede of angelic memory had these
" words engraved upon a fountain; Many, like me, have viewed
" this fountain, but they are gone, and their eyes closed for ever.
" I conquered the world by policy and valour; but could not over-
" come the grave."

The sultan sighed at the recital, and calling his sons Daood and Mahummud before him, said, " This is my last breath, and with it
" I conjure you, as ye value the permanence of the kingdom, to
" agree with each other. Mahummud is my successor; esteem
" submission and loyalty to him as your duty in this world, and your
" surety for happiness in the next." Having said this, he sent for his treasurer, and committed to each of his sons a sum of money to distribute to the poor. When they had obeyed him, and returned, he exclaimed, " Praise be to God!" and instantly resigned his life to the Creator. " Constantly appears some one who boasts, I am Lord,
" shows himself to his fellows, and vaunts, I am Lord. When the
" affairs of mortals have become dependant upon him, suddenly ad-
" vanceth death, and exclaimeth, I am Lord." The death of sultan Alla ad Dien happened eleven years, two months, and seven days

after

---

ᵃ A Garden.
ᵇ A celebrated Persian poet.
ᶜ An ancient emperor of Persia.

after his acceſſion to royalty, and on the firſt of Rubbee al Awul, 759, in the ſixty ſeventh year of his age.

A. D. 1357.

It is related, that ſultan Alla ad Dien being aſked how, without great treaſures or armies, he had acquired royalty in ſo ſhort a ſpace? replied, By affability to friends and enemies, and ſhowing liberality to all, to the utmoſt of his power. Some authors write, that he was deſcended from Bhamen, one of the ancient kings of Perſia; and I have ſeen a pedigree of him, ſo derived, in the royal library of Ahmednuggur: but am inclined to believe, ſuch lineage was only framed upon his acceſſion to royalty, by flatterers and poets, and that his origin was too obſcure to be authentically traced. The appellation of ᵃ Bhamenee, he certainly took in compliment to Kangoh Bramin, which is often pronounced Bhamen, and by tribe he was an Afghaun.

ᵃ Bhamenee is a very common corruption of Braminee in the vulgar pronunciation of Hindooſtan.

## SULTAN

## MAHUMMUD SHAW BHAMENEE.

WHEN sultan Mahummud spread over himself, like Solomon, the royal umbrella, he greatly encreased the magnificence and splendour of the court. He fixed a golden ball, set with jewels, on which was a bird of paradise composed of precious stones, at the top of the umbrella. On the bird's head was a ruby, inestimable in value, which had been presented to the late sultan by the roy of Beejanuggur. He added greatly to the train of his attendants, and divided the nobility and officers into four bands; appointing each a stated service and time of waiting. He formed a corps of bardars, whose employment was to muster the guards, and conduct persons to audience; also one of [a] two hundred youths, chosen among the sons of the nobility, to carry the royal armour and weapons; and instituted a [b] body guard of four thousand men, under the command of a nobleman of high rank, who was stiled meer nobut, or lord of the watch. Fifty sillehdars, and a thousand of the body guard, attended at the palace daily. Every day, except on Fridays, he gave publick audience early in the morning, and continued transacting business till the crier proclaimed noontide prayer, when the court broke up. Before he ascended the throne, he always prostrated himself before it, out of respect to the memory of his father. The throne was of silver, placed under a magnificent canopy, on a rich carpet; and the court before the hall of audience was shaded by an awning of velvet, brocade, or other superb manufacture. The governors of his provinces,

---

[a] They were called sillehdars, or arms-bearers, from their employment.
[b] This corps was named khauseh khiel, or select band.

vinces, he named terruffdars, or holders of a division. In the beginning of his reign, Mallek Syef ad Dien Ghoree enjoyed the distinction of sitting in the presence; but requesting to resign this privilege, he afterwards stood, like the other nobles. The nobut, or band of music, played five times daily, at stated hours; and all persons, when introduced to the sultan, knelt and prostrated their foreheads to the ground. After the dissolution of the house of Bhamenee, the succeeding princes used the umbrella and khootbah; but none struck coins of gold in their own name, or founded the nobut five times, except the sultans of Golconda, stiled Koottub Shawee.

The gold and silver coins of the Bhamenee sultans were of square form and different value, having on one side the [a] creed of testimony and the names of [b] the four holy friends. On the other was the sovereign's title and year of his reign. The Hindoo bankers, at the instigation of the roies of Beejanuggur and Telingana, melting all which fell into their hands, that the coins of the infidels might alone be current in Dekkan, the sultan was enraged; and when they persisted in the offence in spite of his remonstrances, he put all the guilty to death, and restrained the business of exchange to some Kutteries, descendants of Dhellians, who had migrated to Dekkan. After this, the Bhamenee coins alone were current in the Mahummedan dominions; but since the cessation of that dynasty, the coins of the Hindoo princes have been allowed also to pass universally.

In the beginning of the reign of sultan Mahummud Shaw, the roies of Beejanuggur and Telingana demanded from him the territories which had been wrested from them by his father, threatening, in case of refusal, to invade his country, and draw upon him the armies of Dhely. As he was not sure of the attachment of part of his nobility, and his treasury was low, owing to the great sums

D which

---

[a] There is no god but God, and Mahummud is his prophet.
[b] Mahummud, Ali, Aboubekker, Omar.

which he had given to his mother, Mallek'eh Jehaun, who had gone on pilgrimage to Mecca, Medina, and Kerballa, he, during a year and half, kept the ambassadors of the roies at his court, and sent his own to Beejanuggur, to amuse his enemies. In this period he displaced such officers as he suspected, and, his mother being returned, resolved on war, and demanded from the roies all their best elephants laden with jewels, gold, and the most precious manufactures of Dekkan.

The roy of Telingana, upon this, sent his son Nagdeo with an army towards Kolaufs, and the roy of Beejanuggur dispatched a considerable force to join his ally, who was quickly defeated by the troops of Mahummud Shaw, under Bahadur Khan; and that general, having plundered all the country to the vicinity of Warunkul, obliged the roy to pay a contribution of a large sum of money, twenty five elephants, and many valuable effects, which he presented to the sultan at Koolburga.

A.D. 1371. Towards the end of the year 773, some merchants arriving from distant parts, offered horses to the sultan for sale, and he not approving them, observed, that they were unworthy of being presented to a prince; upon which the merchants said, they had lately possessed much finer, which they had intended to bring him, but they had been forced from them, at undervalue, by Nagdeo at \* Velumputtun, though they had signified to him that they were designed for the sultan.

Mahummud Shaw, already offended with Nagdeo, was resolved to revenge this fresh instance of disrespect, and, committing his affairs to the care of Mallek Syef ad Dien Ghoree, repaired immediately to his camp at Sultanpore. Here he continued ten days, to review the army, and receive the prayers of the venerable Mahummud Scrauje

ad

---

\* I don't know where. Perhaps Goa, or Rajapoore.

ad Dien Juneedee for fuccefs in his expedition. On the eleventh he began his march. On his arrival at Kallean, afking an attendant, to whom he allowed great freedom of fpeech, in what time he might reach Velumputtun, the wit replied, that if he continued his prefent fpeed, he might perhaps fee it in twelve months. The fultan, nettled at the repartee, immediately felected four thoufand horfe from his army, and proceeded with fuch rapidity, that in the fpace of a week he advanced near Velumputtun. He then ordered a band of veteran Afghauns to difguife themfelves in torn habits, and repair to the town, as horfedealers who had been plundered by robbers, in order to amufe the guards at the gates. The Afghauns, on their arrival at the town, were queftioned by the guards, and replied, that they were merchants who had been plundered by a numerous banditti not far from the place, and were come to implore protection and juftice from the governor. During this ftory, Mahummud Shaw rufhed on with a thoufand horfe, and the guards attempted to fhut the gates, but were prevented by the Afghauns, and flain. The fultan now entered the town, and commenced a flaughter of the inhabitants without mercy. Nagdeo, who expected nothing lefs than fuch an enemy, was engaged at an entertainment, and, on receiving the alarm, fled with precipitation to the citadel, which the fultan affaulted without delay; when the young roy, after a faint oppofition, tried to make his efcape by a poftern, but was taken prifoner in the city. In the morning he was queftioned by the fultan, why he had dared to feize horfes from merchants on their way to Koolburga? and making an infolent reply, Mahummud Shaw, who had before this refolved to fpare his life, commanded a pile of wood to be lighted before the citadel, and putting Nagdeo in an engine, had him fhot from the walls into the flames, in which he was confumed. The fultan remained fifteen days in the town, and, as his troops came up, encamped them without the gates, while he repofed from his fatigues, and indulged himfelf in pleafure with his favourites.

The sultan, having seized the treasures of Nagdeo, and levied a heavy contribution from the inhabitants, left Velumputtun, and returned towards his capital; but the Telingas, who had now collected in great force, surrounded him on all quarters, and so harassed his march, that he commanded his tents and baggage to be burnt, with all his plunder, except jewels and gold. Thus lightened, he moved in close order from dawn till nightfall every day, procuring from the villages he passed, such provisions as offered, and passing the night in strict vigilance, sleeping on his arms. With all these precautions, the enemy destroyed such numbers of his troops, in passes and woods, that of four thousand, only fifteen hundred men regained Koolburga. The sultan himself received a wound in his arm, and at Kolaufs was obliged to halt from indisposition. Here he was fortunately joined by Mallek Syef ad Dien Ghoree, with the main body of his army, when the Telingas were driven back to the heart of their own country with great slaughter, and several places taken from them; after which the sultan returned to Koolburga.

The roy of Telingana, enraged at the death of his son, sent petitions to the emperor Feerose Shaw of Dhely, acknowledging himself his vassal, and promising, if he would send a force, to act in conjunction with it, for the recovery of the imperial possessions in Dekkan, and pay also a considerable tribute. In this offer he was joined by his ally, the roy of Beejanuggur; but Feerose Shaw, being too much employed with domestic commotions to assist them, did not attend to their representations.

Mahummud Shaw, hearing of the proceedings of the roies, and the weakness of the court of Dhely, from his spies, resolved on the conquest of Telingana. Having again committed the charge of internal government to Mallek Syef ad Dien Ghoree, he marched to Kolaufs, from whence he detached Azim Humaioon, with the troops of Bieder, towards Golconda, and Suffder Khan, with those of Berar,

against

against Warunkul, towards which he followed in person by regular marches. The roy of Telingana, difappointed of affiftance from Dhely, declined engaging the royal army; and, retiring to the woods, fent fome of his chiefs with valuable prefents to Bahadur Khan, entreating his interceffion for peace, which the fultan at firft refufed. The roy then difpatched one of his fons to the royal camp, with declarations of fubmiffion; when Mahummud Shaw, at the earneft perfuafions of his nobility, confented to agree to fuch terms as Bahadur Khan fhould judge confiftent with the dignity of his ftate. It was fixed by him, that the roy fhould prefent to the fultan three hundred elephants, two hundred valuable horfes, and \* thirty three lacs of rupees, and that he fhould cede to him the city of Golconda with its dependancies.

As the fultan had been near two years living with his army in the country of Telingana, the roy was much diftreffed, and faw no relief, but in fulfilling the conditions. It was agreed that Mahummud Shaw fhould retreat from the country of Golconda, and that Bahadur Khan fhould remain at Kolaufs, to receive the offerings of the roy. Mahummud Shaw, having committed the city of Golconda to Azim Humaioon, returned towards his capital. From Bieder, where he halted three months, he difmiffed his nobility and their troops, to refrefh themfelves from their fatigues, into their feveral diftricts.

When the agents of the roy came to Kolaufs, Bahadur Khan conducted them to the fultan; who, when they had prefented the offerings agreeably to treaty, conferred upon them rich khelauts, valuable jewels, and fine horfes. Some days after this, the ambaffadors reprefented to Bahadur Khan, that if his majefty, fixing the boundaries of the ftate of their prince, would fign a treaty, binding his fucceffors to protect the roies of Telingana as their vaffals, they would

\* 33,000l.

would present him with a curiosity, worthy only to be laid at the feet of a great king.

Bahadur Khan having communicated their offers to the sultan, he was impatient to receive the promised gift; and the ambassadors, being introduced, repeated their promise. Mahummud Shaw, finding them sincere, drew up a paper in his own hand, fixing Golconda as the boundary between its kingdom and the roy's possessions, conjuring his successors, as long as the roies of Telingana should refrain from breaking their faith, not to molest them. The treaty, being ratified with his own seal and those of the judges and principal nobility, was given to the ambassadors. In performance of their promise, they presented to the sultan a throne set with valuable jewels, which had been prepared by the roy of Telingana some years before, and intended as a present to sultan Mahummud Tughluk Shaw of Dhely.

Mahummud Shaw was highly satisfied, and dismissed the ambassadors with great marks of honour and approbation. On his return to Koolburga, he made a great festival, and mounted this throne with much pomp and magnificence, calling it, Firozeh, or Cerulean. He conferred presents and honours on those who had merited his notice during the war. The silver throne of his father was ordered to be laid up in the treasury, as a valuable memorial.

I have heard some old persons, who saw the throne Firozeh in the reign of sultan Mhamood Bhamenee, describe it. They said, that it was in length nine feet, and three in breadth; made of ebony, covered with plates of pure gold, and set with precious stones of immense value. The jewels were so contrived, as to be taken off and put on with ease in a short time. Every prince of the house of Bhamenee, who possessed this throne, made a point of adding to it some rich stones; so that when, in the reign of sultan Mhamood, it

was

was taken to pieces, to remove fome of the jewels to be fet in vafes and cups, the jewellers valued it at one [a] corore of oons. I learned alfo, that it was called Firozeh, from being partly enamelled of a fky colour, which was in time totally concealed by the number of jewels.

This feftival lafted forty days; during which the ftrictnefs of religious law was laid afide. The nobility and people followed the example of the fovereign in feftivity and pleafure. At this time, a number of capital muficians, who had learnt the compofitions of ameer Khooffroo, and Khajah Houffun Dhelie, and fome of them heard thofe great mafters, came, attended by three hundred fingers, from Dhely to Koolburga. Mahummud Shaw, regarding their arrival at fuch a juncture as aufpicious, received them with much attention. One evening, in a felect affembly, he permitted Mallek Syef ad Dien Ghoree, and the [b] fuddur al fhereef, to fit at the foot of his throne; as alfo Bahadur Khan, on whom he conferred the title of ameer al amra, and afked his daughter in marriage for his fon, the prince Mujahid Shaw.

Moollah Daood Biederee, author of the Tofet al Sallateen, relates, that he was then twelve years of age, and feal-bearer to the king. He fays, that one evening, when the fpring of the garden of mirth had infufed the cheek of Mahummud Shaw with the rofy tinge of delight, a band of muficians fung two verfes of ameer Khooffroo in praife of kings, feftivity, and mufic. The fultan was delighted beyond meafure, and commanded Mallek Syef ad Dien Ghoree to give the three hundred performers a draft for a gratuity on the treafury of the roy of Beejanuggur. The minifter, though he judged the order the effect of wine, in compliance with the humour of the fultan, wrote it, but did not difpatch it. However, Mahummud Shaw

[a] Nearly four millions fterling.
[b] Chief magiftrate.

Shaw penetrated his thoughts. The next day, he enquired if the draft had been sent to the roy, and being anfwered, not, exclaimed, " Think you a word without meaning could efcape my lips? I did " not give the order in intoxication, but ferious defign." Mallek Syef ad Dien upon this affixed the royal feal to the draft, and difpatched it by exprefs meffengers to the roy of Beejanuggur. The roy, haughty and proud of his independance, placed the prefenter of the draft on an afs's back, and, parading him through all the quarters of Beejanuggur, fent him back with every mark of contempt and derifion. He alfo gave immediate orders for affembling his troops, and prepared to attack the dominions of the houfe of Bhamenee. With this intent he marched with thirty thoufand horfe, three thoufand elephants, and one hundred thoufand foot, to the vicinity of the fortrefs of [a] Oodnee; from whence he fent detachments to deftroy and lay wafte the country of the faithful.

Mahummud Shaw, as his troops in Bieder and Berar had not yet refted from the fatigues of a two years campaign, contented himfelf with calling, for the prefent, Khan Mahummud with the army from Dowlutabad. He fent his fon, the prince Mujahid Shaw, with a fifth part of the plunder of Velumputtun, to Shekh Mahummud Serauje ad Dien, to be diftributed to fyeds and holy men, afking their prayers for fuccefs againft the unbelievers. He called together all the religious of Koolburga, and, upon a Friday went, accompanied by them, to the grand mofque, where he pronounced, with much earneftnefs of heart, a form of invocation for the fuccefs of the army of Iflaam. He then fixed upon the lucky inftant of march, and ordered his camp to be pitched without the city.

The roy of Beejanuggur, by this time was, notwithftanding the rainy feafon and inundation of the Kiftna, arrived before the fortrefs of Mudkul, to which he laid fiege with much vigour. The garrifon,

---

[a] Now called Adoni, alfo Imtiauz Ghur, now poffeffed by Tippoo Saheb.

rison, consisting of six hundred men, of approved valour, left nothing undone for the defence of the place; but the governor, a relation of Mallek Syef ad Dien Ghoree, having imposed some severities on the troops, disaffection arose among them, and the officers grew neglectful of their duty. In consequence, the fort fell into the hands of the enemy, who, with a rancorous cruelty, put men, women, and children to the sword, without sparing any. One man only escaped; who brought intelligence of the capture to the sultan.

Mahummud Shaw, on hearing it, was seized with a transport of grief and rage, in which he commanded the unfortunate messenger to be instantly put to death; exclaiming, that he never could bear in his presence, a wretch, who could survive the sight of the slaughter of so many brave companions. The same day, without waiting for the junction of his whole army, (in the month of Jemmad al Awul, 767) he began his march, and took a solemn oath, that till he should have put to death one hundred thousand infidels, as an expiation for the massacre of the faithful, he would never sheath the sword of holy war, nor refrain from slaughter. When he reached the banks of the Kistna, he swore by the power who had created and exalted him to dominion, that eating or sleep should be unlawful for him, till he had crossed that river in face of the enemy, by the blessing of heaven routed their army, and gladdened the souls of the martyrs of Mudkul with the blood of their murderers. He then appointed his son Mujahid Shaw to succeed him, and Mallek Syef ad Dien regent of his kingdom. He resigned all his elephants, except twenty, to the prince, gave him his advice, and sent him back to Koolburga. He then crossed the river, with nine thousand chosen horse, without delay.

A.D. 1365.

The roy of Beejanuggur, notwithstanding his vast army, was so alarmed, that he sent off all his treasure, valuable baggage, and elephants towards his capital, intending to engage the next morning, or retreat, as he should find it adviseable.* The night being stormy and heavy rain falling, the elephants and other beasts of burthen stuck frequently in the mud, and were not able to advance above four miles from the camp. Mahummud Shaw heard of the enemy's movement during the night, and immediately marched towards them, leaving his encampment standing. Towards the dawn he arrived at the roy's camp, and the alarm being given, so great was the confusion, that the infidels fled with the utmost precipitation towards the fortress of Oodnee, leaving every thing behind them. Mahummud Shaw entered the camp of their market and baggage, putting all to death, without any distinction; and it is said, that the slaughter amounted to seventy thousand men, women, and children. According to the Tofet al Sallateen, two thousand elephants, three hundred pieces of cannon, seven hundred Arabian horses, and a * singhausen set with jewels, were included in the royal share of plunder. The rest of the effects were left to the officers and soldiers.

Sultan Mahummud, regarding this victory as the omen of others, after passing the rains near Mudkul, and being reinforced by Khan Mahummud from Dowlutabad, marched against the infidels towards Oodnee; in the plains of which, on the banks of the Tummedra, the roy of Beejanuggur had taken up his station in his own territories; having given the command of Oodnee to his sister's son. Here he had collected a great army, and brought elephants, and all the splendid insignia of empire, from Beejanuggur.

Mahummud Shaw, by the advice of Khan Mahummud, did not sit down before Oodnee. He collected a train of artillery, which, till now, had never been employed by the faithful in Dekkan, of which he gave the command to Mukkrib Khan, son of Suffder Khan Syestaanee, and attached to him a number of Turks and Europeans, well acquainted with fireworking. As it was common for bands of thieves

---
* A litter in form of a griffin or tiger.

thieves to steal into the camp at night, and murder and maim men and horses, he commanded all the elephants taken from the roy to be sent to Koolburga, desiring the officers to return all their baggage to that place, except what was absolutely necessary. The artillery was placed round the camp, held together by strong ropes and chains every night, and regular patroles and rounds observed.

In a short time the sultan crossed the Tummedra, and entered the domains of Beejanuggur; which were now, for the first time, invaded by a Mahummedan sovereign in person. Roy Kishen Roy, on receiving the intelligence, called together all the first nobles of his court, and consulted on the best mode of opposing the mussulmauns. It was agreed, that Hoje Mul, a maternal relation to the roy, and commander of his armies, should have the conduct of the war. Hoje Mul, vain to excess on receiving his command, asked the roy if he should bring the prince of the mussulmauns alive a prisoner into his presence, or present him only his head upon a spear. Kishen Roy replied, that a living enemy, in any situation, was not agreeable, therefore, he had better put him to death as soon as he should take him. Hoje Mul, having received his disinission, marched to oppose Mahummud Shaw, with forty thousand horse and five hundred thousand foot. He commanded the bramins to deliver every day to the troops, discourses on the meritoriousness of slaughtering the mahummedans, in order to excite zeal for expelling them. He ordered them to describe the butchery of *cows, the insults to sacred images and destroying of temples, practised by the true believers.

Mahummud Shaw, when the enemy arrived within fifteen cosses of his camp, commanded his general, Khan Mahummud, to muster the troops; who were found to be fifteen thousand horse and fifty thousand foot. Ten thousand horse and thirty thousand foot, with all the artillery, he advanced under Khan Mahummud Khan. On

---

* They are regarded as sacred by the Hindoos.

the fourteenth of Zeekaud the armies of light and darkness met. From the dawn till four in the afternoon, like the waves of the ocean, they continued in warm conflict with each other, and great numbers were slain on both sides. Moosch Khan, and Eeefeh Khan, who commanded the right and left wings of Khan Mahummud's line, drank the sherbet of martyrdom, and their troops broke; which misfortune had nearly given a fatal blow to the army of Islaam. At this instant Mahummud Shaw appeared, with three thousand fresh horse. This restored the spirits of Khan Mahummud, as also of the disordered troops, who rallied, and joined him. Mukkrib Khan, advancing with the artillery, was not wanting in execution, greatly disordering the enemy's horse and foot. He asked leave to charge, and complete the rout. Khan Mahummud, upon this, detached a number of the nobility to support him, and permitted him to advance; which he did with such rapidity, that the infidels had no time to use fireworks, but came to short weapons, as swords and daggers. At this time, an elephant, named [a] Sheer Shikar, belonging to Khan Mahummud, refused the guidance of his driver, and rushed into the center of the enemy's line, where he was stopped by the elephants of Hoje Mul Roy, and his driver was killed. Khan Mahummud, with five hundred horse, followed, and the elephant becoming unruly, turned upon the enemy, throwing their ranks into confusion. Hoje Mul Roy, after receiving a mortal wound, fled, and his followers no longer made resistance. The infidels, seeing their center broke, fled on all sides. The scymetars of the faithful were not yet sheathed from slaughter, when the royal umbrella appeared. The sultan gave orders to renew the massacre of the unbelievers. They were executed with such strictness, that pregnant women, and even children at the breast, did not escape the sword.[b]

Mahummud

[a] The tiger hunter.

[b] It may not be unnecessary here to mention, that the wives of soldiers and other females accompany an Indian army.

Mahummud Shaw halted a week on the field, and difpatched accounts of his victory to his own dominions. In performance of his vow of maffacre, he next marched towards the camp of Kifhen Roy, who thinking himfelf unable to oppofe, notwithftanding his numerous force, fled to the woods and mountains for fhelter. The fultan followed him from place to place for three months, putting to death all who came in his way, without diftinction. At length Kifhen Roy took the road of Beejanuggur, his capital. The fultan purfuing, foon arrived with his army near the city. The infidels in the night hovered round the camp giving abufive language, but not daring to attack. At the end of a month, the fultan, finding it impoffible to take the city, or draw the enemy out of their works to engage, pretended violent illnefs, and gave orders to retreat; which were put into execution. The army having moved, Kifhen Roy with his troops followed from the city, conftantly hovering on all fides, fhouting, and crying, " Your king is dead; the prayers of " our bramins have been accepted, and we will not fuffer a fingle " man of you to efcape to his own country." In this manner the army croffed the Tummedra, followed on every fide by the enemy. At length, the fultan entered a fpacious plain, where he commanded a halt; and Kifhen Roy alfo encamped at no great diftance. Mahummud Shaw, now finding opportunity convenient to his wifhes, thought proper to give a general audience, that the fufpicions of his indifpofition might be removed from the troops, who were fomewhat difpirited, being all, except a few confidential officers, unacquainted with the ftratagem. He retired early, under pretence of weaknefs, and calling the principal nobility into privacy, commanded them to arm their troops, and wait his orders at a certain place, to which, about midnight, he repaired armed; and after forming the troops into various parties, proceeded to furprife the enemy.

Kifhen Roy and his officers had paffed the night in drinking, and the amufement of dancing girls and fingers. They were fatigued
with

with pleasure, and drowned in sleep; from which they were awakened in the dawn of morning, by the groans of the dying, and the shouts of the faithful warriors piercing the heavens. Kishen Roy, finding it vain to keep any order among his affrighted troops, fled with his people in dishonour; and did not draw back his reins, till he reached his capital of Beejanuggur.

Mahummud Shaw acquired immense treasures from the plunder of the camp. About ten thousand of the enemy were slain in the pursuit; but this did not satisfy the rage of the sultan, who commanded the inhabitants of every place round Beejanuggur to be massacred without mercy. The bramins and principal Hindoo officers, seeing such devastation, rose against Kishen Roy, complaining that his reign was inauspicious over them, that their honour was lost, ten thousand bramins had been slain, and not a remnant of population would be left. Kishen Roy replied, that he had done nothing without their advice, but that he had no power to controul fate, and was ready to accede to whatever they advised. Upon which they desired him to make peace, as his father had done, with the mussulmauns, and endeavour to appease them. Kishen Roy accordingly dispatched ambassadors to the sultan, confessing his errors, and entreating pardon and peace; but was refused by Mahummud Shaw.

At this time, a favourite remarked to the sultan, that he had only sworn to slaughter one hundred thousand Hindoos, and not totally to destroy their race. The sultan replied, that though twice the number of his vow might have been slain, yet till the roy should submit and satisfy the musicians, he would not pardon him, or spare the lives of his subjects. To this, the ambassadors, who had full powers, immediately agreed, and the money was paid at the instant. Mahummud Shaw then said, " Praise be to God, that what
" I ordered

"I ordered has been performed. I would not let a light word be recorded of me in the pages of time."

The ambassadors, seeing the sultan pleased, bowed their foreheads to the ground, and besought him to hear from them a few words. Being permitted to speak, they observed, that no religion commanded to punish the innocent for the crimes of the guilty, but particularly helpless women and children; if Kishen Roy had been faulty, the poor and wretched had not been partakers in his crimes. Mahummud Shaw replied, that the decrees of providence had so ordered, and that he had no power to alter them. The ambassadors then said, that as the Bestower of kingdoms had conferred upon him the regions of Dekkan, it was probable that his successors and the princes of Carnatic might long remain neighbours to each other, which made it adviseable, to avoid cruelties in future quarrels, that a treaty should be made not to slaughter the helpless and wretched inhabitants. Mahummud Shaw was struck by their remarks, and took an oath, that he would not in future put to death a single enemy after victory, and would bind his successors to observe the same lenity. From that time to * this, it had been the general custom in Dekkan to spare the lives of prisoners in war, and not to shed the blood of an enemy's unarmed subjects. Mahummud Shaw, after he had received satisfaction in all his demands, returned with his victorious army to Koolburga. He on his way, visited shekh Serauje ad Dien, to whose prayers, and the charities sent to Mecca with his mother, he attributed all his successes over the Hindoos.

Mahummud Shaw had not remained above five days at his capital, when he was obliged to advance the royal standard towards Dowlutabad,

---

* It might have been so when Ferishta wrote, but modern warriors have too often stained their victories with unnecessary slaughter, especially Tippoo Saheb; for which he has been punished by our arms, in spite of the pity of some Britons, in opposition, who seem to have had more false compassion for him, than true for their own unfortunate countrymen, made captives in defending the glory of England.

Dowlutabad, a rebellion having broken out in that quarter. When the sultan, pretending illness, had retreated from Beejanuggur, and was hemmed in on all sides by the enemy, a report of his death circulated through every part of his dominions, and several adventurers took the opportunity of exciting disturbances. Among the number was Bahram Khan Mazinderanee, whom the late sultan had honoured with the appellation of son. Finding the country of Dowlutabad empty of troops, he, by the advice of Geodeo ᵃ Mharatta, chief of the Naiks, set up the standard of rebellion, and some of the chiefs of Berar secretly sent troops to assist him, as also the raja of ᵇ Buggellana. Elevated by his successful beginning, he appropriated to his own use some years revenues of Mheerut and Berar, which sultan Mahummud Shaw had deposited in the fortress of Dowlutabad, with which he levied troops. Most of the towns and districts of Mheerut fell into his hands. These he divided among his adherents, who, in a little time, amounted to nearly ten thousand horse and foot.

Mahummud Shaw received intelligence of the rebellion soon after his return to Beejanuggur, and wrote to him, that as he supposed the report of his death, with the temptations of ill-disposed persons had alone led him to be guilty of such daring offences, if he would now repent and return to obedience, he would esteem him and his adherents as formerly, and forget their crimes. This letter he sent by Syed Jellall ad Dien and Shaw Mallek, two principal servants of his court.

Bahram

---

ᵃ From this it appears, that the term Mharatta is of very ancient use, and not introduced, as supposed by some, on the family of Sewajee Bhosélah obtaining power in Dekkan. Ferishta often mentions the Mharattas, as inhabitants of the province of Mheerut, or Mharat, dependant on the government of Dowlutabad, from the earliest part of his history. The Bhosélah family are descendants of the ranas of Odipone, and did not enter Dekkan till centuries after the rebellion here mentioned fell out.

ᵇ A tract in Dekkan, extending from the river Taptee, on the frontier of Guzarat, to Pooneah.

Bahram Khan, upon receipt of the sultan's orders, consulted with Geodeo. That chief observed, that Mahummud Shaw was haughty, and jealous of authority, so that, after having offended him by such acts of disobedience, it was by no means prudent to rely on his mercy; therefore, as they possessed such a fortress as Dowlutabad, and the raja of Buggellana and chiefs of Berar were in their interest, it was safer not to stop, but take every measure to bring their designs to a successful conclusion, by rendering themselves independant. Bahram Khan, by the specious instigations of Geodeo, attended not to the sultan's admonitions, but encreased his preparations for resistance. Syed Jellall ad Dien and Shaw Mallek returned to the sultan, and laid before him the obstinate and insolent behaviour of the rebel.

Mahummud Shaw became filled with rage at this reiterated disrespect, and, upon his return from Beejanuggur to Koolburga, dispatched Musnud Ali Khan Mahummud with the bulk of his army, intending to follow himself shortly after, and enjoy the amusement of hunting on his march. Bahram Khan, with Geodeo and many of the chiefs of Berar and Buggellana, moved to Puttun; where, opening the hand of liberality, they collected a great croud of needy adventurers, eager of opportunity. Musnud Ali, who was a veteran of much experience and tried abilities, not thinking it adviseable to engage hastily, halted at Seugaum. Bahram Khan made an attempt to surprize his camp; but, finding the royalists on their guard, retreated without effecting his design. Musnud Ali, from this, penetrated the inability of the enemy, and marched against them. At the same time he dispatched accounts of his design to Mahummud Shaw, then engaged in the pleasures of the chase in the hills on his frontiers, informing him, that under the royal auspices, he should on such a day attack the camp of the rebels.

Mahummud Shaw, upon receipt of the general's letter, resolved to advance with his attendants, in all about three hundred. His ministers were alarmed for his safety, and represented, that as from Musnud Ali's dispatches the enemy appeared to be in great force, it would be prudent to advance slowly, so that the nobility and army might be at hand to attack the rebels with the whole of the royal power. The sultan allowed the propriety of their reasoning, but said, that it interfered with his resolution: that as he had, with only a thousand horse, penetrated the very center of Telingana, and punished his enemies, also, with only nine thousand horse, drove the hosts of Beejanuggur to the recesses of the hills and woods, and returned successful to the extent of his desires, three hundred were sufficient to repel rebels. He, immediately after, mounted his favourite steed Shubdeez, and moved with such expedition, that he reached Puttun at the instant when Bahram Khan had drawn up to engage the rebels. The news of the sultan's arrival was soon spread abroad, and the raja of Buggellana, clapping the spur of flight to his horse, deserted the enemy, and was followed by all his dependants. Bahram Khan and Geodeo were confounded at the chances of fortune. Without attempting to oppose, or drawing a single bow on the royalists, they fled from the field, and posted with confused expedition to seek shelter in the fortress of Dowlutabad. Mahummud Shaw, while the troops were plundering the rebel's camp, arrived with seventy followers and some elephants, and, at the request of Khan Mahummud, encamped on the field till the next day. He conferred his approbation, with marks of honour, on the troops. In the morning he moved with such rapidity, that before evening he arrived before Dowlutabad, and took measures for commencing the siege.

Bahram Khan and Geodeo now awoke from their dream of pride, and were at a loss how to act. During the night they quitted the fort, and coming to the house of shekh Ein' ad Dien, besought his advice, whether to maintain the fort against the sultan,

or

or fly. The fhekh replied, that as they had fought an afylum from him, he would give them fincerely fuch counfel as tended to their welfare. He faid, that retiring to the fortrefs, and fhutting themfelves up, was far from prudent; that they had better take their wives and children by the hand, and, difregarding their effects, make their efcape, while they had it in their power, to Guzarat. They complied with his advice, and fent meffages to their families, defiring them to repair to the fhekh's without delay. The women, who had previoufly received hints of the defign, brought with them horfes, and neceffaries for flight. The fhekh, fpreading his hands over the heads of Bahram Khan and Geodeo, defired them to depart, faying, that by the bleffing of God they would be fafe; after which they haftened towards Guzarat.

Mahummud Shaw, in the morning hearing of their efcape, purfued them with four hundred horfe; but, not overtaking the fugitives, returned in high wrath to Dowlutabad againft fhekh Ein ad Dien, with whom he was before diffatisfied on the following account. Sultan Mahummud had demanded a declaration of allegiance from all the religious of his kingdom, who had univerfally made it, except the fhekh, who refufed; becaufe the king drank wine, and was guilty of fome errors repugnant to the divine law. The fultan now fent a meffenger to order him to his prefence, and perform his allegiance, or give an affurance under his own hand of his affent. The fhekh wrote in reply, that once, a fcholar, a [*] fyed, and a proftitute were taken prifoners together by infidels, who promifed to give them quarter, if they would fall proftrate before their idols; or if not, put them to inftant death. The fcholar agreeably to the cafuiftry of mental refervation, performed the ceremony, and the fyed followed his example. When it came to the turn of the proftitute, fhe faid, I have been all my life committing crimes, and am neither a fcholar nor a fyed to atone for this fin by my other virtues.

[*] Defcendant of Mahummud.

virtues. She refused to prostrate, and was put to death. The shekh observed, that his case was like her's, that he was resigned to the sultan's resentment, but would neither come into his presence, nor take oaths of allegiance. Mahummud Shaw was enraged, and commanded him to quit the city. The shekh obeyed immediately; and repaired to the tomb of [a] shekh Boorahan ad Dien, upon which he seated himself, and exclaimed, Where is the man who will drive me from hence? The sultan, admiring the resolution of the shekh, repented of his passion, and sent the following verse to him by the suddur al shereef, " I am submissive to thee, be thou submissive to " me."

The shekh replied, that if sultan Mahummud [b] Ghazee would, like his father, promote the observance of religious laws, discourage vice from his dominions, abstain from drinking wine in publick, and permit the judges to execute the laws of the faith against criminals, no one would be dearer to him. He also sent the following verses, written in his own hand: " While I live I would do nought but " good. I can have no views but loyalty and attachment. Even to " those who have done evil against me, if in my power, I would " only do good." Mahummud Shaw was much pleased with the name of Ghazee, given him by the shekh, and commanded it to be added to his titles. [c]

Having committed the government of Mheerut to Khan Mahummud, he returned to Koolburga; where, upon his arrival, he commanded all the distilleries in his dominions to be destroyed, and engaged earnestly in promoting strict observance of religious laws. The banditti of Dekkan, famous through all countries for their daring

---

[a] A saint much venerated in Dekkan.
[b] Engaging in war from religious motives against infidels. It is a title assumed by all Mahummedan sovereigns.
[c] May we not call this shekh the Thomas a Becket of Dekkan?

daring robberies on caravans, he determined to root out entirely. For this purpofe, the royal mandate was iffued to the governors of all the provinces to ufe the utmoft vigilance in clearing their countries of thieves and highwaymen, by putting all to death without diftinction, and to fend their heads to the capital, as proofs of their obedience. Such expedition was made ufe of, that in fix or feven months there remained not a fign of thefe offenders in his kingdom. Near eight thoufand heads were brought to Koolburga from different parts, and were piled up in heaps near the city, as examples of the royal juftice.

Sultan Mahummud Shaw, who had attended to his internal government at the admonitions of fhekh Ein ad Dien, conftantly kept up a friendly correfpondence with that venerable perfonage, and obferved towards him great attention and refpect. The fhekh, in his turn, frequently fent exhortations and admonitions, in which he did not refrain from delivering his fentiments with honeft freedom.

As the roies of Beejanuggur and Telingana, with all the zemindars of Dekkan, were now confined in the path of obedience and fubmiffion, and did not neglect to remit their ftipulated tributes, the extent of the kingdom was free from trouble or diforders. Sultan Mahummud Shaw laid afide ideas of further conquefts, and employed himfelf in promoting the happinefs of his people, and to make his territories flourifh. Every year he made a tour of one quarter or other of his dominions, attended by the governor of it, who efcorted him back to the capital. The excurfion was employed in inveftigating the ftate of the provinces, redreffing complaints, forming plans of publick utility, and the pleafures of the chafe. During the reign of Mahummud Shaw all ranks of people repofed on the couches of fecurity, and enjoyed the fulnefs of eafe and pleafure. Senfible of the value of a juft king, they were grateful and obedient to his authority, and prayed earneftly for his long reigning over them.

them. But as the wolf of death, greedy of prey, conftantly feizes a fresh [a] Jofeph, and a Jacob becomes plunged in grief, the claws of the favage darted on the victim of his life, and on the nineteenth of Zeekaud, 776, fnatched him from the abode of this vain world, and overwhelmed mortals, like Jacob for his fon, in lamentations and tears for his lofs. He was buried by the fide of his father, and "All is vanity," was written on his tomb. Happy the reign that paffed like his, and the king, of whom fuch memorials have remained! He was refpected in his life, and at his death remembered by his virtues.

A.D. 1374.

According to the Seruaje al Towarekh, fuch great treafures and numbers of elephants, as were collected in the houfehold of Mahummud Shaw, were never enjoyed by any other prince of the houfe of Bhamenee. In his time, there were belonging to him, of great and fmall, male and female elephants, three thoufand; and in the reign of any other fultan, we read of never more than two. The fums accumulated by him, according to the fame book, exceeded thofe acquired by other princes a full half. No prince before him ever fo far reduced the roies and zemindars of Carnatic, from whom he wrefted much of the accumulated riches of feven hundred years. It is computed that near five hundred thoufand unbelievers fell by the fwords of the warriors, in defence of the faith of Iflaam; by which the diftricts of Carnatic were fo laid wafte, that they did not recover their natural population for feveral [b] kerruns. Mahummud Shaw reigned feventeen years.

[a] The brothers of Jofeph, agreeably to the Mahummedan tradition, told Jacob, that he was deftroyed by a wolf.
[b] Kerrun is a period of ten years.

SULTAN

# SULTAN

# MUJAHID SHAW BHAMENEE.

---

SULTAN Mujahid Shaw, son of Mahummud Shaw by the daughter of Mallek Syef ad Dien Ghoree, on the death of his father sat on the throne of Dekkan. He was of great bodily strength, tall of stature, and in dignity and majesty of aspect exceeded all the princes of his family. He was unrivalled in valour, fortitude, and strength of constitution. He spoke the Turkish language elegantly, and his favourite companions were Turks and Persians. He was fond of archery from his infancy; and would converse of nothing but discipline and arms. While a youth, he broke open the door of his father's treasury, and taking from it some bags of gold, divided the whole among his play-fellows. The treasurer discovering the theft, informed Muhummud Shaw; who, enraged at such vicious conduct, sent Mubarik, his [a] betel carrier, to call the prince before him. Upon his arrival in the presence, he saw his father angry, and guessed the cause; but, unable to excuse himself, remained silent, though he received from the angry sultan some severe strokes with a whip, that drew blood. When he was dismissed, he went and complained of Mubarik to his mother; observing, that if he had informed him of the affair, he could have made her his intercessor, or have contrived an excuse to evade going to his father's presence, till his passion was abated. The princess observed, that the servant was not in fault, as obedience to the sultan was his duty. The prince made no reply, and took care to stifle every sign of resentment against Mubarik, to whom he behaved with more attention and kindness than

---

[a] An aromatic leaf, chewed by the people of India.

than he had ever shown before. At the end of a week, he took an opportunity of telling him, with much art, that he had heard he was blessed with remarkable bodily strength, and had overcome the most celebrated wrestlers by the force of his grasp, on which account he had a desire to try a fall. Mubarik, to please the prince, consented; and a struggle ensued, in which Mujahid Shaw threw him to the ground with such force, that in the fall he broke his neck, and died immediately. The prince was then in his fourteenth year.

Mujahid Shaw acceded to the throne in his nineteenth year. Immediately upon his accession, he made a pilgrimage to Dowlutabad, in order to pay his respects at the tomb of shekh Boorahan ad Dien; and having chosen shekh Zien ad Dien for his spiritual director, returned to his capital. As he was jealous of the power of Khan Mahummud, he appointed Azim Humaioon governor of Dowlutabad in his room, and recalled him to the presence. He wrote to Kishen Roy, raja of Beejanuggur, that as some forts and districts, between the Kistnah and Tummedra rivers, were held by them in participation, which occasioned constant disagreements, he must for the future limit his confines to the Tummedra, and give up all on the eastern side to him, with the fort of Beekapore, and some other places. Kishen Roy answered to this demand, that the forts of Roijore, Mudkul, and others on the banks of the Kistnah, had for ages belonged to his family, therefore the sultan would do wisely to surrender them, confine himself to the boundary of the Kistnah, and restore the elephants which sultan Mahummud Shaw had obtained from the ill behaviour of his servants; by which concessions their disgusts might be changed into friendship.

Mujahid Shaw, on receipt of this insolent answer, opened the treasures of his father, and made great additions to his army. He entrusted the management of civil affairs to Mallek Syef ad Dien Ghoree, and resolved to march to Beejanuggur. When the troops
of

of Dowlutabad, Bieder and Berar were collected, he moved, carrying with him a great treasure, and five hundred elephants. Having crossed the Kistnah and Tummedra, he arrived before the fortress of Oodnee, in strength unequalled in Dekkan, which he ordered Suffder Khan Syestaanee to besiege with the army of Berar, and sent the ameer al amra Bahadur Khan and Azim Humaioon, with their troops, onwards. Upon hearing that Kishen Roy was encamped on the bank of the Tummedra, he advanced in person towards that river, by slow marches, and with great caution. The Hindoo prince, on the approach of the advanced army, and the motions of the sultan, made preparations for an engagement.

Mujahid Shaw, upon his march, was informed by some zemindars, of an enormous tiger that daily committed great ravages, insomuch that, as a road lay near his den, many travellers had been killed by him, and passengers had, through dread, now left off going the path. Being fond of hunting, he commanded them to conduct him to the forest near his den, which they did. The sultan forbad any person entering without permission, and with seven attendants only on foot, advanced into the forest. The tiger soon perceived them, and roaring horribly, stalked towards them. Mujahid Shaw commanded his attendants to reserve their weapons, and going on some paces, let fly an arrow, which entered the side of the savage animal, who instantly fell down dead. The sultan declared, that had he missed his aim, it was his resolution to have attacked the tiger with sword and dagger. As it was extraordinary that one arrow only should kill him, he commanded his attendants to open the body, that he might view what entrail had been pierced. This being done, the arrow was found stuck into the heart.

The idolaters of Beejanuggur, upon hearing of this exploit, were struck with dread. Though they had advanced, resolved to give battle, they altered their intentions, and determined now on keeping

G close

close in the woods, from the cover of which they might annoy the faithful, and be themselves secure. With this view Kishen Roy quitted Beejanuggur to his ministers, and, with his army, entered the forests to the south of the city.

Mujahid Shaw, having heard great praises of the beauty of the city, advanced to Beejanuggur: but thinking it too strong to besiege at present, he moved in pursuit of the enemy in the field. Kishen Roy fled through the woods and hills towards [a] Seet Bunder Rameffar, followed by the sultan, who cut passages for his cavalry through forests before inaccessible. In this manner the roy fled from place to place, for six months, but never dared to appear without the woods. It was in vain that the favourites of the sultan represented the pursuit as fruitless, and destructive to the troops. He would not desist. At last, his good fortune prevailed. The health of Kishen Roy and his family became affected by the noxious air of the woods, and they were warned to quit them by the physicians. Kishen Roy had entertained hopes that the sultan would have been taken ill from the unwholesome climate, and, instead of himself, been obliged to retreat. Driven by necessity, he retired by secret paths to his capital of Beejanuggur. The sultan dispatched an army after him; while he himself, with the ameer al amra Bahadur Khan, and five thousand men, went to amuse himself with the sight of Seet Bunder Rameffar.

The sultan at this place repaired a mosque, which had been built by the officers of sultan Alla ad Dien Khiljee. He broke down many temples of the idolaters, and laid waste the country; after which he hastened with all expedition to Beejanuggur. To that city there were two roads, one fit for the passage of armies, the other narrow and difficult. As the former was lined with ambushes, he chose the latter; through which he marched with a select body of troops, and appeared

---

[a] A port on the Coromandel coast, opposite the island of Ceylon, and esteemed sacred by the Hindoos, as the scene of great exploits of their god Ram.

appeared suddenly in the suburbs of the city. Kishen Roy was astonished at his boldness, and sent myriads of his people to defend the streets. The sultan drove them before him, and gained the bank of a piece of water, which only now divided him from the citadel, in which Kishen Roy resided. Near this was an eminence, upon which stood a temple, covered with plates of gold and silver, set with jewels, much venerated by the Hindoos, and called in the language of the country, Puttuk. The sultan, esteeming the destruction of it as a religious obligation, ascended the hill, and, having razed the temple, possessed himself of the precious metals and jewels.

The idolaters, upon seeing their object of veneration destroyed, raised their shrieks and lamentations to the sky. They obliged Kishen Roy to head them, and advanced resolutely in astonishing numbers. Upon which the sultan formed his disposition. He laid aside his umbrella, and with one of his arms-bearers, an Afghaun named Mhamood, crossed a small rivulet to observe the numbers and motions of the infidels. A Hindoo, who knew the sultan from the horse he rode, resolved, by revenging the destruction of his gods and country, to gain immortal reputation for himself. He moved unperceived through the hollows and broken ground, along the bank of the rivulet, had gained the plain, and was charging towards the sultan on full speed, when Mujahid Shaw, at a lucky instant perceiving him, made a sign to Mhamood Afghaun, who without delay charged the Hindoo. Mhamood's horse rearing, he fell to the ground. His antagonist, having every advantage, was on the point of putting him to death, when sultan Mujahid Shaw advanced with the quickness of lightning. The Hindoo, changing his object, aimed a heavy stroke at the sultan, giving at the same instant a shout of triumph, which made the spectators believe his blow was effectual. Luckily, a helmet of iron saved the head of the sultan, who now inflicted such a wound on his enemy, that he was divided from the shoulder to the navel, and fell dead

dead from his horse; upon which the sultan remounted Mhamood, and joined his army on the other side of the rivulet, amid the acclamations of his friends and admiration of the enemy, who could not withhold their applause for such gallantry and valour.

Kishen Roy advancing with his army, the sultan committed his right and left wings to the ameer al amra Bahadur Khan and Azim Humaioon. Suffder Khan advancing with the fireworks, began the attack, and, after much struggle and slaughter, the enemy were put to flight. The conquerors had scarce reposed from their fatigue, when the brother of Kishen Roy, arrived at the city from his government, with a reinforcement of twenty thousand horse, and a vast army of foot. Kishen Roy, having collected his broken troops, marched once more against the sultan. Great instances of valour were shewn on both sides, and numberless soldiers fell in each army. Mukkrib Khan, with many principal officers, drank the sherbet of martyrdom. Sultan Mujahid Shaw engaged in person in all parts of the line. Wherever he charged, the enemy fled before him, like flocks of sheep before the sharp-fanged wolf. He tempered the clay with the blood of his enemies. Wherever he guided the reins of his sable steed, the idolaters were prostrated under his spear.

Daood Khan, who had been left with six thousand horse and a great body of foot, to keep possession of a post called Dhunna Sodra, learning that the engagement had begun at dawn, and that the enemy were not yet dispersed; also, that new succours were coming to them every instant, was alarmed for the safety of the sultan. He quitted his station, and joined the battle, in which he behaved with astonishing gallantry. He was three times obliged to dismount, his horses being wounded, and to fight on foot. The sultan, on seeing the standard of Daood Khan, was enraged; but stifled his displeasure till the gale of victory had waved the standards of the faithful. He then called Daood Khan before him, gave him a harsh reprimand for
quitting

quitting a station, so important, that should the enemy gain possession, not a mussulmaun could make his escape from the city.

The sultan now sent a body of troops to secure the post, but the enemy had taken advantage of Daood Khan's absence, and obtained possession; of which, the officers, seeing them too strong to be attacked, sent advice to the sultan. Mujahid Shaw, who though he had slain forty thousand of the enemy, yet had lost great numbers of his own army, did not think proper to remain longer where he was, and moved towards Dhunna Sodra. The enemy fled on the sight of his standards. He then, with a choice body, remained in person at the entrance of the pass, until his whole army had crossed in safety, as he judged Kishen Roy would harass his retreat. All who have beheld this country acknowledge, that sultan Mujahid Shaw, in this expedition, performed an action scarcely possible but from the hand of providence.

The country of Kurrah, called also Carnatic, is in length from north to south, from the Kistnah to Seet Bunder Ramessar, [a] six hundred cofs, and its breadth from west to east one hundred and fifty, along the shores of the Indian ocean to the borders of Telingana. The people speak, some the Kuzzi, and some the Teling language; and are so brave, that they advance to battle with songs and dances; but their ardour does not last for any time. The country is full of fastnesses and woods, almost impenetrable to troops. The princes of the house of Bhamenee maintained themselves by superior valour only;

[a] Twelve hundred miles; but this must be, I fancy, an exaggeration. Major Rennell, in his Memoir, says, the Carnatic anciently comprized all that part of the peninsula south of the Gondegama and Tungbedra rivers, from the coast of Coromandel eastward, to the Gaut mountains westward, and was divided into Balla Gaut and Payen Gaut, or the upper and lower Gauts; the former being the western, and containing the districts which now compose the country of Tippoo Saheb; and the latter eastern, or Carnatic, according to its present definition, the dominions of our ally, Mahummud Alee Khan, navob of Arcot.

only; for, in power, wealth, and extent of country, the roies of Beejanuggur were greatly their superiors, especially in the time of sultan Mujahid Shaw, when as yet the whole of the country of Telingana had not fallen under the yoke of Bhamenee. The \* seaport of Goa, the fortress of \* Malgoan, and other places not included in Carnatic, belonged to the roy of Beejanuggur; and many districts of \* Tulghaut were in his possession. His country was well peopled, and the subjects submissive to his authority. The roies of Malabar, Ceylon, and other islands and countries, kept ambassadors at his court, and sent annually rich presents. The ancestors of Kishen Roy had lineally possessed the empire for seven hundred years; during which, being undisturbed by revolutions, and sparing in expense, their treasures so accumulated, as to equal those of all the kings of the earth. In the time of sultan Alla ad Dien Khiljee, the grandfather of Kishen Roy buried his treasures from religious motives, and a great part fell into the hands of the chiefs of Alla ad Dien, at Seet Bunder Rameffar, where they were concealed.

Sultan Mujahid Shaw, seeing it impossible at present to reduce Beejanuggur, moved from the vicinity of it, with his captives. They amounted to between sixty and seventy thousand persons, mostly women; as, in performance of the commands of his father, he had refrained from slaughter after the fury of battle. As his troops were lying before Oodnee, the sultan marched to that fortress, which he besieged for nine months. A scarcity of water had nearly reduced the garrison to submit, when a heavy shower of rain falling, eased their distress, and they continued to hold out. At this time a want of grain prevailed in the royal camp, and fluxes and cholicky pains carried off great numbers; so that the army in general were dissatisfied, and began to cry loudly for return to their own country.

Mallek

---

\* These are on the Malabar Coast, and, except Goa, belonging to the Mharattas.

Mallek Syef ad Dien Ghoree, hearing at Koolburga of the unpromising state of affairs, petitioned the sultan for leave to join him with his troops, as he had a great desire to view the fortress of Oodnee, of which he had heard so many wonderful accounts. The sultan having consented to his request, he marched with great expedition, and soon had the honour of killing the border of the royal Musnud. After reconnoitring the fortress, he observed to the sultan in private, that the conquest of such a place, which had fifteen forts communicating with each other, was not to be hoped for in a short time; that, preparatory to it, the forts between the rivers, from Goa to Malgoan and Beckapore, should first be taken. Mujahid Shaw upon this consented to retreat, and, through Mallek Syef ad Dien Ghoree, a peace being concluded with the roy of Beejanuggur, the sultan moved towards his own dominions, sending the minister on before him to Koolburga.

When the royal army had crossed the Tummedra, and arrived near the fortress of Mudkul, the sultan with some favourites, the companions of his pleasures, went to take the amusement of hunting, attended only by four hundred horse. Among the number were Daood Khan, Suffder Khan Syestaanee, and Azim Humaioon. He generally hunted all day, and passed the night wherever overtaken by the darkness.

Daood Khan, who could not brook the reprimand given him at Beejanuggur for quitting his post, and also had a view to the throne, had secretly plotted the assassination of the sultan. He was joined in this conspiracy by Khan Mahummud and Musaood Khan; the former of whom was disgusted at having been removed from the government of Dowlutabad, and the preference shown by the sultan to his rival Azim Humaioon. The latter had a desire to revenge the death of his father Mubarik Khan, betel-bearer to the late sultan. The traitors waited impatiently for an opportunity to execute their design,

design, but, such was the vigilance of Suffder Khan and Azim Humaioon, that as yet none had offered. But, as the pen of providence had signed the decree, sultan Mujahid Shaw one day dismissed his two faithful amras, against their earnest and importunate requests, to their governments, and moved with his remaining attendants towards his capital. Arriving at the bank of a river, he halted to amuse himself with fishing, but was suddenly seized with a pain in his eyes. He retired to sleep in a tent, which was guarded by the conspirators.

About midnight, Daood Khan, leaving Khan Mahummud and his followers to watch without, entered the sultan's tent, with Musaood Khan, and two other persons. The sultan was fast asleep, and an Abyssinian slave only was present, employed in * rubbing his feet. He raised a cry of alarm on seeing Daood Khan with a naked dagger in his hand. The sultan started, but could not open his eyes, they being glued together from his disorder. Daood Khan rushing upon him, plunged the dagger into his belly. The sultan in agony seized the assassin by the hand in which he held the dagger, and struggled with him. The slave, though unarmed, attacked Musaood Khan, who struck him dead with one blow of his sabre; and inflicted another on the sultan, with such effect, that he expired immediately. Fortune erects palaces for the body, and then hurls it from the throne to the coffin. The world has beheld numerous events like this; it was not the first treachery of time. She places crowns of gold on the head of one, and resigns another to the dark grave.

Daood Khan, rising from his murdered sovereign, went out of the tent, and the same day called together the nobility and their sons who were present, to acknowledge him as sovereign. As he was heir to the crown, Mujahid Shaw having no children, they agreed to his demands with resignation, and were gratified with honours and employments.

* In the east this is commonly used to promote circulation.

employments. In the morning he difpatched his nephew's body to Koolburga; and, after halting two or three days, fet out for that capital himfelf, in great pomp and magnificence, being joined by the royal army.

The death of fultan Mujahid Shaw happened in the night of the feventeenth of Zeehidge, 779, after a reign of not quite three years. A. D. 1377. The hiftory of Hajee Mahummud Candaharee relates, that he received his laft wound from the fon of Mubarik the betel-bearer. God knows the truth.

# SULTAN

# *DAOOD SHAW BHAMENEE.

THE historians of Dekkan relate, that when the news of sultan Mujahid Shaw's assassination was spread abroad, dissention awoke in every quarter. Suffder Khan and Azim Humaioon, who had reached Beejapore, entering into alliance with each other, repaired to Koolburga; and, having visited the murdered prince's body, they retired towards Elichpore and Dowlutabad, carrying with them all the royal elephants and horses that were stationed at Beejapore. They wrote to Daood Shaw, that they were only retiring to their districts to refresh their troops, and should wait for his gracious encouragement with impatience; but whenever he should give them orders to repair to his presence, they would hasten to court without delay. The army of the roy of Beejanuggur, upon intelligence of the death of the sultan, made great rejoicings; and overrunning the country as far as the Kistnah, sat down before the fortress of Roijore. The inhabitants of Koolburga became divided into two parties; one desirous of the authority of Daood Shaw, and the other of that of Mhamood Khan, the youngest son of sultan Alla ad Dien. This prince had lived confined in the citadel since the accession of Mujahid Shaw.

Mallek Syef ad Dien Ghoree observed to the nobility, that factions could only occasion the ruin of the state, therefore, it was prudent

---

* A younger son of the sultan Alla ad Dien Houssun Khangoh Bhamenee.

dent since Daood Shaw had already placed the crown on his head, to obey him, and avoid a civil war. As Mallek Syef ad Dien was the first minister and prime supporter of the house of Bhamenee, the officers and people of the capital agreed to follow his advice; as did also all the ladies of the haram, except the sister of the late sultan, and grand-daughter, by the mother's side, to the minister himself. She rebuked him for his conduct, and entreated him to change it, but without effect.

Mallek Syef ad Dien read the khootbah in the name of Daood Shaw, and went to meet him, attended by all the nobles, divines, and respectable persons of Koolburga. He conducted the sultan in great pomp to the city, where he ascended the throne Firozeh. Daood Shaw, at the request of the minister, permitted him to retire from his office, and took the direction of affairs into his own hands. He was obeyed by all the nobility so that his authority, seemed fully established. The sister of Mujahid Shaw, \* Rhuperwer Ageh, however, still refused to acknowledge his authority, though Daood Shaw used every means to gain her assent; but she refused to give any answer to his messengers. As she had great influence in the haram, of which she was regarded as chief since the death of Mahummud Shaw, the sultan did not chuse to act towards her otherwise than with attention and respect. At length the princess prevailed upon a young man of great valour, who had stood high in the esteem and favour of Mujahid Shaw, by sacrificing his own life, to revenge the blood of his patron.

On the twenty first of Mohirrim, 780, Daood Shaw, attended A.D. 1378. by Khan Mahummud, going to offer his devotions at the great mosque of Koolburga, was followed by the assassin, who placed himself at prayers behind him. While the king was prostrate in prayer

---

\* Refresher of the soul.

prayer, he drew his fabre, and before the attendants were aware of his defign, wounded him in fuch a manner, that he died inftantly. Khan Mahummud, feeing the fultan dead, let not the murderer make his efcape from the mofque; but, with a ftroke, feparated his head from the body. Daood Shaw reigned only one month and five days.

SULTAN

# SULTAN

# MHAMOOD BHAMENEE.

Upon the death of Daood Shaw, Musnud Alee Khan Mahummud resolved to place on the throne his son Mahummud Sunjer, then in his ninth year. For this purpose, having collected his dependants, he repaired to the palace. Rhuperwer Ageh, being informed of his design, shut the gates, vowing that the son of a traitor who had assassinated his sovereign and her brother, should not be sultan while she had life. At the same time she declared Mhamood, the youngest son of sultan Alla ad Dien, possessor of the throne.

As Mahummud Sunjer was in the palace, and in the power of the princess, Khan Mahummud was distressed how to act. Going to the house of Syef ad Dien Ghoree, he endeavoured to pervail upon him to join his party, but received for answer, that as Mahummud Sunjer and sultan Mhamood were both in the hands of Rhuperwer Ageh, he thought it adviseable to avoid contentions, and leave the choice of a prince in her hands. Khan Mahummud, as he knew both the nobles and the people, mussulmauns and Hindoos, would be guided by the advice of Mallek Syef ad Dien, submitted to his arbitration, and accompanied him to the palace. The princess, after much persuasion, having blinded Mahummud Sunjer to prevent all attempts in his favour, with the concurrence of the ministers and nobility, placed Mhamood on the throne Firozch.

Sultan

* A younger son of sultan Alla ad Dien.

Sultan Mhamood was a prince of sweet disposition, humane, virtuous, and just. He had a penetrating judgment in all affairs of state. In the beginning of his reign he confined Khan Mahummud in the fort of Saugher, regarding him as a sower of seditions; and he died, not long after, in his prison. He commanded Musaood, who had assisted in the murder of Mujahid Shaw, to be impaled alive. Mallek Syef ad Dien Ghoree was prevailed upon, with much entreaty and encouragement, to re-accept the honours of prime minister and governor of the capital. The sultan engaged in no affairs without his advice. This caution proved fortunate; for, during his reign, no disturbances happened in the empire, nor was there any relaxation of the order and œconomy of government.

Bahadur Khan, Suffder Khan, and Azim Humaioon, hastened with the expedition of obedient submission to the capital; where they vowed their allegiance, and made proper offerings of congratulation. The roy of Beejanuggur raised the siege of Roijore, out of respect to the sultan, and agreed to pay him the tribute stipulated in the reign of sultan Mahummud Shaw Ghazee.

Sultan Mhamood had a taste for poetry, and wrote elegant verses himself. He spoke fluently the Persian and Arabic languages. When prosperous events occurred, he was not intoxicated with joy, nor immersed in grief at the attacks of misfortune. He never cohabited but with one wife, and paid great regard to the opinions of divines, of whose company he was very fond. In his reign, the poets of Arabia and Persia resorted to Dekkan, and were benefitted by the gracious flow of the stream of liberality. Meer Fyez Oollah Anjoo, who presided on the seat of justice, once presenting him with an ode, was rewarded with a thousand pieces of gold, and permitted to retire, covered with honours, to his own country. The fame of the sultan's affability, judgment, and munificence, spread so wide, that the celebrated poet of Shiraz, Khaujeh Hafiz, determined to visit Dekkan;

but

but was prevented by a train of accidents, which, with the cause of his intention, are thus related.

Meer Fyez Oollah Anjoo sent this famous poet a present with a letter, intimating, that if he would confer honour on the sultan's dominions by his approach, and make Dekkan the envy of paradise by his bounty-shedding presence, the inhabitants would value properly such an honour, and have him conducted back to Shiraz, enriched to the height of his desires. The poet, from the kindness and assurances of Fyez Oollah Anjoo, became ardently desirous of visiting Dekkan. He disposed of the gifts sent him among his relations and creditors; and, departing from Shiraz, arrived safely at [a] Lar. Here he assisted a friend, who had been robbed, with great part of his ready money. From Lar he was accompanied to Ormus, by Khaujeh Zien al Ab ad Dien Hammadanee, and Khaujeh Mahummud Gazroonee, who were also going to visit Hindooftan. With them he took shipping in one of the royal vessels, that had arrived at Ormus from Dekkan; but he had not weighed anchor, when a storm arose, and the sea became very rough. Hafiz repented of his journey; and, pretending that he had forgotten to take leave of some of his friends at Ormus, left the ship. Having written the following ode, he entrusted it to be given to Fyez Oollah Anjoo; after which he returned to Shiraz.

### ODE.

" The breeze of my garden is not to be purchased by the posses-
" sion of the world.

" My companions rebuked me, and said, Quit this spot. What
" whim hath possessed thee, that thy cell is not to be valued?

" Yonder

---

[a] A port in the Persian gulph.

"Yonder royal crown, on which is fet danger of life, is an
"heart-enticing ornament, but not worth my lofs of head.

"From defire of pearls, the dangers of the fea appeared eafy to
"me; but I miftook; for one wave is not to be appeafed by trea-
"fures of gold.

"Is my heart difpirited in the affembly of friendfhip? All the
"gildings of art are not worth a fingle cup of generous wine.

"If Hafiz chufes to retire from the world, contented with a
"little, hundreds of pieces of gold are not worth one inftant of
"vexation."

When Fyez Oollah received this ode he read it to the fultan, who was much pleafed with the poetry, and obferved, that as Hafiz had fet out with intentions to vifit his court, it was incumbent upon him not to leave him without proofs of his liberality. He then committed a thoufand pieces of gold to Mahummud Cafim Mefhidee, one of the learned in his court, that he might purchafe with it what was moft acceptable of the curious productions of Hind, and fend them to the poet at Shiraz; which was done accordingly.

Sultan Mhamood Shaw was fond of rich and curious apparel, while a youth, but, upon his acceffion to the throne, would wear no other than plain white. He frequently obferved, that kings were only truftees of the divine riches, and that to expend more upon themfelves than neceffity required, was a breach of truft. A famine falling out during his reign, he kept ten thoufand bullocks on his own account conftantly going to and from Malwa and Guzarat for grain; which was fold out to the people at a cheap rate. At the cities of Koolburga, Bieder, Candahar, Elichpore, and Dowlutabad, alfo at Choule, Dabul, and other great towns, he eftablifhed fchools for

orphans,

orphans, with ample foundations for their support. He appointed stipends for the expounders of the scriptures and the prophet's history; and gave monthly salaries to the blind in all his dominions. He paid great attention to shekh Serauje ad Dien, visited him in his last illness, and, going often to his tomb, offered prayers for his happiness; and gave alms to the poor pilgrims.

As the sultan, on his accession, chose the blessings of peace in preference to the tumultuous glories of war, his government passed in ease and security; so that the Dekkanees gave him the title of Aristotle. During his reign of nineteen years nine months and twenty four days, only one disturbance occurred, towards the latter end, which was quelled in a few months.

Baha ad Dien Dowlutabadee pleasing the sultan, was appointed to the command of the fortress of Saugher; and his two sons, the one named Mahummud, and the other Khaujeh, were honoured with the royal confidence. By degrees they ascended the musnud of nobility, and gained so much dignity and power, that their prosperity excited the envy of their rivals, who let loose the tongue of defamation against them, and accused them of breaking the royal trust. Though the sultan lent but little attention to such accusations, deeming them false, yet the brothers were alarmed for their own safety, and setting up the standard of rebellion and disobedience, fled to Saugher, with a thousand faithful adherents. The father, misguided by his sons, joined in the rebellion, and levied troops. He twice defeated the royal army sent against him, and acquired much plunder and power.

Sultan Mhamood Shaw the third time dispatched against him Eusuff Azdir, a Turkish slave, with a powerful army; who lay before Saugher for two months; during which the rebels made several desperate sallies. One day, in particular, the elder brother Mahummud, with four hundred brave companions, charged the rear of the

I royal

royal camp with great fuccefs, till he was wounded in the hand by Mahummud Kallapaharee; whom he in turn difabled, but his troops fled. He would not then quit his horfe; and, his father coming to his affiftance, renewed the fight till night, when darknefs put an end to contention. The two brothers, contrary to their cuftom, paffed this night on the edge of the ditch without the fort, unmindful of the treachery of fortune. A number of the garrifon, in league with the royalifts, took this opportunity of writing to Eufuff Azdir, the general, that the brothers were without the fort, and offering, if he would fend a chofen band, to admit them by a wicket, and put to death the chief rebel Baha ad Dien. Eufuff Azdir having felected a number of refolute foldiers, commanded them, if the head of Baha ad Dien fhould be fent them by the garrifon, to enter and take poffeffion; otherwife, to defift and return to camp. When they arrived at the place of appointment, their friends within threw over to them their chief's head, which fatisfied their doubts; and, entering the fort, they founded the march of victory. At this fignal, the brothers were attacked by the royalifts without. feeing no road of efcape, they chofe to die fighting defperately, with moft of their followers. After performing wonderful acts of valour, they quaffed the fherbet of annihilation. This was the firft and laft time, in which the fword of punifhment was drawn from the fcabbard during the reign of Mhamood Shaw.

A.D. 1396. The fultan, not long after this victory, on the twenty firft of Rejib, 790, died of a putrid fever; and the next day Mallek Syef ad Dien Ghoree, the chief prop of the houfe of Bhamenee, after having trod the path of life for one hundred and feven years, placed the feal of lafting filence upon his lips. He was buried, agreeably to his will, in the court of the tomb of fultan Alla ad Dien Houffiin Kangoh Bhamence, and over his grave was laid a great terrace of ftone.

It

It is recorded, that sultan Mhamood was so strict a promoter of the laws, that no neglects were suffered by him in the smallest point. A woman, convicted of the crime of adultery, was once brought to the court of justice to receive the punishment of the law. The judge made some enquiries why she had been guilty of so great a crime. She replied, "I knew not, O judge, that the act was unlawful; but believed, "that as one man might have four women, I might be indulged, "with equal propriety, with four men; but, as I am now informed "I was guilty of error, I will not offend by repetition of the crime." The judge was perplexed at her answer, and she escaped, by her wit, the punishment inflicted by the law on adultery. Sultan Mhamood reigned nineteen years, nine months and twenty four days.

## SULTAN

## 'GHEAUSE AD DIEN BHAMENEE.

WHEN the kingdom of Dekkan was deprived of the virtuous and just sultan Mhamood, his eldest son, sultan Gheause ad Dien, in his seventeenth year, ornamented the throne of empire by his gracious accession. Observing the rules and customs of his father, he behaved graciously to all; and remembering the old servants and supporters of his family, comforted them with favour and kindness. Intelligence of the death of Suffder Khan Syestaanee arriving at court, the sultan having conferred upon his son Sullabut Khan the title of Mujiliss Alee, together with his offices and estates, dispatched him in great splendour and magnificence to Berar. Ahmed Beg Cazweence, [a] peshwa to Mahun.mud Khan, son of Azim Humaioon, was exalted to the office of meer nobut, or lord of the watches; and the sultan showed him uncommon regard and attention. This excited the jealousy of Lallcheen, one of the most powerful Turkish slaves of sultan Mhamood, who aspired to the dignity of prime minister, and wished the post of meer nobut for his son Houssun Khan. Not succeeding in his views he became discontented, and was reproved by the sultan; who often observed before him, that it was highly injurious to the publick to put slaves in office over the heads of those who were; many of them, descendants of the prophet; or that he should depart from the customs of his royal ancestors.

Lallcheen

---

[a] The protector of the faith.
[b] Agent, or minister, if employed by sovereigns. The title is still retained by the first minister of the Mharatta state.

Lallcheen, angry at the remarks of the fultan, treafured the infults in his mind. He turned all his thoughts on revenge, but openly appeared fatisfied with his condition, and fubmiffive to the king. He had a daughter, celebrated for her beauty, wit, and fkill in mufick, whom the fultan was defirous of poffeffing, and privately fent her profeffions of his love. Lallcheen, foon after his acceffion, invited the young fultan to an entertainment at his houfe. The fultan, in hopes that he would prefent his daughter as an offering before him, condefcended to his requeft with much fatisfaction. Lallcheen treated his royal gueft with much fplendour and magnificence. When he had exhilerated his fpirits with wine, he requefted him to clear the prefence of his followers, making figns, which the fultan interpreted in favour of his wifhes. Eager to enjoy the flave's beautiful daughter, and drowned in the fea of defire, the fultan, without caution, commanded all his attendants to retire. Lallcheen, leaving a eunuch with inftructions to ply the fultan with wine, departed towards his haram, as if for his daughter; but in a little time after re-entered with a drawn dagger. The fultan, though intoxicated, attempted to make refiftance, but could not walk firmly; and, foon falling to the ground, rolled down a flight of fteps. Lallcheen came up with him at the laft ftep, and feized him by the hair. By the help of the eunuch, having thrown him upon his back, he pierced out both his eyes with the point of his dagger; then fending for the royal attendants one by one, as if by the fultan's orders, he put them to death fingly, as they came, to the number of twenty four perfons, all of the higheft diftinction and office; fo that no one remained alive powerful enough to obftruct his defigns. He then placed Shumfe ad Dien, brother to the dethroned prince, on the throne, and fent the latter in confinement to the fortrefs of Saugher. This event happened on the feventeenth of Ramazan, 799, after a reign of only one month and twenty days. A. D. 1396.

SULTAN

# SULTAN

## ᵃ SHUMSE AD DIEN BHAMENEE.

SULTAN Shumſe ad Dien acceded to the throne in his fifteenth year; and, warned by the fate of his predeceſſor, was contented with the name of ſovereign. Lallcheen was honoured with the title of ᵇ mallek naib; and the nobility who had eſcaped the ſword ſeeing no ſafety but in ſubmiſſion, bowed their heads to his authority. The mother of the ſultan, who had been a ſlave, anxious for the ſafety of her child, paid the utmoſt deference to Lallcheen, and inſtructed her ſon to do the ſame. She repreſented to him, that it was by his good offices he was raiſed to the throne, that he had no loyal ſubject but him; ſo that he ſhould be careful not to depart from his advice, or liſten to the malicious reports or inſinuations of intereſted perſons againſt him. Lallcheen behaved to the ſultan's mother with great reſpect, frequently ſending her coſtly preſents of valuable curioſities, and uſing every means to enſure her confidence.

Sultan Daood Shaw had left behind him three ſons, Mahummud Sunjer, blinded, as before related, by the princeſs Rhuperwer Ageh, Firoze Khan, and Ahmed Khan. The two laſt were born of the ſame mother, and at the time of their father's death were between ſix and ſeven years of age. Their uncle, Mhamood Shaw, had behaved with paternal tenderneſs, educated them in a manner becoming their rank

---

ᵃ The ſun of the faith.
ᵇ Lord deputy.

rank, and taken care to have them accomplished in all military exercises, under the preceptorship of Meer Fyez Oollah Anjoo Sheerazee. As Sultan Mhamood Shaw had not then a son, he gave each of the princes one of his daughters, and would sometimes say, that Firoze Khan should be his successor. He frequently seated him by his side on the throne, and would declare, that none of his house was more deserving or accomplished, or likely to add lustre to the throne. When the Almighty blessed him with sons, he appointed the eldest, sultan Gheause ad Dien, his successor in the throne; and conjured Firoze Khan and Ahmed Khan, upon his death-bed, to be loyal and obedient to him. They accordingly served him with submission and fidelity.

When sultan Gheause ad Dien was deposed and blinded by Lallcheen, his sisters instigated their husbands to revenge his cause; which they resolved on doing the first opportunity. Lallcheen learning their intentions, complained of them to the sultan. He accused them of falsehood and treachery; hoping by this means to alarm his fears, and obtain an order for their death, or imprisonment, but all in vain; as sultan Shumse ad Dien would not believe them faithless. Lallcheen then represented to the queen mother, that if she did not get rid of the brothers, her son would be deposed, and she, who was accused of love to his person, be exposed to misery and insult. This art had a full effect on the princess, who at length gained over her son to consent to the murder of his cousins; but they having obtained intelligence of the designs forming against them, escaped from Koolburga to the fortress of Saugher.

Suddoo, a slave of the royal family, who commanded in Saugher, was rich and powerful. He received them into the fort with respect, and left nothing undone to testify his loyalty. Ahmed Khan and Firoze Khan from hence wrote to sultan Shumse ad Dien, and the principal nobility, that their design was only to expel Lallcheen,
whose

whose treachery to sultan Gheause ad Dien, and other crimes, which had cast dishonour on the royal family, were known to all, and demanded punishment; that if that was effected, they should remain loyal, and sumissive to the royal authority, and regard sultan Shumse ad Dien as their lawful prince; but if their wish was not complied with, they would not neglect to use all the power in their hands to obtain their desire.

Sultan Shumse ad Dien, by advice of his mother and Lallcheen, sent back an answer which served only to raise the flames of contention. The brothers, with the assistance of Suddoo, having collected three thousand horse and foot, in hopes that great part of the troops would join them from the capital, marched towards Koolburga. Being disappointed, they halted some time on the banks of the Beemrah, but no one joined from the city. It was, notwithstanding, agreed that they should advance, and the umbrella of royalty was spread over the head of Firoze Khan. Ahmed Khan was exalted to the office of ameer al amra, Suddoo to that of meer nobut, and Meer Fyez Oollah Anjoo was appointed vaqueel, or prime minister. Titles of honour and employments were also conferred on their dependants, according to their rank, quality, and merit.

Upon their arrival within four cofs of the city, Lallcheen having distributed great sums of money in largess to the officers and troops, marched out, with sultan Shumse ad Dien, to oppose them. A severe engagement took place in the vicinity of the town of Merkole, and the brothers being defeated, fled with their remaining friends and adherents to Saugher. The power and haughtiness of the king's mother and Lallcheen at length grew to such an height, that many of the officers about the court privately offered their services to the brothers, whom they advised to procure pardon from sultan Shumse ad Dien, and repair to Koolburga, where they might form plans for forwarding their views at leisure.

Firoze

Firoze Khan, relying on the assurances of his friends, sent Meer Fyez Oollah Anjoo and Syed Kummaul ad Dien, with other respectable persons, to the queen and Lallcheen, representing, that fear only had occasioned their rebellion, of which they now sincerely repented; and if the sultan would send them letters of pardon, they would repair to court, and live under the shadow of the royal munificence. The queen mother and Lallcheen, highly pleased at such a request, sent letters of pardon, filled with the most flattering assurances of favour.

Soon after the arrival of the letters, the two brothers were sitting upon a terrace, and consulting whether they should yet go to Koolburga, when a [a] Cashmirian madman passed by, and exclaimed, I am come, O Firoze of lucky auspices, to conduct thee to Koolburga, and make thee sultan. Regarding this as a happy presage, they marched immediately to Koolburga; where they were honoured by dresses and gifts from the sultan; but Lallcheen and Firoze Khan, still suspicious, were ever on their guard against each other.

About a fortnight after their arrival in the capital, on Thursday, the twenty third of Suffer, anno 800, Firoze Khan came into the durbar, attended by twelve [b] assillehdars firmly attached to his interest, and about three hundred of his other followers obtained admittance into the fort, by one or two at a time. He then sent for his brother Ahmed Khan, and, upon his arrival, told Lallcheen that some of his relations were come from his jaghire, in order to pay their respects to the sultan, whose commands he requested might be given to the porters, to admit whomsoever he should send for.

A.D. 1397.

K            Firoze

---

[a] The Mahummedans regard the rhapsodies of the mad as inspirations; and it is not uncommon for a person meditating an undertaking, to visit a lunatic, and listen to his words, from which he draws an ill, or lucky omen.

[b] Arms-bearers.

Firoze Khan taking care to employ Lallcheen in conversation, his brother went out, on pretence of introducing his relations. Attempting to pass with twelve persons at once, he was stopped by the porters; when, finding that his scheme must be betrayed, he resolved to run all hazards, and attacked them. The porters were cut down, and he rushed into the durbar without delay. Some opposition was made by Lallcheen's sons, but all the rest of the assembly fled. Sultan Shumse ad Dien ran to hide himself in a subterraneous apartment. The three hundred friends of Firoze Khan, agreeably to the plan formed, attacked and put to flight the dependants of Lallcheen in the courts of the palace; so that every thing succeeded according to design.

Firoze Khan having put chains on sultan Shumse ad Dien and his minister, confined them in the apartment to which they had fled for shelter. Then, accompanied by the nobility, he repaired to the hall of audience, where he ascended the throne Firozeh. To fulfil the prediction of the Cashmirian, and as a fortunate presage, he stiled himself Firoze Shaw Roze Afzoon, and girt himself with the sword of sultan Alla ad Dien. When his authority was established, he blinded sultan Shumse ad Dien, and sent him to confinement in the fortress of Bieder. Having sent for sultan Gheause ad Dien from Saugher, he gave up Lallcheen to his resentment. That prince, though quite blind, having ordered him to be placed bound before him, killed him with one stroke of his sabre. He then asked with much earnestness of sultan Firoze Shaw to be allowed to go on a pilgrimage to Mecca. This was granted, and he sailed from Choule, and arrived in safety at the holy city. Sultan Firoze Shaw sent annually for his support five thousand pieces of gold, and quantities of the best manufactures of Hind, till his death, which fell out at Mecca, after many years. Sultan Shumse ad Dien reigned only five months and seven days.

SULTAN

# [a] ABOU AL MUZZUFFIR AL GHAZEE SULTAN FIROZE ROZE AFZOON SHAW BHAMENEE.

FROM various histories we learn, that sultan Firoze Shaw far exceeded his predecessors in power and magnificence; and that in him the house of Bhamenee became most celebrated. He forced the roies of Beejanuggur to give him a daughter of their house in marriage, though against their custom of marrying only in their own tribe. Neither did he neglect the promulgation of the true faith, but made four and twenty glorious campaigns, by the success of which he greatly enlarged his dominions. The fort of [b] Beekapore, and the best part of Telingana, were by him reduced to the Islaam yoke. He was also the first of the Dekkan sultans who wore a crown set with jewels in the form of a turban. On liberality, one of the prime virtues of royalty, he valued himself much, and required a great reputation. He was guilty of no offences against the rules of religion, but drinking wine and listening to music. He fasted often, and regularly observed the prescribed ceremonies of the holy law. He would often express anxiety for his two offences, but said, that as music lifted his mind to contemplate the divinity, and wine did not make him passionate,

---

[a] The victorious servant of God, champion of the faith, the fortunate sultan of happy auspices.
[b] Called also Sanore Bancapore.

passionate, he hoped he should not be questioned hereafter concerning them, but find mercy from a forgiving Creator.

As he was much addicted to women, he consulted the divines and casuists, in what manner he might gratify his passion, without breaking the law, which allowed only four wives. Some said, that he might divorce one and marry another as often as he pleased: but no opinions given were satisfactory to the sultan; who, at last, referred the point in debate to Meer Fyez Oollah Anjoo, his minister. Fyez Oollah observed, that in the time of the prophet and the first Kaliph, the [a] mutteah was allowed; and though abrogated in the reign of the second, it was still legal, according to the tenets of the [b] Sheeah's. The [c] Soonee denied this privilege, and much debate took place among the learned. All the various traditions were quoted in favour of their opinions, by each party. At length the sultan embraced the judgment of the Sheeahs, and took into his haram in one day three hundred women.

According to Hajee Mahummud Candaharee, Firoze Shaw, every fourth day, made a point of copying sixteen pages of the koraun; after which he engaged in publick business. He generally spent his evenings, till twelve o'clock, in company of divines, poets, reciters of history, and chaunters of the [d] shaw namneh, and the most learned and witty among his courtiers. In this assembly he laid aside the royal dignity; observing, that when he sat on the throne to transact business, he was a sovereign, and necessarily obliged to assume state, that his dignity might impress the hearts of the people and the order of government be supported: but that, in their company, he regarded himself as a private person, and wished to be treated

---

[a] The mutteah is a marriage for a time, made by compact between the parties.
[b] Followers of Alee.
[c] The other grand sect of mussulmauns.
[d] Ferdosi's celebrated history of ancient Persian monarchs.

treated without form or ceremony. He defired that all might come or go at will; that each perfon might call for what he chofe to eat and drink, and fpeak freely on all fubjects but two, which he forbad being introduced into converfation; the firft, affairs of ftate, and the fecond, flander of an abfent perfon.

Mullah Eefauk Sirhindee, a man of great learning and wit, obferved one day to the fultan, that his defiring his attendants to ufe no ceremony towards him was contrary to the genius of kings; the truth of which was proved by an anecdote of the emperor \* Mahummud Subuctageen, and the phyfician and aftrologer, Anweree Khan. The fultan defired he would relate the ftory. Having heard it, he laughed, and obferved, that fuch behaviour could only proceed from princes void of juftice, difcernment, or fcience; and that he hoped fuch weaknefs, as could occafion a like conduct, was not in his difpofition. Thofe who frequented the fultan's affemblies, had full experience of his excelling moft princes in uniformity of behaviour, and fteadinefs of conduct.

There are many curious anecdotes of fultan Firoze Shaw by Moolla Daood Biederee, the relation of which would occafion too great prolixity, and perhaps caufe my being accufed of departure from truth; fo that I fhall not give them to my readers; but as Subuctageen and the phyfician Anweree have been mentioned, it may be proper to give the ftory in the words of Moolla Daood Biederee.

"It is related, that the phyfician Anweree Khan was one of the
"wonders of his age, and performed many furprizing deeds. On
"account of his great learning, and the condefcenfion ufed towards
"him by the emperor, he acquired a freedom in his behaviour, that
"in the end grew difpleafing. One day, while the emperor was
"fitting

\* Emperor of Ghuznee, part of Hindooftan, Perfia, and Tartary.

"sitting on the terrace of a lofty building in the palace of Ghuznee, Anweree Khan entered the gate. The sultan commanded him to foretell at which gate of the palace he should go out. Anweree Khan immediately fixing his astrolabe, took an altitude, and having finished his observation, wrote it on a piece of paper, and placed it under a pillow. The sultan gave orders for part of the eastern wall of the fort to be thrown down, and when he had gone out that way, examined the paper, on which was written the very act he had done. The sultan was enraged at the physician's foreknowledge, and ordered him, in his passion, to be cast headlong from the top of the palace. Luckily, a net or some soft substance received Anweree, who escaped without the least hurt. The sultan then asked him if he had foreseen this? to which the physician replied, he had; and calling for his journal, pointed out to the sultan a prediction that he should, upon such a day, fall from a high place, and escape unhurt. This displeased the sultan still more, and he ordered him to be confined. Six months after this, while the physician was still in prison, one of his slaves going to the market, was told by a diviner from omens, that he perceived in his aspect much good fortune, which he would foretell him for a certain sum. The slave gave him his demand; upon which the diviner said he had a master in distress, who in a few days would be delivered from his troubles, and receive a dress of honour. The slave, by way of congratulation, told his master; who reproved him for credulity, and going into such bad company. Three days after, it happened that Houssun Meimundee took opportunity, upon the sultan's conversing with him upon astrology, to mention the unfortunate physician, lamenting, that instead of rewards and honours for his two surprizing predictions, he had been doomed to wretchedness and a gloomy prison. The sultan replied, that certainly he was unrivalled in science, but a complete physician should know better from the human mind that kings are like

"children,

"children, and ᵃ muſt be flattered. After theſe remarks he com-
"manded the phyſician to be releaſed. Anweree, upon his way
"from priſon to the court, met the diviner, and loſt ſomething of his
"ſcientific vanity. The ſultan honoured him with a dreſs, a thou-
"ſand pieces of ſilver, a horſe, and man and woman ſlave; at the
"ſame time he expreſſed his concern for what had happened; he
"deſired that he would now and then ſpeak to pleaſe his humour,
"and not always adhere to the letter of his art."

Sultan Firoze Shaw every year diſpatched veſſels from the ports of Goa and Choule, to bring him the manufactures and curious productions of all quarters; but particularly to invite perſons celebrated for their talents in any, whom, he would frequently obſerve, ſhould be regarded as the choiceſt poſſeſſions of all countries. He ſaid, that kings ſhould draw to them the learned and deſerving of all nations; that from their ſociety they might be able to ſelect the perfections of each, and, in a manner, thus travel the globe. On this account, the celebrated of all parts flocked to his court, and ſhared his royal bounties. The ſultan had ſo excellent a memory, that he could converſe in the languages of many countries; and he always did in their own to ſtrangers. Hearing any thing once, was ſufficient for his retaining it ever after. He was alſo a good poet, and often ſpoke verſe extempore. He was well acquainted with ſeveral ſciences, and particularly fond of natural philoſophy. On Saturdays, Mondays, and Thurſdays, he gave lectures on botany, geometry, and logic, generally in the day, but if buſineſs interfered, at night. It was ſuppoſed that he exceeded ſultan Mahummud Tughluk Shaw in learning.

He

---

ᵃ This idea, at the preſent day, ſufficiently influences the conduct of Indian courtiers; who do not fail to burſt out into the moſt rapturous exclamations of applauſe, on any repartee, or even activity of the prince in his exerciſes, ſuch as hitting a mark, &c. Their children are ſeriouſly taught the following maxim of the poet Saadee. "Should the prince at noon ſay, It is night, declare that you behold the moon and "ſtars."

He was the first king of Dekkan who intermarried with the syeds of Anjoo, taking a daughter of that family for his son Houssun Khan, and giving one of his own in marriage to Meer Shumse ad Dien Mahummud Anjoo, whom he appointed governor of Dowlutabad.

Firoze Shaw built a town on the banks of the Beemrah, which he called Firozeabad. The streets were laid out with regularity, and very broad. Within it, near the river, he erected a citadel of stone, divided into a number of splendid courts, detached from each other, all supplied plentifully with water, conducted by an ample canal from the river. Each of these courts he committed to one of his favourite ladies; and, to avoid confusion and irregularity among his women, formed rules and ordinances to be observed in the haram, which were strictly obeyed during his life. In the apartments where any of his own women resided, he did not allow more than three female attendants to one person, who were to be always of the same nation, or speak the same tongue as their mistress. He had persons constantly employed to buy women slaves of all nations; from whom he chose persons to supply the vacancies occasioned by death, or other causes, among his mistresses or their servants. He had Arabians, Circassians, Georgians, Turks, Russians, Europeans, Chinese, Afghauns, Raajepootes, Bengalees, Guzaratees, Telinganees, Mharattins, and others, in his haram, and could converse with each in her own language. He divided his attention so regularly among them, that each lady fancied herself most beloved by the sultan. He could read the \* Toreet and Anjeel; and respected the tenets of all religions, but acknowledged with raptures the faith of Mahummud superior to all others, as it commanded keeping up women from the eyes of strangers, and forbad the use of wine, contrary to the other systems of religion.

When

---

\* The bible and new testament. From this it is probable, Firoze Shaw learned Hebrew from the Jews, who have been settled on the Malabar coast for many ages, and, as they say, since the captivity of Babylon.

When sultan Firoze Shaw ascended the throne, he appointed his brother Ahmed Khan ameer al amra, with the title of [a] Khan Khanan, and raised Meer Fyez Oollah Anjoo, his preceptor, to the office of [b] vaqueel al sultunnut and title of [c] mallek naib. Honours were also conferred on many of the family of Bhamenee. Historians unitedly agree, that he made twenty four campaigns against the Hindoos, but the particulars of a few only are related by Moollah Daood Biederee in his Tofet al Sallateen.

In the year 801, Dewul Roy, of Beejanuggur, with thirty thousand horse, and a vast army of foot, invaded the royal territories between the rivers, with a design to reduce the forts of Mudkul and Roijore. Sultan Firoze Shaw having intelligence of his motions, moved without delay from Koolburga to Saugher, where he took a muster of his army. After this he put to death a zemindar, with seven or eight thousand Hindoos, who had been always very troublesome and refractory. The armies of Dowlutabad and Berar had joined him, and he was preparing to move against Dewul Roy, when suddenly advice was brought, that Nersing, possessor of [d] Kurleh, at the instigations of the sultans of [e] Mando and [f] Aseer, also the roy of Beejanuggur, had invaded the province of Berar, where he committed every cruelty and depredation on the mussulmauns as far as the walls of [g] Dahoor. Upon this the sultan sent back the forces of Dowlutabad

A.D. 1398.

[a] Lord of lords.
[b] Deputy of the government.
[c] Lord deputy.
[d] A district on the frontier of Berar bordering on Malwa, having a capital of the same name.
[e] The capital of Malwa, then governed by Afghaun sultans.
[f] A strong fortress, then the capital of Khandeshe, under an independant sovereign, claiming his descent from Omar, one of the friends of Mahummud, and the second kaliph. This place and sovereignty were reduced to the Mogul empire by Akber.
[g] A town in Berar.

bad to oppofe Nerfing, and marched with the remainder of his troops againft Dewul Roy.

It being the rainy feafon, and the river Kiftnah very full, Dewul Roy had pitched his camp, in felf-fecurity, on the bank; and ftationed large bodies of foot along the fhore to oppofe the paffage of the muffulmauns. Sultan Firoze Shaw, on his arrival near the river, held a council of war with his chief officers, but received no advice that to him appeared fatisfactory. While the fultan was debating in his own mind how to act, \* Cauzi Serauje, feeing his concern, offered, if the fultan would permit him, to crofs the river with a few of his friends, whom he would felect for the purpofe, to affaffinate Dewul Roy, or his fon, as he found it moft convenient; obferving, when the alarm that would attend fuch an exploit fhould throw the enemy's camp into confufion, the fultan might fend a party acrofs the river, fecure a paffage for the whole army, and make the infidels repent of their infolence and difobedience to the prince of the faithful.

The fultan approving the meafure, fome hundreds of hurdles covered with leather were prepared expeditioufly for the troops to crofs. Cauzi Serauje with feven of his friends, difguifed as holy mendicants, proceeded to the roy's camp, and repaired to the quarter where the dancing girls refided. Here the cauzi pretended to be enraptured with a courtezan, and was guilty of a thoufand extravagancies to fupport his character. In the evening, the girl having adorned herfelf in her richeft ornaments, prepared to go out; on which, the cauzi, like a jealous and diftracted lover, falling at her feet, entreated her to ftay, or let him attend her, and not rend his heart by abfence. The woman upon this informed him, that fhe was ordered to attend an entertainment by the roy's fon, and durft not difobey, nor

---

\* A judge from the laws of the koraun. It was not uncommon among the mahummedans, for fuch a magiftrate to feek, out of regard and zeal for religion, the moft difficult and hazardous exploit in war.

nor could she take him with her, as only musicians and dancers would be admitted. The cauzi upon this replied, that he played on the same instrument as herself, and had, beside, some curious accomplishment that would highly please the roy's son. The dancing girl, thinking him in jest, out of contempt gave him her *mundul, and desired him to play; which he did in so masterly a manner, that she was delighted, saying, that his company would give her superiority over her fellows, and do her honour with the roy's son. Accordingly, he with his companions attended the girl to the tents of the young roy.

As is the custom of Dekkan, many sets of ᵇloolies and dancing girls were ordered to perform at the same time, and having finished their parts, the roy's son called for the players and mummers. The dancing girl now obtained leave for the cauzi and one of his companions to show their feats. Having assumed the dress of women, they entered ogling and smiling, and so well imitated the mummers in playing on the mundul, dancing and mimickry, that the roy's son was charmed with their performances. At length they each drew a dagger, and, like the dancers of Dekkan, continued to flourish them for some time, making a thousand antic postures in advancing, retreating, and turning round. At last, suddenly rushing upon the roy's son, they plunged both the daggers into his breast, afterwards attacking his companions. Their remaining friends, who were watching without the tent, on hearing an alarm, ripped up the curtain, and entered to assist them. Many of the company being much intoxicated, were easily put to death. The cauzi with his friends extinguished all the lights; and, making their escape through the rent, mingled with the crowd. The outcry soon became general round the tents. Great confusion ensued, and various reports and alarms took place. Some said, that the sultan had crossed the river and surprized the camp; others,

---

* A stringed instrument.
ᵇ Youths trained to sing and dance in public.

others, that one of his chiefs, with twelve thousand men, had cut off both the roy and his son. The night was uncommonly dark, and the camp extended near ten miles, so that circumstances were variously reported; and the different chiefs, ignorant of the real cause of the alarm, contented themselves with waiting in their several quarters under arms. About four thousand of the sultan's troops in this interim, crossed the river in boats and rafts, which had been prepared for the purpose. The enemy's foot stationed to oppose the passage, terrified by the alarm in camp and the approach of the sultan's forces, fled in confusion, without waiting to be attacked. Before the morning Firoze Shaw had crossed the river with his whole army, and at dawn assaulted the enemy's camp with great fury. Dewul Roy, grieved by the death of his son, and panic struck at the bravery of the assailants, made but a faint resistance. Before sunrise, having taken up his son's corpse, he fled with his army. The sultan gained immense plunder in the camp, and pursued him to the vicinity of Beejanuggur. Several actions happened on the way, all of which were fortunate to the sultan; and the roads were heaped up with the bodies of the slaughtered Hindoos.

When Dewul Roy had shut himself up in the fort of Beejanuggur, and no enemy remained in the field, Firoze Shaw dispatched Khan Khanan and Meer Fuzzul Oollah to lay waste the districts south of the city, which were uncommonly populous and flourishing. Cauzi Serauje, in reward for his heroic exploit, being raised to a high rank of nobility, was detached with them. They left nothing undone in performance of their instructions; and having taken captives without number, returned to camp.

As great numbers of bramins had fallen into the hands of the mussulmauns, their friends at Beejanuggur offered to assist the roy with large sums of money to purchase peace and ransom the captives. Dewul Roy accepted their offers; and, after much negotiation,

Meer

Meer Fuzzul Oollah agreed to accept [a] ten lacs of oons for the royal treasury, as a ransom for the prisoners, and one lac for his own intercession. Accordingly, the bramins sent six lacs, and Dewul Roy five; all which Fuzzul Oollah laid before the sultan, who greatly praised his disinterested services. A treaty was then concluded between the powers, by which it was agreed, that their boundaries should remain the same as before the war, and that one party should not molest the subjects of the other. Sultan Firoze Shaw released his prisoners, and began his march to his own dominions. When he had passed the Tummedra, he dispatched Folaud Khan to regulate the country between [b] the rivers, and, leaving the army, hastened with a few attendants to Koolburga.

In a few months after the conclusion of this campaign, and the beginning of the year 802, the sultan marched to punish Nersing; and upon his arrival before Mahoor, the governor of that place having obtained quarter at the intercession of some of the nobility, made large offerings, and joined the army with his children. The sultan halted a month and five days at Mahoor, when he moved towards Kurleh. Nersing, who had great wealth and power, being possessed of all the hills of [c] Gondwaneh, and other countries, sent rich presents to the governors of Malwa and Khandeshe, entreating assistance; but though they had, through dread of his power, furnished him formerly with aids, yet as they in fact wished his ruin, they now gave him a positive refusal. Notwithstanding this, Nersing was resolved to engage the sultan; and, marching two cofs from Kurleh, waited for his approach.

A. D. 1399.

Sultan

[a] Near 400,000l. sterling.
[b] The Kisinah and Tummedra.
[c] The part of Berar next Malwa, now belonging to Chimnajee Bhoselah, whose country is also called Nagpore.

Sultan Firoze Shaw was anxious to lead the battle in perfon; but as Khan Khanan and Meer Fuzzul Oollah Anjoo requefted to be allowed to crufh the enemy with their own troops, he confented, and gave them their difmiffion. They firft wrote to Nerfing a letter of remonftrance on the folly of his conduct, and advifing him to fubmit to pay tribute; but he anfwered it only by threats of defiance, and greater preparations for war. Khan Khanan and Meer Fuzzul Oollah then attacked his lines, and a fevere conflict enfued; in which Shujahut Khan, Dillawer Khan, and Bahadur Khan, principal nobles, obtained martyrdom; and, the infidels charging furioufly, the troops of Iflaam were broken. At this inftant it was reported to Fuzzul Oollah, that Khan Khanan was flain. He commanded the informer to keep the report fecret, and advancing with two hundred horfe, ordered the march of victory to beat, crying out, that the fultan was coming to their affiftance. The troops at thefe tidings rallied in great numbers, and he drove off the enemy. He was foon after joined by Khan Khanan, fuppofed to be flain; and they now together charged the remaining enemy with fuch vigour, that they foon put them to flight, and took prifoner Goful Roy, the fon of Nerfing. The fugitives were purfued to Kurleh; about ten thoufand were flain in their flight; and Nerfing, having with much difficulty gained the fortrefs, fhut himfelf up, and was clofely befieged by the victorious army of Iflaam.

At the end of two months, being reduced to great diftrefs he begged terms; but received anfwer from the generals, that they had no power to grant any; and, unlefs Nerfing would throw himfelf at the fultan's feet, he muft expect none. Nerfing, feeing no refource but compliance, went with his family to the fultan's camp at Elichpore; where, expreffing forrow for his offence, and acknowledging himfelf the fultan's vaffal, he offered to give up Kurleh; but if his majefty chofe to admit him among the number of his tributaries, and to draw the pen of forgivenefs over his crimes, he
would

would pay every year the tribute fixed by sultan Alla ad Dien, and remain constant in the paths of obedience.

Sultan Firoze Shaw having pardoned Nerſing, gave him a dreſs of honour, richly embroidered with gold; and having received one of his daughters among his women, with forty fine elephants, a ſum of money, and other valuables and curioſities, ordered the ſiege of Kurleh to be diſcontinued. Upon the junction of Khan Khanan and Meer Fuzzul Oollah with his army, he diſmiſſed Nerſing, and returned in triumph to the capital of Koolburga. As this victory was chiefly owing to Meer Fuzzul Oollah, that nobleman was promoted to the command of the Berar army.

In the year 804, repeated accounts coming from the court of Ameer Timur, of that great conqueror having conferred the throne of Dhely on one of his ſons, with orders to ſubdue all the kingdoms of Hindooſtan, and that he had reſolved to march in perſon to aſſiſt his deſigns, if neceſſary; Sultan Firoze Shaw ſent ambaſſadors to the emperor, with rich preſents, and a letter expreſſive of reſpectful attachment. Timur received the ambaſſadors graciouſly, and accepted the preſents. At the end of ſix months, by means of ſome of the favourites at court, they repreſented to the emperor, that Firoze Shaw was deſirous to be numbered among his ſlaves, and would, whenever his majeſty ſhould march himſelf, or ſend one of the princes, to conquer Hindooſtan, haſten to join from Dekkan with his troops. Timur, pleaſed at his offers of attachment from ſo great a diſtance, pronounced that he gave him the ſovereignty of Dekkan, Malwa, and Guzarat, with permiſſion to uſe the umbrella, and all other inſignia of empire. He alſo delivered to the ambaſſadors a firmaun, containing the grant of the above countries, a ſword ſet with jewels from his own ſide, a royal robe, a Turkiſh ſlave, and four horſes, ſuperior in beauty to any ever ſeen in Dekkan.

A.D. 1401.

The

The sultans of Malwa and Khandēſhe, whoſe power was yet weak, alarmed at the ambition of ſultan Firoze Shaw, ſent ambaſſadors to court his friendſhip; obſerving, that they ought to live together like brothers, and unite in alliance againſt the power of the emperor of Dhely. At the ſame time they privately wrote to the roy of Beejanuggur, that whenever he ſhould need their aſſiſtance againſt ſultan Firoze Shaw, to inform them, that they might lend him all the ſupport in their power.

On theſe overtures, the roy of Beejanuggur changing his behaviour to the ſultan, neglected to pay his tribute for four years; and Firoze Shaw, knowing the ſecret enmity of his neighbours the ſultans of Guzarat and Malwa, did not preſs him, but winked at his neglect, reſolving to puniſh it at his convenience.

There reſided in the town of Mudkul a farmer, who was bleſſed with a daughter of ſuch exquiſite beauty, that the creator ſeemed to have united all his powers in making her perfect. Agreeably to the cuſtom of Hindooſtan, her parents wiſhed in her childhood to betroth her to one of her own caſt; but ſhe requeſted that the ceremony might be delayed, with ſuch earneſtneſs, that to pleaſe her it was put off. Some time after, an old bramin, who had been on a pilgrimage to Banaras, ſtopped on his return at her father's houſe, and was ſo delighted with her beauty, that he adopted her as his daughter, and reſolved to accompliſh her in muſic and dancing, of which he was perfectly maſter. He continued near a year and half with her family; at the end of which, finding her completely ſkilled in muſic and all the graces of dancing, he took his leave, with a promiſe ſhortly to return, with propoſals calculated for the honour of his pupil, and the advantage of her family. The bramin, who had from the firſt reſolved to exalt his adopted daughter to royalty, proceeded to Beejanuggur, and, being introduced to the roy, ſpoke in ſuch praiſe of the beauty and accompliſhments of the young maid, that he was fired

with

with defire of poffeffing her, and entreated the bramin to procure her for him of her parents in marriage. This requeft was what the bramin earneftly wifhed, and he immediately agreed to fatisfy him; upon which the roy difpatched him with rich gifts and great promifes of favour to the parents, and the title of ranee, or princefs, for their beautiful daughter. The bramin loft no time in his journey, and, upon his arrival at the farmer's houfe, delivered to him and his wife the roy's orders that they fhould repair to Beejanuggur with their daughter. The parents were overjoyed at fuch unexpected good fortune, and calling for the young maid, laid before her the rich gifts of the roy, congratulated her on being foon to be united to a great prince, and attempted to throw upon her neck a golden collar fet with jewels, as the token of immediate efpoufals, and which, if done, could not have been broken off.

The beautiful virgin, to their great aftonifhment, drawing her neck from compliance, refufed to receive the collar; and obferved, that whoever entered the haram of Beejanuggur, was afterwards not permitted to fee even her neareft relations and friends; and though they might be happy to fell her for worldly riches, yet fhe was too fond of her parents to fubmit to eternal abfence from them, even for all the fplendour of the palace of Beejanuggur. This declaration was accompanied with affectionate tears, which melted her parents; who, rather than ufe force, difmiffed the bramin with all his gifts, and he returned chagrined and difappointed to Beejanuggur. The maid then obferved to her parents, that fhe had long had an inward perfuafion that fhe fhould become wife to a great prince of the faith of Iflaam, and defired them to wait patiently the decrees of providence. Her parents fmiled at her fuppofed folly; but, as advice and remonftrance had no effect, they fubmitted to be filent, and leave her in the enjoyment of her own thoughts.

When the bramin arrived at Beejanuggur, and related to the roy the failure of his scheme, the prince's love became outrageous, and he resolved to gratify it by force, though the object resided in the heart of Firoze Shaw's dominions. For this purpose he quitted Beejanuggur with a great army, on pretence of going the tour of his countries; and upon his arrival on the banks of the river Tummedra, having selected five thousand of his best horse, and giving the reins of his conduct to love, commanded them, in spite of the remonstrances of his friends, to march night and day with all expedition to Mudkul, and, surrounding the village where Pertal lived, to bring her prisoner to him, with her whole family, without injury.

As the roy had, in the excess of love, lost his judgment, he neglected to send the bramin to prevent the parents of his beloved from being frightened at the approach of troops, and to tempt them to remain in the place, should the alarm be spread time enough for the inhabitants to escape; so that the country round Mudkul being apprized of the enemy's approach, the inhabitants, and among them Pertal's family, fled for shelter to distant parts.

The troops of Dewul Roy, being deprived of their expected prize, returned with expedition; but on their route laid waste several towns and villages, before troops could be collected to oppose them. At length Folaud, governor of the province, marched against them, and the plunderers, seeing themselves greatly superior to him in numbers, stopped to engage, and obliged him to retire. Being however, quickly reinforced, he pursued them a second time; and the invaders, not dreaming of being followed by a beaten enemy, had become careless on their march, so that they were surprized and had not time to form. Folaud Khan completely defeated them, and slaughtered above two thousand, before they recrossed the Tummedra.

Sultan

Sultan Firoze Shaw, on hearing of this unprovoked and infolent invafion, immediately iffued orders for affembling his forces, and his camp to be formed near Firozeabad. In the beginning of the winter of the year 809, he moved in great force, and arrived near Beejanuggur, in which Dewul Roy had fhut himfelf up. An affault was made upon the city, and the fultan got poffeffion of fome ftreets, which, however, he was obliged to quit, his army being repulfed by the Carnatickehs. Dewul Roy, encouraged by his fuccefs, now ventured to encamp his army under protection of the walls, and to moleft the royal camp. As the muffulmauns could not make proper ufe of their cavalry in the rocky unevennefs of ground round Beejanuggur, they were fomewhat difpirited. During this, fultan Firoze Shaw was wounded by an arrow in the hand, but he would not difmount; and drawing out the arrow, bound up the wound with a cloth. The enemy were at laft driven off by the valour and activity of Ahmed Khan and Khan Khanan, and the fultan moved farther from the city to a convenient plain, where he halted till his wounded men were recovered. Laying afide the defign of taking the city, he detached a body of ten thoufand horfe under Khan Khanan and Mean Suddoh his meer nobut, to lay wafte the country to the fouth of Beejanuggur; and fent meer Fuzzul Oollah Anjoo to befiege the fortrefs of Beekapore, the moft important in the Carnatic. The fultan, with the remainder of his army, continued in the environs of the city, to amufe Dewul Roy, and fortified his camp with a circle of cannon and fireworks. Dewul Roy more than once attacked him, but was always driven off with great flaughter. He then defifted from attacks, and difpatched ambaffadors to beg aids of the fultans of Malwa, Khandefhe, and Guzarat.

A.D. 1406.

The fultan continued to employ Dewul Roy for four months, during which Khan Khanan laid wafte the moft flourifhing towns and diftricts of Carnatic, and Meer Fuzzul Oollah fucceeded in the reduction of the fortrefs of Beekapore, with it's valuable dependancies;

the government of which he committed, by the sultan's orders, to Mean Suddoh, and with his army returned to the royal camp. Khan Khanan also joined the army of the sultan with about sixty thousand captives, male and female, and a very rich plunder in treasure and effects. The sultan received them with the favour due to their services, and made a splendid festival in honour of his successes, at which he consulted on further operations. After some debate, it was resolved that Khan Khanan should remain opposed to Dewul Roy, while the sultan, accompanied by Meer Fuzzul Oollah, marched to besiege the fortress of Oodnee, the strongest in possession of the enemy.

Intelligence of the sultan's designs reaching Dewul Roy, as he had been refused assistance from the sultans of Malwa, Khandeshe, and Guzarat, he was plunged into a sea of despair, and sent some of his principal nobility to treat for peace at the royal camp. The sultan at first refused to grant it on any terms; but at length, being moved by the advice and entreaties of Fuzzul Oollah, agreed, on condition that the roy should give him his daughter in marriage, [a] ten lacs of oons, five [b] muns of pearl, fifty choice elephants, and two thousand men and women slaves, singers, dancers, and musicians; also, that the fort of Beekapore, already in his possession, should, to obviate all future disputes, be ceded to him for ever, in part of the marriage portion.

Though the [c] roies of Carnatic had never yet married their daughters but to persons of their own cast, and giving them to strangers
was

[a] Nearly 400,000l.
[b] The Bengal mun, or maund, is eighty pounds weight. The five here mentioned of pearls could scarcely be of that computation; but as the pearl fishery between Dekkan and Ceylon was for ages belonging to the roies of Beejanuggur, great quantities must have been in their possession.
[c] From this it appears, that the roies of Beejanuggur were sovereigns of all the ancient Carnatic.

was highly disgraceful, yet Dewul Roy, out of necessity, complied, and preparations for celebrating the nuptials were made by both parties. For forty days communication was open between the city and the sultan's camp. Both sides of the road were lined with shops and booths, in which the jugglers, drolls, dancers, and mimics of Carnatic displayed their feats and skill, to amuse passengers. Khan Khanan and Meer Fuzzul Oollah, with the customary presents of a bridegroom, went to Beejanuggur, from whence at the expiration of seven days, they brought the bride, with a rich portion and offerings from the roy, to the sultan's camp. Dewul Roy having expressed a strong desire to see the sultan, Firoze Shaw with great gallantry agreed to visit him with his bride, as his father in law.

A day being fixed, he with the bride proceeded to Beejanuggur, leaving the camp in charge of Khan Khanan. On the way he was met by Dewul Roy in great pomp. From the gate of the city to the palace, being a distance of nearly six miles, the road was spread with cloth of gold, velvet, sattin and other rich stuffs. The two princes rode on horseback together, between ranks of beautiful boys and girls, who waved plates of gold and silver * flowers over their heads as they advanced, and then threw them to be gathered by the populace. After this, the inhabitants of the city made offerings, both men and women, according to their rank. After passing through a square directly in the center of the city, the relations of Dewul Roy, who had lined the streets in crowds, made their obeisance and offerings, and joined the cavalcade on foot, marching before the princes. Upon their arrival at the palace gate, the sultan and roy dismounted from their horses, and ascended a splendid palanquin, set with valuable jewels, in which they were carried together to the apartments prepared for the reception of the bride and bridegroom; when Dewul Roy

---

* Or rather, small coin stamped with the figure of a flower. They are still used in India, to distribute in charity, and, on occasion, thrown by the pursebearers of the great among the populace.

Roy took his leave, and retired to his own palace. The sultan, after being treated with royal magnificence for three days, took his leave of the roy; who pressed upon him richer presents than before given, and attended him four miles on his way, when he returned to the city. Sultan Firoze Shaw was enraged at his not going with him to his camp, and said to Meer Fuzzul Oollah, that he would one day have revenge for the affront offered him by such neglect. This declaration being told to Dewul Roy, he made some insolent remarks, so that, notwithstanding the connection of family, their hatred was not calmed. Sultan Firoze Shaw proceeded to the capital of his dominions, and dispatched persons to bring the beautiful Pertal and her family to court; which being done, her beauty was found to surpass all that had been reported of it. The sultan observing that he was too old to espouse her himself, gave her to his son Houssun Khan in marriage, and gratified her parents with rich gifts and grants of land in their native country. Pertal was committed to the care of the sultan's aunt till the nuptial preparations were ready, when the knot was tied, amid great rejoicings and princely magnificence.

A.D. 1407.     In the year 810 Firoze Shaw, as he was a great encourager of astronomy, ordered an observatory to be built on the summit of the pass called Ballaghaut; but this work being interrupted by the death of Hakeem Houssun, the most able professor, it was left unfinished.

A.D. 1412.     In 815 the sultan went, on pretence of hunting, into the country of Gohndwarra, which he laid waste, and brought away near three hundred elephants. Soon after this, the sultan hearing that the celebrated religious syed Mahummud Geesoo-derauz, was arrived near Koolburga from Dhely, ever anxious to honour merit, came himself from Firozeabad to visit him, and sent all the nobility of the court to meet him; but, though he at first treated him with much attention, on finding him unadorned by learning or science, he withdrew the warmth of his favour.

Khan

Khan Khanan, brother to the sultan, entertained for the holy syed the strongest veneration, built for him a superb convent, spent great part of his time in attending his lectures on divinity, and was never absent from his \* wujd, or extacies; at which times he distributed large sums to the servants of the convent, and dirveshes.

In the year 818, the sultan having fixed on his son Houssun, a weak and dissipated prince, to succeed him, conferred upon him a royal cap and vestband, with an umbrella, tents, and elephants, peculiar to royalty. When he invited the nobles to acknowledge him, he requested also of the holy syed to give him his blessing; but he answered, that to one chosen by the sultan the prayers of a fakeer were of no moment. Sultan Firoze Shaw, dissatisfied with his declining the blessing, sent to beg it again, with much importunity; upon which the syed observed, that as the crown after him was decreed to his brother Khan Khanan, by the will of providence, it was vain to try to bestow it on another. The sultan, on hearing this, was much alarmed, and ordered the syed to leave the city, pretending that his convent was too near the palace, and that the crowds of his disciples and students were dangerous to the peace of the capital. The syed immediately obeyed, and retired out of the town to the spot where his tomb now stands, and his followers soon erected for him a magnificent dwelling.

A. D. 1415.

In the year 820 the sultan dispatched ambassadors to the roy of Telingana, demanding some years' arrear of tribute; and he obeying, sent the sums due, with such valuable presents of money and effects, in addition, as satisfied the sultan.

A. D. 1417.

---

\* The Mahummedan dirveshes often fall into real or pretended extacies at their religious assemblies, when verses are recited from their poets; and, when in these fits, what they utter is regarded by their disciples as the effect of prophetic inspiration. During the paroxysms, they dance, tear their clothes, and commit a thousand extravagancies. The wujd is not unlike the described extacy of the ancient Pythian priestess.

In the middle of this year, sultan Firoze Shaw formed the design of reducing the fortress of Mankul, now generally called Bilcondah. Without regarding his relationship to the roy, he marched and commenced the siege, which extended to two whole years; at the end of which, its reduction not being the will of heaven, a pestilence broke out in the royal army, in which men and horses died every day in alarming numbers. Discontent and fear filled the survivors, and many of the first nobility deserted the camp, and fled, with their followers, to their jaghires. At this crisis Dewul Roy collected his army; and having obtained aids from all the surrounding princes, even to the raja of Telingana, marched against the sultan with a vast host of horse and foot.

Firoze Shaw, though he judged his army unequal to opposition, yet impelled by royal jealousy of his glory, in spite of all the remonstrances of his friends, gave battle. Meer Fuzzul Oollah, who commanded the troops of Islaam, charged the infidels with heroic vigour, and, routing their center, proceeded to attack their right wing. He was on the point of gathering the flowers of victory, when one of his own attendants, bribed for the purpose by Dewul Roy, gave him a mortal wound on the head, and he instantly quaffed the sherbet of martyrdom. This fatal event changed the fortune of the day; the sultan was defeated, and with the utmost difficulty, by the most surprizing and gallant efforts, made his escape from the field. The Hindoos made a general massacre of the mussulmauns, and erected a platform with their heads on the field of battle. They followed the sultan into his own country, which they wasted with fire and sword, took many places, broke down mosques and holy places, slaughtered the people without mercy; by their actions seeming to discharge the treasured malice and resentment of ages. Sultan Firoze Shaw, in the exigence of distress, requested aid of the sultan of Guzarat, who, having but just acceded to the throne, could afford none. At last fortune took a turn favourable to his

affairs

affairs, and the enemy, after repeated battles, were expelled from his dominions by the sultan's brother, Khan Khanan. But these misfortunes dwelt on the mind of Firoze Shaw, now old, and he fell into a lingering disorder and lowness of spirts.

During his illness, the sultan gave the reins of government into the hands of two of his slaves, one named [a] Hoshiar Ein al Moolk, and the other [b] Nizam Bedar al Moolk, strengthening their influence with the whole weight of his authority. These ministers, jealous of the popularity and ambition of Khan Khanan, observed to the sultan, that the government of Dekkan could only be secured to his son Houssun Khan, when the kingdom should be cleared of the power and influence of Khan Khanan. The sultan then recollected the prediction of syed Mahummud Geesoo-derauz, and determined to prevent a possibility of his aspiring to the throne, by having his brother blinded. Khan Khanan, being informed of the sultan's design by his spies, prepared for flight. During the night he went with his son Alla ad Dien to the dwelling of the holy syed, to request his advice and blessing. The syed took the turban from his own son's head, and dividing it into two parts, tied one round the head of the father and son, and extending his hands over them, hailed them both with future royalty. Khan Khanan, after this ceremony, returned to his house; and, having spent the remainder of the night in preparation, issued from the gates at dawn of day with four hundred faithful companions. At the gate he was saluted, after the royal form, by a celebrated merchant, named Khulf Houssun Bussoreh, one of his earliest acquaintance, who had heard of his design.

Khan Khanan desired him to hasten to his own dwelling, lest he should be seen by the officers of the court, and suffer trouble on his account. To this Houssun remarked, that to be a companion in the days.

[a] The political eye of the state.
[b] The regulator, watchful of the state.

days of prosperity, and to cast the dust of inconstancy in the eyes of a friend in adversity, was not becoming a virtuous man; that while he had a spark of life within him, he should be loath to quit his patronage; and hoped, if he would receive him among the number of his servants, to perform some services of importance. Khan Khanan, pleased at his attachment, consented to his accompanying him, and said, that if the reins of empire should ever be held in his hands, he should be his guide and minister. He then left the city, and in the evening arrived at Khankhananpore, which he vowed to dedicate to the use of the syeds of Mecca and Medina, Nujeef and Kerballa, should he become king.

Hoshiar and Bedar, on learning the flight of Khan Khanan, went with anxious impatience to the sultan; and, having obtained permission to pursue him, marched with all expedition, attended by four thousand horse and some war elephants. Khan Khanan was for concealing himself in the country, till he could prevail on some of the nobility to assert his cause; but Houssun, dissuading him from it, sent to Koolburga, Bieder, and Kallean, from whence he procured a number of the disaffected and idle to enlist. Some days were passed in moving from place to place, to avoid fighting, when, at last, the ministers were reinforced, and all hope of escape cut off; nor could Khan Khanan hope to engage with success, the enemy being eight thousand strong, and his whole force not amounting to more than a thousand. In this crisis, a band of grain merchants, called in Hindoostan, Bunjarehs, in their way from Berar, with two thousand head of oxen, halted in the neighbourhood of Kallean, as also three hundred horses, which some dealers had brought to sell from Lahore. Khulf Houssun, who was eager for opposition, purchased them all, and making red and green banners, after the custom of Dekkan, mounted a man with a flag on each ox. He placed some cavalry in front of this mock force, with orders to appear at a distance when the engagement should commence, and to proclaim, that some principal

cipal

cipal amras had arrived from their jaghires to affift Khan Khanan. Khan Khanan at firft regarded the fcheme as ridiculous, but at laft confented to embrace it, as he could not avoid fighting. In the morning Khan Khanan moved flowly with his motley army towards the enemy, encouraging his troops by declaring that fuch and fuch noblemen were haftening to join him, and then only a few miles from them. Hofhiar and Bedar alfo dreaded the event of his being reinforced, and eagerly accepted the prefent offer of battle, hoping to prevent it. When the fight had begun, Khulf Houffun, advancing his horfe in front of the oxen, and waving his banners, appeared marching from behind a grove at fome diftance, which ftruck the enemy with a belief that the amras were arrived to Khan Khanan's affiftance; and a vigorous charge being made at the fame time, the right of the enemy broke in confufion. Hofhiar and Bedar, who were in the center, feeing their men on the right fly, and terrified at the fuppofed new troops, after a flight oppofition were routed, and driven from the field. Khan Khanan, thus unexpectedly victorious, purfued the fugitives; and having taken many elephants, horfes, and much plunder, encamped at a fmall diftance from Koolburga, and was joined by numbers of the royal troops from all quarters.

Sultan Firoze Shaw, notwithftanding his indifpofition and weaknefs, fpread the royal umbrella over the head of Houffun Khan, by the advice of his minifters; and having entrufted the citadel to fome faithful fervants, put himfelf in a palanquin (being too infirm to travel otherwife) at the head of many of the nobility, four thoufand horfe, a great number of foot, fome artillery, and many elephants, to oppofe his brother Khan Khanan. An engagement took place a few miles from the city. The body in which fultan Firoze Shaw was, being hard pufhed, a report fpread through the army that he was killed; upon which the nobility and troops came over in great numbers to the ftandard of Khan Khanan. Hofhiar and Bedar, being

alarmed

alarmed at the great defertion, fled with the fultan precipitately towards the citadel, at the gates of which fultan Firoze Shaw recovered from a fainting fit, into which he had fallen from alarm and fatigue.

Khan Khanan, out of refpect, would not allow the fultan to be purfued; but when he heard of his being in the fort, marched to the capital, and encamped under the walls of the citadel. Hofhiar and Bedar, together with Houffun Khan, manned the works, and began to moleft the befiegers with fhot and arrows. A ball entering the tent of Khan Khanan, wounded fome perfons fitting near him, upon which he retreated to a greater diftance.

Sultan Firoze Shaw, at length, calling his fon Houffun Khan before him, obferved, that empire refted on the attachment of the nobility and army, and as they had moftly declared for his uncle, he had better wind up the rolls of oppofition, which could only occafion publick calamities, and fubmit to his power. After this he ordered the gates of the palace to be thrown open, and admitted Khan Khanan, with a number of his attendants. Khan Khanan approaching the bed of the fultan, bowed his head at his feet, when Firoze Shaw expreffed pleafure at feeing him, faying, that he praifed God for letting him behold his brother fovereign, of which high dignity he was truly deferving; that paternal affection had made him wifh his fon for his fucceffor, but as he was difappointed, he left his kingdom to God, and his fon to his care. He then begged he would affume the throne, and take care of his perfon for the little time he might remain his gueft. Khan Khanan, the fame day, put on the royal turban invented by his brother, and mounting the throne Firozeh, ftiled himfelf Sultan Ahmed Shaw, commanding coins to be ftruck, and the khootbah to be read in his name. As fultan Firoze Shaw, ten days after this, refigned his
foul

foul to the guardians of paradife, his body was depofited with great funeral pomp and royal ceremony, near the tombs of his anceftors. He reigned twenty five years, feven months, and fifteen days. It is faid in fome books, that he was put to death through policy, by his brother; but no good foundation appears for the report.

SULTAN

# SULTAN

# 'AHMED SHAW WULLEE BHAMENEE.

SULTAN Ahmed Shaw underſtood well the rules of civil policy and military affairs. Copying his brother, he paid great reſpect to the ſyeds, learned men, and divines, omitting voluntarily nothing for their benefit and encouragement. In the beginning of his reign, on account of the predictions made by him of his ſucceſs, he ſhowered favours on the venerable ſyed Mahummud Geeſoo-derauz, and, as the people generally follow the opinions of their king, the natives or Dekkan choſe him for their guide in religious affairs; ſo that his reſidence became a place of pilgrimage to all ſects. The ſultan withdrew his attachment from the family of ſhekh Serauje ad Dien, to the holy ſyed; to whom he granted in perpetuity ſeveral towns, villages, and extenſive lands near Koolburga, and built for him a moſt magnificent college, not far from the city. ᵇ Though it has now paſſed from the family of Bhamenee to the ſultans of Beejapore, yet moſt of the eſtates, given by the former princes, are ſtill in poſſeſſion of the ſyed's deſcendants. The people of Dekkan have ſuch a reſpect for the ſaint, that a Dekkanee, on being once queſtioned by a humouriſt, who was the greateſt perſonage, Mahummud or he, replied, with ſeeming wonder at his query, that the prophet was undoubtedly a great man, but ſyed Mahummud Geeſoo-derauz a far ſuperior kind of being.

Sultan

---

ᵃ The excellent ſultan, friend of God.
ᵇ Feriſhta wrote in the beginning of Jehaungeer, about the year 1607.

## FERISHTA's HISTORY OF DEKKAN.

Sultan Ahmed Shaw, from the inftant he mounted the throne, turned all his attention to ftrengthen his army, and obtain revenge for the invafions of the roy of Beejanuggur in the laft reign. He appointed Khulf Houffun vaqueel al fultunnut, with the rank of twelve hundred; and, as he was a merchant, conferred upon him the title of ᵃ mallek al tijar. This title is ftill given in Dekkan, where it is efteemed one of the moft honourable. Houffun, admiring the fidelity of the minifters of the late fultan, thought them worthy of confidence, and interceded for them with the fultan, who, at his recommendation, honoured Hofhiar Ein al Moolk with the title of ameer al amra and rank of fifteen hundred; and giving the government of Dowlutabad to Bedar Nizam al Moolk, exalted him to the rank of two thoufand. We are told, that the princes of Bhamenee confined the higheft rank of nobility to two thoufand, in which were admitted only four perfons, the terruffdars, or governors of the four capital divifions of the kingdom. From this, the ranks were continued down as low as two hundred, but none of lefs rank were efteemed noble. An ameer of a thoufand had the privilege of carrying in his fuit the ᵇ toghe, ᶜ ullum, and drums, as infignia of dignity.

The late fultan's fon, Houffun Khan, though legal heir to the fovereignty of Dekkan, Ahmed Shaw, (contrary to the opinions of his minifters, who advifed his being ftrictly confined or put to death,) appointed an ameer of five hundred, and gave him the palace of Firozeabad for his refidence, with an ample jaghire, and permiffion to hunt or take his pleafure within eight miles round his palace, without reftriction to time or form. As this prince was entirely devoted to indolence and pleafure, he was more fatisfied with this power of indulging his appetites, than with the charge of empire.

While

---

ᵃ Prince of merchants.

ᵇ A ftaff with a head of this ◊ form.

ᶜ A ftaff with a head in form of a hand. Each of thefe are carried feparately on an elephant; alfo the drums.

While his uncle lived, he enjoyed his ease, and no difference ever happened between them; but he was afterwards blinded and kept confined to the palace of Firozeabad.

When Ahmed Shaw had, by his virtues, impressed the minds of his people with affection to his government, he stationed a strong force on the frontiers of his dominions towards Guzarat, to prevent invasions from that quarter, and then marched towards Carnatic with forty thousand horse. Dewul Roy without delay collected his troops, and calling the roy of Warunkul to his assistance, marched with a most numerous army, in the hope of extirpating the mussulmauns, to the bank of the Tummedra, where he fixed his camp.

Sultan Ahmed Shaw being arrived on the opposite bank, surrounded his camp with carriages, after the usage of [a] Room, to prevent the enemy's foot from making night attacks, and halted for forty days; during which his detachments of horse laid waste all the country of Dewul Roy on one side the river. He endeavoured to tempt the Hindoos to cross and give him battle on the ground which he regarded as advantageous, but in vain. At length, tired with delay, the sultan summoned a council of his nobility, and finding them unanimous for crossing the river, then fordable, and attacking the enemy on their own ground, resolved on doing it the next morning.

The roy of Warunkul deserted his ally, and withdrew to his own country, with all his troops. Early in the morning, Lodi Khan, Aulum Khan, and Dillawer Khan, who had marched during the night and forded the river at a distance, reached the environs of the enemy's camp. It happened that the roy was sleeping, attended by only a few persons, in a garden, close to which was a thick plantation

---

[a] Turkey in Europe.

tation of fugar cane. A body of the muffulmauns entered the garden for plunder, and Dewul Roy, being alarmed, fled almoft naked into the fugar cane plantation. Here he was found by the foldiers, who thought him only a common perfon, and having loaded him with a bundle of canes, obliged him to run with it before them. Dewul Roy, rejoiced at his being undifcovered, held his peace, and took up the burden readily, hoping that he fhould be difcharged as a poor perfon, or be able to make his efcape.

They had not gone far, when the alarm of fultan Ahmed Shaw's having croffed the river, and the lofs of the roy, filled the camp, and the Hindoos began to difperfe. The fultan entered the camp, and Dewul Roy's mafters, hoping now for more valuable plunder than fugar cane, haftened to join their friends, leaving him to fhift for himfelf. Dewul Roy ran with his own troops, and about noon came up with fome of his nobles, by whom he was recognized and received with great joy. His fafety being made known, his army rallied into fome order; but, as he regarded the late accident as an ill omen, he laid afide all thoughts of engaging in the field, and fled to Beejanuggur.

Ahmed Shaw not ftopping to befiege the city, overran the open country, and wherever he came, put to death men, women, and children, without mercy, contrary to the compact made by his anceftor Mahummud Shaw with the roies of Beejanuggur. Laying afide all humanity, whenever the number of flain amounted to twenty thoufand, he halted three days, and made a feftival in celebration of the bloody work. He broke down the idol temples, and deftroyed the colleges of the bramins. During thefe operations, a body of five thoufand Hindoos, enraged to defperation at the deftruction of their country and the infults to their gods, united in taking an oath to facrifice their lives in attempting to kill the fultan, as the grand author of all their sufferings. For this purpose they employed spies to observe his motions, that they might seize the first opportunity of action.

It happened, that the sultan going to hunt, in the eagerness of chase separated from the body of his attendants, and advanced near twelve miles from his camp. The devoted infidels, informed of the circumstance, immediately hastened to intercept him, and arrived in sight when even his personal attendants, about two hundred Moguls, were at some distance from him. The sultan alarmed, galloped on in hopes of gaining a small mud inclosure, which stood on the plain as a fold for cattle; but was so hotly pursued, that some broken ground falling in his way, he was not able to cross it before his pursuers came up. Luckily some archers at this instant arrived to his aid, so that the enemy were delayed sufficiently to give the sultan time to reach the inclosure with his friends. The infidels attempted to enter, and a sharp conflict took place; all the faithful repeating the \* creed of testimony, and swearing to die, rather than submit. Syed Housfun Buduckshi, Meer Ali Syestaanee, Meer Ali Cabulee, and Abdoolla Khoord, in this fight did such services, as procured them the sultan's lasting praises and gratitude. Their little troop being mostly killed and wounded, the assailants advanced close to the wall, which they began to throw down with pickaxes and hatchets, so that the sultan was reduced to the extremity of distress. At this critical juncture arrived Abd al Kadir, first armourbearer to the sultan, and a body of troops, with whom, fearful of some accident having happened to occasion his absence, he had left the camp in search of his master. The infidels had completed a wide breach, and were preparing to enter, when they found their rear suddenly attacked. The sultan with his remaining friends joined Abd al Kadir in attacking the enemy, who after a long struggle were driven off the field, with the loss of a thousand men, and about five hundred of the mussulmauns obtained martyrdom. Thus the sultan, by the almost inspired caution of Abd al Kadir,

acceded,

---

\* There is no god but God, and Mahummud is his Prophet.

acceded, as it were a second time, from the depths of danger to the enjoyment of empire. It deserves place among the records of time, as a remarkable event, that two sovereigns at the head of armies, should fall into such danger for want of numbers, and both escape uninjured. Sultan Ahmed Shaw, the same day, raised Abd al Kadir to the rank of two thousand, the government of Berar, and title of Khan Jehaun; to which he added the appellations of Life-bestowing Brother, and Faithful Friend. Abd al Luttecf, his brother, was raised to the same rank, with the title of Azim Khan. All who had any share in the sultan's deliverance were amply rewarded with titles, bounties and commands. As the Mogul archers had been of great use, he gave orders to Mallek al Tijaar to form a body of three thousand, composed of the natives of [a] Eerauk, Khorassan, Maweralnere, Turky, and Arabia, and commanded all his officers to practise themselves, children, and dependants, at shooting with the arrow.

After this event, Ahmed Shaw, having laid waste the whole country, marched to Beejanuggur, which he kept so closely blocked up, that the inhabitants were reduced to the greatest distress; when, Dewul Roy, to spare his people, sent ambassadors to the sultan entreating peace; to which he consented, on condition that he would send the tribute of as many years as he had neglected to pay, laden on his best elephants, and conducted by his son, with his drums, trumpets, and all other insignia of state, to his camp. Dewul Roy, unable to refuse compliance, agreed to the demands, and sent his son with thirty favourite elephants, loaded with treasure and valuable effects. The sultan sent some noblemen to meet him, and, after being led in ceremony through the market and great streets of the camp, he was brought to the presence. The sultan, after embracing, permitted him to sit at the foot of his throne; and putting on his shoulders a magnificent robe, and girding him with a sabre set with jewels, gave him twenty beautiful horses of various countries, a male elephant,

---

[a] Provinces of Syria, Persia, and Tartary.

elephant, dogs for the chafe, and three hawks, which the Carnatickehs were till then ftrangers to the ufe of. He then marched from the environs of Beejanuggur, and on his arrival on the bank of the Kiftnah, difmiffed the roy's fon, and returned to Koolburga.

This year, no rain falling, a grievous famine raged through all Dekkan, and multitudes of cattle died on the parched plains, for want of water. The fultan enlarged the pay of his troops, and opened all the royal ftores of grain for the eafe of the poor; but the next year alfo no rain appearing, the people became feditious, complaining, that the ᵃ fultan's reign was unlucky, and difpleafing to God. The fultan was much afflicted, and repaired to pray for the divine compaffion on his fubjects. His prayers were heard, and a plentiful fhower fell almoft immediately. Thofe who had abufed him, now became loud in his praife, calling him ᵇ Wulleh, and worker of miracles. The fultan returned with joy and thankfgiving to his palace, amid the acclamations of his people, who now blamed their own rafhnefs of opinion.

A.D. 1421. In the year 828, the fultan, to be revenged of the roy of Warunkul for joining the roy of Beejanuggur, marched to fubdue his country, and all Telingana. On his arrival at Golconda, he fent an army before him under Khan Azim, and made a halt with the main body for twenty feven days. During this time he received accounts that Khan Azim, notwithftanding his fmall force, had defeated the enemy, killed feven thoufand men, and obtained poffeffion of Warunkul

---

ᵃ Among other fuperftitions, the natives of Hindooftan regard the failure of the ufual rains, as a mark of divine difpleafure to their Sovereigns; and in times of drought, it is ufual for the emperor, or governors of towns and diftricts, to go out, attended by eminent religious and the people, to pray for rain. They generally chufe a time when the clouds hang heavy, and promife the accomplifhment of their petitions. I have heard marvellous ftories from the natives, of the fudden effect of thefe folemn prayers.

ᵇ Friend of God.

unkul, the roy being flain in the action. The fultan moved to Warunkul, and took poffeffion of the buried treafures of ages, which had till now been preferved from plunder, and accumulated yearly by the œconomy of the roies. He conferred on Khan Azim ten large and ten fmall elephants, a girdle fet with jewels, four ftrings of fine pearls, and a large fum of money; after which he detached him to reduce the other towns of Telingana; which having effected in the fpace of four months, he returned to the fultan at Warunkul. He was now ordered to reduce fome ftrong pofts in poffeffion of the deceafed roy's heirs, while Ahmed Shaw returned to Koolburga.

In the year 829, Ahmed Shaw marched to reduce a rebellious zemindar, who had feized the fort of Mahoor from the royal garrifon. The rebel was foon reduced, but the fultan, who had affured him of pardon on fubmiffion, put him to death as foon as he fell into his hands, with five or fix thoufand of his followers, as examples to deter others from rebellion. The fultan poffeffed himfelf of a diamond mine in Gohndwareh, where he raifed many temples of idols, and erecting mofques on their fites, appropriated to each fome tracts of land, to maintain dirvefhes and fupply lamps and oil for divine fervice. He halted near a year at Elichpore, founded Kaween, repaired the fortrefs of Pernalleh, and then returned to his capital Koolburga. A.D. 1425.

As fultan Hofhung Shaw of Malwa dreaded the neighbourhood of Ahmed Shaw, he made propofals to his tributary, Nerfing Roy of Kurleh, to enter into alliance againft the houfe of Bhamenee; and the roy refufing to accede to his demands, Hofhung Shaw twice invaded his country, but was expelled both times with difgraceful loffes. He however made a third attempt, fo unexpectedly, that Nerfing could not gain time to collect his troops, and was obliged to retire to his fortrefs. In the year 830, Nerfing petitioned Ahmed Shaw for affiftance, obferving, that from the day of his having fubmitted A.D. 1426.

mitted to become tributary to Firoze Shaw, he had never wandered from the path of obedience; that he was esteemed by all the surrounding states as a tributary to his house, whom to delay supporting, in the days of misfortune, would be ungenerous.

Ahmed Shaw immediately ordered Khan Jehaun, governor of Berar, to march to the succour of Nersing; and moved himself, with seven thousand horse, to Elichpore, to be ready, if necessary, to support him. Hoshung Shaw, judging the sultan's not being with the army to proceed from fear, advanced to Kurleh, plundered the country round, and opened the tongue of ridicule on the inactivity of Ahmed Shaw; which being informed of, he marched rapidly to relieve Kurleh.

At this time some venerable divines represented to the sultan, that none of his ancestors had ever assisted infidels against mussulmauns, that it was against the laws of the faith, and should be avoided, as indelible disgrace. The sultan, then within forty miles of the enemy's camp, was struck with the remonstrance, and immediately stopped his march; writing to Hoshung Shaw, that, as Nersing was one of his dependants, it would promote friendship to desist from attacking him, and return to his own country; that he himself was, at the remonstrances of the divines, going back immediately to his capital.

Ahmed Shaw begun his retreat before the messenger had arrived in the enemy's camp. Hoshung Shaw was filled with rage and contempt at the message; and knowing his own army superior to the sultan's, as he had only fifteen thousand horse, by double his numbers, resolved to pursue him; which he did with such rapidity, as always to encamp on the ground his enemy had left in the morning, committing great depredations on his route.

Ahmed

Ahmed Shaw, stung at this affront, assembled his divines, telling them, that he thought he had already sufficiently shewn his regard for the laws of the faith, by suffering dishonour to his arms. He then ordered his baggage to go on before, and halted his army in disposition of battle; giving the command of his right wing to Khan Jehaun, the left to Abdoolla Khan, grandson of [a] Ismael Mukh, and committing the royal umbrella to his son, the prince Alla ad Dien, posted him in the center. He then, with two thousand chosen horse and twelve war elephants, retired to a spot he had fixed upon as an ambush for the enemy.

Hoshung Shaw, who had not yet been opposed, expected the Dekkanees were still flying before him, and advanced without any regard to the order of his army. When he came up with them, he had not time to make a disposition; but seeing no remedy for his neglect, but valour, charged in a confused manner with seventeen thousand men. When the lines were engaging, sultan Ahmed Shaw rushed from his ambush, with his elephants and two thousand men, on the rear of the army of Malwa; which, confounded between two attacks, was panic struck, and fled with precipitation. The Dekkanees pursued them, and killed above two thousand men, took all their baggage and two hundred elephants, with the women and all the haram of Hoshung Shaw. Nersing, hearing of the defeat of the Malwes, quitted his fortress, and intercepted them in their passage through his country, killing great numbers. Sultan Ahmed Shaw lamented this misfortune, and having conferred magnificent presents on the women and children of Hoshung Shaw, sent them to Malwa, escorted by some persons of rank and confidential eunuchs, without demanding any ransom. Nersing came to pay his respects to the sultan, accompanied by his sons; and having prevailed upon him to visit

---

[a] For a short time sultan Nasir ad Dien, as related in the account of the first Bhamence sovereign.

visit Kurleh, entertained him with princely splendour, making rich offerings, among which were many valuable diamonds, rubies, and pearls. He conducted the sultan back as far as Mulhoora, from whence he received leave to return home, after having been favoured with honorary dresses, and other marks of the sultan's approbation.

It is written in the history of Malwa, that another battle happened between the two sultans, on account of Nersing's calling Hoshung Shaw to his assistance, when Ahmed Shaw besieged Kurleh; but as the writers of Dekkan do not record it, God only knows the truth. The sultan, in his march from this war, on his arrival at Bieder took the amusement of hunting; and coming to a most beautiful spot, finely watered, resolved to build upon it a city to be called after his own name, Ahmedabad. A citadel of great extent and strength was erected on the very site of Bieder, the ancient capital of the princes of the country, who, according to the Hindoo books, five thousand years back possessed the whole extent of Meerhut, Carnatic, and Telingana. Raja Bheem-Sein was one of the most celebrated of this house; and the history of the loves of his daughter and Raja Nul, king of Malwa, are famous through all Hindoostan. Their story was translated from the Hindoo language by shekh Fiezee, under the title of Nul and Dummun, into persian verse, at the command of the emperor Akber.

Sultan Ahmed Shaw, willing to strengthen his family by alliance, asked the daughter of Nusseer Khan, prince of Khandeshe, who prided himself on his descent from* Omar Farook, in marriage for his son sultan Alla ad Dien. Nusseer Khan, who dreaded the king of Guzarat, regarded the offer of this alliance as fortunate, and, readily consenting to the marriage, sent his daughter in great pomp with ambassadors to Ahmedabad Bieder, and sultan Ahmed Shaw prepared

* One of the friends of Mahummud, and third caliph.

prepared a palace without the city for her refidence, till preparations were finifhed for her entry. The nuptials were then celebrated with great rejoicings and magnificent feftivals, which lafted for two months.

The fultan now thought proper to make a divifion of his territories among his children. Ramgeer, Mahoor, and Koollum, with part of Berar, were allotted to Mhamood Khan, whom he difpatched to take poffeffion. To Daood Khan he gave royal infignia, and fent him with a number of the nobility to eftablifh himfelf in Telingana. Alla ad Dien he appointed to fucceed him in the throne, and his youngeft fon, Mahummud, to be his colleague in power. He took the oaths of his fubjects to obferve this arrangement, thinking by them to fecure what was impoffible could ever ftand. Mallek al Tijar was raifed to the rank of two thoufand, and appointed governor of Dowlutabad.

In the latter end of the year 833, the fultan ordered Mallek al Tijar to march into the country of [a] Kokun, extending along the coaft of the Indian ocean, and to clear it of rebels and difturbers. Mallek al Tijar in a fhort time executed his inftructions fo fully, that he delivered the whole country from confufion, and fent feveral elephants and camels loaded with gold and filver, the fruits of his conquefts, to court. Ahmed Shaw, in reward of his fervices, conferred upon him a fuit of his own robes, a fword fet with jewels, and other gifts, with which, before this, no fervants of the houfe of Bhamenee had ever been diftinguifhed.

Mallek al Tijar, from his excefs of zeal for the fultan's glory, reduced the ifland of [b] Mahaim, belonging to the kings of Guzarat;

P                                                                          upon

[a] At prefent in the hands of Tippoo and the Mharattas principally. I apprehend the term to be applied here to the whole extent of what we call the coaft of Malabar below the paffes.

[b] I apprehend Bombay, which the Indians call Mahaimbee. Mahe is too far fouth

upon which, sultan Ahmed Shaw Guzaratee sent his son Zuffir Khan, with an army, to retake it. Upon this, the sultan of Dekkan also dispatched his son Alla ad Dien to reinforce Mallek al Tijar. Both armies remained some time encamped in sight of each other, on opposite banks of an inlet of the sea, without either having the boldness to attack. At length, prince Alla ad Dien, being affected greatly in his health by the unwholesome air and water of the country, removed some days' journey, for a change of air. Zuffir Khan, during his absence, attacked Mallek al Tijar, and after a very desperate conflict of the two armies, the brother of the Dekkan general was taken prisoner, and two chief officers killed. The army of Dekkan received a total defeat; and effects innumerable, with tents, elephants, and horses, fell into the hands of the Guzaratees. In the [a] Tarekh Mhamood Shawee it is written, that sultan Alla ad Dien was in this action, and displayed proofs of heroic bravery; but, as victory depends not solely on human exertions, he, with Mallek al Tijar, was obliged to fly with precipitation.

Sultan Ahmed Shaw, in a short time after the defeat, having recruited his army, marched towards Guzarat; and sultan Ahmed Shaw Guzaratee hastened with his forces to meet him. The Dekkanees laid siege to the fortress of Tunbole; but the sultan, on hearing of the enemy's march towards him, raised the siege, and moved to oppose him. Both armies lay near each other for some time inactive; till at length the divines and learned men on both sides extinguished the flames of mutual enmity between the kings, by the pure waters of admonition, and it was agreed, that each should rest satisfied with the districts and forts in his possession, nor in future covet the territories of the other.

The

south on the coast of Malabar, for us to suppose it ever in the hands of the Guzarat sultans.

[a] A history of Guzarat.

The author of the ᵃ Tarekh Alfee relates, that in the year 835 A.D. 1431. the sultan, hearing that Mahummud Khan, son of the sultan of Guzarat, was employed on a distant expedition to Nudderbar, marched against him; upon which Ahmed Shaw Guzaratee hastened to assist his son; but the Dekkanees, on his approach, retreating four stages, he returned towards his capital, and encamped on the banks of the Taptee. Here he learned that the Dekkanees had returned and laid siege to Tunbole; upon which he moved against them, and an engagement ensued, which lasted from morning till night, without decision in the favour of either army; but both the sultans in the night retreated to their own country, without proposals of peace or any agreement. Some other historians relate the particulars of the siege of Tunbole; but, as copying them would occasion prolixity, I pass them over.

In this year was finished the citadel of ᵇ Ahmednuggur, built with stone, for which the sultan ordered publick rejoicings. He put to death his sister's son, Sheer Khan, whose life he regarded as prejudicial to the interests of his own children. In the year 837, A.D. 1433. Hoshung Shaw, taking opportunity of the disagreements between Guzarat and Dekkan, invaded the country of Nersing, whom he killed in battle, and the fort of Kurleh with its dependancies came into his possession.

Sultan Ahmed Shaw, upon receiving intelligence of this loss, marched towards the Malwa army; but Nusseer Khan, prince of Khandeshe, interfering, by his mediation the two sultans were prevented from coming to action; and, after much negotiation, it was agreed, that the fort of Kurleh should belong to Hoshung Shaw, and

---

ᵃ A general history, written at the command of Akber, comprising the events of one thousand years from the Mahummedan æra.

ᵇ Called Ahmedabad, to distinguish it from another Ahmednuggur, founded long afterwards by the Nizam Shawee sovereign.

and all the province of Berar to Ahmed Shaw. A treaty was concluded, and obfervance of it fworn to in a folemn manner, by the two fultans, who afterwards returned to their feveral capitals. Not long after, the fultan marched into Telingana, to quell a rebellion of fome powerful zemindars againſt his fon Daood Khan, and in a ſhort time reduced them to obedience. After a reign of twelve years and two months, fultan Ahmed Shaw died on the eighth of Rejib, A.D. 1434. 838. He was eminent for his juſtice and regard to religion.

SULTAN

## SULTAN

## ALLA AD DIEN 2ᵈ· BHAMENEE.

SULTAN Alla ad Dien afcended the throne at Ahmedabad Bieder, agreeably to the will of his father. He did not neglect his brother Mahummud Khan, but allowed him elephants, horfes and confiderable eftates. Dillawer Khan, one of the firft amras of the court, he appointed vaqueel al fultunnut, and Khajeh Jehaun Afterabadee vizier. Ummad al Moolk Ghoree, an ancient nobleman, who, after performing great fervices to the royal family, had retired from bufinefs, he prevailed upon to accept the office of ameer al amra; and difpatched him, together with his brother Mahummud Khan and Khajeh Jehaun, with a very powerful army, againft the infidels of Beejanuggur, the roy of which had withheld his tribute for five years, and refufed to pay the arrears. They laid wafte the country in fuch a manner, that the roy in a fhort time was glad to procure peace, by giving twenty elephants, a great fum of money, and two hundred female flaves fkilled in mufic and dancing, befides a valuable prefent to Mahummud Khan.

On the return of the army near Mudkul, fome of the difcontented Dekkan nobility, reprefented to Mahummud Khan, that as his father had left him partner in the empire, it was but juft that fultan Alla ad Dien fhould either admit him to fit with him on the throne, and have a joint direction of ftate affairs, or make a divifion of the territories between them; but, as he fhowed no inclination to perform either, the prince had a right to do himself justice, and by force of arms possess himself of half the kingdom. Mahummud Khan, led by their arts, used much persuasion to draw Khajeh Jehaun over to his designs, as also Ummad al Moolk Ghoree; but both strenuously refusing; and setting before him the criminality of his intentions with a noble freedom, he put them to death. After this, being assisted by a considerable army from the roy of Beejanuggur, he took Mudkul, Roijore, Sholapore, Beejapore, and Nuldirruk, from the sultan's governors.

Sultan Alla ad Dien was much affected at the death of Ummad al Moolk Ghoree, saying, that he had performed invaluable services to his ancestors, was dear to him as his father, and that no advantages could accrue to the murderer of so worthy and distinguished a personage. He then opened the doors of his treasury, and, having collected an army, marched from the capital to engage the rebels. Upon meeting, such a severe conflict was sustained by the brothers, that even the \* warrior of the sky relented at the numbers of the slain; but the gale of victory at last waved the standards of sultan Alla ad Dien, most of the amras who had been the fomenters of the rebellion were taken prisoners in the action, and Mahummud Khan fled, with a few attendants, to the hills and woods for shelter. The sultan returned to the city of Ahmedabad Bieder, and, soon after, passing over the crimes of the guilty amras, released them from their chains. He, by his assurances of pardon and safety, prevailed upon his brother to deliver himself up, and on his arrival treated him with affection and encouragement; not long after conferring upon him the fortress and territory of Roijore, vacant by the death of his brother Daood Shaw, governor of Telingana. Mahummud Khan lived long in the undisturbed possession of his countries, spending his time in a round of pleasures.

On

---

\* The planet Mars.

On the first day of the year 840, sultan Alla ad Dien conferred A.D. 1436. robes of honour on Dillawer Khan, and dispatched him to reduce the country of ᵃ Kokun, inhabited by a stubborn and hardy race of men. The rajas of Amede and Sungeer being soon humbled, agreed to pay regular tributes; and Dillawer Khan having taken the beautiful daughter of the latter for the sultan, returned with her and some years' arrear of tribute to the capital. The sultan, at first, was pleased at his services, and charmed with the raja's daughter, who was without her equal in beauty, disposition, and knowledge of music. He gave her the title of ᵇ Pericherah, and the fame of their loves became noised abroad. At length, finding that Dillawer Khan had received bribes from the rajas of Kokun, and not done his utmost to reduce their fortresses, he became cool to the minister; who seeing his disgust, resigned, of his own accord, the ring of the vaqueelut, and by so doing saved himself from danger. This important dignity was then conferred on the eunuch Dustur al Moolk, but all ranks of people soon became disgusted at his tyrannical behaviour; which though daily represented to the sultan, made no impression on his mind, as he regarded the complaints against the minister as proceeding from envy and the self-interest of faction; on which account he shewed him every day more countenance and favour. At length, Humaioon Shaw, the sultan's son, desiring the eunuch to grant some petition he had recommended, he replied, he could not immediately, but in a day or two would take it under his consideration. At the expiration of two or three days the prince sent him a message, observing, that the business was still unfinished, and desiring that he would conclude it without delay. To this the minister insolently returned for answer, that the case did not come under his department, and that it was unbecoming in the prince to interfere.

The prince, naturally violent in his temper, lost all patience at this affront; and calling to him in privacy one of his arms-bearers,
ordered

ᵃ Written by most Europeans, Concan.
ᵇ Angel-faced.

ordered him to assassinate the eunuch, and promised to protect him from all danger of the consequences. The sillehdar, who had suffered from the minister's tyranny, accepted the commission; and accordingly, the same day, as he was coming from the court, having approached him as if to present a petition, suddenly drew a dagger, and stabbed him to the heart. The prince's guards, who had waited the event, by the instructions of their master favoured his escape among them; and a scuffle arose between them and the minister's attendants, who pursued the assassin. The noise reached the sultan's apartments, and Humaioon Shaw went out as if to enquire the cause of the disturbance. Upon his return, he told the sultan that a sillehdar of long service, and much claim to the royal favour, having been contemptuously treated by Dustoor al Moolk, and now particularly with abusive language, being inflamed with passion, had stabbed him, and was seized by the troops, who waited orders concerning his disposal. The sultan, who in the first part of his reign would not pass sentence of death on any one, and also, from his son's manner, guessing the truth, only ordered the murderer to be confined, and immediately conferred the vacant dignity upon Meamun Oollah Dekkanee, one of the learned of the time of Firoze Shaw, who possessed great qualities and virtues.

A.D. 1437.   In the year 841, Mallekeh Jehaun, wife to the sultan, and daughter of Nusseer Khan, prince of Khandeshe, jealous of her husband's preference of Pericherah, and his coldness to herself, wrote complaining letters to her father. Nusseer Khan was enraged at sultan Alla ad Dien, and, by the approbation of Ahmed Shaw of Guzarat, planned the conquest of Berar. He wrote privately to the nobility of that province, offering great rewards if they would join his standard, and with so much success, that they became unanimous in their resolve of supporting his pretensions; observing, that as he was descended from the great Omar, if they fell in battle fighting against his enemies, they should be honoured as martyrs. They accordingly sent

sent him assurances of loyalty and attachment, with an invitation to take possession of the province; upon which Nusseer Khan entered Berar, with all the troops of Khandeshe, and a considerable force was sent to his aid by the raja of Gohndwareh. The treacherous nobles conspired to confine Khan Jehaun, their governor, who was firmly attached to the house of Bhamenee, and join the invaders; but Khan Jehaun, being luckily informed of their designs in time for his escape, fled to the fortress of Pernalleh, where he shut himself up, and wrote accounts of the state of affairs to court. The traitors having joined Nusseer Khan, read the Khootbah in his name, as sultan of Berar, and marched with him to besiege Pernalleh.

Sultan Alla ad Dien, on receiving this intelligence, summoned the ministers and nobility at the capital to consult on measures to be taken in such a critical juncture of affairs. The Dekkan lords recommended, that the sultan should march in person against the enemy, as it was probable the sultans of Guzarat and Malwa, also the roies of Gohndwareh, would join in assisting Nusseer Khan. The sultan, thinking he perceived disaffection to his person in this advice, appointed Mallek al Tijar, governor of Dowlutabad, to conduct the war.

Mallek al Tijar having accepted the commission, observed, that servants could have no rule but submission and resignation of life at command of their masters; but remarked, that it was well known the defeat at Mahaim was occasioned entirely by the enmity of the Dekkanee and Abyssinian amras, who could not bear to see a [a] foreigner distinguish himself in the service of the sultan; that if his majesty,

---

[a] As this word will frequently occur in the following pages, it may be proper to mention, that the author means by the term foreigner, Turks, Persians, or Arabians, newly settled in Dekkan, and their descendants of one or two generations.

majesty, from that consideration, would give him the command of the body guards, and all the foreigners, without any Dekkanee or Abyssinian officers, he hoped that, by the blessing of the Almighty, and the royal auspices, he should be able to bring affairs in Berar to a prosperous issue.

Sultan Alla ad Dien consenting to his proposals, appointed three thousand Mogul archers from the body guards to attend him; as also many Mogul amras, who had been bred up under Firoze Shaw and Ahmed Shaw. Among them were two princes, Mujnou Sultan and Shaw Koolli Sultan, lineal descendants from the great conqueror * Chungeez Khan.

Mallek al Tijar proceeded first to Dowlutabad, from whence he dispatched a force to guard the frontiers towards Guzarat and Malwa. He then entered Berar with a well supplied army of seven thousand veteran Moguls; and Khan Jehaun having found opportunity to quit Pernalleh, came to meet him at Mhaker. Mallek al Tijar dispatched Khan Jehaun with his troops to Elichpore, in order to prevent the roy of Gohndwareh from entering that way to the assistance of Nusseer Khan, and then moved with the main army towards the district

---

As the Abyssinians appear, from this history, to have had great power in Dekkan, it is necessary to relate, that formerly great numbers of slaves were brought by Arabian merchants from the coast of Abyssinia, and sold throughout India to the sultans and principal chiefs, who employed them frequently in high offices, when they again purchased their countrymen offered for slaves; by which means, colonies (if they may be so called) of them were established in many parts of Hindoostan, but particularly on the two coasts of the peninsula and in Bengal, where a few Abyssinians, at one period, assumed royalty. Mr. Bruce, in his travels, mentions this trade from Abyssinia, but seems to think eunuchs only were sold from thence. Many were, but numbers also in a perfect state.

* Called by some European writers, Zingis, and Jengeeze Khan. He was emperor of Tartary, also ancestor of Timur and the Great Moguls. All the continent of Asia, Turkey in Europe, and part of Russia, were conquered by him; from whom are also descended the present royal family of China.

district of Rohker, in which the enemy was encamped. At the pass of Rohker, he was opposed by a detachment of the Khandeshees, whom he routed with great slaughter; and Nusseer Khan, thinking this defeat an ill omen, retreated with precipitation from Rohker to Boorahanpore, to which he was pursued by Mallek al Tijar, and, not thinking himself safe at the capital, he fled to the fortress of Telung.

Mallek al Tijar having levied heavy contributions from the citizens of Boorahanpore in jewels, money, and effects, proceeded to lay waste the province of Khandeshe; which having done to the extent of his wishes, he returned to Boorahanpore, burned down the royal palace, dug up the foundations, and then marched as if towards Dekkan. During the night he changed his route, and by a forced march arrived suddenly before Telung, with four thousand horse. Nusseer Khan, who had with him twelve thousand, thinking he must have the advantage of an enemy so inferior in number and exhausted with fatigue, marched out to give battle. The Khandeshees, however, were totally defeated; many principal chiefs of Nusseer Khan and the rebellious amras of Berar were killed. Mallek al Tijar, with a great plunder, among which were seventy elephants and some artillery, returned in triumph towards Ahmed-abad Bieder.

Sultan Alla ad Dien, in honour to his merits, sent the prince Humaioon, attended by all the court, to meet him at a distance from the city; where, upon his arrival, he gave him a suit of the royal robes, elephants, and sabres set with jewels, with permission to go to his government of Dowlutabad; and all the chiefs who had accompanied him were gratified with titles, promotion, and grants of lands. To Shaw Koolli Sultan, who had particularly distinguished himself, he gave his daughter in marriage, and ordered that the Moguls should take place of the Dekkanees and Abyssinians. From the day of this distinction, till the present time, the most rooted hatred has been kept up between the Dekkanees and Moguls; which the former have gratified, on several occasions, by cruelties on the latter, whenever they had opportunity.

About this time, Deo Roy of Beejanuggur called a general council of his nobility and principal bramins, observing to them, that as his country of Carnatic, in extent, population, and revenue, far exceeded the territories of the house of Bhamenee; and in like manner, his army was far more numerous, he wished therefore to explore the cause of the mussulmauns' successes, and his being reduced to pay them tribute. Some said, that the Almighty had decreed a [a] superiority of the mussulmauns over the Hindoos for thirty thousand years or more yet to come, which was plainly foretold in their scriptures; that, therefore, the Hindoos were generally subdued by them. Others said, that the superiority of the mussulmauns arose from two circumstances: one, all their horses being strong, and able to bear more fatigue than the weak, lean animals of Carnatic; the other, a great body of excellent archers always kept up by the sultans of the house of Bhamenee, of whom the roy had but few in his army.

Deo Roy, upon this, gave orders for the entertainment of mussulmauns in his service, allotted them jaghires, erected a mosque for their use in the city of Beejanuggur, and commanded that no one should molest them in the exercise of their religion. He also ordered a koraun to be placed before his throne, on a rich desk, that the mussulmauns might perform the ceremony of obeisance in his presence, without sinning against their laws. He also made all the Hindoo soldiers learn the discipline of the bow; in which he and his officers used such exertions, that he had at length two thousand mussulmauns,

[a] At present this prophecy seems to be suspended; the Hindoo Mharattas having the emperor of the Mahummedans, and many of his provinces, under their government.

muſſulmauns, and ſixty thouſand Hindoos, well ſkilled in archery, beſides eighty thouſand horſe and two hundred thouſand foot, armed in the uſual manner, with pikes and lances.

With this hoſt he reſolved on conquering the Bhamenee princes; and, accordingly, in the year 847, croſſed the Tummedra ſuddenly, A. D. 1443. took the fortreſs of Mudkul, ſent his ſons to beſiege Roijore and Beekapore, encamped himſelf along the bank of the Kiſtnah, and ſent out detachments, who plundered the country as far as Saugher and Beejapore, laying waſte by fire and the ſword.

Sultan Alla ad Dien, upon intelligence of this invaſion, prepared to repel it, and commanded all his forces from Telingana, Dowlutabad, and Berar, to repair to the capital of Ahmedabad without delay. Upon their arrival he reviewed the whole, and found his army compoſed of fifty thouſand horſe, ſixty thouſand foot, and a conſiderable train of artillery. With this force he began his march againſt the enemy; and Deo Roy, upon his approach, ſhifted his ground, and encamped under the walls of the fortreſs of Mudkul, detaching a large body to haraſs the ſultan.

The ſultan halted at the diſtance of twelve miles from Mudkul, and diſpatched Mallek al Tijar, with the troops of Dowlutabad, againſt the ſons of Deo Roy; alſo, Khan Zummaun, governor of Beejapore, and Khan Azim, commander of the forces of Berar and Telingana, againſt the main body of the enemy. Mallek al Tijar, going firſt to Roijore, gave battle to the eldeſt ſon of Deo Roy, who was wounded in the action, and fled towards Beekapore, from whence he was joined by his younger brother, who quitted the ſiege of that fortreſs.

In the ſpace of two months, three actions happened near Mudkul between the two grand armies; in the firſt of which multitudes were
ſlain

slain on both sides, and the Hindoos having the advantage, the mussulmauns experienced great difficulties. The sultan was successful in the others; and, in the last, the eldest son of Deo Roy was killed by a spear thrown at him by Khan Zummaun, which event struck the Hindoos with a panic, and they fled with the greatest precipitation into the fortress of Mudkul. Mujeer al Moolk and his brother, officers of note, following the fugitives, in the ardour of pursuit entered the fort with them, and the infidels, admiring their valour, took them both prisoners without injury, and carried them before Deo Roy, who ordered them to be kept in confinement. Sultan Alla ad Dien, upon this, wrote to him, that the two chiefs were regarded by him as of equal importance to two hundred thousand common men; therefore, as it was a rule with the princes of his family to kill a hundred thousand Hindoos in revenge for the death of a single mussulmaun, should he take away their lives, till he had revenged the death of each, by the slaughter of an hundred thousand Hindoos, he would not leave the country.

Deo Roy, who knew by experience the resolution of the princes of this house, dispatched to the sultan confidential persons, proposing, that if he would promise not to molest his territories in future, he would bind himself to pay annually the stipulated tribute, return the two prisoners, and never again withdraw his feet from the circle of obedience. The sultan acceded to his request, a treaty was executed, and Deo Roy immediately sent back Mujeer al Moolk and his brother, also an offering of forty war elephants, and valuable effects to a great amount, with the tribute due for some years past. The sultan then honoured the roy with a rich dress, and horses in furniture set with jewels; after which he began his return home; and, during the rest of his reign, Deo Roy regularly remitted his tribute, while the sultan also strictly observed his part of the treaty.

In the first part of his reign, sultan Alla ad Dien erected at Ahmedabad Biedar an infirmary, to support the expenses of which he granted considerable tracts of land, and established in it both mussulmaun and Hindoo physicians. To every part of his dominions he sent ᵃ censors and just judges; and, though he drank wine himself, he forbad the use of it by others, as also gaming. He put chains on the necks of ᵇ collinders, and idle, dissipated vagabonds, and punished them by employing them in removing filth from the streets, drawing heavy stones, and all kinds of laborious works, that they might reform, and get a livelihood by some calling, or else quit the country altogether. If any one, after admonition and moderate correction, was convicted of drinking wine, melted lead was poured down his throat. The rank of offenders was no security from punishment.

One of the grandsons of ᶜ Mahummud Geesoo-derauz, being captivated in the snares of a courtezan, and tempted by her to drink wine, became quarrelsome from the effects of it, and, beating the woman, cut off her side locks. The affair was complained of to the cutwal, who confined both parties; but, considering the rank of the syed, he thought proper to refer the decision of the cause to the sultan; who being much enraged, ordered the offender to be carried to the most publick square of the city, there to receive two hundred blows on the soles of his feet, and to take a solemn oath against drinking wine. The courtezan was led through the streets dressed in an ass's skin, and afterwards banished from the city.

The

---

ᵃ Called mhatussubs, whose office was to examine weights and measures, to prevent intoxicating liquors being sold, and to punish offences against morality. Since the death of Aurungzebe, this office has become a sinecure.

ᵇ Wandering religious, many of whom are the most dissipated characters.

ᶜ The holy personage mentioned in the two last reigns.

The sultan so wisely regulated his civil and military departments, that the actions of [a] Feredoon and Nosherowan lost their lustre, when compared with his justice. On Fridays, and all holidays, he attended at the mosque, and heard sermons. He was averse from shedding the blood of man. He destroyed many idol temples, and erected mosques in their room. He held no conversation with [b] Nazarenes or bramins, nor would he permit them to hold civil offices.

After the war of Beejanuggur the sultan changed his conduct, being captivated in luxurious enjoyments. Giving up the total management of government to ministers, he all at once entertained a thousand beautiful women; to accommodate whom, he erected a magnificent palace, and laid out elegant gardens round it, on the banks of a piece of water. This he called the abode of bliss, and in it spent most of his hours in drinking ruby-coloured wines, pressing the lips of silver-bodied damsels, or listening to the melody of sweet-voiced musicians. During this intoxication of pleasure, he only appeared in the publick audience hall once every four or five months, and the Dekkanee amras exercised the powers of government uncontrouled.

At this time, Meamun Oolla Dekkanee formed a plan for reducing all the fortresses along the sea coasts; to perform which, he sent Mallek al Tijar, with seven thousand Dekkanee and three thousand Arab horse, besides his own troops. Mallek al Tijar fixing upon [c] Jagneh as his seat of government, raised a fort near the city of [d] Jeneah, from whence he sent detachments at different times into Kokun,

[a] Two ancient Persian kings.
[b] Christians are so called in India, on the coasts of which they were numerous at an early period, and supposed to have been converted by St. Thomas, whose sepulchre is said to be near Madras, on an eminence, called from thence, St. Thomas's Mount.
[c] On the coast of Malabar.
[d] This was afterwards a principal residence of Sewajee, founder of the modern Mharatta state.

Kokun, and reduced several rajas to subjection. At length he moved to that country in person, and laid siege to a fort, the raja of which was named Sirkeh, whom he speedily obliged to deliver himself and family, with his possessions, into his hands.

Mallek al Tijar insisted, that Sirkeh should embrace the faith of Islaam, or be put to death; upon which the subtle raja, with much humility, represented, that there existed between him and roy [a] Songeer, who owned the country round the fortress of [b] Kalneh, a family competition and rivalry, and that they were near relations. Should he therefore enter the order of Islaam, and his rival remain secure on the musnud of power, he would, on the general's return, extend the tongue of mockery on his change of faith, and raise up his whole family and subjects to rebel; so that he should lose the countries his ancestors had held for ages in independance. He added, that if Mallek al Tijar would reduce his rival, and give his country either to himself, or one of his amras, which might be effected with little trouble, he would then readily pronounce the creed of the true faith, enroll himself among the slaves of the sultan, and annually remit a tribute to his treasury, as well as assist in reducing those roies who might hereafter fail in their duty and allegiance.

Mallek al Tijar to this replied, that he had heard the road to the roy's country was full of woods, and difficult passes: to which Sirkeh answered, that while there was with the army so faithful and capable a guide as himself, not a single skirt should receive injury from

R

[a] I apprehend this to be Soneda, a district near Bidenore, and reduced latterly by Tippoo Saheb.
[b] This place is often mentioned in the account of Aurungzebe's war in Dekkan. I cannot find it in any map; but as Jeneah, the head quarters of Mallek al Tijar, is situated on the upper part of Malabar, and an inlet of the sea is mentioned as in the roy's country during the war, it is most probably not very far from Jeneah, and near the coast.

from the thorny woods, and that the rose of accomplishment would be gathered without trouble.

A.D. 1453.
Mallek al Tijar, relying on the promises of the raja, in the year 858 began his expedition; but was in the outset deserted by most of the Dekkanee and Abyssinian officers and troops, who declined entering the woods. Sirkeh, agreeably to his promise, for the two first days conducted him along a broad, easy road; so that the whole army praised his zealous services; but on the third, he led them through paths so horrible, that a male tiger, through dread of the terrors of it, would have become a female; fuller of windings than the curly locks of the fair, and narrower than the path of love. Demons would have started at the precipices and caverns, and the ᵃ ghole have been panic-struck at one view. The sun never enlivened the vallies, nor had providence fixed bounds to its extent. The grass was tough as the teeth of serpents, and the air fetid as the breath of dragons. Death dwelt in the waters, and poison in the breeze. After winding, fatigued, weary, and alarmed, this dreadful path, they entered a dark forest, a passage through which was difficult even to the gale, bounded on three sides by mountains, that seemed to have their heads above the clouds, and on the other an inlet of the ocean, so that there was no path to advance, and none to go back, but that by which they had entered.

Mallek al Tijar was at this crisis ill of a bloody dysentery, so that he could not attend to the regular march and order of his troops; who, being excessively fatigued, about nightfall flung themselves down to rest wherever they could, nor was there a spot allowing of two tents to be pitched upon it near each other. At this time, while the troops were eager of rest, Sirkeh made his escape by the sea, and sent a message to the roy of Songeer, that he had lured the game into his toils. The roy, with a great force, with which also was the treacherous

---

ᵃ An evil spirit of the woods.

erous Sirkeh, about midnight rushed from dens, passes, and caverns, on the musfulmauns unsuspicious of surprize, and buried in the sleep of wearinefs and fatigue. Nearly seven thoufand of the faithful were put to death like sheep, with knives and daggers; for the wind being high, the clashing of the trees, which feparated them from one another, prevented their hearing the groans of their fellow-fufferers. Mallek al Tijar fell, with five hundred noble fyeds of Medina, Ker-balla, and Nujeef; as alfo fome few Dekkanee and Abyssinian nobles, with about two thoufand foldiers of thofe countries. When the roy thought his bloody revenge had been glutted fufficiently, he retired with his people from the foreft.

The furvivors of this dreadful maffacre, with much difficulty travelled back the path they had advanced, and joined the Dekkanee and Abyssinian amras, who had remained encamped on the plains. They advifed them to retire to their jaghires, that they might repofe a little from their fatigues, and fupply themfelves with neceffaries for future fervice; but this the Moguls refufed doing, as the town of Jagneh was nearer, and they might in a fhort time recruit themfelves, and be able to rejoin the army. Some of the Moguls alfo imprudently obferved, that the defection and treachery of the Dekkan amras had principally occafioned the deaths of Mallek al Tijar and the fyeds, of which, on their arrival at Jagneh, they would write full accounts to court.

The Dekkanees, alarmed at this remark, refolved to be the firft accufers; and therefore wrote by exprefs to the fultan, that Mallek al Tijar, at the inftigation of a zemindar named Sirkeh, and the councils of the fyeds and Moguls, had entered on a wild plan, in defiance of their moft earneft remonftrances, and that he had fuffered the punifhment of fuch imprudence, by his own death and of moft of his followers; that the furvivors, inftead of agreeing to remain with them till another general fhould be appointed by his majefty, majesty, to take revenge on Sirkeh and Toy Songeer, had behaved with insolence, spoke disrespectfully of the sultan, and were gone in a body to the fortress of Jagneh, intending to serve the rajas of Kokun, and tempt them to raise the standard of rebellion.

These complaints they forwarded to Sheer al Moolk Dekkanee, and Nizam al Moolk, son of Ummad al Moolk Ghoree, who were thirsting for the blood of the Moguls, as their rivals in the sultan's esteem. They presented them to Alla ad Dien when heated with wine, and related the defeat of Mallek al Tijar, and the behaviour of the surviving Moguls, with a thousand aggravations and malicious remarks. The sultan was inflamed with passion, and, without a moment's reflection on the probability of the guilt of the Moguls, commanded the two amras to repair to Jagneh, and put them all to the sword.

Like \* Abdoolla Zead, or Shumse al Joshhun, putting on armour against the descendants of the prophet, they moved towards Jagneh with a great force. The syeds and Moguls hearing of their approach, shut themselves up in the mud fort, and sent off petitions, relating the truth of affairs and their own innocence, to court. Their messengers were intercepted by Sheer al Moolk, who tore the pacquets. They also dispatched other letters, but as none of their own companions could pass, they entrusted them to two natives of Hindoostan, who had been for years fed amply with their bounty. These wretches, black in heart as complexion, giving way to their natural treachery, carried the letters to Sheer al Moolk, who tore them, as he had done the former, and rewarded the traitors with gifts. He then closely blocked up the roads, so that no person could pass without search; and the unfortunate syeds, like their great ancestor Houssein, were reduced to the extremity of despair, but, with the Moguls,

---

\* Two chiefs sent against the sons of Alee by Yezeed.

Moguls, resolved to stand out as long as possible. Sheer al Moolk upon this summoned the Dekkan amras from Kokun to assist him, and arrived before Jagneh with a great army. The siege continued for two months without effect, during which time he wrote frequently to court, that the syeds and Moguls, continuing in obstinate rebellion, had asked assistance of the king of Guzarat, offering to give him up Jagneh, and assist his invasions. The Dekkanee ministers backed these letters with their own assurances, and procured repeated orders from the sultan to punish the rebels in such a manner, that their fate might remain an example of terror to others. If now and then a letter from the accused found its way to the capital, the ministers took care to prevent its being seen by the sultan, who, they pretended, was so enraged, that he would not even hear or read a word from them.

When provisions in the fort grew scarce, the besieged resolved, that leaving a sufficient number to defend their families, they would make a sally, fight their way through the enemy, and, flying to the capital, lay the truth of affairs before the sultan, and implore justice. The Dekkanees learning their design, dreaded the event, as they knew they would fight desperately, and that some must make their way good to court, which would immediately occasion a discovery of their treachery. They therefore had recourse to stratagem to get the besieged in their own power. They sent a message to them, that being followers of the prophet, and pitying their misfortunes and the children and women of the syeds, they had interceded with the sultan for their pardon, who at last complying with their petition, had given orders that they should be permitted to retire unmolested out of his dominions, with their families and effects. A forged order was produced, as a proof of the sincerity of their declaration, and both chiefs, like Yezeed, swore by the Almighty, the koraun, and the prophet of God, that they would not injure them in person or property.

Relying

Relying upon their oaths, the unfortunate, in number about two thousand five hundred, of whom twelve hundred were fyeds of unmixed defcent, evacuated the fort, with their wives, children, and property, and encamped at a little diftance, to provide carriage and conveyance for their march. The Dekkan chiefs for three days abided by their promifes, and ufed every endeavour to gain their confidence, and lull fufpicion, by kind offices and offers of affifting their wants. On the fourth day, they prevailed on the chief among them to come to an entertainment in the fort. All the principal men, about three hundred, excepting Kafim Beg, Suff Skekunn, Kirra Khan Khoord, and Ahmed Beg Meccæ, attended. While they were eating, a number of armed men, on a fignal given by Sheer al Moolk, rufhed from ambufh upon them, and put every man to the fword. At the fame inftant, four thoufand Dekkanees without the fort attacked their camp, and put every male they found to death, even to infants at the breaft. After this tragedy, they plundered the tents, and treated the women with all the infult that luft or brutality could infpire. Since the time of Houffein, the fyeds were never before fo abufed; but is it not aftonifhing that men, who called themfelves fervants of the prophet, fhould fo bafely treat his defcendants?

Kafim Beg, and the Moguls who had encamped about two miles from the reft of their unfortunate companions, on hearing the alarm, armed themfelves, and, putting even their women in foldiers' habits, fled towards the capital. Sheer al Moolk inftantly difpatched two thoufand horfe to purfue them, under Daood Khan, and wrote to all the jaghiredars and farmers to intercept them as rebels, or cut them off, under pain of the fultan's difpleafure. Kafim Beg, with three hundred followers, pofted on without halting, except when the Dekkanees coming near, obliged him to difperfe them, which he did frequently with defperate valour. He paffed the nights on the plain, and in this manner proceeded for fome days; till at length, near the town of Sirkeh he was clofely preffed by Daood Khan, who had
summoned

summoned Houssun Khan, the jaghiredar, to his succour. This nobleman had once been relieved from great danger in a battle by Kasim Beg, whom he now resolved to assist in turn. He told Daood Khan, that it was impossible the Moguls could be rebels, as they were hastening of their own accord to the capital. Daood Khan finding he would not join him, attacked the Moguls with his own people, and Kasim Beg, with his followers, resisted like men fighting for life. Daood Khan was luckily killed by an arrow in the first onset; but this spurred on the Dekkanees to revenge, and they had almost overcome the Moguls by numbers, when Houssun Khan came to their assistance; upon which the Dekkanees fled with their chief's body towards Jagneh. Houssun Khan conducted the brave sufferers to his residence, where they were supplied with relief by his indulgence, and wrote representations of their case to the sultan, who, in answer, commanded Kasim Beg and his companions to repair to court.

Upon their arrival, sultan Alla ad Dien commanded them into his presence, and examined into the whole affair; which being explained to his satisfaction, he was enraged at his treacherous ministers, and ashamed of his own fatal confidence. He ordered Mustapha Khan, who had kept the letters from his perusal, to be beheaded on the spot, and his body to be exposed to view through the streets. He appointed Kasim Beg to the government of Dowlutabad and Joneer, with all the honours of Mallek al Tijar, and raised all his followers to rank, ordering fresh levies of Moguls to be made under them. He seized the houses of Nizam al Moolk and Sheer al Moolk to his own use, and commanded them, with all the other capital aggressors, to be brought walking on foot, loaded with heavy chains, to the capital. Such as had been instrumental in forging the first accusation, he put to death in various ways, and deprived their children of their estates, so that they wanted even a meal. According to the Tubbukkat Mahmood Shawee, Sheer al Moolk and

Nizam

Nizam al Moolk were afflicted with leprofy the fame year, and their fons walked the markets for fhameful purpofes, among the outcafts of fociety.

A.D. 1446. In the year 850, fhekh Azzree, the fultan's preceptor, for whom when a youth he had great refpect, wrote him a long letter of advice from Khoraffan. The fultan was much affected with the perufal. He forfwore the ufe of wine, and anfwered the letter with his own hand and a valuable prefent. He now reftored all the inftitutes of Ahmed Shaw, attended regularly to the adminiftration of affairs, and expelled all Dekkanees from offices of truft.

A.D. 1453. In the year 857, a dangerous eruption breaking out in the fultan's foot, which would not fubmit to medicine, he was prevented by it from quitting his private apartments, and reports were often fpread through the provinces of his death. Jellall Khan, fon in law to the fultan, being affured of his deceafe, poffeffed himfelf of many diftricts round his government of Bilcondah, which he gave in charge to Secunder Khan, grandfon by the mother's fide to fultan Ahmed Shaw. Khan Azim, governor of Telingana, dying at this crifis, and no officer of fufficient influence being on the fpot to take the charge of affairs for the fultan, many of the nobility of the province fubmitted to the authority of Secunder Khan, offering to acknowledge him chief of the country.

Sultan Alla ad Dien, notwithftanding his indifpofition, prepared to march for the reduction of the rebels; upon which Jellall Khan and Secunder Khan agreed, that the former fhould remain in Telingana, and the latter proceed to Mahoor, to watch the motions of the royal army, as it lay conveniently between Telingana and Berar. The fultan fent frequent offers of pardon, if they would lay down their arms; but Secunder Khan, confcious of his deferving punifhment for having joined in Mahummud Khan's rebellion, and

and many other offences befides the prefent, was not to be fatisfied of the fultan's faith to his promifes, and therefore refolved to fecure himfelf by new crimes from refentment. He reprefented to the fultan of Malwa, Shaw Mhamood Khiljee, that fultan Alla ad Dien had been long dead, but that the minifters, to fecure their own intereft, pretending he was ftill alive, had turned all their endeavours to deftroy the principal nobility, and divide the kingdom among themfelves and adherents; that if he would march, the provinces of Berar and Telingana would fall, without a blow, into his hands.

Sultan Mhamood crediting thefe affurances fo flattering to his ambition, by the advice of the fultan of Khandefhe, in the year 860, A. D. 1455. moved towards Dekkan with a great army, and was joined by Secunder Khan, who advanced with a thoufand horfe, as a body guard, fome days' journey to meet him.

Sultan Alla ad Dien, upon receiving intelligence of this invafion, changed his defign of going in perfon to Telingana. He fent Khajeh Mhamood Geelanee, commonly entitled Gawan, firft promoting him to the rank of a thoufand, with feveral of the nobility, to that quarter, againft Jellall Khan. He difpatched Khan Jehaun, governor of Berar, to obferve the motions of the prince of Boorahanpore, and ordered Kafim Beg, governor of Dowlutabad, to advance with a corps of obfervation towards the enemy. He himfelf followed, with the troops of Beejapore, at the diftance only of ten miles, carried, by reafon of his illnefs, in a palanquin.

Sultan Mhamood, having received fatisfactory accounts of the fovereign of Dekkan's being alive, and marching againft him, retreated fuddenly, with the greateft part of his attendants; leaving an ameer, under pretence of affifting Secunder Khan, but giving fecret inftructions, that if that chief fhould attempt to join the Dekkanees, not

not to permit him, but bring him prisoner to Mando, with all his treasures and effects. Secunder Khan, being timely informed of the intended treachery, made his escape from the Malwa army, with two thousand Afghauns and Raajepoots, to the fortress of Bilcondah; but as Khajeh Mhamood Gawan was then besieging it, it proved but a temporary asylum. Shortly after, he, by the intercession of Khajeh Gawan, obtained his pardon from the sultan, delivered up the fortress, and, going to court with that chief, was again honoured with Bilcondah in jaghire. The sultan having left Fukhir al Moolk Turk in the government of the Mahoor districts, and Ferreh al Moolk in command of the garrison, returned to his capital, where, in the year 862, the disorder in his foot encreasing to a mortification, he left this world of vanity for another, after a reign of twenty three years, nine months, and twenty days.

A. D. 1457.

Sultan Alla ad Dien is said to have been eloquent, of great wit, and fond of learning. He would sometimes ascend the pulpit in the grand mosque on Fridays and holidays, and read the khootbah, in which he mentioned himself by the following titles; The monarch just, merciful, patient, and liberal to the servants of God, chief in worldly and religious affairs, son of the distinguished among kings, Ahmed Shaw Wullee Bhamenee. One day, an Arabian merchant who had sold some horses for the sultan's use, the payment for which was delayed by the officers of the household, being present when the sultan read the above titles, inspired by vexation at ill usage, and the slaughter of the innocent syeds, exclaimed with a loud voice, Thou art neither the just, the merciful, the patient, nor the liberal king, but the cruel and the false; who hast massacred the prophet's descendants, yet darest to assume such vaunting titles in the pulpit of the true believers. The sultan was struck with remorse, and commanded the merchant to be paid on the spot; saying, that those would not escape the wrath of God, who had thus injured his reputation

tation among mankind. He then retired to his palace, which he never left till he was brought out a corpse to be interred. The sultan finding himself dying, appointed his son Humaioon his successor, against the wishes of all his court, who dreaded his cruel and sanguinary temper; and several of the amras made their escape to Guzarat before the sultan's death, to avoid the tyranny of his successor.

# SULTAN

## HUMAIOON SHAW BHAMENEE,

#### COMMONLY CALLED,

### *ZALIM,* or, *THE CRUEL.*

---

WHILE sultan Alla ad Dien was breathing his last, the prince Humaioon was in his own palace. Syef Khan and Mulloo Khan, two chief amras, concealing the king's death, privately seated his youngest son Houssun Khan on the throne. They were joined by Hubbeeb Oolla, and some other amras, who regarded the measure as an unexpected blessing. A body was detached to plunder the palace of sultan Humaioon and secure his person, when great clamour and confusion took place. Humaioon Shaw opposed his enemies with resolution, obliged them to retire, and pursued them towards the royal apartments. On the way, the elephant drivers, [a] perdehdaurs, sillehdars, and body guards, with other persons of the household, who were ignorant of the plan for his destruction, joined Humaioon, so that he entered the grand hall of audience without opposition, and seized his brother, who sat panic-struck and trembling upon the throne. Humaioon ascended in his room, and was acknowledged sultan without farther opposition. He ordered Syef Khan, the contriver of the plot, to be dragged through the city chained to the foot of an elephant, and confined Hubbeeb Oolla.

Agreeably

---

[a] Guards of the private apartments.

Agreeably to the will of his father, he gave the office of vaqueel al fultunnut to Khajeh Mhamood Gawan, with the title of Mallek al Tijar, and the government of Beejapore. Mallek Shaw, faid to be defcended from the great Chungeeze Khan, he appointed governor of Telingana, with the title of Khajeh Jehaun; and conferred jaghires in that province, with the rank of a thoufand and title of Nizam al Moolk, on the nephew of Ummad al Moolk Ghoree, a young nobleman of diftinguifhed abilities. Secunder Khan, fon of Jellall Khan, a favourite companion of the fultan before his acceffion, being difgufted at not having the government of Telingana, of which he was ambitious, fled from court to his father at Bilcondah, and began to raife troops in rebellion.

Humaioon Shaw immediately fent againft him Khan Jehaun, governor of Berar, who had come to court to congratulate his acceffion; and that chief being defeated by the rebels, the fultan thought it neceffary to march againft them in perfon. He hoped, upon his arrival in the vicinity of Bilcondah, that Jellall Khan and Secunder Khan would fee their error, and fubmit: but the latter made a fudden attack upon his camp by night with fome fuccefs, which determined the fultan next day to lay fiege to the fort. Secunder Khan having great dependance on the attachment and bravery of his troops, marched out to offer battle with eight thoufand Dekkanees and Raajepoots. Humaioon, in regard to their former friendfhip, fent him a meffage, importing, that though appearing in arms againft his fovereign was an heinous offence, yet he wifhed not to deftroy fo brave a fubject, would forgive him, and grant him in jaghire any diftrict he fhould chufe in the province of Dowlutabad. Secunder Khan returned in anfwer, that if Humaioon was the grandfon of Ahmed Shaw, he was alfo himfelf his grandfon by his daughter, confequently, his partner in the kingdoms of their grandfather, fo that he muft refign the fovereignty of Telingana to him, or prepare for battle.

Humaioon

Humaioon Shaw was enraged at this infolent reply to his offers, and commanded the march of attack to be founded. Secunder Khan, exalting the ftandard of rafhnefs, advanced to battle, and repeatedly repulfed the vigorous charges of the royal army. The action continued long indecifive. At laft, Mallek al Tijar Gawan, with the Beejapore troops, and Khajeh Jehaun Turk, with the army of Berar, charged from the right and left wings at the fame inftant, and made a great flaughter among the rebels, who began to give way to the fhock. The fultan obferving their confufion, drew from the center five hundred archers and five hundred fpearmen, at the head of whom, mounted on an elephant, he rufhed on the enemy, among whom a dreadful carnage was made. The rebel, undaunted, oppofed fo firmly with the troops about his perfon, that the fultan was deferted by his followers, who fled in confufion. Secunder Khan then advanced fingly, and with his fpear charged the fultan, whofe elephant, by the critical direction of the driver, feized the rebel in his trunk, drew him from his horfe, and dafhed him forcibly on the ground. His followers, who were on full fpeed to fupport his charge, not able to ftop their career, rode in great bodies over him, by which accident he was foon crufhed to death. Upon the lofs of the chief, his army fled; and the fultan, rallying his troops, purfued the fugitives, with great flaughter, a confiderable diftance from the field of battle.

The next day the fultan commenced the fiege of Bilcondah, and at the end of a week Jellall Khan, feeing no refource but fubmiffion, offered to furrender. By the mediation of Mallek al Tijar and Khan Jehaun, having obtained pardon, he threw himfelf at the fultan's feet, with an offering of the accumulated wealth of forty years of high and profitable employment; and, though he was confined, efteemed a few days of life a fufficient prize for the forfeiture of all his poffeflions.

Humaioon

Humaioon Shaw, on the fall of Bilcondah, meditated the reduction of the fortrefs of Dewercondah, belonging to a zemindar of Telingana, who had lent his fupport to Secunder Khan. For this fervice he detached Khajeh Jehaun and Nizam al Moolk, while he marched himfelf to Warunkul. The Telingas uniting, fought feveral battles in the field, but were in all defeated by Khajeh Jehaun, and at length retired within the fortrefs; which was clofely befieged on every fide, though fituated among high mountains and difficult woods. The Telingas applied for affiftance to the roies of Oriffa and \* Oureah; who, being tempted by offers of great fums of money, fent a confiderable body of troops, with many war elephants, to fupport them, promifing to advance quickly themfelves with their whole force. The Telingas, infpired by hopes of fpeedy relief, held out obftinately; and the two generals, hearing of the negotiation, became doubtful how to act. Nizam al Moolk was for raifing the fiege for the prefent, and marching out of the hills and paffes to engage the auxiliaries to advantage on the plain, and prevent their junction. To this Khajeh Jehaun objected, faying, that the Telingas would attribute a retreat to fear only, iffue from the fortrefs, and moleft their march; fo that it was better to continue the fiege, and oppofe the junction, where they were. Nizam al Moolk was obliged to fubmit to this opinion of his fuperior officer. The very next day, the troops of Oriffa and Oureah, alfo the Telingas from the fort, attacked them at the fame inftant, and the cavalry being unable to exert themfelves from the badnefs of the ground, a total defeat was fuftained by the army of Iflaam, in which great numbers were flain. The two generals with the greateft difficulty made their efcape from the field, and did not halt till they arrived at Warunkul, being purfued for eighty miles by the infidels. Humaioon Shaw, enquiring into the caufe of the difafter, Khajeh Jehaun, to fave his own life, falfely accufed Nizam al Moolk as the advifer of the meafure he had difapproved, and the fultan in his rage, without examination into the

truth

* On the fea coaft of Oriffa.

truth of the charge, ordered that gallant nobleman to be put to death inftantly in his prefence; which was done. His relations and followers fled, entering into the fervice of fultan Mhamood of Malwa. Khajeh Jehaun was difgraced, and fent clofe prifoner to one of the royal fortreffes, by the fultan.

Humaioon Shaw, determined on revenging the infult to his arms, was bufily preparing a frefh army to go againft Dewercondah, when fuddenly, advices were brought him from the capital of his dominions, Ahmedabad Bieder, that Eufuff Turk had fet at liberty the blind prince Houffun Khan and Hubbeeb Oolla, and had fled with them into the country. The fultan, upon this, cafting the reins of patience from his hands, and leaving Mallek al Tijar to protect Telingana, in the year 864 returned by forced marches to his capital, and lighting up the fire of tyranny, fet no bounds to his rage; but it is neceffary, before his cruelties are recorded, to mention their original caufe.

A.D. 1459.

Shaw Hubbeeb Oolla, an eminent divine, had been imprifoned for his attachment to the prince Houffun Khan. Upon the fultan's marching againft Secunder Khan, towards Bilcondah, feven of the fhaw's difciples formed the refolution of procuring his liberty. For this purpofe they addreffed Eufuff Turk, flave to the late fultan Alla ad Dien, a man generally beloved, and celebrated for his virtue, integrity, piety, and extenfive charities, alfo a firm difciple and friend to the fhaw's family. He promifed his aid, and corrupted fome of the guards and porters of the palace. The number of the confederacy encreafed to twelve horfemen and fifty foot, all bent upon facrificing their lives to the fervice of the fhaw. Eufuff, advancing in the path of fortitude, one evening went with his friends to the gate of the royal haram, in which the prifoners were confined. Moft of the guards were abfent on their occafions, but he was queftioned by the few on duty. He replied, that he had the fultan's orders

orders to enter the prison, and blind such and such criminals, producing a forged firmaun to prove his assertions; at seeing which, they were silent, and suffered him to pass in. Upon his arrival at the second gate, the guards refused to admit him; and, though he showed the firmaun, insisted that the cutwal's order was necessary before he could be allowed entrance; upon which he rushed upon them with his friends, put them to death, with some resistance, and passed on. Eusuff first hastened to the apartments of the capital prisoners, and took off the chains from Hubbeeb Oolla. Houssun Khan and Yiah Khan, sons of the late king, and Jellall Khan Bokharee, entreated him to break their chains, and take them with him; to which petition he consented. After this he went into every apartment of the prison, proclaiming aloud, that all who wished to be freed from captivity, should repair to the gate of the palace, and join him. About seven thousand unfortunate captives, of all conditions, rose upon their keepers, and, arming themselves with clubs, or whatever came to hand, ranged themselves at the gate as directed. By this time the cutwal of the city, having received the alarm, had advanced to the palace with his people; but the captives, desperate for freedom, received him so warmly with showers of stones, and clubs, that they were defeated. The prisoners, during the night, dispersed to different quarters among their friends. Jellall Khan, near eighty years old, and the prince Yiah Khan, fell into the cutwal's hands again in a few hours, and were put to death. Houssun Khan and Hubbeeb Oolla took shelter in the house of a barber, where they shaved their beards, and put on the dress of beggars. The latter now advised making their escape to some humble retirement; but the prince observed, that the people in general being wearied and disgusted with his brother's cruelty, and attached to himself, it was likely he could soon raise an army, and regain the throne he had lost. Hubbeeb Oolla consented to assist his views. When they had got out of the city to some distance, Houssun Khan made himself known, and adventurers and the disaffected joined him from all quarters. Eufuff Turk alfo joined his ftandard; and in a few days the prince was able, with an army of three thoufand horfe and five thoufand foot, to advance to the garden of Kumtaneh, only fix miles from the capital, in hopes of being able to take it. Finding this, however, impoffible, he retreated to the town of Peer, which he poffeffed himfelf of, with the country round, and levied frefh troops. Such was the ftate of affairs when the fultan arrived at Ahmedabad with his army.

The firft bufinefs of the fultan was to punifh the garrifon of the city; all the foldiers of which, above two thoufand, he put to death in various ways, the moft cruel that could be devifed. The cutwal he confined in an iron cage, every day cutting off fome member from his body, which he obliged him to eat, fo that he died fhortly of his maims. He then difpatched eight thoufand horfe and foot againft the rebels, who at firft were victorious; upon which the rage of the fultan was extreme. He reinforced his army, but confined the women and children of the officers; vowing to put them to death if they fhould be defeated, or defert to the prince Houffun Khan.

In the next battle the rebels fuffered a total defeat, and Houffun Khan, after a defperate refiftance, quitted the field with his adherents, hoping to find an afylum at Beejanuggur. Upon his arrival near the fort of Beejapore, with about eight hundred horfe, the governor, Serauje Khan Juneedee, fent out a meffage to invite him in, declaring, that he would give him up the fort and all its dependancies. Houffun Khan, by the advice of Hubbeeb Oolla and Eufuff Turk, entered the fort of Beejapore, then only of mud. Serauje Khan received them with officious refpect and attention. At nightfall he came, with all his attendants, to the prince's apartment, under pretence of paying his refpects, and furrounded it. The next day he attempted to take his guefts prifoners, and Hubbeeb Oolla fuffered

martyrdom

martyrdom in the refiftance. At length, the prince Houffun Khan, Eufuff Turk, and his other followers, even to carpet-fpreaders, watermen, and fweepers, were feized, and fent prifoners, by the treacherous Serauje Khan, under a ftrong efcort to Ahmedabad.

Humaioon Shaw, letting loofe the bridle of punifhment, and mad with rage, ordered ftakes to be fet up on both fides of the king's market, and vicious elephants and beafts of prey to be ftationed in different parts of the fquare; in others were placed cauldrons of fcalding oil and boiling water. Then, afcending a balcony to view the fpectacle, he firft caft his brother Houffun Khan before a voracious tiger, who foon tearing the wretched prince in pieces with his teeth and claws, left fcarce a relic remaining. Eufuff Turk, and his feven friends, were beheaded before him; and their innocent and helplefs families, being dragged from their houfes, were violated and otherwife tortured in the court of the palace by ruffians, in ways too indecent to mention. Punifhments invented by the fultan were inflicted on young and old, women and children; who fuffered fuch tortures as the imaginations of [a] Zohaak and the tyrant Hijaaje never could have conceived. About feven thoufand of the unhappy prince's women and fervants, who had not the moft diftant concern in his rebellion, even to cooks, waiters, fcullions, and other menials, were fome ftabbed with daggers, others cut in pieces with hatchets, and the reft killed in cruel methods by fcalding oil and water. This tragedy happened in Shauban, the fame year as the rebellion.

The author of the Tarekh Mhamood Shawee fays, he heard from the royal attendants, that upon learning the efcape of Houffun Khan, rage and paffion fo overcame the fultan, that he fometimes tore his robes, at others, bit his pillows, and often his own lips, in fuch a manner that they dropped with blood. Alarmed at the example of Houffun Khan, he put to death feveral innocent perfons of the royal family,

---

[a] A Perfian and Tartar tyrant.

family, who were confined in different fortresses. Nor did he stop here. He became suspicious of all his court, and the innocent and guilty were undistinguished by his savage tyranny. He extended his hands to the children of his subjects, tearing them from their parents to satisfy his lusts. He would frequently stop nuptial processions in the street, and seizing the bride, after deflowering her, send her back to the husband's house. He put his women to death on trivial occasions; and when any of the nobility were obliged to attend him, so great was their dread, that they took leave of their families, as if preparing for death.

At last the Almighty took pity on the sufferings of his people, and listened to the complaints of the wretched. The tyrant was taken ill, and judging he should die, appointed his eldest son, Nizam Shaw, then only eight years of age, his successor; and calling Khajeh Jehaun Turk from Berar, and Mallek al Tijar from Telingana, made his will; constituting them regents and guardians to his son during his minority; commanding them strictly to transact no affair without the advice of the queen mother. He died on the twenty eighth of [a] Zeekaud, 865, according to some; but others relate, that he recovered from this illness, and was assassinated in a fit of intoxication by his own servants, wearied out with his inhuman cruelties. His reign was three years, six months, and six days.

A. D. 1460.

[a] The eleventh month of the Mahummedan year.

SULTAN

# SULTAN

# NIZAM SHAW BHAMENEE.

WHEN Humaioon left the world, out of pity to mankind, and his son Nizam Shaw acceded to the throne of Dekkan, the queen mother, a woman of great abilities, did nothing without consulting Khajeh Jehaun and Mallek al Tijar Mhamood Gawan; admitting no other amras to share in the administration. Mallek al Tijar was appointed vizier, with the government of Berar, and Khajeh Jehaun to the office of vaqueel and [a] terruffdaree of Telingana. These two ministers attended every morning at the palace, and through a female messenger communicated their opinions to the queen mother; who, after she had given her approbation to the measures of the day, sent the young sultan out of her apartments to the hall of audience, where he sat on the throne. On his right hand stood Khajeh Jehaun, and upon the left Mallek al Tijar; who with fidelity and dispatch transacted business. By the happy co-operation and agreement of these three personages, the injuries occasioned by the tyranny of the late sultan were soon repaired; but the surrounding potentates, both mussulmauns and Hindoos, hearing that the throne of Dekkan was filled by a child, and that the nobility and officers were disaffected from the cruelties of their late sovereign, cast their eyes towards his dominions with avidious looks. First, the roies of Orissa and Oureah, in conjunction with the zemindars of Telingana, invaded the country by the way of Raajmundree, plundering and laying waste as far as Kolaufs.

The

[a] Government.

The queen mother and the ministers, did not suffer despondency to find a place in their minds; but, collecting an army of forty thousand men, marched with the young monarch against the enemy. The roy of Orissa kept advancing, and at length arrived within six miles of the royal army, and ten of the capital of Ahmedabad; it being his design to demand the country of Telingana altogether, and a tribute for the rest of his dominions, from the infant sultan. The two ministers sent him a message, importing, that their master had designed to conquer Orissa and Jaajnuggur; but, now he had advanced so far with his army, he should be able to do it, by defeating him, without the trouble of marching to those countries in person; and he had resolved, that not a man should escape, unless the amount of the injuries done to his dominions should be paid, and the raja agree to become his tributary. With this message Shaw Mohib Oolla was dispatched. With one hundred and sixty horse he charged the roy's advanced corps with such pious zeal and courage, that, after skirmishing from morning till midday, the gale of victory waved the standards of the holy champions, and the Hindoos fell back to their main army. The roies of Orissa and Oureah, alarmed at this gallantry in so small a part of the royal army, left their heavy baggage on the ground, and retreated during the night. Khajeh Jehaun followed in pursuit; while the sultan and Mallek al Tijar made easy marches after him. The roies seeing that they lost two or three thousand men in every day's march, from the activity and bravery of Khajeh Jehaun, took protection in a fort; from whence they sent to Mallek al Tijar, entreating pardon; and, after much debate, on paying a large sum of money, they were permitted to retire, without further pursuit, into their own territories. Nizam Shaw returned in triumph to his capital; and, having conferred honours and rewards on the nobility and soldiers, dismissed them with his thanks to their several stations.

Soon

Soon after this, Mhamood Shaw, sultan of Malwa, invaded the territories of Bhamenee, with eight and twenty thousand horse, by the route of Khandeshe; and the roies of Oureah and Telingana, upon this irruption, entered again into alliances, and renewed their depredations on the countries of the mussulmauns. The ministers, upon this, ordered the army of Telingana against the roies, and attended Nizam Shaw, with the troops of Beejapore, Dowlutabad, and Berar, against sultan Mhamood, whose camp they soon approached, and both armies prepared for battle.

Nizam Shaw, notwithstanding his extreme youth, appeared at the head of his army. Mallek al Tijar, with ten thousand horse, formed the right wing, and Nizam al Moolk Turk, with other amras, the left wing, with a similar force. The sultan himself took post in the center, with Khajeh Jehaun, Secunder Khan, his foster brother, eleven thousand horse, and one hundred war elephants.

Sultan Mhamood committed the charge of his right wing to his son prince Gheause ad Dien, and the left to Mahabut Khan, governor of Chunderee, supported by Zaheer al Moolk; while he himself took post with his best troops in the center.

Mallek al Tijar first advanced, and began the battle by a furious charge upon the enemy's left wing, which, after some resistance, fled; Mahabut Khan and Zaheer al Moolk being both killed. Nizam al Moolk Turk, with the left wing, charged the right of the Malwa army under sultan Gheause ad Dien; whose fame for courage and conduct had been long founded throughout Hindooftan. It happened in the height of action, that the two generals came to close combat with each other. The sword of Nizam al Moolk breaking, he threw the hilt in the face of his antagonist with such violence as to wound him in the eye, which bled exceedingly, and he
fell

fell from his horfe with agony. The troops of Malwa, feeing him fallen, turned their faces to flight, and were purfued four miles by the Dekkanees, who made a great flaughter among them, and took much plunder, with fifty elephants. Sultan Mhamood, obferving the defeat of both his wings, was ready to retreat, but another of his fons and fome of his nobles perfuaded him to wait. At this time Khajeh Jehaun charged him with ten thoufand horfe, and fultan Mhamood, ftanding the fhock with great refolution, wounded the elephant of Secunder Khan Turk with an arrow. The huge animal, mad with pain, turning back, trod down many of his own troops, and had nearly feized Nizam Shaw himfelf. Secunder Khan, either out of fear, or enmity to Khajeh Jehaun, drew off his troops, and the fultan with him, to a little diftance from the action; upon which the Dekkanees, miffing the royal ftandard, fled, and did not ftop till they reached the capital. Khajeh Jehaun, now feeing that the right and left wings were gone in purfuit of the enemy, and that the fultan with the Dekkanees had fled, thought it beft to retire; and, with much conduct, quitting the fight, brought off the royal horfes and elephants to Ahmedabad. Mallek al Tijar and his troops, on viewing this ftrange change of fortune, retired alfo. Secunder Khan Turk, on his arrival at the capital, was at firft rewarded by the queen mother for bringing her fon off the field in fafety; but upon her hearing the truth from Khajeh Jehaun, was confined for his cowardice and difgracing the fultan, by taking him from the field on the point of victory. The friends of Secunder Khan complained to the queen, affirming that he had faved the fultan from deftruction, as the two wings had difperfed to plunder, and no troops remained for his fecurity, and declaring, that they would no longer fubmit to be ufed with indignity by the Moguls, who had ufurped the guidance of the royal authority. As the times would not allow the punifhment, Khajeh Jehaun releafed the culprit.

Sultan

Sultan Mhamood, hearing of the dislike of the Dekkanees to the ministers, marched to besiege the capital of Ahmedabad; upon which the queen, jealous of Khajeh Jehaun, to whose remissness she attributed the defeat of the army, by the advice of Mallek al Tijar committed the charge of the citadel of Ahmedabad to Mulloo Khan Dekkanee, and, with the sultan, retired to Firozeabad.

Sultan Mhamood now laid siege to the city, which he took in seventeen days; upon which, great part of the country submitted to his authority, and it was the general opinion, that the power of the house of Bhamenee would pass into that of Khullije; when, suddenly, the standards of sultan Mhamood of Guzarat advanced from that kingdom. Nizam Shaw had, before his retreat, by the advice of Mallek al Tijar, sent ambassadors to request his assistance; in hopes of which he had, at Firozeabad, collected together his scattered army, to defend himself and harass the enemy. Intelligence arriving that the sultan of Guzarat had reached the frontiers of Dekkan, with an army of eighty thousand horse, the queen mother dispatched Mallek al Tijar to his presence to beg speedy relief. The sultan immediately supplied him with twenty thousand horse, under some of his principal nobility; and the allied armies, in a short time, moved towards the capital.

Sultan Mhamood Shaw, who had not been able to take the citadel, upon this raised the siege, and retreated with precipitation towards Malwa. Mallek al Tijar immediately sent two thousand Dekkanee horse to harass his retreat by the way of Berar, while he took post himself, with ten thousand horse and his allies, between Candahar, Beer, and the road to Mando, so that the enemy were shut in on all quarters. He harassed their foraging parties, and cut off all supplies of provision. Sultan Mhamood, who, according to the best accounts, had near thirty thousand horse, frequently tried to bring on an action; but Mallek al Tijar was not to be led from his design,

design; till at length famine grew to the greatest pitch in the Malwa camp, and sultan Mhamood was left, without remedy, to the clamours of his troops.

In this exigence, having killed numbers of his elephants, and set fire to all his heavy baggage, he moved unincumbered towards Ghondwareh, to the confines of which country he was pursued, and constantly harassed on his march, by Mallek al Tijar; so that he lost numbers of his men, and great part of his remaining baggage. Upon his arrival in Ghondwareh, sultan Mhamood commanded a zemindar of that country to conduct him by a route, which would free him from the pursuit of the Dekkanees, and afford some repose to his fatigued army. The zemindar represented, that there was no road easy of passage for an army, but one, on which there was but little water for some stages. The sultan, thinking this a lesser difficulty than the pursuit of an enemy, commanded him to shew the road he mentioned. The first day's march, from the burning winds and excessive thirst, about six thousand men miserably perished; and the next, the natives of the mountains, taking advantage of the distressed army, plundered the helpless of their effects; for the troops, dispirited by their sufferings, made little resistance. A single cup of water sold for [a] two rupees, and frequently was not to be had for money. When sultan Mhamood, after enduring inexpressible hardships, had at length wound out his way from this dreadful labyrinth, suspecting that his miseries had proceeded from the treachery of his guide, he commanded him to be put to death. The Ghonde chief, disregarding life, abused the sultan, boasting, that he had anticipated revenge by destroying twelve thousand men with thirst; that his death was of no consequence, as he had three sons, and should himself be soon transmigrated into one of their offspring. From this we learn, that the Ghondees, like the rest of the Hindoos, believe the transmigration of souls. This gives them a contempt of death

[a] Nearly five shillings.

death, they believing that good conduct in their prefent body will enfure their reanimation in a better ftate.

Sultan Mhamood, before the fall of the city of Ahmedabad Bieder, committed every cruelty of war on the country; but when he had refolved on eftablifhing himfelf in Dekkan, changed his conduct, and treated the inhabitants with gentlenefs. He was always particularly cautious in his drefs and diet, agreeably to the rules of things pure and impure, laid down in the canons of divine law. On this account he had his rice, wheat, oil, and other neceffaries for his own table, from certain farms in his own hereditary dominions, and had vegetables planted or fown in wooden frames filled with foil, carried with him wherever he marched. His halt at Ahmedabad being long, he fent for Molana Shumfe ad Dien, a religious, who attended the tomb of Shaw Khulleel Oolla, to whom he complained of his diftrefs for vegetables, defiring that he would point out fome gardener to him, whofe land was his own, agreeably to the divine laws, that he might purchafe from him at a high price. The Molana replied, " You " fpeak, O king, what can only excite ridicule and fcorn. To invade " the territories of true believers, lay wafte their dwellings, and rob " them of their property, and to pretend obfervance of the law in the " trifling points of drefs and diet, is folly and hypocrify." Sultan Mhamood fhed tears, acknowledged the juftice of his remark, but faid, that empire could not be fupported without fuch contradictory actions.

After the retreat of the fultan of Malwa, Nizam Shaw difpatched ambaffadors to Mhamood Shaw of Guzarat, with valuable prefents, and thanks for the friendly part he had taken in his caufe. Sultan Mhamood returned to Guzarat, and Nizam Shaw to the capital of Ahmedabad Bieder. The fultan of Malwa the next year invaded Dekkan again, advancing as far as Dowlutabad; but was soon obliged to retreat, by the timely assistance of the sultan of Guzarat to Nizam Shaw.

It being the custom of the house of Bhamenee for the children to wed in their early years, the queen mother asked in marriage for her son one of her own relations, and prepared the nuptial feast with royal magnificence and pomp. On the night of consummation, when the assembly of mirth was adorned, and the court full of pleasure and rejoicing, suddenly screams were heard from the royal apartments, and the voice of sorrow complained, with loud sobs, that Nizam Shaw had departed this life, and left the world to other masters. The unblown rose of the royal tree suddenly perished by a destructive blast. The down of beauty had not yet grown on the flower, when death shed upon it the killing mildew. This event happened after a reign of two years and one month, on the night of

A. D. 1462. the thirteenth of Zeekaud, 867.

SULTAN

# SULTAN

# *SHUMSE AD DOONNIA WAL DIEN

# ABOU NUSSUR, AL GHAZEE

# MAHUMMUD SHAW BHAMENEE.

MAHUMMUD Shaw afcended the throne of Dekkan in his ninth year, and the affairs of government were conducted as in the late reign, by Khajeh Jehaun and Mallek al Tijar, under the direction of the queen mother. Ahmed Shaw, younger brother to the fultan, had an ample eftablifhment fettled for his fupport. Khajeh Jehaun took the charge of educating Mahummud Shaw, who made great progrefs in all branches of learning under Shoofteree, the moft celebrated fcholar of his age; fo that, next to Firoze Shaw, he became the moft accomplifhed prince that ever filled the throne of Bhamenee. Khajeh Jehaun acquiring great power and influence in every department of the ftate, directed affairs as he thought proper, without regarding any other authority. He deprived many old nobles of their jaghires, and gave them to creatures of his own raifing; extended the hands of peculation on the royal treafury, and took care to keep his colleague, Mallek al Tijar, employed on the frontiers, fo that he could interfere but little in adminiftration. The queen mother, a

princefs

---

\* Sun of the world and the faith, fon of victory, the champion of religion. He was next brother to the laft fultan.

princess of great prudence and difcernment, alarmed at this behaviour, put the fultan on his guard againſt him, and refolved on his deſtruction. For this purpofe ſhe inſtructed her fon, on the Khajeh's coming next to council, to order his attendants to put him to death. Khajeh Jehaun the next day, according to cuſtom, without fufpicion attended the Durbar; where feeing Nizam al Moolk Turk with fome guards, he was alarmed, but could not properly retire, and as ufual took his poſt near the fultan. Suddenly two female fervants appeared, and faid to the fultan, in a loud voice, It is proper to perform what the queen requefted you. Upon which the fultan, turning to Nizam al Moolk, exclaimed, That wretch is a traitor, put him to death. Nizam al Moolk, who was an enemy to Khajeh Jehaun, without hefitation dragged him from his place, and cut him down with his fabre in the fultan's prefence.

After fome days, Mahummud Shaw conferred upon Mallek al Tijar the title of Khajeh Jehaun, by the advice of his mother, adding the office of vaqueel al fultunnut to his other dignities. When the fultan reached his fourteenth year, his marriage with a princess of his own family was celebrated with royal fplendour; and the queen mother then delivering over to him all power, betook herfelf to a life of devotion: but the fultan ſtill continued to confult her opinion on all matters of importance, and went every day regularly to pay her his refpects.

A.D.1467. When fultan Mahummud Shaw had reached maturity, he became anxious for revenge upon his enemies, and to clafp the bride of conqueſt in his embrace. On this account, having appointed Nizam al Moolk governor of Berar, he fent him in the year 872, with a powerful army, againſt the fortrefs of Kurleh, in the poffeſſion of the fultan of Malwa. Nizam al Moolk laid fiege to the place, and feveral times defeated armies fent to relieve it. The laſt was a very obſtinate engagement, as twelve thoufand Raajepoots and Afghauns fought

fought defperately in the Malwa army, and great numbers were flain on both fides, but victory, in the end, declared for the Dekkanees. A great number of the troops belonging to the fort, who had joined the enemy, were fo clofely purfued by Nizam al Moolk, that his foldiers entered the gates with them, and a paffage being fecured to the army, he made himfelf mafter of the place. As is the cuftom of the common foldiers of Dekkan, they gave abufive language to the conquered garrifon; which fo enraged two brothers, Raajepoots, that they refolved to fhew their enemies an example of defperate bravery. When the confufion was over, and the Malweans had evacuated the fort, the Raajepoots addreffed Nizam al Moolk's attendants, faying, they had paffed their whole lives in the army, feen many brave men, but none equal to their general in heroifm, and begged they might be permitted to kifs his feet before they departed. Nizam al Moolk, feeing them unarmed, ordered them to approach his perfon; upon which they came up in a fubmiffive manner; but turning fuddenly, and fnatching the fabres from the hands of the neareft guards, mortally wounded him; after which they fought in defpair, till they were both cut to pieces. Nizam al Moolk had two adopted brothers, Adil Khan Sewai and Direa Khan Turk, who, after eftablifhing a ftrong garrifon in the fort, took up the general's body, and marched with a valuable plunder to court. The fultan, approving their fervices, appointed them both to the rank of a thoufand, with the fortrefs of Kurleh and its dependancies in jaghire.

The fultan of Malwa now feeing the fpirit of the Dekkanees, and fearing their refentment for the infults offered to them in the late reign, fent an ambaffador, named Sherf al Moolk, with valuable prefents to Mahummud Shaw, to court his friendfhip and alliance. He reprefented, that fultan Ahmed Shaw Bhamenee, and fultan ª Hofhung, had entered into folemn treaties, by which it was agreed
that

---

ª Sultan of Malwa.

that the province of Berar should belong to the former, and the fortress of Kurleh to the latter; and that a lasting peace should subsist between them and their heirs for ever; that the amras of Dekkan had possessed themselves of Kurleh, but, if Mahummud Shaw chose, the treaty might still be observed, and the subjects of both states be saved from contention, and join in mutual interest and alliance.

Mahummud Shaw dispatched shekh Ahmed Sudder with Sherf al Moolk to Mando, representing, that he was firm and true to the rules of friendship and alliance; and while Carnatic abounded in every quarter with strong holds possessed by infidels, for the employment of his arms, he had no occasion for the fortress of Kurleh. He praised God, that the breach of treaty had not happened on the part of the house of Bhamence; it being clear, that in the late reign of his brother, an infant, the Malwa sultan, taking advantage of the weakness of administration, had invaded his dominions, and committed such ravages on the possessions of the faithful, as had not been perpetrated by the destructive Chungeeze Khan in his conquests; what was passed, however, had passed, and could not be recalled; therefore, whatever shekh Ahmed, who was a true promoter of the repose of the faithful, should agree to, from that he would never deviate in the smallest point. Shekh Ahmed was met near Mando by a deputation of the principal nobility of Malwa, and conducted with much respect and ceremony into the city; where, being introduced to sultan Mhamood Khiljee, he delivered his commission. The Malweans acknowledged that the breach of treaty proceeded from themselves, but they hoped that the Almighty, out of his abundant mercy and goodness, would not call them to account for it. Sultan Mhamood also said, that he had been tempted to act improperly, but hoped it would be forgotten; and that such treaties might now be formed, that his successors, and those of Bhamenee, would in future never act towards each other contrary to the laws of religion and humanity. Shekh Ahmed on the part of Mahummud Shaw, and

shekh

shekh al Iflaam on that of Mhamood Shaw, drew up a treaty, to which were affixed the feals of the divines and learned men of both ftates. Both princes wrote on the margin, in their own hands, that whoever fhould deviate from the contents of the treaty, would be curfed by God, and rejected by the prophet. The fum of the alliance was, that both parties fhould refrain from molefting each other's dominions; that the fortrefs of Kurleh, as in the reign of fultan Ahmed the Juft, fhould be delivered up to the Malwa fovereign; and that whatever countries might be conquered from the Hindoos, by either ftate, fhould not be coveted by the other. When the negotiation was concluded, fhekh Ahmed wrote to the governor of Kurleh, which was immediately given up to the deputies of the fultan of Malwa. Shekh Ahmed then returned to Dekkan; and there never happened afterwards any difagreement between the two royal families.

In the beginning of the year 874, Mallek al Tijar Khajeh A.D. 1469. Jehaun Gawan marched with a powerful army againft the roies of Songeer, Khalneh, and other rebels in Kokun. The troops of Joneer, Jagneh Khurrull, Dabul, Ghoule Mapun, Damaun, and other parts, were ordered to join him on this fervice. The roies of Songeer and Khalneh conftantly had a \* fleet of three hundred veffels at fea, to diftrefs the trade of the faithful. Upon the report of Mallek al Tijar's approach, the infidels made alliances with each other, and affembled in great numbers at the head of the paffes; but Mallek al Tijar by degrees forced them from the enemy's poffeffion. Seeing that his cavalry was ufelefs in the mountainous countries, he fent back what horfe he had brought from the capital, and, contenting himfelf

---

\* Thefe rajas were in all probability the anceftors of thofe who ftill maintain pirate fleets on the Malabar coaft, and the defcendants of thofe whom Rennell, in the Memoir to his Map, fays, Pliny notices as committing, in his time, depredations on the Roman Eaft India trade. The places mentioned, as furnifhing troops for their reduction, are on the Malabar coaft. Damaun is at prefent a Portuguefe fettlement; the others are in the hands of the Mharattas.

himself with the troops under Afaud Geelance and his own dependants, made his way by fire and the axe through the woods. He lay five months before the fort of Khakeh without effect, and the rains setting in, relinquished the siege; when, committing the guard of the passes to ten thousand men, on whom he could depend, he descended the mountains, to pass the wet season in the district of Kolapore, where he reduced the fort of Muknch. After the rains he again ascended the passes, and by stratagem, with unbounded gifts of money, obtained the fortress of Khakeh, which had never been conquered by the mussulmauns. At the approach of the rains, he took the same measures as he had done the former season; and at the expiration of the four wet months marched into the country of Songeer, which he reduced with great case, taking ample revenge for the slaughter of the [a] former Mallek al Tijar. He then moved against the port and island of [b] Goa, belonging to the roy of Beejanuggur; sending an hundred and twenty vessels to attack it by sea, while he marched with his army to act against it by land. Before the roy of Beejanuggur could oppose his design, he made himself master of the place. Mahummud Shaw, on information of this important conquest, ordered the nobut to beat the march of triumph for seven days, and made other rejoicings successively.

Khajeh Jehaun, having fixed a strong garrison in the fort, and laid in plentiful stores of every kind, returned after an absence of three years to the capital of Ahmedabad. Mahummud Shaw condescended to honour him with a visit of a whole week, conferring upon him the highest titles, with a suit of his own robes; and the queen mother gave him the appellation of brother. One of his dependants, named Khoosh Kuddum, who had behaved with distinguished gallantry in the different campaigns, was at his recommendation promoted to high rank, with the title of Kishwer Khan, and the

---

[a] *Vide* reign of Ahmed Shaw, stiled Alla ad Dien 2d.
[b] Now the principal settlement of the Portuguese.

the forts of Goa, Bundoch, Khundwal, and Kholapore were granted him in addition to his other governments. When Mahummud Shaw left his house, Khajeh Jehaun, retiring to his chamber, disrobed himself of his splendid dress, threw himself on the ground, and wept with much lamentation; after which he came out, put on the habit of a dirvesh, and calling together all the deserving learned men, divines, and syeds of Ahmedabad, distributed most of his money, jewels, and effects, excepting his elephants, horses, and library, among them; saying, that praise be to God, he had escaped the temptations of his evil passions, and was freed from danger.

Moolla Shumse ad Dien asked him why he had given away every thing but his library, elephants, and horses? He replied, that when the sultan honoured him with a visit, and the queen mother called him brother, his evil passions began to prevail over his reason; and the struggle of vice and virtue was so great in his mind, that he became distressed even in the presence of his majesty, who kindly enquired the cause of his concern; on which he was obliged to feign illness in excuse for his conduct; when the sultan advised his taking repose, and returned to the palace. He had therefore parted with wealth, the cause of his temptations, that his library he had designed for the use of students, and his elephants and horses he regarded as the sultan's, lent only to him for a season. After this, he always wore plain apparel; and, when at leisure from state affairs, retired to his own mosque and college, where he spent his time in the society of the learned, and persons eminent for piety and virtue. On Friday nights he went disguised through the different wards of the city, and distributed alms to the poor, saying, as he gave them, This is sent by the sultan.

In the year 876, Himber, uncle's son to the roy of Oureah, complained to Mahummud Shaw that the roy being dead, Mungul Roy, a slave, his adopted son, had usurped the government, in defiance of his legal

A.D. 1471.

legal claim of inheritance, and promifed, if the fultan would affift him with troops to regain his right, he would become his tributary. Mahummud Shaw, who had a ftrong defire to poffefs Oureah, [a] Raajmundree, and Cundapul, thought this requeft favourable to his views; and, by the advice of Khajeh Jehaun, having conferred the title of Nizam al Moolk on Mallek Houffun Bheheree, difpatched him with a confiderable army to thofe parts. On the borders of Oureah he was joined by Himber with his troops, who became the guide of the army; and Mungul Roy, having collected a great body of troops, advanced in oppofition, but was foon defeated with great flaughter, and Himber put in poffeffion of his hereditary dominions. Nizam al Moolk proceeded without delay, accompanied by Himber, againft Cundapul and Raajmundree; both which he quickly reduced, and by the orders of Mahummud Shaw, having eftablifhed proper ftations of troops for their fecurity, he difmiffed Himber to his own country, and returned with the plunder of his campaign to court; where, by the recommendation of the queen mother and Khajeh Jehaun, he was honoured with the government of Telingana. Ummad al Moolk was appointed governor of Berar. A few months afterwards, Eufuff Adil Khan Sewai, one of the flaves of Khajeh Jehaun, eminent for his great prudence and other qualities, on which account the minifter had adopted him as his fon, was appointed to the government of Dowlutabad, the moft important in the ftate. Mahummud Shaw, confiding in his abilities, fent him to reduce the fortrefs of Weragur, and to recover that of [b] Antore, which, during the Malwa invafion, had fallen into the poffeffion of a Mharatta, who did not pay proper fubmiffion. Adil Khan, upon his arrival at Dowlutabad, difpatched Cafim Beg Suff-fhekun to reduce Antore, and Direa Khan againft Weragur. The chief of the former

[a] Parts of what are now called the Northern Sirkars, and in poffeffion of the Eaft India company.
[b] Moft probably the fame with Attore in Major Rennell's Map. Weragur was perhaps a neighbouring diftrict.

former delivered up the place without oppolition, on receiving quarter; but the raja of the latter held out againſt the beſiegers for ſix months; at the end of which, ſeeing no hopes of relief, he ſent a meſſage to Adil Khan, promiſing, if his life ſhould be ſpared, to make an offering of all his effects in the fort, and evacuate it with his family. Adil Khan agreeing to theſe terms, ordered Direa Khan to permit the inhabitants to retire without hurt to their perſons or honour; and, accordingly, the [a] roy Jey Sing, with his family and dependants, quitted the ancient abode of his anceſtors, leaving behind him his treaſures and all his hereditary poſſeſſions. Adil Khan, who had come poſt to the camp, entered the fort the ſame day, and took poſſeſſion of the treaſure and valuable effects; after which he encouraged the principal inhabitants and farmers of the country, by aſſurances of protection and juſtice. He then marched againſt the fort of Ranjee, the chief of which, whoſe father was lately dead, after little oppoſition, on promiſe of quarter, ſurrendered it with all the contents. Adil Khan having ſelected elephants, horſes, and what richer effects he eſteemed fit for the ſultan's uſe, received the chief among the amras, and gave him back his fort and country in jaghire. He then returned to Amedabad Bieder, and laid before the ſultan ſuch ſums of money, jewels, valuable effects, elephants, and horſes, that the plunder of Raajmundree and Bilcondah appeared trifling when compared to this offering. Mahummud Shaw on this account conferred upon him great honours, ſaying, Whoever had [b] Khajeh Jehaun for a father, could not fail of performing important ſervices. He ordered Khajeh Jehaun to entertain Adil Khan for a week at his own houſe, with all poſſible magnificence; but the miniſter obſerving,

[a] From the circumſtance mentioned, of Jey Sing's leaving the ancient abode of his anceſtors, it is probable he was the roy of the country by deſcent; and the being ſtiled a Mharatta, proves, that the people ſo called were inhabitants of provinces in parts of Dekkan, long before the family of Sewajee or Bhoſela became their chiefs. Jey Sing's family, doubtleſs, were reduced by the Bhamenee ſovereigns, and he had rebelled during the Malwa invaſion in Nizam Shaw's reign.

[b] Alluding to the adoption of Adil Khan by Khajeh Jehaun, as before mentioned.

FERISHTA's HISTORY OF DEKKAN.

serving, that without his majesty's presence the feast would be incomplete, the sultan said, that to partake of an entertainment prepared for another had no charms, but that he would honour his house with a visit of a week, after that of Adil Khan was ended.

Accordingly, on the eighth day, Mahummud Shaw went to the minister's palace, where he passed a week in continued feasting, and admitted Adil Khan to the honour of drinking wine with him. Khajeh Jehaun treated the king with uncommon splendour, and presented him with so many rich curiosities, that beholders were astonished at the sight. Among these were fifty dishes of pure gold, with covers set with jewels, each large enough to hold a roasted lamb; one hundred slaves of Circassia, Georgia, and Abyssinia, most of them accomplished singers and musicians; one hundred horses of Arabia, Syria, and Turky; and one hundred pieces of superb china, not to be seen, but in the palaces of a few great princes. On the last day he made rich presents to the sultan's sons and all the court; then giving the sultan a schedule of all his property, which he said belonged solely to his majesty, he desired him to take possession. Mahummud Shaw admired his behaviour, and accepted of his offer, but conferred upon him anew all he had seen. After this, the credit and favour of Khajeh Jehaun and Adil Khan became so great, that they were courted and envied by all the nobility; and the Dekkanees, like wounded vipers tormenting themselves, ª bound up the waistband of enmity against them.

A.D. 1472. In the year 877, Perkna, roy of the fortress of Balgoan, at the instigation of the prince of Beejanuggur, marched to retake the island of Goa; as did also the general of Bankapore, with a great army, stopping all supplies of provisions. Mahummud Shaw, immediately upon intelligence of this irruption, collected his forces, and moved against

---

ª This expression means the same as that of girding the loins, so frequently occurring in holy writ. Most Asiatics wear a cloth of many folds round the waist.

against Balgoan, a fortress of great strength, having round it a deep wet ditch, and near it a pass, the only approach, defended by redoubts. The sultan sat down before it, and roy Pirkna, out of regard to his future welfare, sent privately persons to Khajeh Jehaun to beg terms of peace, which were presented to the sultan for his acquiescence; but Mahummud Shaw, in order to shew his power, and deter others by example, would not consent to them, and resolved to take the fort by storm. He commanded the artillery, as they valued their own safety, to effect a practicable breach in fourteen days; and committed to Khajeh Jehaun the charge of filling up the ditch, saying, that he expected to have it passable for the troops when the breach should be ready. Though Khajeh Jehaun during the day threw great quantities of wood and earth into the ditch, the enemy in the night always removed them; upon which he changed his operations to another quarter, and began to erect batteries, and dig mines, which till now had not been used in Dekkan. Pirkna, confiding in his wet ditch as a sure protection, was self-secure, when, suddenly, three mines from the posts of Khajeh Jehaun, Adil Khan, and Fatteh Oolla Ummad al Moolk, were conducted under the fort wall, and sprung with success. The troops of Pirknah advanced to defend the breaches. Nearly two thousand of the sultan's troops were slain in storming, and the besieged had nearly filled up the breaches with wood and stones, when Mahummud Shaw himself advanced to the assault, and with great gallantry drove the enemy from the breach, and gained the fort. While he was attacking the citadel, Pirkna having disguised himself, came to the royal attendants, and requested to be introduced to the sultan as a messenger from the roy. Being permitted to advance, as soon as he arrived before the sultan, throwing his turban upon his neck, he declared his quality, saying, that he had come with his family to kiss the foot of the throne. Mahummud Shaw, admiring his fortitude, pardoned his crimes, and received him into the order of his nobility. When opposition had ceased, the sultan entered the citadel, and gave God
thanks

thanks for the success of his arms. Having added Balgoan and its dependancies to the jaghire of Khajeh Jehaun, he returned towards the capital. Soon after this expedition, in which she had accompanied her son, died the queen mother, by whose prudence the state had acquired new splendour. The sultan sent her corpse in great pomp to be interred at Ahmedabad Bieder.

When the royal standard reached the city of Beejapore, Mahummud Shaw, at the request of Khajeh Jehaun, in whose jaghire it was, halted to repose himself from his fatigues, and, to divert his grief at the death of his mother, engaged in pleasures. Liking the situation of the place, he resolved to remain at it for the rainy season; but it happened that this year a drought prevailed through all Dekkan, so that the wells of Beejapore were dried up, and the sultan, against his inclination, was obliged to move to Ahmedabad. No rain fell the next year, when the cities, towns, and villages became almost destitute of population. Many of the inhabitants died of famine, and numbers migrated for food to Malwa, Jaajnuggur, and Guzarat. In Telingana, Meerhutt, and all the Bhamenee dominions, no grain was sown for two years successively; and the third, when the Almighty showered his mercy upon the earth, scarce any farmers were left to cultivate the lands.

Not long after this dreadful visitation of famine, while the country was reviving from depopulation, intelligence came that the garrison of Cundapul had mutinied, and having killed their governor, who was tyrannically oppressive, and seized the property and women of his dependants, had given up the fort to roy Oureah, who was protected by Mahummud Shaw. Oureah, on this acquisition, sent agents to the roy of Orissa, representing, that if he wished to recover his hereditary dominions in Telingana, now was the crisis, as Dekkan had been ruined by two years of famine, and the armies were reduced to a small body; that he would join him on consideration of being

FERISHTA's HISTORY OF DEKKAN.

being admitted to share in the conquests of the muſſulmauns, and for the preſent give him up the fort of Cundapul, with the dependant country. The roy of Oriſſa, tempted by theſe offers, having collected ten thouſand horſe and eight thouſand foot, alſo ſummoned the rajas of Jaajnuggur to his aſſiſtance, entered Telingana without delay. Nizam al Moolk, governor of Raajmundree, unable to cope with ſo great a force, ſhut himſelf up in that fortreſs, and ſent expreſs accounts of the ſituation of affairs to court.

Mahummud Shaw, by the advice of Khajeh Jehaun, reſolved to oppoſe the infidels in perſon. Having advanced one year's pay to the troops, he began his march with great expedition. Upon his arrival near Raajmundree, the enemy not thinking it adviſeable to meet him in the field, roy Oureah retired to the fortreſs of Cundapul, and the roy of Oriſſa croſſed the lake of Raajmundree, and retreated towards his own dominions. Mahummud Shaw, enraged at this unprovoked invaſion, having left Khajeh Jehaun with the prince Mhamood Khan at Raajmundree, marched with twenty thouſand horſe to puniſh the deceitful idolater. In the latter part of the year 882 he penetrated to the capital of Oriſſa, and uſed no mercy in ſlaughtering the inhabitants and laying waſte the country of the enemy. As the roy had retired to the very extremity of his poſſeſſions, the ſultan had unmoleſted range for operation, and collected vaſt ſums from the people; after which he determined to ſend for his ſon and Khajeh Jehaun, and eſtabliſh them in the province.

A. D. 1477.

The roy of Oriſſa, hearing of the ſultan's intentions, ſent repeated embaſſies, with elephants and other valuable preſents, to open the door of forgiveneſs, declaring ſolemnly, that he would never in future, in any manner, aſſiſt the zemindars of Telingana. To this the ſultan replied, that if he would give him up twenty five noted elephants, which had belonged to the late roy his father, he would grant him peace. The roy valued theſe elephants next to his life, yet durſt not refuſe, and therefore ſent them in rich trappings, and chains

chains of gold and silver; upon which the sultan began his march from Orissa.

The sultan on the march, when engaged at some distance from his route in hunting, saw a fort upon a high hill, and going to view it nearer with his attendants, asked some of the country people to whom it belonged. They replied, that it was the property of the roy of Orissa, and that no power dared be so rash as to cast even a look of conquest upon it. The sultan, inflamed at this insolent reply, halted at the foot of the hill, and the next day began the siege, which continued a month and half without effect. At the expiration of that time, the roy sent an apology for the rudeness of his people, who were clowns and unacquainted with politeness, entreating that his majesty would regard the fort as his own by conquest, and bestow it upon him as one of his vassals. This apology pleased the sultan, who raised the siege, and continued his march.

Mahummud Shaw next sat down before Cundapul; and roy [a] Oureah after six months, being much distressed, sued for pardon; which being granted at the intercession of some of the nobility, he surrendered the fort and city to the royal troops. The sultan went to view the fort, and broke down a temple of idols, killing some braminee devotees who officiated at it with his own hands, from a point of religion. He then gave orders for a mosque to be erected on the foundations, and ascending a pulpit, read some prayers, distributed alms, and commanded the khootbah to be proclaimed in his name. Khajeh Jehaun represented, that as his majesty had slain some infidels with his own hands, he might now properly assume the title of Ghazee; which he did. He was the first of the Bhamenee family that killed a bramin; and it is the belief of the Dekkanees, that this

[a] The raja seems here to be called by the name of the province; as in Europe some times personages are by the places giving their titles.

this act was inauspicious, and conducive to the troubles which soon after perplexed the affairs of himself and his family, to their dissolution.

Mahummud Shaw, according to the advice of Khajeh Jehaun, remained near three years in Raajmundree, to settle the conquered country and establish proper posts of defence on the borders. Having secured the whole country of Telingana, by expelling all the refractory zemindars, he resolved on the conquest of [a] Nersinga, and consulted Khajeh Jehaun on establishing a governor for the province of Telingana. The minister replied, that no one was more capable of such a charge than Nizam al Moolk Beheree; and the sultan approving of that nobleman, committed to his care Raajmundree, Cundapul, and several other places. Warunkul, and other districts, he conferred on Azim Khan; and, after these regulations, began his march towards Nersinga. Nizam al Moolk, disgusted at Azim Khan's appointments, represented to the sultan, that he wished to leave his government in charge of one of his sons, and attend the royal stirrup. To this the sultan replied, that his only aim was the protection of the country, and that he was indifferent by whom that should be effected. It is said, that Khajeh Jehaun perceiving Nizam al Moolk to be of great ambition, did not wish that his son Mallek Ahmed, who had married a lady out of the sultan's haram, and was more aspiring than his father, should be stationed with him in the same jaghire; therefore, when Nizam al Moolk was before appointed governor of Raajmundree, he persuaded the sultan to station Mallek Ahmed with Khodawund Khan Hubshee, and give him a jaghire in Mahore, with the rank of three hundred. Mahummud Shaw now complying with the request of Nizam al Moolk, called Mallek Ahmed to camp, and having promoted him to the rank of a thousand, dispatched him, as his father's deputy, to Raajmundree.

[a] A country dependant on Beejanuggur, called by Europeans, Bisnagar, but then in rebellion against that state.

Nerfing was a powerful raja, possessing the country between Carnatic and Telingana, extending along the sea coast to Matchiliputtun, and had added much of the Beejanuggur territory to his own by conquest, with several strong forts. He had frequently excited the frontier zemindars of Bhamenee to rebel; and the amras on the borders, unable to curb his insolence, had frequently represented it to court, which at length determined the sultan to reduce him.

Mahummud Shaw, in the beginning of this expedition, marching by a ruined fort, and being told that it had been erected by the emperors of Dhely to awe the borderers, halted, and commanded it to be repaired without delay. Khajeh Jehaun used such activity, that the common work of two years was accomplished in the space of six months; a garrison appointed, and ample stores of all kinds laid in for defence. He then conducted Mahummud Shaw to view the works completed; and so sensible was the sultan of his merit, that he exclaimed, " The Almighty hath bountifully conferred upon me " two great blessings, an important empire, and a servant unequalled." Having said this, he took off his upper robe, and putting it on the shoulders of Khajeh Jehaun, took his in return, and put it on his own person. Such an honour being done by a sultan to his servant, we read not of in any history.

Mahummud Shaw, having stationed three thousand horse near the fort to protect his rear, marched on. Wherever he came he laid waste the country, and slaughtered those inhabitants who made resistance. Upon his arrival at Ghondpore, he was informed by the country people, that at the distance of ten days' journey was the temple of [a] Kinjee, the walls and roof of which were plated with gold, ornamented with precious stones, and that the sultans of Islaam, as yet, had never seen it, nor heard of its name.

Mahummud

[a] Or, Conjeveram.

Mahummud Shaw, having selected six thousand horse from his army, made forced marches towards Kinjee, but moved so rapidly himself, that only forty horsemen could keep up with him, among whom were Nizam al Moolk Beheree, and Yeghrush Khan Toork. When they appeared before the temple, from it advanced some Hindoos, one of whom appeared above the rest of uncommon stature, mounted on horseback, and brandishing a drawn sabre by way of defiance. Advancing full speed towards the sultan, he aimed a blow at him without effect; when Mahummud Shaw, with great agility, struck him with his scymetar with such force, as to cleave him in two. Another infidel then attacked the sultan, whose little force was engaged man against man, but he had the good fortune to slay him also, upon which the rest of the Hindoos fled into the temple. Crowds, like bees, now issued from within, and ranged themselves under the walls to defend it. The troops coming up, the sultan assaulted the place, which was carried with great slaughter of the Hindoos. An immense plunder fell to the victors, who took nothing away but gold, jewels, and silver, so abundant were those valuable commodities. The sultan then plundered the city of Kinjee, and after reposing in it for a week, returned to his grand army.

After this, Mahummud Shaw sent many of the foreign officers, with the troops of Dowlutabad and Joneer, against the capital of Nersinga, going himself against [a] Matchiliputtun, which he reduced, with all the dependant country, and then returned to Ghondpore. Nizam al Moolk, Zireef al Moolk, and others, had bribed several of the most confidential servants about the sultan's person to throw out hints, now and then, prejudicial to Khajeh Jehaun, and these traitors lost no opportunity of alarming the royal mind with suspicions of his aspiring views, and peculation of the royal revenue; till, at length, they brought that great minister to destruction, by contriving the following infamous forgery: but it is necessary, before the particulars are

[a] Or, Massulipatam.

are related, to difplay the caufes of the enmity of the nobility, who contrived his ruin.

The dominions of Bhamence having in the reign of Mahummud Shaw become very extenfive, Khajeh Jehaun thought it political to make feveral alterations in the rules eftablifhed by fultan Alla ad Dien Kangoh, which were formed for a fmall ftate; and having convinced the fultan of their utility, he was permitted to carry them into execution. The whole kingdom, originally divided into four terruffs, or provinces, under four chief governors, he diftributed into eight. Berar was portioned into two governments; Kaweel under Fatteh Oolla Ummad al Moolk, and Mahore under Khodawund Khan Hubfhee. Dowlutabad was conferred on Adil Khan, and Joneer, with the diftricts of Alore, Baeen, Ban, the port of Goa, and Balgoan, on Fukhir al Moolk. Beejapore, with many diftricts as far as the Beemrah, alfo Roijore and Mudkul, were conferred upon himfelf. Ahfiunabad, Koolburga, with Saugher, as far as Nulderruck and Sholapore, were entrufted to the Abyffinian eunuch, Duftoor Deenar. The country of Telingana, which had been left entirely to Nizam al Moolk Beheree, was alfo divided. Raajmundree, Matchiliputtun, Bilcondah, Oureah, and other places, were continued under his charge; and the government of Warunkul was conferred on Azim Khan. Several places in each of the eight divifions were referved as peculiar revenues for the fultan's private expenfes, and particular collectors appointed to manage them.

From the time of fultan Alla ad Dien to the prefent reign, it had been the rule of the ftate, to leave all the forts in each province to the charge of the governor, or terruffdar, who appointed his own deputies and garrifon, without reftriction. In confequence of this impolitic indulgence, the governors of provinces had fometimes rebelled againft the royal authority, and it had as often been found difficult to reduce them. By the new regulation, one fortrefs only was left in the

chief

chief governor's hands for his own refidence, and all the reft were garrifoned by officers and troops paid and appointed by the fultan, without any intervening authority over them.

Another change of the rules of fultan Alla ad Dien, was in the pay of the troops. By them, the amras of five hundred had one lack of * oons per annum; of a thoufand, two lacks in ready money, or a jaghire producing an equal revenue. Khajeh Jehaun, after the entire conqueft of Telingana, to encourage the army, fettled the pay of an amra of five hundred, at one lack and twenty five thoufand oons; of a thoufand, at two lacks and fifty thoufand; and the jaghires were fo eftablifhed, that if the revenues were one oon lefs than the allowed pay, it was fupplied from the royal treafury; and if the amras kept one foldier under their fixed numbers, a fum equal to his pay was deducted from their allowances. By thefe rules, fuch a confiftent order and dependance was maintained, that government acquired full force, and all ranks of people enjoyed their rights in fecurity and repofe; but this ftrictnefs was difgufting to thofe of afpiring minds, who conceived a rooted hatred for the minifter.

Khajeh Jehaun faw their malice; but as all his view was the fultan's intereft and profperity, he regarded it not; and as a fincere attachment fubfifted between him and Adil Khan, whom he had adopted as his own fon, no one dared, while they were together, to attempt openly the fmalleft injury againft them. At length, Adil Khan going upon the expedition againft Nerfinga, the two friends were feparated; and a number of Dekkanees and Abyffinians, who had been raifed to high offices at the recommendation of Khajeh Jehaun, entered into confederacy with Nizam al Moolk Beheree againft their patron; advifing, that advantage of Adil Khan's abfence fhould be taken, to effect his deftruction.

Zireef

* Called pagodas by Europeans, a lack of which makes fomewhat above forty thoufand pounds.

Zireef al Moolk Dekkanee and Miftah Hubſhee being charged with the plot againſt their patron, paid their court to one of his Abyſſinian ſlaves, who had the care of his ſeals; and having gained his friendſhip by large preſents, haſtened to finiſh their deſign. One day, after drinking wine together, Zireef al Moolk and Miftah Hubſhee produced a folded paper, ſaying, that it was the account of one of their friends, and had received the ſeals of moſt of the heads of offices, only requiring the Khajeh's, which if he would affix, they ſhould regard it as a great obligation. The ſlave, being intoxicated with liquor, complied with their deſire; and, without the caution of unfolding the paper, \* ſtamped the ſeal on the part they pointed out to him. The two wretches, overjoyed at their ſucceſs, went the ſame night to Nizam al Moolk, who, in conjunction with them, wrote on the paper a letter, as if from Khajeh Jehaun to the roy of Oriſſa, in theſe words: " I am weary of the drunkenneſs and " cruelty of Mahummud Shaw. Dekkan may be conquered with " little trouble, as at Raajmundree and that frontier there is no " general of any note. You may invade that quarter without oppo-
" ſition; and as moſt of the nobility and troops are devoted to me, " I will join you with a powerful army. When we have in con-
" junction reduced the ſultan, we will divide his territories equally " between us." Zireef al Moolk and Miftah Hubſhee delivered this letter to the ſultan, in the preſence of Nizam al Moolk. Mahummud Shaw, ſeeing the ſeal of his miniſter, was inflamed with rage. Nizam al Moolk finding opportunity to ſpeak, by falſe accuſations ſo raiſed his paſſion, that he loſt all command over his reaſon, and without weighing probability, or aſking to ſee the meſſenger, who, it was pretended, had been intercepted carrying the letter to the roy of Oriſſa, ſent for Khajeh Jehaun to the preſence. His friends who had heard the cauſe, informed him of it, and remarked, that it would be prudent to form ſome excuſe for not obeying that day, and to wait till the ſultan ſhould recover his reaſon, when the

forgery

---

\* The natives of India commonly put their ſeal inſtead of ſignature to papers.

forgery would be easily detected, and the criminals punished. Khajeh Jehaun in reply, repeated a verse to this effect: "As martyrdom "to love is glorious here and hereafter, happy should I be to be "carried dead from the field immediately." He then said, "This "beard has grown white in the auspicious service of the father, and "it will be honourable should it be dyed with my blood by the "fortunes of the son; there is no evading the decrees of fate, and to "draw the neck from its sentence is impossible." Many capital amras, attached to his cause, now sent messengers to him, informing, that they had heard alarming reports, and had ten thousand horse ready for his service; that if he would fly to Guzarat, they would attend him, and sacrifice their lives in his defence. He answered, that he had for many years enjoyed honourable repose in his master's service, in which he had been guilty of no crime; and that, on account of the mere accusations of his enemies, the sultan could not believe him unfaithful; but if, impelled by providence, he should punish him innocent, it was best to submit to the decree. That what they had proposed as duty and friendship, was ingratitude and rebellion.

Having said thus, he instantly went to court. Mahummud Shaw sternly exclaimed, "When any one is disloyal to his sovereign, and "his crime is proved, what should be his punishment?" The Khajeh replied, "The abandoned wretch who practises treachery. "against his lord, should meet nothing but the sword." The sultan then shewed him the letter; upon seeing which he, after repeating the verse of the koraun (O God, this is a great forgery) said, "The "seal is mine, but not the letter, of which I have no knowledge." He concluded by repeating the following verses: "By the God "whose commands the just have obeyed with their blood, false as "the story \* of Eusuff and the wolf, is that my enemies have forged "of me." As the sultan was intoxicated with wine, and had
resigned

\* Alluding to Joseph's brethren telling Jacob that he was torn by a wild beast.

resigned his reason to anger, and the decline of the house of Bhamenee was near, he attended not to the examination of facts; but rising from the assembly, ordered Johir, an Abyssinian, to put the minister to death on the spot. Khajeh Jehaun addressed the sultan, saying, " The death of an old man like me is of little moment " to myself, but will be to you the ruin of an empire, and your own " glory." The sultan attended not to his words, but abruptly retired into his haram. The slave then drawing his sabre advanced towards the Khajeh; who, kneeling down facing the * Kibleh, said, " There " is no God but God, and Mahummud is the prophet of God." When the sabre reached his neck, he cried, " Praise be to God for " the blessing of martyrdom," and resigned his soul to the divine mercy. Asaad Khan Geelanee, an amra of high rank, and friend to the Khajeh, happening to be present, was put to death by the slave also, without orders. Khajeh Jehaun at the time of his death was seventy eight years old. A little before, he had written a poem in praise of Mahummud Shaw.

A.D. 1481. His death happened on the fifth of Suffur, 886, and Moolla Abd al Kerreem Sindee, author of the Tarekh Mhamood Shawee, one of the servants of the Khajeh, composed the following verses on his martyrdom.

" The innocent martyr, truly deserving veneration, by whose " bounty the world was made glad; if you wish to know the " date of his death, read the ᵇ record of the unjust slaughter." Again he says, " If any are desirous to know the year of his death, " say, without guilt Mhamood Gawan was martyred."

There are in Dekkan many remains of the munificence of this great man; particularly a college, built by him at Ahmedabad two years before

---

* The point of prayer, Mecca.
ᵇ This expression in numerical letters composed the date.

before his death, containing also a mosque and a large square of shops, which, at the date of this history, were as entire as if just finished. Khajeh Jehaun had great learning, and much judgment in composition of prose and verse. In arithmetic he was unequalled; and his [a] Rozet al Insha and poems are still extant in some libraries in Dekkan. He annually remitted valuable presents to the learned in Khoraffan and Eeraak, and the princes of those parts bestowed honours upon him. Molana Jami Abd al Rahmaan corresponded with him, and some of his letters are to be seen in his works. There is also in the Molana's poems one written in his name. Moolla Abd al Kerrun Tummdee has given an account of him from his birth to his death, part of which is inserted as worthy of a place in history.

Khajeh Jehaun's ancestors in former ages, for generations successively, held the post of vizier to the princes of Geelan in Persia, and one of them became sultan of Rishd; which territory, according to Hajee Mahummud Candaharee, continued in his family till the time of Shaw Tahmasp Suffewi. Khajeh Jehaun, as he was of royal extraction, alarmed at the jealousy of Tahmasp, persuaded his mother to quit his birth-place; and, though invited to the high office of vizier by the princes of Eernak and Khoraffan, refused the honour, chusing rather to become a merchant. In this capacity he travelled through many countries, and made acquaintance with celebrated and learned men in each. In his forty third year, partly to trade, and partly to visit the religious of Dekkan, he came by sea to the port of Dabul, and from thence over land to Ahmedabad, intending to proceed from that capital to Dhely. Sultan Alla ad Dien the second, seeing his great qualities, with much entreaty prevailed upon him to become enrolled among his nobility. In the reign of Humaioon Shaw Zalim, he was honoured with the title of Mallek al Tijar, and rose to the first office in the state. Mahummud Shaw added several other honours to his name, and among them the title of Khajeh Jehaun.

[a] Garden of composition. Insha is a directory for correspondence on all subjects.

Jehaun. He entertained two thousand Moguls in his own pay, and ten thousand horse from the sultan were under his command. The following reason is given for his being called ᵃGawan. Being one day in the sultan's company sitting on a terrace of the palace, a cow happened to bleat underneath, when one of the assembly laughingly said, O vizier, what says the cow? To which he replied, She says I am one of her species, and should not sit among asses. When he received the title of Gawan he prophetically observed, that he feared it was unlucky, as all who had held it suffered unnatural deaths. He was by sect a sunnee of the strictest order. His loyalty to Mahummud Shaw was sincere, and the fame of his liberality spread over Asia; there being scarce a town or city, the deserving of which did not taste of his bounty. His behaviour was affable to all ranks, and his justice in his dealings unimpeached.

Mahummud Shaw having heard frequent reports of the vast wealth of Khajeh Jehaun, sent for his treasurer, Nizam ad Dien Houssun Geelanee, and demanded where his money, jewels, and plate were deposited. The treasurer, alarmed, told the sultan, that if he would promise to spare his life, he would discover all; upon which, thinking to receive a great treasure, he took an oath and promised, if he concealed nothing, to reward him with royal bounty. The treasurer then said, " O sultan, my lord had two treasuries, one of which he " called the sultan's, from which were issued the expenses of his " troops, stables, and household: in this there are now ten thousand " laarees, and three thousand oons. The other he named the trea- " sury of the poor, and in this there is a sealed bag, containing three " hundred laarees." The sultan said, " How comes it that the " Khajeh, whose revenues equalled that of many kings, should only " have such a small sum?" The treasurer replied, " Whenever " money came from his jaghire, having taken for the king's trea- " sury the pay of his troops and stables, he gave the remainder, in

" your

ᵃ Cows.

"your majesty's name, to the poor, not reserving a [a] cowrie for his
"own use. A sum of forty thousand laarees, which he brought with
"him from Persia to Dekkan, he employed, by means of agents, in
"trade; and preserving always that capital, expended two laarees
"each day for his kitchen and apparel out of the profits, the
"remainder of which was carried into the poor's treasury, and issued
"from thence in sums, remitted to his mother, relations, and
"worthy persons, with whom he had made acquaintance in his
"travels, and who would not come to Hindoostan."

The minister's enemies were confounded at this account, but enviously remarked, that the Khajeh was a cautious man, and suspecting his expenses might betray his riches, had left them secreted at the capital. To which the treasurer replied, that if one laaree, his property, should be found there, or any where, beyond the sums he had mentioned, he would submit to the severest punishment. The sultan then assembled all the head servants; and first questioned the chief [b] feraash; who said, that all the tents and carpets his lord had, were now in the camp, except some mattings in the city on the floors of his mosque and college, and that the Khajeh always slept himself upon a bare mat. The overseer of the kitchen was then called, who declared, that all the utensils and vessels were with him, but that the victuals for his master's own eating, were always dressed in earthen pots. The librarian lastly stood forth, and acknowledged that there were in the library three thousand volumes, but all in trust for the students of the college. The sultan now became melancholy, and the treasurer took courage to say, " O sultan, may thousands
"such as Mhamood Gawan be ransoms for thy safety! but why
"didst thou not regard the claims upon thee for his services? why
"call not before thee the bearer of the letter to the roy of Orissa,
"that his treachery might appear to us and all mankind clear and
                                            " undoubted?"

[a] A small sea shell, current as money.
[b] Tent-keeper.

"undoubted?" Mahummud Shaw, struck with this query, awoke from the trance of stupefaction, and called to the accusers of the unfortunate minister to bring the bearer of the letter before him. None could be found. He then rose trembling with horror, retired into his haram, full of remorse and sorrow, at his rash credulity and unjust sentence against his faithful friend. The hearse of the deceased was sent off, in melancholy pomp, to Ahmedabad for interment; and three days after, the prince Mhamood Khan and many of the nobility were ordered to visit the grave.

The sultan now prepared to march, but the night of the orders being issued, Ummad al Moolk and Khodawund Khan, with the troops of Berar and Mahore, separated from the camp, and moved four miles distant. Mahummud Shaw upon this account deferred his march, and sent to them to enquire the cause of their movement. They answered, that as the servants of his majesty had by their machinations destroyed such a character as Khajeh Gawan, they could not but be fearful of their own safety, if they remained at court. The sultan, upon this, sent a private message, desiring them to come to his presence, that by their assistance he might punish the traitors who had abused his confidence by such forgeries; but to this they replied, that whenever Adil Khan should arrive, they would come with him, and kiss his majesty's feet. The sultan, seeing that nothing but patience and complying behaviour would succeed, sent a firmaun to Adil Khan; who came with all expedition to Ghondpore, and pitched his camp close to that of the two disgusted chiefs. All three obtained whatever they chose to ask, without reserve. The jaghire of Khajeh Jehaun, Beejapore, was conferred on Adil Khan, who was appointed terruffdar, and Direa Khan, Fukhir al Moolk, and Mulloo Khan, with most of the mogul amras attached to him, obtained jaghires in that division. Ummad al Moolk and Khodawund Khan were fixed in their governments, and obtained all their demands. When they had attended the sultan to Ahmedabad, they

encamped

encamped without the city, and would not enter it; upon which the fultan, feeing his authority vain, did not give way to unavailing rage, but held his peace, and difmiffed them honourably to their feveral jaghires, arming himfelf with patience and forbearance. In hopes that Nizam al Moolk would imitate the conduct of Khajeh Jehaun in his vigilant policy, he ftrengthened his power daily, loading him with benefits, which only ferved to difguft the nobility.

Some months afterwards, the fultan, in hopes that Adil Khan, Ummad al Moolk, and Khodawund Khan would join him with their armies, marched; but though they accompanied him, they always encamped at a diftance, and paid their refpects only on the road, ftanding far from him, furrounded by guards. Mahummud Shaw, a thoufand times in an hour, regretted the lofs of Khajeh Jehaun; but as there was now no remedy, he held his tongue from complaints, while he fuffered inwardly extreme anxiety. When he arrived at Balgoan, and had feen the city and fortifications, though the amras repeatedly urged him to vifit Goa and Kokun, he would not confent, and began his return to the capital. At this time intelligence arrived, that Sewa-roy, prince of Beejanuggur, had fent a large army againft Goa; upon which the fultan difpatched Adil Khan with the troops of Beejapore, to oppofe him, and went himfelf by regular marches to Firozeabad; but Ummad al Moolk and Khodawund Khan quitted the army on the route without leave, and retired to their governments in Berar.

Mahummud Shaw, knowing that civil war could be attended with no benefit, refolved to be paffive, and halted three months at Firoze-abad; feemingly fpending his hours in pleafures, but inwardly a prey to grief and forrow, which wafted his ftrength daily. He appointed his fon Mhamood Khan his fucceffor, and conftituted Nizam al Moolk regent. A declaration to this effect was made out in writing, teftified by the fignatures and feals of the learned and pious men in the court. While this paper was drawing out, he would
frequently

frequently say, If they obey not me, who reigned gloriously for many years, and conquered nations with my sword, how will they stoop to submit to a child? His weakness daily encreased; but, upon his return to Ahmedabad, he grew better, and presuming upon it, indulged in debauches. His fever had not entirely left him, when one day he drank a large cup of wine, and retired to his haram, which brought on a severe fit. The physicians administered to him medicines immediately, and, seeing him somewhat recovered, retired. In their absence, the sultan, from the vulgar maxim that nothing is so good to remove the lassitude from intoxication as a fresh cordial, drank wine, and instantly fell into strong fits; during which he frequently cried out, that Khajeh Jehaun was tearing him to pieces: till at length he trod the path of mortality, on the first of Suffur, 887, after a reign of twenty years. The date of his death is comprized in the following verses.

A.D. 1482.

" The king of kings, sultan Mahummud; when suddenly he
" plunged into the ocean of death, as Dekkan became waste by his
" departure, \* the ruin of Dekkan was the date of his death."

\* These words are in numerical letters.

SULTAN

# SULTAN

# MHAMOOD SHAW BHAMENEE.

SULTAN Mhamood Shaw afcended the throne of Dekkan in the twelfth year of his age; and the amras then at court, Nizam al Moolk Beheree, Kowaam al Moolk, Cafim Bereed Turk, and others, fwore allegiance. His inauguration was conducted with much ceremony. The throne Firozeh was placed in the grand hall of audience, and on each fide of it a chair of filver. Shaw Mohib Oolla and Syed Hunneef, the two moft celebrated divines of Dekkan, having offered prayers for his profperity, placed the crown on the fultan's head; then, each holding an arm, helped him to afcend the throne, which at this time, in magnificence and intrinfic value, exceeded every other in the world. This done, they feated themfelves on the filver chairs. Nizam al Moolk and Cafim Bereed then advancing, made offerings of congratulation, and their, example was followed by all the nobility and officers prefent. Some of the affembly obferved, that Adil Khan Turk, Fukhir al Moolk, Direa Khan, and Mulloo Khan, who were among the prime Turkifh nobility, not being prefent, the ceremony was not binding. To this Nizam al Moolk replied, that to keep the throne vacant would caufe diffentions; but when they returned from Kokun, the ceremony might be repeated, and titles and honours be conferred. Moolla Abd al Kerrum Tummdee, who was prefent, writes, that the people regarded this difpute as ominous of evil; and fo it proved, as the reign of Mhamood Shaw, though a long one, paſſed in troubles and civil wars, and the royal authority fell from the houſe of Bhamenee.

When the late ſultan Mahummud Shaw aſcended the throne, being but a child, the chief nobility had aſpired to independance; but by the able conduct of the queen mother and Khajeh Jehaun, their deſigns were overthrown, and they dared not openly ſhew their wiſhes. That prince, from his abilities, ſoon became capable of managing affairs in perſon, and by degrees the power of the nobility was reduced to proper bounds. He had encouraged a number of Georgians, Circaſſians, Calmucks, and other Turkiſh tribes, beſides two thouſand ſlaves, Abyſſinians and Hindoos. From theſe were ſelected the officers of government, and by degrees many of them roſe to high power. Nizam al Moolk Beheree, one of the Hindoo ſlaves, was conſidered by the Dekkanees and Abyſſinians as their head; while the Turks attached themſelves to Adil Khan, originally a Turkiſh ſlave. As Khajeh Jehaun favoured the Turks, Adil Khan was permitted to ſtand at court above Nizam al Moolk, which hurt his pride, and, in the end, led him to plan the deſtruction of that great miniſter, as before related; but Adil Khan, by his prudence, eſcaped his ſtratagems, and being appointed terruffdar of Beejapore became daily more powerful.

Upon the death of Mahummud, and the acceſſion of Mhamood Shaw, Adil Khan, and the nobility with him, having entered into alliance to ſupport each other, came from Kokun in great force to felicitate the young ſovereign, and encamped without the walls of Ahmedabad. Adil Khan, Direa Khan, Fukhir al Moolk, Yeghruſh Khan, Azdauh Khan, and Ghuzzunfir Khan entered the city with a thouſand Mogul and Turkiſh horſe, to pay their allegiance to the ſultan. When they arrived at the palace, though it was againſt the etiquette of the court for noblemen to enter with attendants, yet, fearful of treachery in Nizam al Moolk, they took with them two hundred

hundred armed followers. Nizam al Moolk, with five hundred select attendants, met them with much ceremonious attention, and introduced them to the fultan's prefence. Adil Khan, having paid his refpects in form, took his place as formerly above Nizam al Moolk and all the nobility. Dirca Khan fat between the Nizam and his fon Mallek Ahmed, that, in cafe of treachery, they might be firft revenged on the perpetrators, and truft to fortune for the reft. Ahmed Khan attempted to move next his father, who forbad him; and to prevent difturbances, which he faw, from the caution of his rivals, would be hazardous to his perfon, haftened the ceremony of beftowing khelauts from the fultan, and rifing of the court. Eufuff Adil Khan, at coming out, led Nizam al Moolk by the hand, under pretence of converfation, to the outer gate of the citadel; where, being joined by his force, he parted from him with profufe affurances of regard and friendfhip, and took up his refidence at his houfe in the city, with a guard of a thoufand chofen men for his protection; giving orders to Dirca Khan and his other friends to return to camp, and be upon their guard.

Nizam al Moolk the next day vifited Adil Khan; and, after many declarations of friendfhip, defired that he would, with all the Mogul and Turkifh amras, refide in the city, that they might attend with him at court, and affift in the management of the royal affairs.

Adil Khan replied, that his affurances of friendfhip accorded with his own wifhes; but for his daily attendance at court, there was no occafion, as he and his friends were only foldiers, and ignorant of the political arcana of government. Agreeably to the will of their late fovereign, he defired he would conduct adminiftration, and leave him the military execution of the fultan's orders; that his friends had better remain encamped without the city, as they were rude and ignorant, and quarrels might arife, dangerous to the publick repofe of the town between them, the Abyffinians and Dekkanees. It was

was at length agreed, that Nizam al Moolk should have the post of vaqueel al sultunnut, and leave the various great offices which he had held under Mahummud Shaw, to others. By this plan the vizarut was conferred on Kowaam al Moolk, senior, and Warunkul on Kowaam al Moolk, junior. Raajmundree, with the [a] nizarut, was given to Dillawer Khan Hubshee. Every post was shared by mutual consent among their friends. They then repaired together to court, where the sultan's assent being passed, and khelauts of confirmation given, Adil Khan returned to his own house, and never after concerned himself in the internal management of the royal affairs.

For a short time the Moguls and Turks lived amicably with the Dekkanees and Abyssinians; but Nizam al Moolk and Kowaam al Moolk, senior, at length infringed the treaty, as they wished to remove Eusuff Adil Khan Turk, and fill his place with Adil Khan Dekkanee, then deputy governor of Warunkul. With this design they called him to court, with Fatteh Oolla Ummad al Moolk, on pretence of felicitating the sultan's accession. They came accordingly, with a great army, and encamping without the walls, entered the city with a few attendants to pay their compliments and offerings to the sultan, who received them very graciously, and honoured them with khelauts.

About three weeks after this, Nizam al Moolk, who had lulled the weak Ummad al Moolk Turk into a reliance on his friendship, told him, that he wished, with the assistance of the Dekkanee nobility, to destroy Eusuff Adil Khan Turk, that they might both be secured from his machinations, and send off his partizans to their different stations; that the Dekkanee amras could not leave their houses for fear of the Turks, so that, if he approved the plan, it would be adviseable for him on the day of its execution to order the Turkish troops under him to keep within their habitations. Kowaam al

[a] Superintendance of the royal seraglio.

al Moolk approved of the defign, and the following day, Nizam al Moolk having feated the fultan upon one of the towers of the citadel, fent orders to Adil Khan Dekkanee and Futtch Oolla Ummad al Moolk to pafs in review with their troops before the fultan, in order to receive their khelauts and audience of difmiffion to their governments. Ferraud al Moolk, the \* cutwal, hearing by fome means of the defign, informed Kowaam al Moolk that Nizam intended treachery againft all the Turks without exception, and that the plot to affaffinate Eufuff Adil Khan was only a cloak to his defigns; fo that for the Turks to remain paffive in their houfes, on fuch a day, would be the height of folly. Kowaam al Moolk, who wifhed the deftruction of Eufuff Adil Khan, and relied on the fincerity of Nizam al Moolk's friendfhip to himfelf, would not believe the information.

Adil Khan Dekkanee and Ummad al Moolk came into the city, with all the troops of Telingana and Kaweel, and drew up before the citadel. The fultan Mhamood Shaw, who was merely a tool in the hands of his minifters, by the inftruction of Nizam, having called the two chiefs to him in the tower, faid, that as the Turks were become difobedient to his authority, and committed great difturbances in the city, he thought it neceffary to employ their forces in punifhing them without delay. Ummad al Moolk, who had a fincere regard for Eufuff Adil Khan, having placed him in fecurity, fent his army with Adil Khan Dekkanee to deftroy the Turks. Kowaam al Moolk was made the firft facrifice; and the gates of the city being kept fhut, a great flaughter was made among the Turks, who were unprepared for fuch an attack; but Yeghrufh Khan, Kuddim Khan, and other officers who were friends of Eufuff Adil Khan, maintained a running fight to the gates, which they forced; and Direa Khan, informed of the attack on his companions, entered the city with a great force, which made the combat equal. It is faid, that fkirmifhes

---

\* A magiftrate who has the regulation of the markets, collects the town duties, and fuperintends the police.

mishes occurred in the streets of the capital for twenty days succeffively, and about four thoufand men were flaughtered on each fide. At length the divines and holy men interfered as mediators; and, as many Turkifh officers of rank had fallen, Eufuff Adil Khan confented to peace, and quitting the capital, with his dependants, retired to Beejapore.

Nizam al Moolk having now the fole power of adminiftration in his hands, conferred Beer, Darwer, and many other diftricts, upon his own fon Mallek Ahmed. Fukhir al Moolk Dekkanee, the fon of a flave of Khajeh Jehaun, a gallant and learned man, was raifed to the rank of a thoufand, and his fon exalted to the title of Khajeh Jehaun. Ummad al Moolk was honoured with the vizarut, and his fon Shekh Alla ad Dien fent to command on the part of his father in Berar. Cafim Bereed, who had fhewn great activity againft the Turks, was made cutwal of the city and meer nobut. Kowaam al Moolk, junior, was difmiffed to Telingana. Nizam al Moolk and Ummad al Moolk, during four years, in conjunction with the mother of fultan Mhamood, tranfacted all the affairs of government.

'At length, Dillawer Khan Hubfhee, envying their power, reprefented to the fultan, that his minifters paid no regard to his authority, and, in league with the queen mother, ufurped all the power of the ftate, regarding him ftill as a weak infant. This obfervation provoked Mhamood Shaw to action, and he ordered Dillawer Khan to affaffinate the minifter. One night, when both were gone to the queen mother's apartments, to confult her on fome urgent bufinefs, Dillawer Khan placed himfelf in the paffage with another perfon armed, and, as the minifters came out, rufhed upon them with their fabres. Nizam al Moolk received a wound, but as both were perfect in the art of defence, they kept up a running fight, and made their efcape out of the palace. Having fent word to Cafim Bereed that the fultan intended his affaffination alfo, they fled with their followers

out

out of the city. Cafim Bereed having fhut the gates of the palace, prevented any perfons from going to the fultan; who was at length reduced to fuch diftrefs, that he wrote to the minifters, apologizing for his conduct, and inviting them back; but they infifted that, prior to their return, Dillawer Khan fhould be put to death; which refolve coming to his hearing, he made his efcape with his family to Boorahanpore. Nizam al Moolk with his fon Mallek Ahmed returned to the capital; but Ummad al Moolk retired to his government of Berar.

Nizam al Moolk now, in order to ftrengthen his party, raifed Mallek Wujjeh and Mallek Afhruff, formerly dependants on Khajeh Jehaun, to high rank; appointing the firft governor of Dowlutabad, and the other his deputy; and having exacted promifes of attachment and fidelity from them to his fon Mallek Ahmed, fent them to Dowlutabad. He alfo committed the fortrefs of Porundeh and Sholapore to Mukhdoom Khajeh Jehaun Dekkanee, binding him by a fimilar oath of attachment. At the expiration of three months, having procured the fultan's permiffion, he difpatched his fon Mallek Ahmed to Joneer, as his deputy.

In the year 891, Adil Khan Dekkanee, governor of Warunkul, A. D. 1486. dying, Kowaam al Moolk, junior, haftened, by forced marches, from Raajmundree to that city, and fetting up the ftandard of rebellion, poffeffed himfelf of all Telingana. Nizam al Moolk, taking the fultan with him, marched towards Warunkul; upon which, Kowaam al Moolk retreated to Raajmundree, and wrote privately, complaining of the ufurpations of the minifter, to the fultan; who having refigned himfelf to wretchednefs, through fear of his guardians, returned no anfwer, but fent immediately the petition to Nizam al Moolk. When the royal ftandard had reached Warunkul, advice came from Mallek Ahmed, that the port of Goa, which in the late reign had been granted to Kifhwer Khan, and was deputed

by

by him to the charge of Nujum al Dien Geelanee, on his death, had been seized by one of his officers, named Bahadur Geelanee, as also Dabul, Kolapore, Kulher, Punnalleh, Serwaleh, and Balgoan, and that, at the instigation of Eusuff Adil Khan, he daily grew more insolent, and committed insults on the port of Choule and other places; also, that Zien ad Dien, the jaghiredar of Jagneh, had rebelled.

Nizam al Moolk commanded his son, first to reduce Zien ad Dien, and sent orders to Khajeh Jehaun Dekkanee, governor of Porundeh, and Mallek Wujjeh of Dowlutabad, to march to his assistance. Upon this Zien ad Dien applied for protection to Eusuff Adil Khan of Beejapore; who sent six thousand horse to join him, commanding them to encamp near the fort of Indapore; and if Mallek Ahmed should move towards Jagneh, to hasten there, and assist in opposing him.

When this news reached Warunkul, the influence of Nizam al Moolk visibly declined. He was treated with slight by the sultan, and the attachment of Casim Bereed, Dustoor Deenar, and all the Abyssinian amras to him fell off. The sultan, who earnestly wished his destruction, encouraged the change, by complaints of the minister, and ordered them to assassinate him on the first opportunity that should occur. Nizam al Moolk being informed of the plot against his life, fled from the camp at midnight; but, instead of taking shelter with his son at Joneer, hastened to Ahmedabad, hoping to secure the royal treasury. Pussund Khan Dekkanee, who had been raised from the depth of wretchedness to nobility and the government of the capital by Nizam al Moolk, received him into the city, with assurances of strict obedience to his orders. The minister, thinking himself secure, wrote to Mallek Ahmed to join him from Joneer, and opening the royal treasures, distributed them with a lavish hand to levy troops and support his rebellion.

Mhamood

Mhamood Shaw, upon intelligence of this proceeding, appointed Koottub al Moolk, governor of Telingana, and with the reft of his nobility haftened towards Ahmedabad. Nizam al Moolk, finding his influence in the city decline, refolved to feize as much of the royal treafure as he could, and join his fon. Puffund Khan contrived to delay him by artful flatteries, and wrote privately to the fultan, defiring him to advance without delay, as he would give up the rebel into his hands. Mhamood Shaw fent for anfwer, that if he was fincere he fhould fend the traitor's head to him, as a proof of loyalty. Puffund Khan, attended by five hundred followers, went to Nizam al Moolk, who refided in the palace, and pretended that he wifhed to converfe with him in private, on affairs of importance. The minifter complying with his requeft, they retired into a room together. Puffund Khan, who was young and ftrong, fell upon the old, defencelefs minifter, and feized him by the neck with fuch force that he was foon ftrangled. Having then cut off his head, he brought it out; and, expofing it to the people, cried out, Such is the reward of traitors to their fovereign. After which he fent it by exprefs meffengers to the royal camp.

Mhamood Shaw now entered the city with his friends, and entrufted them with the direction of public affairs; but, impelled by the indifcretion of youth, and a ftrong attachment to pleafure, he devoted his time to drinking, mufic, and love, without attending in the leaft to the care of his kingdom. He took many of the jewels from the throne Firozeh, to fet in falvers, vafes, and cups for banquets.

In the year 896, envy poffeffed the minds of the Dekkanees and Abyffinians, who tried every art to prejudice the fultan againft his favourites, but in vain. Puffund Khan at length united with the Dekkanees to affaffinate Mhamood Shaw, and place another prince of the royal family on the throne. The confpirators repaired to the palace

A. D. 1490

palace armed; and, left the Mogul troops should come to the sultan's affiftance, fhut the gates after them. It was late in the night, and the fultan was engaged in feftivity, when they rufhed towards the royal apartments. This occafioned fome noife, but before Mhamood Shaw could know the caufe, a number of Dekkanees, admitted by the porters, rufhed in upon his privacy. Yezeez Khan Turk, with four other flaves, Houffun Ali Subzwaaree, and Syed Mirza Mefhidee, though unarmed, threw themfelves between the villains and the fultan, giving their lives a ranfom for his fafety. The fultan had time to gain the terrace of the [a] royal tower, except which, and the haram, all the palace was now in the poffeffion of the traitors, who purfued their fuccefs, but were gallantly oppofed by Mhamood Shaw with a few Turks and Moguls, the conftant companions of his pleafures, with ftones, darts, and clods of earth. The fultan alfo fortunately difpatched a meffage to the Turkifh and Mogul troops, of the dangerous fituation he was in from the confpirators, and his hopes of preferving himfelf till they fhould come to his relief. Cafim Bereed, with fome other noblemen, and about five hundred followers, haftened inftantly to the palace, but found the gates faft. Eight perfons with great difficulty fcaled the walls, and founded trumpets on their entrance. Many of the Dekkanees and Abyffinians, thinking all the Moguls had entered the fort, fled, and opened the gates to make their efcape. Eight and twenty Moguls of Subzwaar received them with fhowers of arrows, which drove them back, and they attempted to re-fhut the gates; but the Moguls rufhed on and prevented them. Skirmifhing now enfued, and Kifhwer Khan, who had gone round to the foot of the king's tower, hearing of the gate being opened, entered without delay. The traitors took fhelter in the [b] agate mahal. A great difturbance now arofe in the city, of which

---

[a] Moft probably over a kind of bow recefs, in which the fultans fat (as common in India) to receive the congratulations of the publick on feftival days, or to fee reviews, fights of elephants, &c. on the fpace before the palace.

[b] An apartment fo called, from the walls being lined or inlaid with agate.

which no one knew the cause, and the common people began to break open and plunder the houses of the Turks and Moguls. At length the moon rose, when friends and enemies could be distinguished. The servants of the palace, who had admitted the conspirators, now turned against them, from a shew of loyalty, and set fire to the [a] straw roofs, under which numbers had been concealed, putting them to the sword as they ran out. It now became known, that about three hundred were waiting together in an apartment, for an opportunity to rush out, and, by resolute charges, force their way through the gate at dawn of day. Sultan Jehangeer Khan Turk, upon this, took charge of the gates, and dispatched Khan Jehaun to guard the city and markets. The horses from the royal stables were taken out, and divided among the sultan's friends. At sunrise sultan Mhamood ascended the throne, and ordered the Moguls to enter the houses of the treacherous Dekkanees and Abyssinians, to slay all without distinction, and seize their effects for the royal use. For three days successively, the flames of slaughter and devastation raged in the city, no one daring to intercede with the sultan for pardon; till, at length, one of the sons of [b] Shaw Mohib Oolla requested that the massacre might be stopped, and was successful in his application.

Mhamood Shaw, to celebrate his escape from this danger, held a magnificent festival of forty days, and went in solemn procession through the city, the streets of which were [c] adorned on the occasion. As he regarded the royal tower as auspicious, he erected upon it a splendid pavilion, in which, when finished, he spent most of his time in a continued round of voluptuous amusements. To the affairs of government he paid no attention; leaving them entirely to the direc-

tion

---

[a] Probably of temporary erections in the outer squares, for the accommodation of guards and other attendants. The most superb buildings in India are disfigured constantly by these huts.

[b] A venerated religious.

[c] It is common in India, on the publick entrance of a prince, to ornament the shops and houses, by hanging out silks, &c. &c.

tion of his favourites. Muficians and dancers flocked to his court from Lahore, Dhely, Perfia, and Khoraffan; as alfo ᵃ ftory tellers, ᵇ reciters of the Shaw Nammeh, and all other minifters of pleafure. The people, copying the example of the prince, ftudied nothing but diffipation; reverend fages pawned their decent robes at the wine cellars, and holy teachers, quitting their cells, retired to the taverns, and prefided over the cafk. The governors of provinces, feeing the court thus employed, acted independantly; fo that the royal officers only who joined their views were allowed to hold their pofts, and thofe who refufed to wink at their encroachments, were expelled with difgrace. In a fhort time, except the province of Telingana and the diftricts adjacent to Ahmedabad, no parts of the kingdom properly remained in poffeffion of the fultan. The terruffdars, however, ex- except Mallek Ahmed Beheree, openly acknowledged the royal authority; but their fubmiffion was only fhewn in this point; If the fultan, at the defire of his minifter Cafim Bereed, took the field, and they faw advantage to themfelves in the expediton, they accompanied the royal ftandard, but with a force and fplendour, before which the fultan's funk to wretchednefs of appearance; and upon a return, they quitted him on the route for their feveral countries, without even the ceremony of afking leave. That they might not undergo the mortification of ftanding in the royal prefence, or performing the cuftomary obeifance to the fultan, they evaded vifiting the court.ᶜ ᵈ Mallek Ahmed Beheree never accompanied the royal ftandard at all, but affumed independance; founded the city of ᵉ Ahmednuggur; and

---

ᵃ They generally attend when their employer goes to repofe, and repeat fometimes portions of hiftory, but commonly tales fimilar to thofe of the Arabian nights.

ᵇ Thefe have by heart the poems of Ferdofi, author of the Shaw Nammeh, or hiftory of ancient Perfia, and the works of other poets. I apprehend, they may be compared to our minftrels.

ᶜ The above is a picture ftrongly refembling the ftate of the prefent empire of Hindooftan.

ᵈ Governor of a province now called Dowlutabad.

ᵉ Now in the hands of the Nizam.

and taking upon himself the honours of majesty, sent ambassadors to
[a] Eusuff Adil Khan and [b] Fatteh Oolla Ummad al Moolk, to prevail
upon them to copy his example, and read the khootbah in their
own name. It was accordingly resolved by all three, to avow their
claims to royalty.[c]

Casim Bereed, who had obtained, or rather chosen for his establishment, the terruffdaree of Ahmedabad and its vicinity, wished that the forts of his government should be garrisoned by his own dependants, but was denied possession by several governors. As he regarded their refusal as proceeding from the private orders of the sultan, he also threw off his allegiance, and endeavoured to reduce them by force. He twice defeated the royal army, and was near driving the sultan from his capital, when Dillawer Khan Hubshee, who had taken shelter at Boorahanpore from the resentment of Nizam al Moolk, hastened with an army to his sovereign's relief. Casim Bereed was defeated, and fled towards Golconda, and Dillawer Khan pursued him closely, hoping to take him prisoner, when providence decreed a change of fortune. In the heat of pursuit, near Kolaufs, a vicious elephant of Dillawer Khan's refused the guidance of his driver, and ran back upon his own army, trampling many persons to death, which occasioned much confusion. Dillawer Khan, taking a spear in his hand, with some of his attendants,
attempted

[a] Governor of the province of Beejapore.
[b] Governor of Berar, now shared by the Nizam and Mharattas.
[c] From this period, the sovereignty of the house of Bhamenee became almost nominal; the ministers of the territory still left to it usurping the real authority. This has in fact been also the case in the modern empire of Hindoostan, since the year 1712, when Jehaundar Shaw, grandson of Aurungzebe, ascended the throne. The ruin of the empire and desolation of India has been falsely imputed to the English servants, either because their idle countrymen at home envied the success of their active brethren, or from ignorance of Indian history. When we have lost (and not till then) our eastern possessions, the calumnies of self-interested orators will be refuted by the cool judgment of the unbiassed historian.

attempted to turn him, but in vain. The elephant rushing on, the soldiers fled, and Dillawer Khan was seized by the furious animal with his trunk, and crushed to death. Cafim Bereed foon hearing of this event, turned back upon the yet victorious army, who fled, difpirited by the lofs of their chief, and all the baggage and effects fell into his hands; after which he carried his rebellion still farther with impunity. As the fultan could not refift his power, he admitted him into the capital; a feeming reconciliation took place, and the minifter, feated fecurely on the mufnud of adminiftration, left nothing but a nominal royalty to Mhamood Shaw. The hiftorians of the Bereed dynafty reckon the eftablifhment of it from this period.

Cafim Bereed wrote to the roy of Beejanuggur, that Eufuff Adil Khan, having rebelled againft the fultan, had affumed royal honours, and if he would invade his country, he fhould be rewarded by the reftoration of the forts of Mudkul and Roijore. The roy being a child, his minifter Ramraaje fent a powerful army againft Adil Khan, and having committed great devaftation, obtained poffeffion of the promifed forts. Eufuff Adil Khan, at length, having effected a peace with Ramraaje, marched to take revenge on Cafim Bereed, who being much alarmed, applied for affiftance to Mallek Ahmed Nizam al Moolk; offering, when his enemy fhould be expelled, to affift him with the royal influence to obtain poffeffion of Goa, Kokun, Punnalleh, and Mangalore, from the hands of Bahadur Geelanee, and to leave them entirely at his difpofal. Mallek Ahmed, approving the conditions, marched in great force to Ahmedabad, and Cafim Bereed being thus ftrengthened, moved with the fultan, whofe inclinations he never confulted, againft the enemy. A fevere engagement enfued, in which the minifter and fultan were defeated. Mallek Ahmed and Adil Khan, who had previoufly fettled their difputes privately, without attacking each other, retired to their own countries.

In

In the year 899, fultan Mhamood Guzaratee fent an ambaffador A. D. 1493. to the fultan, reprefenting, that Bahadur Geelanee, who commanded on the fea coaft of Malabar, had feized many rich fhips belonging to the Guzarat merchants; and, not ftopping at fuch exceffes, had fent his flave Yacoot Hubfhee, with twenty fhips of war, to Maheem, which he had laid wafte, without mercy; imprifoning the people, and burning mofques and other buildings, intending next to proceed againft Surat; that an army from Guzarat could not march into the country of the rebel Bahadur, without fome injury to Dekkan; and to convey a fufficient force by fea was impoffible; therefore it was incumbent on the fultan to punifh the exceffes of the rebel: but fhould he find himfelf unequal to the tafk, if he would acquaint his friend, fuch meafures fhould be taken in Guzarat as would prove effectual.

Mhamood Shaw, roufed by this meffage, refolved to march to reduce Bahadur Khan, and applied for fupport from his vaffals; who, as they feared the refentment of the king of Guzarat, and hoped to fhare in the plunder of the rebel, complied with his orders. Adil Khan fent his general Kummaul Khan, with five thoufand horfe to the royal ftandard. Mallek Ahmed Beheree fupplied the fame number under Muttubba Khan, and Ummad al Moolk alfo furnifhed fome troops under the command of one of his chief officers.

Mhamood Shaw difpatched firft a firmaun to Bahadur Geelanee, informing him of the complaints of his ally the king of Guzarat, and demanding reftitution of the places, fhips, effects, and captives he had feized from that ftate. Bahadur, hearing that a confidential fervant had been difpatched with a firmaun, gave orders for his being detained on the road in the town of Mirch, and fpoke infultingly of the royal authority and the fultan's perfon; upon which Mhamood Shaw immediately began his march, and pufhed on without delay. Upon his arrival before the fortrefs of Jamcondah, he ordered Koottub al Moolk, terruffdar of Telingana, to befiege it; but that general being

being killed by an arrow from the walls, as he was reconnoitring, the fultan conferred his office and titles on Sultan Koollee, with Khongeer, Terkee, and other diftricts of Telingana, in jaghire, to fupport his dignity. Jamcondah being taken, and delivered over to the troops of Eufuff Adil Khan, the fultan moved to Mangalore, where Bahadur had fixed his refidence; but before the royal army could arrive he deferted the place, which was taken from his garrifon in three days, the works not being completely finifhed. Sultan Mhamood, by the advice of Bereed, moved next againft Mirch; and the troops of Bahadur met him in the field, but were defeated with great flaughter. The furvivors retired into the fortrefs. After a long fiege, the governor feeing no hopes of relief, begged quarter, which was granted by the approbation of Bereed; who received twenty five horfes belonging to Bahadur, and affurances were given to his followers that fuch as chofe to enter into his fervice fhould be entertained, and the reft allowed to depart, but without either their horfes or arms. All the Moguls replied, that after furrendering the fort, without horfes or arms they could not approach their chief, and would rather be put to death. The fultan, admiring their fortitude and fidelity, gave them up their horfes and arms, with permiffion to join Bahadur unmolefted.

The fultan, on the fall of Mirch, marched towards Baloeh; and in the interim Bahadur, liftening to the advice of his friends, fent Khajeh Neamut Oolla Geelanee to make offers of fubmiffion for him to the fultan. The fultan, by the approbation of Cafim Bereed, agreed to pardon Bahadur, alfo to reftore fome of the conquered places, and confirm him in his remaining poffeffions, if he would come to the prefence, and give a fum of money, with two elephants for the royal ufe. Neamut Oolla wrote him of the fuccefs of his embaffy, and advifed his repairing to the royal camp without delay.

Bahadur,

Bahadur, on the receipt of his agent's letter, thinking that the sultan's generosity proceeded from weakness, was again filled with pride; and sharpening the tooth of avidity on the royal baggage, vaunted insolently, that he intended that year to have the khootbah read in his own name at the capital of Ahmedabad, and, in the next, in Guzarat. Mhamood Shaw, enraged at this insolence, marched from Baloeh to Kulher, which he took; and followed his success with such rapidity, that Bahadur's affairs declined daily; and at length he fled to the fortress of Punnalleh, the strongest in his possession. The sultan, not wishing to sit down before it, went to Kolapore, intending to proceed from thence to Dabul, and amuse himself on the sea: upon which Bahadur quitted Punnalleh, with design of lying in ambush for the sultan on his route; but in the end, not having courage to execute his plan, fled, and numbers of his people leaving him, some joined the sultan, and others went to Adil Khan. Mhamood Shaw, by the advice of Bereed, sent Khajeh Jehaun, governor of the fort of Porundeh, to prevent Bahadur's re-entering Punnalleh; and on his arrival at Kolapore, as the rainy season had set in, resolved to halt for some time.

Bahadur now became humble, and again sent Khajeh Neammut Oolla and Mujd ad Dien with petitions to the sultan, declaring, if a promise of pardon should be sent him under the royal hand-writing and the seals of Casim Bereed and the principal chiefs, he would come to the presence, and during the remainder of his life never depart from the path of loyalty. The sultan complied with his request; and, to calm the fears of the rebel, dispatched some respectable persons to conduct him to court. On their arrival at Bahadur's camp, his ill fortune would not allow him to submit, and he started new difficulties; upon which the sultan called Khajeh Jehaun from the siege of Punnalleh, and sent him, with other amras, against him. Bahadur advanced to meet the royalists, with two thousand horse and fifteen thousand foot. A severe action ensued, and Bahadur being

being killed by an arrow, his troops fled. Khajeh Jehaun cut off the rebel's head, and marched to the royal camp, where the fultan honoured him with a fuit of his own robes, elephants, and horfes.

Two or three days after the victory, the fultan went to view the fortrefs of Punnalleh, and difpatched Mallek Ein al Moolk Cananee to Goa, to confole Mallek Saieed, and bring him to the prefence. By the approbation of Bereed, Bahadur's jaghire was conferred on the former; and the fultan, with a few of his principal nobility, having gone to Dabul and failed for his amufement along the coaft, returned towards his capital. On the route he fpent fome time at Kallabaug, near Beejapore; and, on his arrival at Ahmedabad, difpatched ambaffadors with rich prefents to fultan Mhamood of Guzarat, as alfo Kummaul Khan, Suffder Khan, and all the prifoners taken by the rebel Bahadur, with the twenty fhips and cargoes that he had feized.

A. D. 1495.  In the year 901, Sultan Koolli Koottub al Moolk Hammadance, was appointed terruffdar of Telingana, and Golconda and Warunkul, with their dependancies, added to his jaghire. Duftoor Deenar was conftituted governor of Saugher and Ahffunabad Koolburga. The fultan being perfuaded that the munfubdars ftationed with the great amras ftrengthened their power, withdrew all who were with Duftoor Deenar, and ordered them to remain on duty at court. Duftoor Deenar, difgufted at the removal of the munfubdars, in conjunction with Yezeez al Moolk Dekkanee, raifed a rebellion; and having collected between feven and eight thoufand Abyffinians and Dekkances, feized the country near Koolburga. Mhamood Shaw, by advice of Cafim Bereed, demanded the affiftance of Eufuff Adil Khan, who joined him with an army. An engagement happened near the town of Mhundree, in which the rebels were defeated, and Duftoor Deenar taken prifoner. The fultan would have put him to death, but was prevailed upon, at the interceffion of Adil Khan, not only to pardon, but reinftate him in his governments. As fome of the rebels

rebels had taken shelter in the fort of Saugher, the sultan laid siege to it, and on its reduction, gave it to Adil Khan; after which he returned to his capital.

In the year 902, Eusuff Dekkanee, Yeghrush Khan, Mirza Shumse ad Dien, and others who had the sultan's confidence, entered into a plot with some of the Turkish officers to destroy Casim Bereed; but he, gaining intelligence of their designs, put them to death, with all their abettors. The sultan was enraged at this presumption, would not admit him into his presence, and became his own minister. At length, by the mediation of Shaw Mohib Oolla, he was with much difficulty prevailed upon to forgive and receive him again into favour; after which he relapsed into his usual indolence and debaucheries. [A.D. 1496.]

In 903, the sultan asked the infant daughter of Adil Khan in marriage for his son sultan Ahmed, then fourteen years of age. After much negotiation, it was settled that the nuptial ceremonies should be performed at Koolburga. Accordingly, the sultan repaired to that city, where Adil Khan entertained him with great splendour. The knot of marriage was tied by Abd al Summie Cauzee of the royal camp, and it was agreed that the bride should be delivered to the prince as soon as she should reach the age of ten years. The festival was still celebrating, when Dustoor Deenar and Adil Khan quarrelled about the government of Koolburga, but the sultan would not interfere in the dispute. Dustoor Deenar retired to Porundeh, and contention grew high between Adil Khan and Casim Bereed, who opposed his pretensions. Koottub al Moolk siding with the former, Bereed was alarmed, and retired with his eldest son and his followers to Allind; upon which Adil Khan, leaving the festival unconcluded, took the sultan with him, and together with Koottub al Moolk, Mallek Elias, and Ein al Moolk, marched against Bereed, [A.D. 1497.]

who, being defeated in an action, fled to Porundeh. By this fuccefs, the power of Adil Khan became fo raifed, that the fultan, in his prefence, did not afcend his throne. All the allies having by his influence obtained their demands, retired to their diftricts. Cafim Bereed then venturing to return to court, obtained the vaqualut as before; but conducted himfelf fo haughtily to his unfortunate fovereign, that he could not even fatisfy his thirft without permiffion.

A. D. 1498.  In 904, Adil Khan led an army againft Duftoor Deenar, who fled from Koolburga, and by advice of Cafim Bereed took protection with Mallek Ahmed at Ahmednuggur. That ameer furnifhed him with auxiliaries; upon which Adil Khan, unable to oppofe, came to Ahmedabad, and the fultan defired Mallek Ahmed to defift from war, which he did; only fending a petition to the fultan, reprefenting that Duftoor Deenar was an old fervant of the throne, whom Adil Khan was eager to deftroy, fo that if his majefty would command him to quit his unjuft perfecution, it would be worthy of the royal generofity and care of his fubjects.

A. D. 1504.  In the year 910, Cafim Bereed dying, his fon Ameer Bereed fucceeded him in office; and, affuming ftill greater power, deprived Mhamood Shaw of what little authority had been left him by his father. This year, Adil Khan having put Duftoor Deenar to death, poffeffed himfelf of Koolburga and all his country. He read the khootbah in Beejapore, agreeably to the forms of the fheiah fect; which, having never been done before in any part of Hindooftan, turned the minds of all the Dekkanees againft him. Sultan Mhamood, at the defire of Ameer Bereed, wrote to Koottub al Moolk, Ummad al Moolk and Khodawund Khan, that Adil Khan, having thrown off all allegiance, had not only exalted the enfigns of rebellion, but introduced the cuftoms of heretics in the countries of Iflaam; fo that it was neceffary they fhould repair to the royal ftandard

ftandard with their armies, in order to expel him. In the margin of each firmaun the fultan wrote the following verfe: " He is grown fo " vain in the pride of his riches, that the fun, to his eyes, appears " but an atom."

Koottub al Moolk, with the amras of Telingana, repaired to court without delay; but Ummad al Moolk and Khodawund Khan made excufes: upon which, Ameer Bereed applied for fuccours to Mallek Ahmed Beheree, who, with Khajeh Jehaun Dekkanee and a great army, came to Ahmedabad, and joined the fultan. Adil Khan, thinking it vain to oppofe fo powerful a league in the field, having committed Koolburga and Allind to the charge of Direa Khan and Fukhir al Moolk Turk, and fent his fon Ifmaeel, then an infant at the breaft, with his women and treafures, to Beejapore under the care of Kummaul Khan Dekkanee; went, attended by five thoufand chofen horfe, into Berar. Sultan Mhamood and the allies purfued him with great expedition. Upon Adil Khan's arrival at the camp of Ummad al Moolk, that ameer refufed to protect him, as it would be difre-fpectful to oppofe the fultan in perfon; upon which he retired to Boorahanpore.

Ummad al Moolk now hinted privately to Mallek Ahmed, that Ameer Bereed wifhed the ruin of Adil Khan, merely to poffefs him-felf of Beejapore; which if he fhould effect, and keep the fultan in his hands, he would then meditate the deftruction of others; that, therefore, he had better retire to his own country, and leave him to watch the minifter. Mallek Ahmed and Koottub al Moolk, approv-ing this advice, fuddenly marched homewards, without taking leave of the fultan; and the next morning Ummad al Moolk fent petitions to court in favour of Adil Khan, begging the fultan to pardon his crimes, and return to the capital.

The

The fultan, at the inftigation of Ameer Bereed, refufed to comply; upon which Adil Khan, hearing of the retreat of the two powerful amras, returned to Ummad al Moolk, and, in conjunction with him, moved to attack the royal camp; which Ameer Bereed thinking himfelf unable to defend, left ftanding, and fled with the fultan to Ahmedabad. Adil Khan and Ummad al Moolk, having divided the plunder of the camp, returned to their feveral capitals.

A.D.1510.
A.D.1512.
A.D.1514.

In the year 916, Adil Khan being dead, Ameer Bereed marched to reduce Beejapore; but all his attempts proved vain, and the family on that throne encreafed daily in power. In the year 918, Koottub al Moolk, affuming royal independance, caft the fultan's name out of the khootbah. He continued however to fend fultan Mhamood, privately, every year a prefent in money. In 920, Ameer Bereed levied a great army with the royal treafures, and marching with the fultan, took Koolburga from the garrifon of Ifmaeel Adil Khan, and gave it to Jehangeer Khan, fon of Mallek Deenar, for whom he procured the title of Duftoor al Moolk. This chief having collected troops, took all the forts on one fide of the Beemra, from Saugher to Nuldirruk; and Ameer Bereed, receiving reinforcements from Nizam al Moolk and Koottub al Moolk, croffed the river with twenty thoufand men, and proceeded by regular marches to Beejapore. Ifmaeel Adil Khan gave him battle near the city, and totally defeated him, fo that he fled in the greateft confufion; and Mhamood, who had fallen from his horfe and received a fevere bruife, with his fon fultan Ahmed, was left defencelefs on the field. Ifmaeel Adil Khan obferving the refpect due to princes, treated the fultan with attention, providing him with all conveniences becoming his high rank.

Mhamood Shaw fhortly after went with Ifmaeel Adil Khan to Koolburga, where the ceremony of the nuptials between Sultan Ahmed and Bibi Suttee, fifter to Ifmaeel Adil Khan, was celebrated with

with great pomp and magnificence. The fultan having obtained five thoufand Mogul horfe to affift him, marched to Ahmedabad, which Ameer Bereed evacuated on his approach, and retired to the fort of Oufeh. Mhamood Shaw now took poffeffion of his capital; but foon after, the officers of Ifmacel Adil Khan, on hearing that Ameer Bereed had received aids from Boorahan al Moolk, deferted the fultan, and the minifter returning, put him under greater reftraint than before. Tired of his fituation, the unfortunate Mhamood Shaw found means to make his efcape to Kaweel in Berar, and beg affiftance of Ummad ad Dien, who marched with him towards the capital. Ameer Bereed, fhutting himfelf up in the citadel, applied for relief to Nizam al Moolk, who difpatched Khajeh Jehaun to join him with a confiderable force, and he entered the citadel.

Ameer Bereed and his ally now fallied forth againft the fultan and Ummad al Moolk, who prepared to receive them, and drew up their troops for action. It happened that the fultan was bathing, and the meffenger fent by Ummad al Moolk to inform him of the enemy's approach, infolently obferved, that it was no wonder, a prince who could be fo employed at fuch a critical time, fhould be the fport of his nobles. The fultan, ftung with the remark, and enraged at what he thought the infolence of Ummad al Moolk, joined the line as foon as poffible; but fuddenly fpurring his horfe, galloped over to Ameer Bereed's army. Ummad al Moolk immediately retreated with precipitation towards his own country, and the minifter returned triumphantly into the city with the fultan.

Ameer Bereed now put the fultan in fuch clofe confinement, that he could not poffibly efcape again. Mhamood, wearied with difappointments, old, and weak in mind, gave up the ftruggle for authority, and contented himfelf with the pleafures of wine, women, and the external pageantry of royalty. In the year 923, A.D. 1517.

Ameer

A.D. 1518. Ameer Bereed found it neceffary to march with him to Mahore againft Bufheer Khan; who, with his fon, was flain in battle, and the fultan gave the place to Ghalib Khan, after which he returned to his capital, where he died on the fourth of Zeekidge, after a reign of thirty feven years and twenty days of conftant viciffitude and trouble.

SULTAN

## SULTAN AHMED SHAW BHAMENEE.

AMEER Bereed, as he had but a ſmall territory in his poſſeſſion, and dreading, ſhould he aſſume open independance, that the ſurrounding powers would attack him, placed ſultan Ahmed, ſon of Mhamood Shaw, upon the throne, leaving him the palace, with the uſe of the royal jewels, and a daily allowance of money for his ſupport; which not being equal to his expenſes, the ſultan privately ſold ſeveral valuable jewels. The miniſter having information of this, put many muſicians and others to death, for being concerned in the ſale; but he never could recover the jewels, as the purchaſers had fled with them to Beejapore. Sultan Ahmed ſent agents privately to Iſmaeel Adil Khan, complaining of the ill uſage of Bereed; and Adil Khan diſpatched ambaſſadors with preſents to court; but, before their arrival, ſultan Ahmed died, two years after his acceſſion to the throne, in the year 927.

A. D. 1520.

# SULTAN ALLA AD DIEN 3ᵈ BHAMENEE.

AMEER Bereed kept the throne vacant near fourteen days after the death of Ahmed Shaw, and then seated upon it sultan Alla ad Dien. This prince, warned by the fatal consequences of the debaucheries of his predecessors, refrained from pleasure, and turned his thoughts to humble Bereed, whom he conciliated so much, as to throw him in the end off his guard. He then privately placed near his apartments a band of armed men, resolved to take the minister prisoner, when he should repair to visit him at the following new moon. Bereed, agreeably to custom, came with his sons to congratulate the sultan; but just as he had reached the apartment, one of the concealed persons happening to sneeze, he was alarmed, and turning back, sent in guards to examine the avenues. The plot was discovered, and all who were concerned in it put to death except the sultan, whom he confined strictly, and seated another prince on the throne, by the title of sultan Wullee Oolla, whom after two years he deposed, and put to death, having conceived a passion for his queen, whom he forced to submit to his desires.

# SULTAN

# KULLEEM OOLLA BHAMENEE.

SULTAN Kulleem enjoyed nothing but the name of sovereign, and never was allowed to leave the palace. In the year 933 the emperor Baber conquered Dhely; upon which, Ismaeel Adil Shaw, Boorahan Nizam Shaw, and Koottub Shaw, sent ambassadors to his court. Sultan Kulleem Oolla dispatched one of his companions in disguise with a petition to the emperor, setting forth, that his kingdom had been usurped and his person confined by rebellious servants; also offering, if the Mogul would relieve him from his distress, to cede to him Dowlutabad and the province of Berar. As Baber was yet unconfirmed in his conquests, and the sultans of Malwa and Guzarat were his enemies, he did not attend to the request; of which Ameer Bereed coming to the knowledge, treated him with great rigour. The sultan made his escape to his uncle Ismael Adil Khan, who received him honourably, in hopes of using his name to his own advantage; but not satisfied, he fled to Boorahan Nizam al Moolk. That prince at first behaved to him respectfully, even submitting to stand in his presence; but being told, that such homage was acknowledging a defect in his own title to royalty, he discontinued it. Sultan Kulleem died shortly after at Ahmed-

A.D. 1526.

FERISHTA's HISTORY OF DEKKAN.

Ahmednuggur, and with him ended the dynafty of Bhamenee. Dekkan was in fact, before this event, divided into five kingdoms; Adil Shawee, or Beejapore; Koottub Shawee, or Golconda; Ummaud Shawee, or Berar; Nizam Shawee, or Ahmednuggur; and Bereed Shawee, or Ahmedabad Bieder; the hiftory of which forms the fubject of the following pages.

FINIS OF THE BHAMENEE DYNASTY.

# PART II.

# *HISTORY*

OF

## THE BEEJAPORE, AHMEDNUGGUR,

AND

## GOLCONDA SOVEREIGNTIES.

# SULTAN EUSUFF ADIL SHAW BEEJAPOREE.

ABOU al Muzzuffir Eufuff Adil Shaw, the founder of the Adil Shawee dynafty, was a fon of one of the emperors of Turky, of the Othomaun family. His father, fultan Morad, dying in 854, was fucceeded by his eldeft fon, fultan Mahummud; upon whofe acceffion the officers of ftate advifed, that as in the beginning of the late reign a perfon had called himfelf Muftapha, fon of* Ælderrum Bayazeed, and occafioned great infurrections in the empire; in future, only one prince of the family fhould be fuffered to live. Sultan Mahummud, affenting to the propofal, gave orders for his brother fultan Eufuff to be put to death; and the executioners came to demand him from his mother, that, having ftrangled him, the body might be expofed for publick information. The fultana entreated them to fpare the innocent child; or, if the policy of ftate demanded fo fevere a facrifice, to indulge her with deferring it a day, that fhe might prepare her mind to take a laft leave. The minifters confented to the delay, and fhe improved it to fave the life of her fon. She fent for Khajeh Ummad ad Dien, a merchant, who had conftantly fupplied her houfehold with the products of Perfia, and enquired how many male flaves he had for fale. He replied, five Georgians and two Circaffians; one of the latter of whom fhe chofe,

A. D. 1450.

as

* The celebrated Bajazet.

as he bore the ftrongeft refemblance to the prince. She then committed fultan Eufuff to the merchant's care, with a large fum of money, entreating him to haften with him to a place of fecurity out of the Turkifh dominions. The Khajeh, moved by her tears and gratitude for former favours, accepted the commiffion; and began his journey, with the infant prince, the fame night. The next morning, the minifters came to the door of her apartments to demand her fon, when fhe admitted one, on whom fhe could depend; and informing him of the deception, bound him to favour it by large gifts. The Circaffian flave was ftrangled, and brought out, wrapped in a fhroud, by the minifter, whofe integrity not being fufpected, the body was buried without examination.

Khajeh Ummad ad Dien arrived with the young prince at ᵃ Ardebeel, and made rich offerings, enrolling Eufuff among the difciples of the venerable ᵇ fhekh Suffi; after which he carried him to the city of Saweh; and, as he was feven years of age, explained to him the neceffity of keeping his illuftrious birth a fecret, and put him to fchool with his own children. The next year, the fultana fent a perfon to Saweh to enquire after the fafety of her child; and the meffenger, after a ftay of nine months, departed; but was taken fo ill at Alexandria, that he remained there a year and half; after which he returned to the fultana, and prefented a letter, written by Eufuff himfelf, with flattering accounts of his progrefs in the acquirement of every accomplifhment. The princefs beftowed great charities, in gratitude for the prefervation of her fon; and fhortly after fent his nurfe with her fon Ghuzzunfir Beg, and her daughter Dil-fhaad Aga, alfo her former meffenger, and a large fum of money for the ufe of the prince, to Saweh. Here he continued till his fixteenth year, when he took the refolution of going to try his fortune in Hindooftan; and

accordingly,

---

ᵃ A town in Perfia.
ᵇ Founder of the Suffee royal family; and hence the emperors have been called in Europe, fophis of Perfia.

accordingly, having taken shipping at ᵃ Jerroon, arrived without accident at ᵇ Dabul, in the year 864. From thence he proceeded, A.D. 1458. under protection of Khajeh Mhamood Kohjukkanee, to Ahmedabad Bieder, and was recommended by him to Khajeh Ummad ad Dien Mhamood, who introduced him as one of his Turkish slaves into the royal houshold, as the best method of acquiring speedy promotion.

After two or three months Khajeh Jehaun, by the approbation of the queen mother, committed Eusuff to the protection of Yezeez Khan, master of the horse; who finding him accomplished for the task, and being old and infirm himself, committed to him the whole conduct of his employment; which gave Eusuff frequent opportunities of going into the presence of Mahummud Shaw, and acquiring his notice. On the death of Yezeez Khan, he, at the recommendation of Khajeh Jehaun, succeeded to the office; but, not agreeing with the bramin who superintended the accounts, resigned his post, and attached himself to Nizam al Moolk Turk, one of the chief nobles; whose friendship he acquired to such a degree, that he honoured him with the appellation of brother.

When Nizam al Moolk was appointed governor of Berar, he procured for his friend from the sultan the title of Adil Khan, with the rank of five hundred, and took him with him. ᶜ Nizam al Moolk being killed at Kurleh, Eusuff Adil Khan, leaving a strong garrison in the fort, conducted safely to court all the rich plunder of a very successful campaign, with thirty elephants, which procured him the sultan's approbation; and from that time the star of his fortune began to shine with encreasing splendour.

D d            When

---
ᵃ A port in the gulph of Persia.
ᵇ A port in Dekkan.
ᶜ *Vide* reign of Mahummud Shaw Bhamenee.

When fultan Mahummud Shaw left this vain world, and diffentions began to prevail in the kingdom, moft of the foreign officers and foldiers attached themfelves to Eufuff Adil Khan; who, feeing the minifters of fultan Mhamood bent on his deftruction, withdrew himfelf from Ahmedabad, with his family and followers, to his government of Beejapore. Refolving now to be the founder of a kingdom, he began to add to his territories by conqueft.

A.D. 1489. When the eagle of profperity had fpread the fhade of his wings over his head, he, with the affent of Mallek Ahmed Beheree, in the year 895, under authority that, [a] " The fword is his who can ufe it, " and dominion for him who conquers," read the khootbah of Beejapore in his own name, and fpread the umbrella of empire. All the Turks and foreigners acknowledged his title to royalty. He now conquered many of the forts from the governors of fultan Mhamood; and brought within the circle of his authority all the country from the river Beemrah to Beejapore, the inhabitants of which acknowledged his royalty; and he was alfo joined by many Dekkanee amras, who had formerly deferted him on his retiring from Ahmedabad, fo that great fplendour began to reign in his court.

The flames of envy rifing in the breaft of Cafim Bereed, who had entertained hopes of founding a kingdom for himfelf in Beejapore, he wrote to Heemraaje, the minifter of Beejanuggur, who had ufurped that fovereignty, leaving the roies only nominal power, that fultan Mhamood would cede to him the forts of Mudkul and Roijore, if he could wreft them from Adil Khan; and at the fame time to Bahadur Geelanee, who poffeffed Goa and all Direabar, in the language of Dekkan called Kokun, tempting him to invade the country of the ufurper.

Heemraaje,

[a] A verfe from the koraun.

Heemraaje, with a great army, crossed the river Tummedra, and after laying waste the country, took Mudkul and Roijore without advancing farther; and Bahadur Geelanee reduced the fortress of Jamcondah. Adil Shaw's power was too weak to resist by force this double attack. He made peace with Heemraaje, and drove Bahadur Geelanee from his dominions; but, without attempting to recover Jamcondah, led his army, composed of eight thousand Turks and foreigners, against Casim Bereed, towards the capital of Ahmedabad Bieder.

Bereed, in this exigence, applied for aid to Mallek Ahmed Beheree, who joined him, with Khajeh Jehaun Dekkanee, governor of Porundeh. The allies, with sultan Mhamood, marched from the capital, and were met by Adil Shaw at the distance only of ten miles. Direa Khan commanded the right wing, Fukhir al Moolk Turk the left, and Adil Shaw the center. Ghuzzunfir Beg, his foster brother, commanded a reserved corps of a thousand Turkish archers, to assist wherever there might be occasion. Casim Bereed fled with the sultan at the first onset; upon which Adil Shaw and Mallek Ahmed discontinuing the fight, entered into a treaty on the field, both retiring to their own dominions. This action however is differently related by an historian, who says, Mallek Ahmed was not in the field, but his general Khajeh Jehaun only; that Adil Shaw was defeated, and retired to Beejapore, where he effected a peace with all his enemies; and soon after, learning that dissentions prevailed in Beejanuggur, marched against Roijore.

Upon his arrival on the banks of the Kistnah, being tempted by the beauty of the country, he amused himself for some time in pleasure, and excess brought on an ague and fever, which confined him to his bed for two months; during which, his brother Ghuzzunfir Beg directed all publick affairs. In this interval, Heemraaje, having settled his dissentions, advanced with the young roy at the head

head of a great army to Roijore, which struck terror into the army of Adil Shaw, for whose recovery fervent prayers were offered up by his subjects. The arrow of entreaty reaching the mark of acceptance, weakness was changed to strength, and Adil Shaw recovering, distributed sixty thousand rupees among holy men and syeds of Medina, Kerballa, and Nujiff. He also committed a considerable sum to Khajeh Abdoolla Herdee, who had come with him to Hindooftan in the same ship, directing him to go and build a mosque at Saweh, and to give the surplus of the money among the poor of that city.

Intelligence arriving that Heemraaje had crossed the Tummedra, and was advancing by hasty marches, Eusuff Adil Shaw ordered a general review of his army, which was found to consist of eight thousand * doaspeh and seaspeh horse, also two hundred elephants, great and small. He, after the review, addressed himself to Ghuzzunfir Beg, Mirza Jehangeer, and Daood Khan Lodi, his favourite nobles, saying, that he had confident hopes of being able to beat the enemy with this force, and thought it adviseable to advance towards them. His opinion being approved, he moved immediately, and encamped at a little distance from their army. Dividing the ground among his amras to the best advantage, he threw up intrenchments round his camp, to prevent surprize. Several days passed inactively, till on Saturday in Regib, 898, both armies drew out, and in the beginning of the action near five hundred of Adil Shaw's troops being slain, the rest were disordered and fell back, but were rallied again by the sultan. One of the officers, who had been taken prisoner and made his escape, observed, that the enemy were busily employed in plunder, and might be attacked with advantage. The sultan relished his advice, and proceeded; when Heemraaje, not having time to collect his whole army, drew out with seven thousand horse and a considerable number of foot, also three hundred elephants. Adil Shaw charged his center with such

A. D. 1492.

* Doaspeh is a soldier having two horses, and seaspeh one having three.

such fury, that Heemraaje was unable to stand the shock. Victory waved the royal standard, and the infidels fled, leaving two hundred elephants, a thousand horses, and [a] sixty lacks of oons, with many jewels and valuable effects, to the conquerors. Heemraaje and the young roy fled to Beejanuggur; but the latter died on the road of a wound he had received by an arrow in the action. Heemraaje seized the government of the country; but some of the principal nobility opposing his usurpation, dissentions broke out; which gave Adil Shaw relief from war for some time from that quarter.

Dustoor Khan relates, that the victory was gained by the following stratagem. Adil Shaw, after the disorder of his troops, sent a messenger to Heemraaje, entreating peace, and offering to acknowledge allegiance to the roy for the country he held; upon which the minister and roy came, attended by three or four hundred followers, and their principal nobility, to a conference in the field; when Adil Shaw fell upon them by surprize with his whole army, and routed them, killing seventy persons of rank. Their troops, alarmed at the death of their chiefs, fled, and left the camp to be plundered by the victors.

Adil Shaw, after his success, conferred on Soobjung Bahadur Khan fifty elephants, with one [b] lack of oons, and detached him with a force to reduce the forts of Mudkul and Roijore, which he effected in the space of forty days, and the sultan then returned to his capital of Beejapore. This victory, and the great accession of wealth, strengthened his power, extending far the acknowledgment of his royalty. He, out of respect to sultan Mhamood Bhamenee, sent him two splendid vests, the borders of which were adorned with precious stones, two horses shod with gold, and saddles and bridles set with jewels.

Adil

[a] About one million eight hundred thousand pounds sterling.
[b] Thirty thousand pounds.

Adil Shaw was preparing to march against Jamcondah, which Bahadur Geelanee had taken from him; but sultan Mhamood, upon receipt of an embassy from the king of Guzarat, going in person against that chief, he laid aside the design, and sent his general Kummaul Khan Dekkanee, with five thousand horse, to attend the sultan; for which service Jamcondah was delivered up to his troops, as soon as taken from the rebel. When sultan Mhamood returned from his expedition against Bahadur, Adil Shaw went to meet him; and having conducted him to Beejapore, then newly surrounded with a wall of stone, entertained him for ten days with royal magnificence. At his departure, he laid before him an offering of twenty elephants, fifty horses, four arm bracelets set with jewels, and other rare and valuable articles to a great amount. Sultan Mhamood having made choice of one elephant, sent back every thing else, with a private message, that as they would not remain with him, but be seized by Casim Bereed for his own use, he had returned them, to be kept for him in trust, till such time as Adil Shaw, like a faithful servant, should deliver him from the usurpation of his minister.

Adil Shaw, though he had it in his power to effect the desires of sultan Mhamood, did not think it accorded with his own interest, and answered, that such an undertaking could not succeed, unless Mallek Ahmed should agree in promoting it, as also Ummad al Moolk; but that when his majesty should reach his capital, he would prevail upon those chiefs to join with him in punishing the insolent minister. Mhamood Shaw was satisfied with this declaration, and departed for his capital; but, before his march, Adil Shaw conveyed to him privately a large sum of money, and made considerable presents to Casim Bereed and Koottub al Moolk, who had attended the sultan.

A.D. 1495.    In the year 901, Dustoor Deenar, an Abyssinian eunuch, who held the governments of Koolburga and Saugher, with Allind, and other

other forts and pergunnahs between the river Beemrah and Telingana, afpired to royal power: for this purpofe he commenced a friendfhip with Mallek Ahmed Beheree, and obferved to him, that as Fatteh Oolla Ummad al Moolk had, by the fupport of Adil Shaw, affumed royal titles in Berar, it would be agreeable to friendfhip to fupport him in his claims to equal honours in his own territories. Mallek Ahmed, as Duftoor Deenar was the adopted fon of his father Nizam al Moolk, and had alfo high demands on his own gratitude, agreed to fupport him; and accordingly the eunuch fpread over his head the umbrella of majefty; and feizing many diftricts dependant on the capital of Ahmedabad, drove out the officers of Cafim Bereed in a difgraceful manner.

Cafim Bereed, through fultan Mhamood, having required the affiftance of Adil Shaw againft the rebel, he fent his brother Ghuzzunfir Beg, with Direa Khan and other chiefs, to join the royal ftandard; writing to fultan Mhamood at the fame time, that he fhould have attended in perfon, did he not forefee in that cafe, that Mallek Ahmed would join Duftoor Deenar with his whole force, which would prolong the war. Soon after this, intelligence came that Khajeh Jehaun Dekkanee, at the inftigation of Mallek Ahmed, had moved from Portindeh to Koolburga with a confiderable force, and that Mallek Ahmed alfo was preparing to march, fhould he fee a neceffity for his affiftance. Eufuff Adil Shaw now thought it prudent to join his amras, and accordingly did fo with great expedition. Sultan Mhamood and Cafim Bereed having joined him, the allied armies moved againft Duftoor Deenar without delay. The eunuch advanced to receive them with eight thoufand horfe, moftly Abyffinians, and twelve thoufand auxiliaries, under Mallek Ahmed and Khajeh Jehaun; but, after a brave ftruggle, was defeated and taken prifoner. Sultan Mhamood would have put him to death, by defire of Cafim Bereed; but Adil Shaw, from motives of policy, not wifhing to ftrengthen the power of the minifter, interceded for his pardon,

and

and obtained for him restoration of his government of Koolburga. Adil Shaw then, without paying his respects to Mhamood Shaw, returned to Beejapore, and the sultan and Dustoor Deenar to their several residencies. Mallek Ahmed, who had begun his march to join the eunuch, hearing of the peace, returned to Ahmednuggur.

A.D. 1497.   In the year 903, Mhamood Shaw demanded the daughter of Adil Shaw, Bibi Suttee, then an infant in the cradle, in marriage for his son sultan Ahmed; and chusing Koolburga for the place of espousals, both princes repaired to that city, which much alarmed Dustoor Deenar. Adil Shaw privately informed sultan Mhamood, that if he wished to displace Casim Bereed, he must cede to Beejapore the districts then under Dustoor Deenar, as they lay between it and the jaghire of the minister, which would afford a pretence for advancing his troops into them, and easy opportunities would offer of expelling Casim Bereed, before Mallek Ahmed or any other power could hear of such a design being on foot. Mhamood Shaw approving the plan, gave the required grants, and dispossessed the officers of Dustoor Deenar; who, unable to resist, by the mediation of sultan Koollee Koottub al Moolk, made a treaty with the victor for the rest of his territories. Casim Bereed, alarmed at this proceeding, quitted Mhamood Shaw, and retired to Allind with his dependants.

Adil Shaw upon this moved with Mhamood Shaw, Koottub al Moolk, and Mallek Elias, to reduce Bereed, whom he defeated near the town of Kinjoutee, and the fugitives took shelter in various forts. A rich carpet of cloth of gold, after the victory, was spread on the field, and Mhamood Shaw taking Adil Shaw by the hand, commanded him to sit; which honour he would not accept till after repeated orders. It was determined now, that the following year they would march and extirpate Casim Bereed. As Mallek Elias had fallen in the action, Adil Shaw conferred his estates upon his eldest

son

fon Mahummud, with the title of Ein al Moolk; and, having taken leave of Mhamood Shaw, returned to Beejapore.

The next year, Adil Shaw marched againſt Duſtoor Deenar, but Mallek Ahmed coming to his aſſiſtance, he retired towards Bieder, where he received aſſurances of ſupport from Koottub al Moolk, and Ummad al Moolk; upon which Duſtoor Deenar and Ahmed Mallek retired, without hazarding an action, to their capitals. The year following, Adil Shaw ſent embaſſies to Mallek Ahmed and Ummad al Moolk, obſerving, that Dekkan was too ſmall a country to maintain ſo many independant powers, that therefore they, out of regard to the happineſs and ſecurity of their poſterity, ſhould form a ſtrict alliance, and endeavour, in conjunction with each other, to extend their dominions. After much negotiation, it was agreed among the three princes, that Ummad al Moolk ſhould have Mahore, Ramgeer, and all the territory then in poſſeſſion of Khodawund Khan Hubſhee; that Mallek Ahmed ſhould have Dowlutabad, Antore, Kalneh, and all the country beyond them to the borders of Guzarat. Adil Shaw for his ſhare was to take the territories of Duſtoor Deenar and Ein al Moolk. Caſim Bereed was to have the country of ſultan Koollee Koottub al Moolk, with the capital of Ahmedabad Bieder, and a ſmall circle of lands round it. By this treaty, no power was to interfere with the plan of the other, but all join to enforce that laid down in the partition agreement.

Adil Shaw, in purſuance of the plan, to be certain if Ein al Moolk was attached to his views, diſpatched a firmaun, commanding him to his preſence, which, before, he had always done by letters of equality and requeſt. Ein al Moolk received the firmaun with joyful ſubmiſſion, declaring, that now he was convinced Adil Shaw regarded him as loyal, from his putting his attachment to the teſt of trial. He made a feſtival of a week in the fort of Goa on the occaſion, and repaired with ſix thouſand horſe to Beejapore, where Adil Shaw received

received him as his subject, exacting royal salutations from him, and conferring upon him an honorary dress, which he respectfully received, and swore allegiance.

Dustoor Deenar, apprehending his own destruction, applied to Ameer Bereed, who had just then acceded to the ministry of sultan Mhamood's affairs, on the death of his father Casim Bereed, for his protection from the schemes of his enemies; and the minister sent three thousand horse to his assistance. Dustoor now encamped on the banks of the Beemrah, and Khajeh Jehaun, who had parted from Mallek Ahmed on the partition treaty, from which he was excluded as a principal, thought it political to join the eunuch; which he did, with his brother and five thousand horse; Mallek Ahmed being then engaged in taking Dowlutabad, and defending himself against invasions from Guzarat.

Adil Shaw, unmoved by the present superiority of the enemy's numbers, collected his troops; and dividing liberally among them the treasures he had taken from the Beejanuggur army, marched from Beejapore, and encamped within ten miles of the enemy. The day following, he prepared his army for battle, sending on an advanced corps of two thousand chosen horse under Yas Koolli, brother of Ghuzzunfir Beg, with directions to encamp within two miles of the enemy's line, and divert their attention by hovering parties. At the same time he sent a message to Dustoor Deenar, assuring him, that should he, directed by the kinder influence of his stars, agree to submit to his authority, both he and his dependants should receive the highest honours in his government; but if, impelled by folly and ill fortune to refuse his gracious protection, he should turn away his head from his offers, and be blinded by the veil of pride, he must abide by the chance of war.

Dustoor

Duftoor, blinded by vanity to his real intereft, fent back a difrefpectful anfwer, and detached a large body of Abyffinian cavalry to attack the advanced corps of Adil Shaw; but they were defeated with great flaughter, and many elephants and horfes fell into the hands of the victors. Adil Shaw the next morning advanced upon the enemy, and drew up his army near their camp, in the following order: Ghuzzunfir Beg commanded on the right wing, Hyder Beg Tubbreezee on the left, and Mirza Jehangeer Koomi had charge of an advanced body. The fultan, with a chofen band, took his poft in the center. Duftoor Deenar alfo, proud of his numbers, drew out his troops, moftly covered with iron armour, after the manner of Hind; difpofing his elephants in different parts, and all his artillery and machines for battering in front. The anxious for reputation on both fides now lighted up the flames of conflict. Mirza Jehangeer advanced firft, with the velocity of lightning, on the enemy, and fcorched up the ftores of their exiftence with the burning blaft of annihilation. Ghuzzunfir Beg and Hyder Beg, charging from the right and left, attacked together, with fuch refiftlefs fury, that nothing could withftand their charge. By the blefling of the eternal aufpices and the royal fortune, Duftoor Deenar fell in the field, and his troops fled, overwhelmed in defeat and terrors. Ghuzzunfir Beg, who had received a fevere wound, kneeling down with the reft of the amras, performed the ceremonies of congratulation, and waved money and jewels over the fultan's head in offering for the victory. Adil Shaw, kifling his eyes and forehead, clafped his noble brother in embrace, and fuperintended the drefling of his wounds; but all was vain; and the hero, according to the declarations of holy writ, (When their death comes, they fhall not delay an inftant nor abide) after three days and nights, having drank the fherbet of martyrdom, fpeeded to the world eternal.

Adil Shaw was fincerely affected at this heart-rending lofs; but, having performed the funeral rites, brightened his countenance with the

the crimson of patience and fortitude, from necessity, and attending to the important affairs of empire, possessed himself of Koolburga, Saugher, and all the forts and territories of the defeated amra, which he committed to officers in whom he could confide, and then returned in triumph to Beejapore. On his arrival in that city, he raised Mirza Jehangeer and Hyder Beg to the highest rank of nobility, as they had shewn great gallantry in the action; and conferred honours and gifts on all the officers and soldiers who had deserved them during the war.

A.D. 1502. Being now arrived at the height of his wishes, as to worldly power, Adil Shaw resolved to execute a work of religion, which he had determined on in his mind for many years. In the year 908, he held a grand assembly of his principal subjects, and calling Mirza Jehangeer and Hyder Beg, who were of the [a] sheea sect, as also syed Ahmed Herdee and other learned men of that persuasion, addressed them, saying, that when the prophet, appearing to him in a vision, had hailed him with the presage of his present dignity, he had then vowed, if his dream proved true, to promulgate the faith of the [b] Imaums, and grace the pulpit with proclamation of their titles; that also, when Heemraaje and Bahadur Geelanee had invaded his territories, and nearly seized the reins of government from his hands, he had renewed his vow, therefore wished to have their opinions if the present was a fit time for performance.

The assembly unanimously broke out into prayers for the prosperity of his house; after which, some approved of his holy zeal, others,

[a] The Mahummedans are divided into two grand sects, soonis and sheeas. The former contend, that Omar was the legal successor of the prophet as head of the church; and the latter give it to Alee, Mahummud's son in law. This division, which also gave rise to many other differences, has often caused much bloodshed among the mussulmauns.
[b] Immediate descendants of Alee.

others, more cautious, obferved, that his power was yet but in infancy; that fultan Mhamood, though weak, was ftill the acknowledged lawful monarch of Dekkan; that moft even among his own nobles, were Turks, Dekkanees, and Abyffinians, of the fooni fect, as were alfo the furrounding powers of Dekkan, Mallek Ahmed, Ummad al Moolk, and Ameer Bereed, all zealous for their faith; therefore, that it was more than probable an oppofition too great to be overcome by his fingle authority, would attend an invafion of the eftablifhed religion. Adil Shaw, after a fhort paufe of reflection, replied, that he had pledged himfelf to God, who had raifed him by his bleffings to royal power, and did not doubt but, on performance of his vow, the fame gracious arm would be his protector. At this inftant news arrived, that Shaw Ifmaeel Suffewee had eftablifhed the fheea rites in Perfia, which confirmed Adil Shaw, who was a difciple of that houfe, in his determination; and he took meafures without delay to put it into execution.

On an appointed day, he went in great pomp to the grand mofque in the citadel of Beejapore; and Nukkeeb Khan, one of the venerable fyeds of Medina, by his command afcending the pulpit firft, in the call to prayer cried aloud, agreeably to the fheea faith, " I bear teftimony that Alee is the friend of God:" after which he read the khootbah in the names of the twelve Imaums. Adil Shaw was the firft perfon who dared to perform thefe ceremonies of the fheea fect publickly in Hindooftan. Notwithftanding this bold attempt, out of prudence, he did not permit the populace to utter fcandalous and abufive expreffions of the [a] Sahabeh; fo that fanaticifm and overbearing zeal were prevented from fpreading their poifonous venom. The learned difciples of [b] Jaffier, and the eminently verfed in the tenets of [c] Hunnefi and Shafee, lived together in friendfhip; and

in

---

[a] Companions of the prophet, Omar, Aboubekker, and Ofman, whom the fheeas abufe in their devotions, as ufurpers of the rights of Alee.
[b] A doctor of the fheea fect.
[c] Doctors of the fooni fect.

in the mosques of different sects, each worshipped the true God, according to his own faith, without interference in the ceremonies or opinions of each other. The holy teachers and pious recluse were astonished at this well-regulated moderation, and attributed it to an almost miraculous ability in the wise sultan. The author of these sheets recollects an anecdote applicable to this circumstance, which he thinks proper to insert for the information of his readers.

Molana Gheaus ad Dien, a very celebrated divine of Persia, much respected for his abilities and purity of life, was once asked by sultan Ibrahim, Which was the best of all the various sects of Islaam? He replied, Suppose a great monarch to be seated in a palace, with many gates leading to it, and through whichever you enter you see the sultan, and can obtain admission to his presence. Your business is with the prince, and not with those at his gate. Sultan Ibrahim again asked him, Which, in his opinion, was the best of all faiths? He replied, that the best man of every faith in his idea followed the best faith. This observation pleased Ibrahim, who conferred upon the Molana large gifts.

It is related, that when Eusuff Adil Shaw read the khootbah after the ceremonial of the sheeas, and established their tenets at Beejapore, many of the principal chiefs, as Direa Khan, Fukhir al Moolk Turk, and others, embraced the same faith as their sovereign; but some being rigid soonis, were much disgusted, and expressed desires of quitting his service; of which Adil Shaw being informed, laid before them the tolerating maxim of " My faith for myself, and " your faith for yourselves," in such a convincing manner, that they became satisfied. But as he was jealous of the great influence and power of Ein al Moolk, he deprived him of the chief command of his army, and the districts he had held from Bahadur Geelanee; giving him Sukker, Ahrra, and Balgoan in their room, with leave to retire from court, and follow his own opinions in religious matters.

All

All the fooni nobility had licenfe alfo in their own jaghires to read the khootbah in the names of the Sahabeh; and no oppofition was made to their exercifing their publick worfhip. Notwithftanding this compliance, the fultan kept fpies over every nobleman, that he might be informed of all his motions.

Mallek Ahmed Beheree and Ameer Bereed, who were ftrict and zealous followers of the foonnut, were much enraged at the innovation on the eftablifhed faith of Dekkan, fpoke openly of it in reproachful terms; and at length, forming an alliance, invaded the dominions of Adil Shaw, to punifh him for what they deemed apoftacy. Ameer Bereed poffeffed himfelf of Kinjoutee and many of the diftricts taken from Duftoor Deenar, and Mallek Ahmed fent ambaffadors to Beejapore peremptorily demanding the delivery of the fortrefs of Nuldirruk. Adil Shaw, fired by this attack upon his dominions, fent back a fharp anfwer, and moving immediately to Kinjoutee, regained poffeffion. Sultan Mhamood and Ameer Bereed now requefted aids from Koottub al Moolk, Ummad al Moolk, and Khodawund Khan Hubfhee. Koottub al Moolk, though fecretly of the fheea fect, yet, in compliance with the times and at the inftigation of the amras of Telingana, moved towards the court of Mhamood Shaw; but Ummad al Moolk and Khodawund Khan made excufes, and would not join in the league. Ameer Bereed upon this difpatched his fon Jehangeer Khan to Ahmednuggur, with fuch powerful remonftrances, that Mallek Ahmed without delay marched to join him with ten thoufand horfe and a powerful train of artillery; which, added to the troops of Bereed and Khoottub al Moolk, made a very formidable army. Sultan Mhamood was placed nominally at the head of the allies. Adil Shaw thinking it unfafe to engage them in a pitched battle with his inferior force, fent his fon Ifmaeel, then an infant of five years, with all his treafures and elephants, from Allind to Beejapore; committing the care of that city and the fole direction of affairs to Kummaul Khan Dekkanee.

Having

Having ftationed Direa Khan and Fukhir al Moolk Turk to protect Koolburga, he himfelf, attended by Ein al Moolk Canaanee and many foreign officers, with fix thoufand horfe firmly devoted to his fervice, marched with expedition towards Beer, burning and deftroying the country as he paffed. Mallek Ahmed, feeing his territories attacked, moved with fultan Mhamood and the allies in purfuit of Adil Shaw, who had taken this meafure to prevent the invafion of his own country. Adil Shaw always avoided an engagement, but hovered round the allied army, haraffing their followers and cutting off their fupplies. Being however at length exhaufted with fatigue, he, after plundering the environs round Dowlutabad, retired into Berar, depending on the friendfhip of Ummad al Moolk, who was encamped with an army near Kaweel, refolved to obferve a ftrict neutrality, and attend only to the protection of his own territories. He received Adil Shaw with kindnefs; but as he knew the allies would invade Berar if he kept him with him, advifed his retiring to Boorahanpore, till fome fcheme could be devifed of breaking the league formed againft him; which might eafily be done, if he would for the prefent order the fooni rites to be re-eftablifhed at Beejapore. Adil Shaw complied with his advice, fent proper orders to Kummaul Khan, and taking leave of his friend, departed for Boorahanpore, where he was received with kindnefs by the fultan of Khandefhe.

Ummad al Moolk now fent one of his neareft relations to Mallek Ahmed and Koottub al Moolk, obferving, that it was clear to him, Ameer Bereed had ufed religion only as a pretence to ruin Adil Shaw and poffefs himfelf of the kingdom of Beejapore; that if, now he was mafter only of a fmall territory, he performed fuch plans by the nominal authority of the fultan as none of them were equal to, their remaining independant in Dekkan would become impoffible, fhould he acquire fo rich a territory. He obferved, that no man had any concern in the religious opinions of another, and that every one

wou¹

would be called to account for his actions at the day of resurrection; but that, laying aside that confideration, Eufuff Adil Shaw had retracted his profeffion of the fheea opinions, and fent orders to reftore the fooni rites in Beejapore; fo that no pretence now remained for continuing the war. Therefore he advifed them, inftead of injuring themfelves by being made the dupes of an artful minifter, to retire to their own dominions. Mallek Ahmed and Kocttub al Moolk, who paid great refpect to the advice of this aged and experienced ftatefman, were convinced of its propriety; and on the fame night in which they received it, without taking leave of Mhamood Shaw, began their retreat to their own territories.

Ameer Bereed, not warned by this defertion of the allies, had the folly to apply to Ummad al Moolk for his affiftance to invade Beejapore, and fuffered himfelf to be kept fome days in negotiation; till, at length, Adil Shaw arriving at Kaweel from Boorahanpore, he faw the dangerous fituation to which he was betrayed by his credulity, and fled with the fultan, attended only by a few followers, leaving his camp ftanding, which was plundered by the two friends. Adil Shaw, having taken leave of Ummad al Moolk, returned to Beejapore after an abfence of three months; and, being now fecure from all enemies, reftored the publick exercife of the fheea faith, and bent his mind to the improvement of his dominions, without meditating further conquefts. He fent fyed Ahmed Herraee, with prefents and declarations of attachment, to Shaw Ifmael Suffewi, emperor of Perfia, with accounts of his fuccefs in eftablifhing the fheea religion.

In the year 915, the chriftians (Portuguefe) furprized the town A.D. 1509. of Goa, and put to death the governor, with many muffulmauns. Upon intelligence of which, Adil Shaw, with three thoufand chofen men, Dekkanees and foreigners, marched with fuch expedition, that he came upon the Europeans unawares, retook the fort, and put many to death; but fome made their efcape in their fhips out to fea.

FERISHTA's HISTORY OF DEKKAN.

The government and fecurity of Goa being provided for, Adil Shaw returned to his capital, and died in that city of a droplical diforder, after he had reigned with great profperity twenty one years, in the feventy fifth year of his age. Tahir Shaw relates, that he was informed by fyed Ahmed Herraee, who had lived long at the court of Adil Shaw, that he was a wife prince, well acquainted with mankind, very handfome in his perfon, and eloquent of fpeech, eminent for his learning, liberality, and valour. He wrote elegantly, and was a good judge of poetical merit, often compofing verfes himfelf. His tafte and fkill in mufic were fuperior to thofe of moft of the mafters of his time, whom he encouraged by princely rewards to attend him; and he performed exquifitely on the [a] timboor and [b] oqde. He would frequently fing to them extempore verfes. He mixed pleafure with bufinefs, but never for the former neglected the latter; always warning his minifters to act with juftice, integrity, and honour, and by his own example and attention exciting their emulation. He invited many learned men and valiant officers from Perfia, Tartary, and Turky, alfo eminent artifts, to his court, and made them eafy under the fhade of his bounty. He furrounded Beejapore with a ftrong wall of ftone. He left behind him four children, the prince Ifmaeel and three daughters, all by one mother, originally a Hindoo, fifter to a Mharatta chief, taken in war. Being of exquifite beauty, great underftanding, and engaging manners, Adil Shaw, after her embracing the Iflaam faith, married her, and gave her the title of Boobojee Khanim. His eldeft daughter was married to Nizam Shaw, the fecond to Shekh Alla ad Dien Ummad al Moolk, and the third to fultan Ahmed Shaw, fon of Mhamood Shaw Bhamenee.

SULTAN

[a] A fort of lute.
[b] A fmall kind of guitar.

# SULTAN
## ABOU AL FATTEH ISMAEEL ADIL SHAW.

ISMAEEL Adil Shaw upon his acceffion being too young to direct the affairs of his kingdom, the guidance of adminiftration was committed to Kummaul Khan Dekkanee. He had been one of the principal nobles of Mhamood Shaw Bhamenee, but, on Eufuff Adil Shaw's affuming independance, was won over to his intereft, and appointed his [a] meer nobut; after which, fhewing diftinguifhed gallantry and activity in the battle againft Heemraaje, he rofe in credit and influence above all the other minifters. Eufuff Adil Shaw, upon his death bed, added the office of regent, during the minority of his fon, to his former dignities; and earneftly advifed and entreated Direa Khan, Fukhir al Moolk, Mirza Jehangeer, Hyder Beg, and the reft of the nobility, to a ftrict friendfhip and agreement with him, as alfo among themfelves. On this account the above amras held him as their fuperior, and, leaving all affairs to his direction, obeyed him as regent.

Kummaul Khan, on the commencement of his authority, difplayed good conduct. He reftored the fooni exercife of religion, ftudied to gain the affections of the publick, and by his condefcenfions procured the attachment of the nobility. He obferved moderation and agreement with the families of Nizam Shaw, Koottub Shaw, and Bereed Shaw. He made peace with the Europeans, who, after the

[a] Commander in chief.

the retreat of Eufuff Adil Shaw, had befieged Goa, and regained it by giving large bribes to the governor, juft on the acceffion of the infant king, on condition that they fhould be fatisfied with the ifland alone, and not moleft the towns and diftricts. Accordingly, fince that time, the Portuguefe have kept poffeffion of Goa, and, obferving the treaty, have not made any encroachments on the Adil Shawee territories.

Kummaul Khan, after thus fettling the welfare of the kingdom, held the regency with eafe and fatisfaction; and Direa Khan and Fukhir al Moolk dying the year following, he divided their jaghires among his own relations and dependants, procuring for each honours and offices; taking alfo fome pergunnahs from the eftates of Mirza Jehangeer and Hyder Beg, to beftow upon his own followers. The lands of thofe officers who died, or were convicted of crimes, he confifcated, and gave them to his own creatures; by thefe means encreafing and confirming his power till at laft he became giddy with dreams of vanity, and his evil imagination formed ambitious defires of royalty.

The ambition of treacherous minifters had already proved fatal to the [a] lawful kings of Dekkan. Heemraaje was the firft ufurper. He had poifoned the young raja of Beejanuggur, fon of Sheoroy, and made his infant brother a tool to his defigns; by degrees overthrowing the ancient nobility, and at length eftablifhing his own abfolute authority over the kingdom. Cafim Bereed and others had reduced fultan Mhamood to nominal royalty, and at length read their own names in the khootbah.

Kummaul Khan, tempted by thefe fuccefsful examples, when he had gained the requifites to power and dignity, addreffed himfelf artfully to Ameer Bereed, obferving, that if he wifhed to extend his poffeffions,

[a] The Bhamenee dynafty.

poffeffions, the favourable opportunity now offered, as Ahmednuggur was held by the hands of a weak infant; and Uinmad al Moolk, fovereign of Kaweel, being immerfed in youthful pleafures, had no inclination for military glory; therefore, if he would receive him among the number of his friends, and allow of his claims to royalty, he would in return affift his views of conqueft. Ameer Bereed embraced the propofal with joy, as he had for years been fecretly wifhing for opportunity to extend his power; and a treaty of alliance, offenfive and defenfive, was immediately concluded. It was ftipulated, that all the country conquered from Duftoor Deenar, as Koolburga, Allind, Kinjoutee, and Nuldirruk, to the banks of the Beemrah, fhould be ceded to Bereed; and Beejapore, Kokun, Mudkul, and Roijore, with other places, be confirmed to Kummaul Khan, who might depofe, or even put to death, Ifmaeel Adil Shaw, and proceed to reduce Sholapore and the country belonging to Zien Khan.

Ameer Bereed, having confined fultan Mhamood in his palace under charge of his fons, moved to Koolburga; and Kummaul Khan, imprifoning Ifmaeel Adil Shaw, with his mother Boobojee Khatoon, in the citadel of Beejapore, marched with a great force to Sholapore, which he befieged for three months; and no relief coming from Ahmednuggur, Zien Khan, on receiving fecurity for the fafety of his family and wealth, delivered it up to him, with the five dependant diftricts. Bereed, who was then befieging Koolburga, after receiving from the Adil Shawee officers the places ceded to him by Kummaul Khan, fent him a congratulatory letter on his fuccefs; upon which the regent, more haughty than before, returned to Beejapore to finifh the ufurpation he had meditated, by dethroning his fovereign, and feizing the kingdom.

Kummaul Khan, upon his arrival at Beejapore, brought the young fultan once for form fake to receive the compliments of the court in

the

the durbar. To strengthen his own party, he suddenly issued orders to reduce the *khasseh khiel from three thousand foreign troops to three hundred; commanding all the rest to quit Beejapore in a week, under penalty of forfeiting life and property to the state. The unfortunate exiles hastened with all speed to various parts, to avoid his tyranny, and the regent, as no obstacle now lay in his way, imitating the rules of the court of Nizam Shaw, to give more consequence and dignity to his service, ordered the amras of a thousand to be stiled nobles of three thousand, and to establish the korawat, or hiring of temporary cavalry. When Kummaul Khan, by this manœuvre, had raised an army of twenty thousand horse, he called together his creatures on the first of Suffir, in the year 917, to consult with them upon a lucky day for his deposing Ismaeel Adil Shaw, and proclaiming his own name in the khootbah at Beejapore. After much debate, the first of the ensuing month, Rubbi al Awul, was fixed as the day propitious to his designs; the traitor little supposing, that the recorders of providence were then penning the concluding pages of the journal of his vain-glorious life.

A.D. 1511.

The young sultan and his mother, though much alarmed at the intelligence of the regent's daring ambition, notwithstanding the small number of their friends, raised their minds to destroy the ungrateful rebel. As providence had decreed the preservation of the Adil Shawee family, and its long sway of royal power, some astrologers represented to Kummaul Khan, that from the appearance of the heavenly bodies, certain days of the present month were very unfavourable to his designs; therefore he would do well to clothe himself with the armour of caution, and strictly avoid the company of any persons he had the least cause to suspect of disaffection. The regent, impressed with their remarks, on the days pointed out as unlucky, committed the charge of the city to his own dependants; and having chosen an apartment in the citadel close to the royal palace,

* Corps of royal guards.

palace, shut himself up, with only his own family and principal officers, keeping all the gates of the fort strongly barred within, and guards without. He himself remained in one room constantly for some days, pretending a severe head-ache, to excuse his retirement; thinking by this prudence, which providence smiled at, to evade its decrees.

The queen mother, inwardly rejoicing at the measures of the regent, so favourable to the plan she had formed to destroy him, prepared to carry her designs into execution, and applied for assistance to Eusuff Turk, the foster father of Ismaeel Shaw, who had been treated with great indignity, and mortally hated Kummaul Khan. The old officer, in reply to the queen's request, said, that instead of one life devoted to the service of his prince, he lamented he had not a thousand to sacrifice for him; but that against eight thousand Dekkanees and Abyssinians, it was clear to all, one man could effect nothing. The queen replied, that if he would risque his single life for his master's safety, the traitor and his schemes would fall together. Eusuff Khan answered, that as he knew his life would be taken the instant Kummaul Khan should ascend the throne, he preferred giving it honourably in ransom for his sovereign's, which would acquire him immortal reputation among the illustrious faithful, and desired to be informed how he could be useful.

The queen then sent for an old female attendant of her own, whom she knew to be employed as a spy upon her actions by Kummaul Khan, and pretending to be under great uneasiness at the reports of his indisposition, sent her with \* a sum of money, as an offering for his safety, to make enquiries of his health. When the old woman had left her and gone some paces, she called out, as if on sudden recollection, that Eusuff Turk was very much depressed, and wished

---

\* It is customary in India, when princes are ill to send them money, which is distributed to the poor.

wished to make a pilgrimage to Mecca; therefore she desired she would take him with her, and prevail on Kummaul Khan to give him leave, and a [a] betel of dismission with his own hand, which she should regard as a favour done to herself. The spy consented; and going first in to Kummaul Khan, delivered the queen's present and message in such a manner, that the regent was highly pleased, and gave orders to admit Eusuff. The Turk on his entrance, with great humility, made his obeisance, and uttered several flattering speeches, which pleased Kummaul Khan, who called him nearer to him, at the same time reaching out his arm to give him a betel. Eusuff advanced, [b] putting his hands under the cloth that covered his shoulders, as if to receive it with the customary respect. The regent had stretched his hand to put the betel on the cloth, when Eusuff, with the quickness of lightning, plucking out a dagger concealed underneath, stabbed him in the breast with all his force, so that he fell down and expired immediately with a loud groan; upon which the attendants rushed upon Eusuff, and cut him to pieces with their swords, together with the old woman, who they supposed had acted in concert with the murderer.

The mother of Kummaul Khan, a woman of daring spirit, commanded the attendants to refrain from clamour; and placing the body dressed out, supported by pillows, on a musnud, in a balcony of the palace, as if to receive compliments from the court, instructed the regent's son, Suffder Khan, to go down and command the guards, as if from his father, to surround the royal haram and seize Ismaeel Adil Shaw; also to send orders to the troops without the citadel to assemble under arms, as his father would shortly assume the royal dignities, and appear on a bastion of the citadel to receive the compliments of the people and army, as their sovereign prince.

Suffder

---

[a] The betel is given by superiors, on dismission to their servants, as a token of regard.

[b] An inferior presenting or receiving any thing, puts a cloth on his hands, as if their touch would contaminate the offering or gift.

Suffder Khan thinking the force within fufficient to take the young fultan prifoner, kept the gates of the citadel fhut, and with his relations and followers, armed with mufquetry, fabres, fpears, bows and arrows, advanced to the apartments where the prince refided with his mother and family. The queen, apprehending that Eufuff Turk had failed in his attempt, and that Kummaul Khan out of refentment had haftened his operations to dethrone her fon, thought it beft to pretend ignorance of Eufuff's defigns, and endeavour to avert the ftorm by flattery and fubmiffion; but the fultan's fofter aunt, Dilfhaad Aggeh, who had come from Perfia to Hindooftan in the latter part of the reign of Eufuff Adil Shaw, remarked, that in fuch a crifis as the prefent valour and fortitude were required, inftead of fubmiffion and entreaties. She then ordered the doors to be fhut, and fent out her eunuch Mallek Sundul to the few of her countrymen on duty in the outer court of the haram, informing them, that Kummaul Khan, meditating the depofal of Ifmaeel Adil Shaw their fovereign, and of the fame nation as themfelves, was advancing to affaffinate him with the whole royal family, and convert the garden of empire to a rooft of ravens and birds of prey; that if they were men of honour, they fhould not regard the fuperiority of the enemy, but valiantly affift their prince againft the traitor; who, by the divine blefling, would be overwhelmed in the enormity of accurfed ingratitude, and that they would gather the flowers of glorious victory in the field of fidelity.

The guards bound the belts of refolution on their waifts, and touching the ground of loyalty with their foreheads, declared their vows of fupport and defence of their young fovereign. Dilfhaad Aggeh and Boobojee Khatoon now came out, in the dreffes of men in compleat armour, with bows and arrows in their hands attending on Ifmaeel Adil Shaw, who had the yellow umbrella of his father held over him by a Turkifh woman, named Murtuffeh Aggeh, and joined the guards.

Suffder Khan, who was endeavouring to force the gates, was oppofed by the Turks from the wall with arrows, and the young fultan, with the women, affifted in perfon; but the enemy's fuperiority was fo great, that the little band of gallant Turks had no chance, many of them were killed by mufquet balls, and the reft falling back, a mournful cry of defpair iffued from the apartments of the women. Juft then, Muftapha Khan and Secunder Khan Koomi, who had formerly the charge of the citadel, and whom Kummaul Khan thinking weak and humble had not molefted, hearing of the difturbance, haftened with fifty Dekkanee matchlock men to the wall of the mahal, and, hailing Dilfhaad Aggeh, afcended the terrace, and joined her party againft the rebels; who, though now kept at bay, could not be driven off, and many perfons fell on both fides. Dilfhaad privately fent a fervant over the wall into the city to inform all the foreigners and others of the danger to which the fultan was expofed from the treachery of his minifter, entreating them to haften to his affiftance, and fhe would admit them over a baftion behind the palace. The rebels not knowing of this accefs, many of her friends mounted by ropes thrown over by Dilfhaad, till at laft they amounted to one hundred and fifty foreign archers, fifty matchlock men, nineteen Turkifh flaves, and twenty five Abyffinians, all refolute to defend their prince. Dilfhaad, with a veil on her head, fought with them, and by animating fpeeches encouraged their ardour, promifing that the fultan would reward them all by high honours. Suffder Khan, feeing that the defenders encreafed in numbers, fent out a party to prevent more entering, and made a fierce attack with five hundred men, bringing alfo cannon to batter down the walls of the haram. Many of the defendants fell, and all the Dekkanees and Abyffinians threw themfelves in a panic over the battlements. The foreigners now, by the advice of Dilfhaad, fat down filent under cover of the parapet wall; and Suffder Khan, judging they had fled alfo, broke open the outer doors of the mahal, and entered the court; but as he was endeavouring to force the other, the gallant Dilfhaad fired a

volley

volley of shot and arrows from the terrace above, which did great execution, killing and wounding some principal rebels. An arrow also pierced the eye of Suffder Khan, who ran under a wall over which the sultan himself was standing; and the royal youth, knowing his person, rolled down a heavy stone from the terrace, which crushed him to death as he lay couched to avoid the shot. The troops, seeing their chief killed, ran to the house of Kummaul Khan, where they learned that he also was dead; upon which they opened the gates of the citadel and fled different ways. Khusseroo Khan Turk, a faithful slave of the late sultan, dreading the numbers of the enemy without, shut the gates again, and by the orders of Dilshaad sent the heads of the father and son with a guard by a sally port, to be carried through the streets of the city, for the information of the people. Mahummud Ein al Moolk, who had given his daughter to Suffder Khan in marriage, and all the principal friends of the regent, quitting their houses and effects, made their escape as expeditiously as possible out of the city. When the capital was cleared of the rebels, the sultan came out with the funeral procession of his foster father Eusuff, whose body he deposited near the tomb of the venerable \* Ein ad Dien Junceaee, at which he also paid his respects; and distributing great alms, ordered a dome to be erected over it, and a mosque near, for the support of which lands were allotted. During his whole reign, he went constantly once a month to visit the tomb of the faithful Eusuff. Towards evening he returned mounted on an elephant into the citadel.

The next day, early in the morning, the sultan ascended the throne, and gave general audience, at which all the officers of the court and inhabitants of the city paid their compliments, and made offerings according to their rank and ability. Express letters were dispatched to the surrounding powers, with accounts of the punishment of the regent, and the happy escape of the sultan from his treacherous

---

\* A celebrated mussulmaun divine.

treacherous defigns. Ameer Bereed, upon receiving the information, immediately raifed the fiege of Koolburga; but Heemraaje, who had taken advantage of the times to invade the fultan's dominions, ftill continued before Roijore; which at laft was given up to him by the garrifon, Ifmaeel Adil Shaw being too much employed in reftoring the domeftic affairs of government, to afford it timely relief.

The fultan firft raifed thofe who had affifted him in the late crifis to high honours, and fent letters of invitation to Mirza Jehangeer, Sobejung, Hyder Beg, and other noblemen, who had fled from the perfecutions of Kummaul Khan to different parts, to return to his court and refume their employments. With mercy, becoming a great king, he drew the line of forgivenefs over the crimes of the regent's mother and his family, who had been taken prifoners, and, giving them a confiderable fum of money, ordered them to leave his territories. The aftrologers, who had foretold fo truly the danger of Kummaul Khan, he took into his own employment. The veterans of his father flocking from all quarters to his court, he had foon a gallant body of Turks and Moguls in his fervice. Khufferoo Turk, who had affifted in his late deliverance, was honoured with the title of Afiud Khan, and had Balgoan conferred upon him in jaghire. The fultan had vowed that he would not entertain any Dekkanees or Abyffinians in his fervice; and he kept this promife for near twelve years, keeping none but foreigners; till at length, at their requeft, he admitted their children to be received into the army, and afterwards by degrees confented to entertain fuch Afghauns and Raajepoots as were not born in Dekkan, the rule againft whom was rigidly obferved till the reign of Ibrahim Adil Shaw.

Mirza Jehangeer, on his return to court, having the diftricts of Koolburga conferred upon him, drove out the forces of Ameer Bereed with the flaughter of four hundred men, retook the forts of Nufferutabad, Saugher, and Ahngur, wholly regaining all the country

country taken from Beejapore during the regency of Kummaul Khan. Ameer Bereed, fired with his loffes, fent firmauns in the name of fultan Mhamood to all the fovereigns of Dekkan, demanding affiftance; upon which, ᵃ Boorahan Nizam Shaw, ᵇ fultan Koolli Koottub Shaw, and ᶜ Alla ad Dien Ummad Shaw, each fent troops to join the royal ftandard. In the year 920, Ameer Bereed obliged the fultan to A.D. 1514. move from Ahmedabad at the head of the allies, confifting of twenty five thoufand horfe, towards Beejapore, and committed every wafte and depredation on the country in his route.

Ifmaeel Adil Shaw, out of policy, remained in his capital; letting the enemy advance without oppofition to Allapore, a town built by Eufuff Adil Shaw, within a mile and half of Beejapore; when he marched out of the city at the head of twelve thoufand horfe, all foreigners. Notwithftanding the great fuperiority of the enemy, he defeated them fo completely, that the allies fled, leaving behind them Mhamood Shaw and his fon fultan Ahmed, who had fallen from their horfes in the action. All the baggage of the fugitives fell into the hands of the victors; and Ifmaeel Adil Shaw, on hearing of the fituation of the princes, went to pay his obeifance to them as his fuperiors, prefented offerings of horfes with furniture fet with jewels, and would have conducted them in magnificent palanquins to Beejapore, that they might be freed from the oppreffion of Ameer Bereed. Mhamood Shaw not confenting to enter the city, encamped near Allapore; where he remained fome time to recover of a bruife he had fuftained in his fall, and afterwards demanded Bibi Sutti, fifter to Ifmaeel Adil Shaw, for his fon fultan Ahmed, to whom fhe was efpoufed. Ifmaeel Adil Shaw confenting, Koolburga was appointed for celebrating the nuptials, and both fultans repaired to it in company with great pomp. The ceremony of marriage was performed
with

ᵃ Of Ahmednuggur.
ᵇ Of Golconda.
ᶜ Of Berar.

with royal magnificence, and the bride being delivered to sultan Ahmed, Ismaeel Adil Shaw sent five thousand horse to attend them, with the sultan Mhamood Shaw, to Ahmedabad, which was deserted by Ameer Bereed on their approach; so that the sultan for some time had the pleasure of liberty, and release from the controul of a minister: but the Beejapore troops had no sooner left him, than Ameer Bereed returned, and resumed the charge of affairs, as before.

Some years before this, the emperor of Persia, Shaw Ismaeel Suffewi, had sent ambassadors to the powers of Hindoostan, who had been received with due respect by the roy of Beejanuggur and the king of Guzarat. Sultan Mhamood also had received an ambassador to him with proper attention, and wished to dismiss him with royal presents; but Ameer Bereed not consenting, the ambassador wrote to Ismaeel Adil Shaw, complaining of his being detained at Ahmedabad. The sultan immediately demanded his dismission; and accordingly, having obtained his audience of leave, the ambassador came to Beejapore, where he was met by Ismaeel Adil Shaw at Allapore, honoured with rich presents, and escorted as far as the port of Dabul by a proper guard, on his return to Persia. The emperor of Persia, in acknowledgment of this service to his ambassador, in the year 925, sent Ibrahim Beg Turkoman, an officer of his court, with letters and presents to Ismaeel Adil Shaw, and among the latter was a sabre set with valuable jewels. The emperor in his letter addressed him as a sovereign prince. Ismaeel Adil Shaw went twelve miles to meet the ambassador; and being highly gratified at the acknowledgment of his royalty by so great a monarch, received Ibrahim Beg with extraordinary honours, ordered the march of victory to be sounded, and commanded the officers of his army to wear scarlet caps of twelve points, it being the distinction of the disciples of shekh Suffi. He also ordered, that on Fridays and holidays a prayer should be recited at the mosques for the royal family of Persia.

A. D. 1519.

In

FERISHTA's HISTORY OF DEKKAN.

In the year 927, Ifmaeel Adil Shaw made preparations for marching to recover Mudkul and Roijore from the roy of Beejanuggur; who gaining early intelligence of his defigns, moved with a great force, and ftationed his camp on the banks of the Kiftnah, where he was joined by many of his tributaries; fo that his army amounted at leaft to fifty thoufand horfe, befides a vaft hoft of foot. The fultan would now have delayed his expedition, as the enemy poffeffed all the ferries of the Kiftnah, but that his tents were pitched, and it would have been difgraceful to retract from his declarations. He therefore marched with feven thoufand horfe, all foreign, and encamped on the bank of the river oppofite to the enemy, waiting to prepare floats to crofs and attack them. Some days after his arrival, as he was repofing in his tent, he heard one of his courtiers without the [a] fkreens reciting this verfe; " Rife, and fill the golden goblet with " the wine of mirth, before the cup itfelf fhall be laid in duft." The fultan, infpired by the verfe, called his favourites before him, and fpreading the carpet of pleafure, amufed himfelf with mufic and wine. When the banquet had lafted longer than reafonable, and the fumes of the wine had exercifed their power, a fancy feized the fultan to pafs the river and attack the enemy. He called his officers before him, and enquired the reafon for the delay in preparing the floats, and was anfwered, that one hundred were already finifhed, and the reft would be ready in a few days. The fultan, warm with wine, refolved to crofs immediately; and mounting his elephant, without making his intentions known, proceeded to the river, as if to reconnoitre, but fuddenly gave orders for as many of his troops as could to go upon the rafts, and others to follow him on elephants through the river. The officers reprefented the folly and danger of precipitation; but the fultan, without reply, plunged his own elephant into the ftream, and was followed involuntarily by the amras and their followers, on about two hundred and fifty elephants. By great good fortune, all reached the oppofite fhore in fafety, and as many

A. D. 1520.

[a] The tents of the great in India are enclofed by walls, or fkreens of cloth.

many troops as could crofs on the floats at two embarkations had time to arrive, when the enemy advanced to battle in fo great force, as excluded every probable hope of efcape to the fultan, who had not more than two thoufand men ready to oppofe thirty thoufand. The heroes of Iflaam, animated with one foul, made fo gallant a refiftance, that above a thoufand of the infidels fell, among whom was Sungeet Roy, the chief general of Beejanuggur; but at laft, harafied beyond all power of oppofition, by cannon fhot, mufquetry, and rockets, which deftroyed near half their numbers, the furvivors threw themfelves into the river, in hopes of efcaping, and Nurfoo Bahadur and Ibrahim Beg, who rode on the fame elephant with Ifmaeel Adil Shaw, drove the animal acrofs the ftream; but fo great was the current, that except the royal elephant and feven foldiers, all the reft were drowned. The fultan's rafhnefs was heavily punifhed by fo great a lofs. He took a folemn vow never to indulge in wine, till he had revenged his defeat; and then, throwing away defpair, bufied his mind in repairing this unfortunate mifcarriage.

As Mirza Jehangeer had fallen in the action, the fultan confulted with Affud Khan on what meafures would be beft to take in the prefent crifis of his affairs. Affud Khan replied, that as his lofs was great, and the troops difpirited, it would be proper to retreat for the prefent to Beejapore, and lay afide thoughts of revenge on the roy of Beejanuggur, till he could ftrengthen himfelf by alliances with Nizam Shaw, and remove his natural enemy Ameer Bereed from his borders; after which, the punifhment of the infidels might be eafily effected. The fultan, approving the advice, marched from the Kiftnah to Beejapore, and conferring the dignity of [a] fippeh fallar on Affud Khan, added feveral diftricts to his jaghire, and made him his principal advifer in all important affairs.

Syed Ahmed Herraee, who had formerly been fent as ambaffador from the fultan to the emperor of Perfia, was now difpatched in that

capacity

[a] Commander in chief.

capacity to Ahmednuggur, to strengthen the bonds of agreement with that state; and being met near the city by Shaw Tahir and all the principal nobility, was introduced to sultan Boorahan Nizam Shaw, and received with great favours. When letters and civilities had been repeatedly interchanged by the two sultans, an interview was fixed upon, and accordingly they met at the town of Sholapore. Boorahan Nizam Shaw having asked in marriage the sister of Ismaeel Adil Shaw, and the latter agreeing to grant his request, nuptial festivals were prepared, the princess Mariem was espoused to him, and the ceremonies of marriage concluded with great pomp and magnificence. Presents of valuable curiosities, elephants, and horses, were given by both kings; and the royal rejoicings for the accomplishment of the alliance continued the whole month of Rejib, of the year 930; after which the royal brothers took leave, and returned each to the capital of his own dominions. A.D. 1523.

It is related, that it was stipulated in the treaty of alliance that Ismaeel Adil Shaw should give up, as the marriage portion of his sister, to Boorahan Nizam Shaw, the fort of Sholapore with its five districts, taken by the late regent from Zien Khan; but that this article he delayed to perform, and Boorahan Shaw for some time took no notice of the breach of treaty; but having the next year secured the assistance of Ummad Shaw, sultan of Berar, and Ameer Bereed, regent of Bieder, he marched to besiege Sholapore, and seize the ceded pergunnahs, with forty thousand horse.

Ismaeel Adil Shaw having collected ten thousand foreign cavalry, moved to oppose the invasion; and both armies lay forty days between the forts of Sholapore and Nuldirruk, at the distance of four miles from each other, without coming to action. Three thousand foreign archers of Adil Shaw exerted themselves daily in hovering round the enemy's camp, and cutting off supplies of provisions; in which, and harassing the foraging parties, they were very successful.

H h          Khajeh

Khajeh Jehaun Dekkanee, governor of Porundeh, vexed at this difgrace and the inactivity of Nizam Shaw, without orders feparated from the camp with four thoufand felect Dekkanee cavalry, refolved to furprize the archers. The following evening, the archers, after a fatiguing excurfion round the enemy's camp, had chofen their poft for the night on the banks of a rivulet; and having picketted their horfes, were unarming, and waiting for their fervants to drefs their victuals, unfufpecting any attack. The night had juft fhut in, when Khajeh Jehaun arrived near, but was perceived at a little diftance from the outpofts, by one of the foldiers, who had gone in front on fome occafion. He immediately ran back and gave the alarm; upon which the archers took to their horfes, but before they could all mount, Khajeh Jehaun charged, and killed about three hundred. The reft made their efcape, by the fwiftnefs of their horfes, and the Dekkanees returning from purfuit to the fpot on which the archers had been encamped, difmounted, and employed themfelves in plunder and eating the victuals, which had been left in the pots on the fires. The archers, when they had rode out of danger of purfuit, rallied; and judging the Dekkanees would be off their guard, refolved to furprize the camp of Nizam Shaw. They accordingly moved, and the centinels, taking them for Khajeh Jehaun's detachment returning to camp, which was alfo the cafe, let them pafs. The archers, letting fly a fhower of arrows, wounded Khajeh Jehaun, who fled with his followers into the camp. The archers purfued, and made great flaughter in their way to the tents of Nizam Shaw. A ftrange confufion now prevailed, friends could not be diftinguifhed from foes, and the archers, when fatiated with flaughter and plunder, retired with very little lofs. Early in the morning, Ifmaeel Adil Shaw advanced to give battle to the enemy, not recovered fully from the night's alarm. Nizam Shaw and Ummad Shaw drew up their line in great diforder and precipitation; but could not long ftand againft the fierce attack of the Beejapore troops. Ummad Shaw, being charged by Affud Khan, fled from the field

almoft

almoft without making any oppofition, and did not halt, except at night, till he had reached his fort of Kaweel in Berar. Nizam Shaw being joined, as he was on the point of giving way, by Ameer Bereed, with fix thoufand horfe, all frefh, continued to oppofe for fome time longer. At laft Kooldi Aga and Ifmaeel Aga, Turkifh chiefs, with two thoufand horfe, gained the enemy's rear, and Affud Khan attacked the right wing at the fame time. This confufed the enemy much; and Boorahan Nizam Shaw, overcome by the weight of his armour, was near falling from his horfe through faintnefs; upon which, fome Turkifh flaves, feeing his condition, led him from the field, and the route of his army immediately became general. About three thoufand men were flain in the purfuit, and the royal ftandard of Nizam Shaw fell into the hands of Affud Khan. Forty elephants, with many pieces of cannon, and all the tents and baggage, became the prize of the victors. Many principal officers and nobles fell on the fide of the vanquifhed. Ifmaeel Adil Shaw, after his victory, returned in triumph to Beejapore, where he made rejoicings for a month together, and conferred rewards and magnificent dreffes on his nobility. He gave Affud Khan five large and fix fmall elephants, taken from Nizam Shaw, and doubled the pay of every foldier in his army. To enable him to bear this expenfe, he divided all the lands appropriated for the fupport of the royal haram among his officers, and alfo half the duties of all his forts. Being one day told that fome officers were ftill unprovided for, and the minifters, in anfwer to his injunctions to fatisfy them, obferving, that the treafury could not maintain fo many troops on the eftablifhed pay, he afked, what number of farms were collected under the heads of his wardrobe and kitchen? It was anfwered, four and twenty. Upon which he commanded half to be divided to the troops, faying, that it was better he fhould fuffer fome inconveniences, than they have reafon to complain.

A. D. 1528.   In the year 935, Nizam Shaw, with Ameer Bereed, again invaded the territories of Ismaeel Adil Shaw, againſt the ſtrongeſt remonſtrances of his own miniſters. He was completely defeated, within twenty cofs of Beejapore, by Aſſud Khan, when Khajeh Jehaun, and ſeveral officers of the firſt diſtinction, were taken priſoners in the action. Aſſud Khan purſued the fugitives as far as Porundeh, and took much baggage and twenty elephants, among which was that which carried the throne of Nizam Shaw. Ismaeel Adil Shaw gave him all the elephants, except one named Alleh Bukſh, or the gift of God, and honoured him with the title of ſon in all his firmauns. The ſultan, by his advice, this year gave his ſiſter Khadijah Sultana to Alla ad Dien Ummad Shaw of Berar; and the two ſultans had a meeting in the town of Oorjaan to celebrate the nuptials; after which they took leave of each other with mutual preſents and profeſſions of regard and ſupport.

This year alſo, ſultan Bahadur of Guzarat invading the territories of Nizam Shaw, Ismaeel Adil Shaw ſent [*] ten lacks of oons and ſix thouſand horſe to aſſiſt the latter, in conjunction with Ameer Bereed. Theſe troops, after the retreat of ſultan Bahadur, returning to Beejapore, informed their ſovereign, that Ameer Bereed had endeavoured to corrupt their fidelity, and prevail on them to join him in an attack on Beejapore, promiſing to reward them with a ſhare of territory. Ismaeel Adil Shaw, juſtly provoked, reſolved to puniſh his treachery;
A. D. 1529.   and in the year 936 ſent intelligent ambaſſadors to Nizam Shaw, complaining that Ameer Bereed had frequently conſpired againſt his family, and more than once induced his enemies to invade his dominions; which treachery he had as yet declined puniſhing, but that now he had reſolved to requite his behaviour, led to it by both religious and political arguments; for, to uſe the wolf with gentleneſs, or the ſnake with favour, was contrary to the dictates of wiſdom. He obſerved, that if Nizam Shaw, out of regard to their connection.

[*] Three hundred thouſand pounds and upwards.

connection and friendship, would remain neutral, he would in a short time give him a full retribution for his evil deeds. Nizam Shaw, who lay under obligations to the sultan for his late succours, acquiesced in all his desires; observing, that whatever he wished to effect would undoubtedly be pleasing to his friends. The ambassadors returned with this answer, and Ismaeel Adil Shaw immediately prepared for his intended expedition.

The sultan having formed an army of ten thousand cavalry, consisting of Arabians, Persians, Turks, Usbeks, Koords, and other foreigners, whom his liberality had bound to his interest, marched towards Ahmedabad. On his approach, Ameer Bereed, who was very old and infirm, by the advice of Heemaje, a bramin, his minister, committed the citadel of Bieder to the charge of Ali Bereed, his eldest son, and the rest of his family, going himself to reside at the fortress of Oudegur.

Ismaeel Adil Shaw, upon his arrival before Ahmedabad, blocked up the city on all sides; but the garrison made repeated sallies, and, being nearly equal in numbers to the besiegers, greatly retarded their operations, and at length the sons of Ameer Bereed, with five thousand horse, came out of the city, resolved, as the Beejaporeans were only archers, to charge upon them covered with shields, and cut them to pieces in close combat, with the swords of the Dekkanees; but Ismaeel Adil Shaw, who had foreseen such an attack, had provided three thousand cavalry, expert in the use of the sabre, and both men and horses covered with iron armour, under the command of Syed Houssein, an Arab chief of great reputation. A very severe action ensued on the plain before the gate of the bramin suburb, and foreigners and Dekkanees both displayed the highest examples of valour in rivalry of each other. Adil Shaw, in spite of the remonstrances of Assud Khan, engaged in the action, and killed two brothers of Ameer Bereed, who had attacked him in single combat.

Both

Both armies were loud in the praises of the sultan's valour, and his own officers, alighting from their horses, kissed his stirrup. At this instant, four large bodies of troops were seen upon the right, which appeared about four thousand. Assud Khan sent off one of his attendants, named Goderz, to learn who they were, with forty horse. It proved that they were four thousand horse detached by sultan Koollee for the assistance of Ameer Bereed. Ismaeel Adil Shaw ordered Assud Khan to oppose them, and prepared to engage the troops of Ali Bereed himself; when Syed Houssein Arab earnestly requested to be honoured with that charge, and observed, that the sultan should not too much expose his person. The sultan, moved by his remonstrances, consented to his request, and presented him with his own sword, yet reeking with the blood of his enemies. Both generals were successful, and the troops of the allies, after losing about five hundred men each, fled in disorder, leaving the field of victory to Ismaeel Adil Shaw. Assud Khan in this battle gained great honour, as, after driving off the four thousand Telinganees of Koottub Shaw, he came to the assistance of Syed Houssein. On this account, when the sultan after the victory dismounted upon an eminence to thank his officers, he honoured Assud Khan above all the rest, by clasping him in his embrace. To Syed Houssein he gave the horse he had rode in the action. Two sons of Ameer Bereed, and Gusthum Beg, commander of the Koottub Shawee auxiliaries, were slain.

Ismaeel Adil Shaw now blockaded the city closer than before; and Ameer Bereed, being reduced to great distress, wrote to Ummad Shaw, earnestly requesting him to come and mediate a peace for him; upon which he, without repairing to Oudegur, came and encamped within a mile of the sultan. Ismaeel Adil Shaw went to visit him with his principal nobility, and Ummad Shaw, after congratulations on the late success, declared, that he had marched merely for the purpose of sharing in his victories, but that he hoped to be able to obtain his forgiveness of the faults of Ameer Bereed.

The

The fultan replied, that Bereed had done his family more injuries than could be enumerated, and that in this war many gallant men had fallen, who had great claims to his efteem; therefore he wifhed not to hear of peace, till their lofs was fully revenged on the infidious enemy. Ummad Shaw, feeing his refolution firm, did not prefs him farther; and the two princes, after fpending a week together in feftivity, parted. Ameer Bereed now left Oudegur, and travelling with great expedition, came to the camp of Ummad Shaw, entreating him to procure peace for him; but being informed no other offer than the furrender of the city would be liftened to by Ifmaeel Adil Shaw, he retired in difguft to his own camp, near that of Ummad Shaw; and to relax his cares engaged in drinking and mufic. His troops alfo, fatigued with long marches, were carelefs of duty, and even the outpofts lay down to fleep, not dreading any danger; while many, following the example of their chief, had recourfe to wine to drown their forrows.

Ifmaeel Adil Shaw having heard of the arrival of Ameer Bereed, ordered Affud Khan, with feveral chiefs and two thoufand chofen horfe, to furprize his camp. Affud Khan prepared the troops, as if to relieve thofe at the trenches; but when he had got without the camp made known his intentions, and proceeded as filently as poffible towards the tents of the enemy. Being arrived clofe to the outpofts, and hearing not the fmalleft noife or challenge, he ordered his troops to ftop and obferve the ftricteft filence, fending fpies to learn the fituation of the enemy; who foon returning, declared, that they had advanced uninterrupted to the tents of Ameer Bereed, where the few on guard were all afleep. To prove their affertions they prefented fome turbans and fabres they had ftolen from them. Affud Khan then ordering his troops to remain in profound filence on the borders of the camp for his further orders, advanced himfelf, with twenty five horfemen and a few foot, through the fleeping enemy to the tents of Ameer Bereed. Here he faw the guards lying about in
ftrange

strange postures, snoring amid the broken vessels of liquor. Assud Khan, thinking it ungenerous to murder them in such an helpless condition, ordered some footmen with drawn sabres to stand over them, in case any should awake, to prevent them giving the alarm. He then dismounted, and entered the tents with some part of his followers, hoping to take Ameer Bereed alive, but if he could not, intending to put him to death, and carry his head to the sultan. Those within he found as fast asleep as their friends without. Ameer Bereed lay senseless on a bed, round which the dancers and singers, male and female, were jumbled together in strange postures, amid their own filth, broken vessels, and spilt liquors, snoring in concert. Assud Khan observed, that to murder such persons was ungenerous, therefore it would be more glorious to carry their chief alive on his bed to the sultan, without injuring any of his followers. The bed of this old, experienced, and wily minister, was then lifted up by the attendants of Assud Khan, who was moving out of the tents with his prize, when one of the lamp-men, called deotees in Dekkan, and who have the body watch of the chief at night, awaking, was going to cry out, but Assud Khan clapped his hands timely on his mouth, and his people strangled him; after which he reached his troops on the border of the camp without accident. He then represented to them, that as their chief end was obtained, it was better to desist from farther enterprize, as in the darkness of the night the Hindoo could not be distinguished from the mussulmaun; and consequently many of the faithful must be slain, which he wished to avoid. All the detachment approved of his generosity, and Assud Khan moved towards the royal camp, carrying his prisoner on his bed in jocose triumph. Ameer Bereed awaking on the road, and finding himself in motion, thought he was among evil spirits, or genii, and began to cry out in terror to God for relief from enchantments; but Assud Khan told him who he was, and after relating his exploit at large, upbraided him with his imprudence; observing, that for a reverend old man, experienced as he was in the arts of government,

to

to have suffered himself to be intoxicated so near an enemy, was highly derogatory to his character and wisdom. Ameer Bereed, as he was covered with shame and sorrow, returned no answer; but Assud Khan, desiring him to be comforted, assured him of his influence with the sultan to procure kind treatment and forgiveness.

The detachment arriving at the royal camp, Assud Khan without delay presented his important prize to the sultan, who was overjoyed at the possession of his enemy, whom he asked, How, with such art and cunning as he had displayed in a long life, he could fall into such a snare? Ameer Bereed said, Fate and providence had thus decreed; therefore to question him on the subject was useless, as he could give no satisfactory answer. The sultan then delivered him over to Assud Khan, whom he ordered to bring him to the Durbar in the morning.

Ismaeel Adil Shaw in the morning, being seated on his throne in full court, Ameer Bereed was placed opposite to him, with his head bare, and his hands tied behind his back, exposed to a hot sun. When he had stood for two hours in this manner, the sultan gave orders for his being put to death, and an executioner advanced to do his duty with a drawn scymetar. Ameer Bereed, seeing his dangerous situation, now opened his lips to entreaty; saying, that undoubtedly he had been guilty of many insults to the sultan and his late father of blessed memory, and was conscious of deserving death at his hands; but if the sultan could forget his crimes, and suffer him to live and repent, he would surrender to him the city of Ahmedabad, with the fortress of Bieder, whose battlements the ladders of royal ability had never yet scaled; and also all the treasures and effects of the royal family of Bhamenee.

The king having consented to mercy on this condition, Ameer Bereed dispatched one of his attendants to his sons, acquainting them with his situation and the agreement he had made. They returned

I i for

for anſwer, that as he was very old, and the ſun of his exiſtence near ſetting, to ſurrender ſuch a fortreſs for a few remaining days of life, would be unbecoming his character or their own intereſt. Their intention in this meſſage was only to gain time, in hopes of aſſiſtance from their allies, for they ſent out privately an intelligent perſon with inſtructions to make terms of ſurrender, ſhould their father be in real danger. Ameer Bereed knew this, and with much art complained of the cruel neglect of his ſons; but Iſmaeel Adil Shaw, who ſuſpected the ſcheme, without delay ordered him to be thrown before a vicious elephant, reſolved to puniſh his treachery, and truſt for gaining the city to an aſſault of his troops. Bereed had again recourſe to entreaty, begging that he might be carried before a certain tower of the fort, that his ſons might behold his miſery, and be moved to ſave his life by ſurrender. This was done accordingly, and the ſons, ſeeing no other means but ſubmiſſion to procure the ſafety of their parent, offered to reſign the city and fortreſs, on condition that they and their women ſhould be allowed to depart with the clothes on their perſons without ſearch. Their demand being agreed to, they loaded themſelves and women as heavily as they could bear with the valuable ornaments and robes of the royal family of Bhamenee, and with their followers retired unmoleſted to the fortreſs of Oudegur.

Aſſud Khan now entered the city, with ſome choſen troops, to prevent plunder, and collect the treaſures and effects belonging to the vanquiſhed. Iſmaeel Adil Shaw at a lucky inſtant, attended by all the princes and nobility on foot from the gate of the city to the palace, entered the grand hall of audience, and aſcended the throne of the Bhamenee ſultans. Having given God thanks for his glorious ſucceſs, he diſpatched his ſon Mulloo Khan, with Aſſud Khan, and other amras, to invite Ummad Shaw to his court; and he aſſenting, came in royal ſtate to the fort. Iſmaeel met him at the ſteps of the palace, and the two kings then ſat down together on one muſnud.

The

The treasures of the fort were now laid before them. [a] Ten lacks of oons, valuable jewels, gold and silver plate, magnificent china, and rich effects innumerable were found, and the sultan desired Ummad Shaw to take whatever he chose. To avoid the scandal of having possessed himself of the riches of the Bhamenee family, he divided every thing into presents to the surrounding powers and to his own army, not keeping a single coin for himself. He entrusted fifty thousand oons to Syed Ali Ukheel, a person celebrated for learning and integrity, to be distributed in charity to the poor inhabitants of Nujiff, Kerballa, and Meshid, and gave fifty thousand to Syed Ahmed Herraee, to be bestowed on the deserving in his own dominions. He then desired the poet Molana Shied Koommi to go to the treasury and take as much gold as he could lift; but the poet, who was very ill and infirm, observing, that when he first came to his court he was as strong again as at present, the sultan desired him to take as much as he could carry away at two attempts, laughing at his ready invention: and the poet still desiring to wait till he should recover, before he made the effort, the sultan repeated the following verse; "There is danger in delay, and it hurts the petitioner." The poet made shift to lift at twice as many bags as contained [b] twenty five thousand oons, and the sultan being told the amount by his treasurer, replied, The molana spoke truth in complaining of his weakness. He then, declaring that he would not rise till he had disposed of all the plunder, commanded Assud Khan to make a division among the troops; which was effected in such a just manner, that every person was contented with his share.

Ummad Shaw now again requested his pardon for Ameer Bereed; and the sultan consented to receive him among his amras, upon Assud Khan's becoming pledge for his fidelity. He had Kallean, Oudegur, and other pergunnahs out of the collection of the city lands, allotted

---

[a] Three hundred thousand pounds and upwards.
[b] Nearly ten thousand pounds.

allotted for his jaghire, on condition of attending the sultan with three thousand horse on his expedition to Roijore. The sultan a week after put his army in motion, attended by Ummad Shaw and Ameer Bereed with their forces; and the affairs of Beejanuggur being in confusion, owing to the death of Heemraaje, who was newly succeeded by his son Ramraaje, against whom rebellions had arisen by several roies, met with no interruption to his arms. Roijore and Mudkul were taken, after a siege of three months, by capitulation, after they had been in possession of the infidels for seventeen years.

Ismaeel Adil Shaw, who had vowed to refrain from wine till the reduction of these fortresses, at the request of his nobility now made a splendid festival, at which he drank wine and gave a full loose to mirth and pleasure. Ummad Shaw and Ameer Bereed partook of the banquet, and Assud Khan was also admitted to sit and drink out of the same cup with his prince, who helped him, and received wine in return from his hands. At his request, fifteen hundred captives were released, and received presents of scarlet caps and vests. Many of them chose to remain in his service, which the sultan permitted. At this festival also, the sultan promised on his return to Beejapore, to give Ameer Bereed the government of Ahmedabad Bieder. The camp continued in constant rejoicings for a whole month, and Moolla Ibrahim Isferanee wrote a poem of a thousand verses descriptive of them. As intelligence arrived that sultan Bahadur of Guzarat was preparing to invade Dekkan, Ismaeel Adil Shaw, having dismissed Ummad Shaw to his capital, returned in triumph to Beejapore, and agreed to return the city of Ahmedabad, six months after Ameer Bereed should resign to him the forts of Kallean and Candahar; giving him leave to go and prepare for the exchange. It is related, that in this expedition the sultan, being one day entertained by Ummad Shaw, was presented with several trays of valuable jewels, which were pressed upon him against his inclination. The sultan a few days afterwards invited him to a banquet, and upon

Ummad

Ummad Shaw's rising to go, drew up twelve thousand of his foreign cavalry before him, observing, that they were the jewels he had acquired during his reign, and he might take his choice of a number from among them. Ummad Shaw praised his observation, and said with a sigh, had he taken care to acquire such jewels, he should not have lost his fortress of Mahore.

In the year 938, Ameer Bereed having neglected to send the keys of the fortresses of Kallean and Candahar, Ismaeel Adil Shaw resolved to reduce them by force, and sent his tents with one of his sons out of Beejapore to prepare for march. Ameer Bereed applied for assistance to Boorahan Nizam Shaw; who sent ambassadors to Beejapore to represent, that as Bereed had lately done him great services, he wished he would lay aside his enmity against him, which would oblige his friend. Ismaeel Adil Shaw observed in answer, that on Boorahan Shaw's attack of Mahore, he had never interfered with requests, and to oblige him had refrained going against Goa ; that as it was the cool season, and he did not chuse to remain at home, he should make a tour of his dominions, and particularly visit Sholapore and Nuldirruk; therefore he hoped Boorahan Shaw would issue orders to his amras on that frontier not to be alarmed or conceive imaginary terrors. Boorahan Nizam Shaw, being perfectly easy from apprehensions on the side of Guzarat and Berar, replied to Ismaeel Adil Shaw, that he would do well not to depart from his desire, and esteem remaining unmolested at home as the luckiest event for his interest.

A.D. 1531.

Ismaeel Adil Shaw, who had marched from Beejapore, received this message at Bahmen Ali, while at evening prayers; after which he moved with only four hundred horse and forty foot, and reached the river flowing under Nuldirruk before evening prayer the next day. He then dismissed the ambassadors of Nizam Shaw, telling them, he had performed every office incumbent on friendship, and should

now

now wait for his royal brother to come, as he had done repeatedly before, and amufe himfelf with a view of the tempeftuous fea of battle.

Boorahan Nizam Shaw did not refufe the invitation; but in conjunction with Ameer Bereed, marched fpeedily with twenty five thoufand horfe and a great train of artillery to the frontiers of Beejapore. Ifmaeel Adil Shaw left the difpofition of his army to Affud Khan, who formed all the fons of foreigners and Raajepoots into one body, as a light corps, under command of Sunjir Khan, fon of Mirza Jehangeer Koomi, obferving, that their fathers were moftly old, fo that this was a day for the fons to fhew their activity. He took, as ufual, command of the right wing, leaving the left to Muftapha Aga, Secunder Aga, and Khoofh Kuldee, Turkifh amras of diftinguifhed abilities. The center was commanded by the fultan in perfon, who joined as foon as the line was formed. When the umbrella, ftandard, and flags of the enemy, which were formerly white, appeared green, the fultan afked the caufe, and was told, they were given to Boorahan Nizam Shaw by fultan Bahadur of Guzarat. While he was fpeaking, the light corps began to engage. Ifmaeel Adil Shaw, upon this, advanced brifkly with his whole line, and an engagement enfued, fo well fupported, that victory hung on the balance between both parties for fome time. At length Khoorfheed Khan, commander in chief of the Nizam Shawee army, being killed, his troops fled in the utmoft diforder. Boorahan Shaw was totally furrounded by the Mogul horfe, and in danger of being killed or taken prifoner, when fome of his body guards, by a defperate effort, freed their fovereign, and carried him from the field with the utmoft precipitation to his capital of Ahmednuggur, without waiting to collect the fcattered army. Much plunder fell into the hands of the victors; and the fuperiority of Ifmaeel Adil Shaw became eftablifhed over all Dekkan. This victory he called the victory of the foreigners' fons, who now rofe in his efteem; and many of them were

raifed

raifed to the rank of nobility, in reward for their fervices. This was the laft conteft between Ifmaeel Adil Shaw and Boorahan Nizam Shaw. An alliance was formed between the two fultans, who had an interview on their frontiers, in which it was agreed that the former fhould have full right to reduce the country of Koottub Shaw, and the latter to add Berar to his poffeffions.

In confequence of this agreement, Ifmaeel Adil Shaw, in the year 940, having brought over Ameer Bereed to join him, marched into Telingana, and laid fiege to Kowilcondah, one of the capital fortreffes on the frontiers of that kingdom. When he had nearly reduced it to furrender, he was taken ill of a violent fever which obliged him to take to his bed. Finding his diforder encreafe, the fultan fent for Affud Khan and Ameer Bereed, who were detached to lay wafte the country of Telingana, and expreffed his defire that they fhould continue the fiege, while he retired to Koolburga for change of air, till his recovery fhould enable him to rejoin his army. It was accordingly fixed that the fultan fhould begin his journey the next morning in a palanquin; but, before day, a fevere fit returned, and joined him to the elect on the fixteenth of Suffir, 941, after a glorious reign of twenty five years. A.D. 1533.

A.D. 1534.

Affud Khan having embalmed the royal corpfe, placed it in a clofe litter, and fent it privately to Kookee. He concealed the fultan's death for two days; at the end of which he communicated the fatal event to Ameer Bereed and all the principal nobility, whom he advifed, to avoid difputes between the two young princes, fons of the deceafed, in an enemy's country, to raife the fiege of Kowilcondah, and defer fettling the fucceffion till their arrival at Koolburga, where they might feek infpiration to direct their choice at the tomb of the bleffed ᵃ Syed Mahummud Geefoo-derauz, who lay buried near that city. All the amras approving the advice, both the princes, with
Affud

ᵃ A celebrated muffulmaun devotee.

Affud Khan at the head of the army, began their march from Kowilcondah.

Ameer Syed Herraee relates, that Ifmaeel Adil Shaw was prudent, patient, and liberal. He did not jealoufly infpect the payments and receipts of his treafury. He was generous, fond of forgiving criminals, never liftening to flander. He never ufed paffionate language. He had much wifdom, added to a found and penetrating judgment. He was a complete artift in painting, varnifhing, making arrows and faddle cloths. In mufic and poetry he excelled moft of his age. He was fond of the company of learned men and poets, numbers of whom were elegantly fupported at his court. He was delighted with repartee in converfation, and had a great fund of humour, which he often employed among his courtiers. No other fultan of Dekkan ever equalled him in the ftrength and wit of his remarks. He was fonder of the Turkifh and Perfian manners, mufic, and language, than the Dekkanee, which he feldom ufed. This partiality was owing to his being kept while young under the tuition of his aunt Dilfhaad Aggeh, who by defire of his father kept him as much as poffible from the company of Dekkanees, fo that he had little relifh for the people or their manners. He was buried at Kookee, near his father Eufuff Adil Shaw.

# SULTAN

# MULLOO ADIL SHAW BEEJAPOREE.

WHEN fultan Ifmaeel Adil Shaw was about to take his departure from this temporary manfion of care, he addreffed Affud Khan, obferving, that although he feared his eldeft fon, Mulloo Khan, had not abilities to govern, yet paternal affection led him to wifh he might fucceed him, according to birthright. He appointed Affud Khan regent of the kingdom, with the fulleft powers, and inftructions to eftablifh the prince in the fucceffion; conjuring him to remain ftedfaft in loyalty to him, as he had full reliance on his abilities to balance the folly and imprudence of his fon.

Sultan Ibrahim, the youngeft fon, had long entertained ambition of the throne, and had brought over many of the nobility to his intereft; fo that at their father's death, the brothers were near coming to open war, though in an enemy's country, and carrying on the fiege of Kowilcondah. Koottub Shaw, learning the difputes of the brothers, thought them favourable to his caufe, and commanded his troops to hover round the camp and ftop fupplies of provifions; alfo to cut off the ears and nofes of their prifoners, and then let them go, to terrify their fellows by fhewing their miferable conditions. All the amras being engaged in one party or other, none would lead detachments againft the enemy, left advantage fhould be taken by their rivals of their abfence; and the camp followers, after having fuffered by the attacks of the Telingas, refrained from bringing in forage

forage or grain, so that famine soon began to rage in the camp, and discontent and dread seized the whole army. Assud Khan, who was respected by all ranks, finding the disorders daily encreasing, resolved to put an end to them by the exercise of his authority. He first put to death some evil minded persons who had excited the princes to enmity, and confined others. Then calling together all the amras, he strictly forbad them to visit either of the princes, and attend him, as usual during the life of the sultan, at the audience tents, that they might conduct publick affairs till a lucky instant should arrive for seating one or other of the princes on the throne. Both the princes and the whole army approved of the orders of Assud Khan, and agreed to acquiesce in his determination. The regent now detached a force to dislodge the Telingas from the vicinity of the camp, and placed strong guards of his own dependants over the princes, informing them, that the astrologers had unanimously declared ten days must yet pass before an instant favourable for accession to the throne would arrive, and that it was his opinion, remaining so much longer in an enemy's country would be imprudent; therefore he advised the immediate march of the army to Koolburga, where they might invoke the blessed spirit of Syed Mahummud Geesoo-derauz to influence the inauguration.

The princes consenting to follow his advice from necessity, the siege of Kowilcondah was raised without delay, and the army moved to Koolburga, where Assud Khan consulted with the principal ladies of the haram of his late sovereign and the nobility on the choice of a king. Most of them being of opinion that his last will should be followed, he acquiesced; and confining sultan Ibrahim, to prevent disturbances, placed Mulloo Adil Shaw on the throne, who was immediately acknowledged by the nobility and army. Assud Khan, on his return to Beejapore, being disgusted at the behaviour of the new sultan, gave up sultan Ibrahim to the care of his grandmother, Boobojee Khatoon, and resigning his employment at court,
retired

retired to his jaghire of Balgoan, with all his family. Mean Hmacel Dekkanee was raifed to the office of prime minifter in his ftead.

Sultan Mulloo, now left without a check on his inclinations, gave himfelf up to the pleafures of wine, mufic, dancing, and low vices; in gratifying which he fpent the whole of his time, leaving the direction of affairs to his abandoned favourites. He foon became difguftful to all the worthy part of his fubjects, whofe children, if they pleafed him, he feized by force, and dragged to his palace for fhameful purpofes. At length he demanded the fon of Eufuff Khan, a nobleman of high rank among the Turkifh officers, who fpurning at the tyrannical order, the anger of the fultan was raifed, and he fent guards with orders, if Eufuff refufed complying with his demands, to bring him his head. The Turk beat off the royal fycophants, and the fame day retired, in fpite of great oppofition, to his own jaghire of Kuppore, with all his family and troops. Other perfons of honour following his example, left court, and repaired to their eftates; but the fultan, notwithftanding thefe commotions, did not alter his conduct.

Boobojee Khatoon, mother to the late king, difgufted at the fultan's fhameful vices, refolved to depofe him, for the eafe of the fubject and fecurity of government to her family. She wrote to Eufuff Khan, that as Mulloo was unworthy of the throne fhe wifhed he would affift in depofing him, and proclaim fultan Ibrahim. Eufuff Khan, difpatching one of his friends to Balgoan without delay, advifed Affud Khan, that, forced by the tyranny of Mulloo Khan, he had fled from Beejapore, and had received fuch orders from the dowager queen. Affud Khan in reply obferved, that as the behaviour of the fultan was difgufting to all ranks of men, the fafety and honour of the ftate required that he fhould follow the advice of Boobojee Khatoon without delay. Eufuff Khan now fent back her meffengers with affurances of implicit compliance with her commands;

mands; and shortly after, on a day appointed between them, making a forced march to Beejapore, suddenly entered the citadel with two hundred friends well armed. Noor Khan, the commander of the garrison, made but little opposition. Mulloo Khan was seized, and blinded, by orders of his grandmother, together with his youngest brother, Ulloo Khan, after an inglorious reign of only six months. Sultan Ibrahim was immediately after seated on the throne, amid the acclamations of the nobility and people.

SULTAN

# SULTAN

# ABOU AL NUSSER IBRAHIM

# ADIL SHAW BEEJAPOREE.

IBRAHIM Adil Shaw, immediately on his accession to the throne, rejecting the names of the Imaums from the khootbah, restored the exercise of the sooni ceremonies; and commanded that no person should wear the scarlet cap of twelve points, which had been worn by all the troops of his father, in imitation of the Persians. He entertained Dekkanees in his service, and admitted only four hundred foreigners to remain in his body guard. All the foreign nobility, except Assud Khan Laree, Khoosh Kuldie Aga Roomi, and Shujahut Khan Koord, were degraded. Dekkanees and Abyssinians were promoted to their offices. All the foreign troops being dismissed, but four hundred, they entered into the services of different princes. Ramraaje of Beejanuggur took three thousand of them into his pay, gave them great indulgences, and allowed them to erect a mosque in their quarters at Beejanuggur. He had the koraun placed before him when they came to pay their compliments, that they might salute him without breach of the rules of their religion.

Ibrahim Adil Shaw, by his new regulations, obtained an army of thirty thousand cavalry, but mostly hirelings who rode his horses. The customs of Ismaeel Adil Shaw were totally laid aside, and the publick accounts, which had been kept in Persic, were changed

to

to Hindooeh, under the management of bramins, who soon acquired great influence in the adminiſtration of government. Aſſud Khan was ordered to keep Dekkanees in his ſervice, and follow the ſooni faith. He out of a thouſand foreigners diſcharged ſix hundred; but refuſing to change his religion, in camp and on his own jaghire publickly encouraged the ſheea ceremonies, and the ſultan thought it prudent to wink at his diſobedience. Ibrahim Adil Shaw the year after his acceſſion led his army to Beejanuggur, on the requiſition of the roy; but before the particulars of the expedition are recited, it is neceſſary to diſplay the cauſes which led to it, and give ſome account of the revolutions of Beejanuggur.

The government of Beejanuggur had remained in one family, in uninterrupted ſucceſſion, for ſeven hundred years; when Seoroy dying, was ſucceeded by his ſon, a minor, who did not live long after him, and left the throne to a younger brother. He alſo had not long gathered the flowers of enjoyment from the garden of royalty, before the cruel ſkies, proving their inconſtancy, burned up the earth of his exiſtence with the blaſting wind of annihilation. Being ſucceeded by an infant, only three months old, Heemraaje, one of the principal miniſters of the family, celebrated for great wiſdom and experience, became ſole regent, and was cheerfully obeyed by all the nobility and vaſſals of the kingdom for forty years; though, on the arrival of the young king at the age of manhood, he had poiſoned him, and put an infant of his family on the throne, in order to have a pretence for keeping the regency in his own hands. Heemraaje at his death was ſucceeded in office by his ſon Ramraaje, who having married a daughter of the ſon of Seoroy, by that alliance greatly added to his influence and power. By degrees raiſing his own family to the higheſt ranks, and deſtroying many of the ancient nobility by various intrigues, he at length aſpired to reign in his own name, and totally extirpate the family of Seoroy. Many of the nobility, however, refuſing to acknowledge his authority, he, in

com-

compliance with their prejudices, placed on the throne an infant of the female line, and committed his perfon to the care of his uncle Hoje Termul Roy, who was not without a caft of infanity in his mind, and from whofe weaknefs he apprehended no danger of competition. Ramraaje, in the fpace of five or fix years, by treachery cut off all thofe chiefs who had declared againft his claim to the throne; and, having left the city of Beejanuggur under charge of a flave whom he had raifed to high rank, marched with a great army againft fome roies of the country of Malabar, who had withheld their tributes. Thefe he foon reduced, and deprived them of their fortreffes; after which fuccefs, he moved againft a powerful zemindar to the fouth of Beejanuggur, who held out for fix months without the fmalleft impreffion, though feveral general actions were fought.

Ramraaje, having expended all the treafure of his military cheft, wrote to his flave to fend him a fupply from Beejanuggur, to enable him to continue the war. The flave, on opening the vaults of the treafury, was overcome with the defire of poffeffing fuch immenfe wealth as they contained, and refolved on rebellion againft his patron. He fet at liberty the young roy, and having procured Hoje Termul Roy to embrace his intereft, affumed the office of minifter, and began to levy troops. Several tributary roies, who were difgufted with Ramraaje, flew with fpeed to Beejanuggur to obey their lawful king; and in a fhort time thirty thoufand horfe, and vaft hofts of foot, were affembled under his ftandard at the city; where now, by the advice of Hoje Termul Roy, they put the flave to death, left he fhould repent of his rebellion to Ramraaje.

Ramraaje hearing of this revolt, inftantly patched up a peace with his enemy, and returned towards Beejanuggur; but being deferted by feveral of his firft nobility, who left him on the route to join their lawful fovereign, he thought it advifeable at prefent to defift from war, and reft contented with his extenfive jaghires. A treaty was accordingly

accordingly concluded between him and the young roy, by which he was allowed to remain in independant poffeffion of his country; and quiet being now reftored, the nobility who had fupported the revolution, left their fovereign under the care of his uncle Hoje Termul Roy, and returned to their feveral diftricts. Not long after this, the uncle becoming ambitious of royalty, ftrangled his nephew, and feized the throne of Beejanuggur. As he was of the royal family, the nobility, preferring his authority to that of Ramraaje, as the more honourable, became fubmiffive and obedient; but in a fhort time, as he governed with tyranny and oppreffion, they became difaffected, and invited Ramraaje to return, and take upon him the adminiftration of affairs.

A. D. 1535.

Hoje Termul Roy having intelligence of the defigns forming againft him, difpatched ambaffadors, with a large fum of money and many valuable prefents, to Ibrahim Adil Shaw, begging he would march to his affiftance; in return for which he would acknowledge himfelf his tributary, and pay down a fubfidy of [1] three lacks of oons for every day that his army fhould march. Ibrahim Adil Shaw, tempted by the greatnefs of the offer, and the glory of having the roy of Beejanuggur for a tributary, in the year 942, by advice of Affud Khan, moved from his capital, and arrived at Beejanuggur by regular marches, without oppofition. He was conducted into the city by Hoje Termul Roy, who feated him on the mufnud of the raaje, and made rejoicings for feven days. Ramraaje and the confederate nobility now fent letters to the roy, expreffive of forrow for their rebellion, and affuring him of their future firm allegiance. They reprefented in ftrong colours the evil confequences of the muffulmauns remaining in the country; that their holy places and gods would be defiled and deftroyed, and the children of all ranks of people, as in the times of the Bhamenee fultans, be made captives. They fwore, finally, never more to depart from obedience, if he

[1] Forty thoufand pounds.

he would procure the retreat of the fultan to his own dominions. Hoje Termul Roy, thinking he had now no farther ufe for his allies, requefted the fultan to return, and paid down *fifty lacks of oons, the amount of the fettled fubfidy, befides making prefents to a vaft amount; among them were twelve fine elephants and fome beautiful horfes.

Ibrahim Adil Shaw had not yet recroffed the Kiftnah, when Ramraaje and the confederates, who had bribed many of the troops in the city, broke their newly made vows, and haftened towards Beejanuggur, refolved to put the roy to death, on pretence of revenging the murder of his predeceffor. Hoje Termul Roy, feeing he was betrayed, fhut himfelf up in the palace, and becoming mad from defpair, blinded all the royal elephants and horfes, alfo cutting off their tails, that they might be of no ufe to his enemy. All the diamonds, rubies, emeralds, other precious ftones, and pearls, which had been collected in a courfe of many ages, he crufhed to powder between heavy millftones, and fcattered them on the ground. He then fixed a fword blade into a pillar of his apartment, and ran his breaft upon it with fuch force, that it pierced through and came out at his back; thus putting an end to his exiftence, juft as the gates of the palace were opened to his enemies. Ramraaje now became roy of Beejanuggur without a rival.

Ibrahim Adil Shaw, hearing of this revolution on his arrival at Roijore, difpatched Affud Khan with the greateft part of his army to reduce the important fortrefs of Oodnee, which was on the point of furrender, when Negtadcree, the younger brother of Ramraaje, marched from Beejanuggur with a great army to relieve it. Affud Khan, upon his approach, raifed the fiege and moved towards him. A fharp engagement enfued, and Affud Khan, finding that he was likely to have the worft of the action, from the vaft fuperiority in numbers

* Seventeen hundred thoufand pounds and upwards.

numbers of the enemy, retreated in good order, but was followed fourteen miles by the victors, when he encamped; and Negtaderee, in order to be ready to harafs the retreat the next day, halted in full fecurity at the diftance of only two miles from him. Affud Khan, who had ardently wifhed for fuch an event, towards the dawn of day, with four thoufand chofen horfe, furprized the camp of Negtaderee, whofe felf-confidence had left him wholly off his guard againft fuch a manoeuvre. Affud Khan penetrated to his tents before he received the alarm, and he had fcarce time to make his efcape, leaving his treafures, family, and elephants, to the mercy of the victors. When the day had fully cleared up, Negtaderee collected his fcattered troops, and drew up as if to engage; but feeing Affud Khan refolute to maintain his advantage, and fearing for the perfonal fafety of his wife and children, he declined hazarding a battle, and, retiring fome miles off, fixed his camp; from whence he wrote Ramraaje an account of his difafter, and requefted reinforcements to enable him to repair it. Ramraaje immediately fent fupplies of men and money, openly declaring his intentions of carrying on the war, but privately informed his brother, that he had reafon to imagine Ibrahim Adil Shaw had not been led merely of his own will to befiege Oodnee; that he fufpected the zemindars of that quarter had invited him to make war, and that many of the nobility with him were fecretly in his intereft; therefore, he thought he would act prudently by making peace with the muffulmauns at prefent, and procuring the releafe of his wife and family from Affud Khan. Negtaderee, in confequence of the defires of his brother, having procured the mediation and influence of Affud Khan, addreffed the fultan for peace; which being granted, and all affairs fettled to the fatisfaction of both ftates, Ibrahim Adil Shaw returned to Beejapore, with Affud Khan, and the reft of his nobility and army.

In this expedition, fome malicious perfons told the fultan that Affud Khan had received an immenfe fum of money, befides jewels,

and

and gold and silver plate to a great amount, from Ramraaje, as a present for the release of his prisoners and mediation of the peace. Ibrahim Adil Shaw, instead of being displeased, or coveting the great sum said to have been received, reproved the informers for their dishonourable proceeding; saying, He returned God thanks that he had a servant, whom great kings feared so, as to pay him contributions and wear the collar of his submission on their necks. He then, in presence of the informers, called for Assud Khan, and honoured him with a suit of his own robes, and other distinguishing marks of favour; which confounded his enemies, and for some time prevented their machinations against him.

The sultan having on his return to the capital made Assud Khan prime minister and commander in chief of his armies, added still more to the envy of his enemies, who took all opportunities of hinting to the sultan, that his influence was growing to a dangerous pitch. Though these insinuations had for a long time no effect, yet at length some impression was made by them on the royal mind, and the sultan, in private, expressed his wish to humble the minister. Eusuff, a companion of the sultan's pleasures, thinking this a fit instant to alarm the fears of his master, observed, that Assud Khan, from a similarity of religion, held friendly correspondence with Boorahan Nizam Shaw, to whom he meditated resigning the fort of Balgoan, and becoming his servant. This report alarmed Ibrahim, and he asked his confidant the surest method of ruining his minister. Eusuff advised that he should invite Assud Khan to court from Balgoan, on pretence of the festival of the circumcision of the young prince Ali, when, if he came, it would be easy to confine his person, or reduce his authority. The sultan's water-cooler happened to be present at this consultation, and told it in confidence to his own family, who revealed it to their friends; so that in a short time the sultan's displeasure at the minister became the topic of conversation among all ranks; and Assud Khan became on his guard. When the royal order was sent commanding him to court, he excused himself from attending, on pretence of illness. Attempts were then made to corrupt his servants to poison him, but all in vain; only serving still more to guard him from the effects of treachery. At last it was determined, that Eusuff should have grants of lands in the vicinity of Balgoan, and retire to them with his dependants, to be at hand to seize any favourable opportunity that might offer of surprizing the minister.

Assud Khan, who was experienced and cautious, was not to be deceived by the arts of his enemies. One day, however, he chanced with few attendants to visit a garden-house at some distance from Balgoan, leaving orders for four hundred horse to follow him. A spy of Eusuff's, who was ignorant of this order, hastened to inform his employer that the minister had gone out almost alone, and might with ease be taken prisoner, if he would be speedy in his motions. Eusuff immediately advanced towards the garden, which, to his disappointment, he found surrounded by troops. Seeing however his own force superior, he resolved to effect his design by force; but was shamefully beaten off by Assud Khan, who returned triumphant to Balgoan, with many prisoners.

Ibrahim Adil Shaw pretended that this attack was made without his consent; and to make it so believed, ordered Eusuff to court, and confined him; at the same time writing to Assud Khan that he was much displeased at the imprudent boldness of a mistaken servant, and would punish him in any manner the faithful minister of his kingdoms should desire. Assud Khan, who knew fully the sultan's real wish, sent back a petition, respectfully setting forth, that he himself was the guilty person, and wished to come to court to implore pardon for his faults; but that as his majesty from his gracious disposition had been pleased of his own accord to overlook his transgressions, he was at a loss for words to express a sense of such bounty. He with his
letter

letter sent back all his prisoners, after having presented them with khelauts, and committed to their charge a valuable offering for the sultan.

This disagreement of the sultan and the minister being known through all Dekkan, Nizam Shaw and Ameer Bereed cast their eyes on the dominions of Beejapore, and circulated a report that Assud Khan had promised to deliver up Balgoan, whenever they should approach with an army. In the year 949 they invaded the territories of Ibrahim Adil Shaw, and having wrested the five districts dependant on Sholapore from his officers, gave them up to the servants of Khajeh Jehaun Dekkanee, afterwards moving towards Balgoan. Assud Khan, though he had originally not the least share in the invasion, out of necessity, to save his estates from devastation, joined them on their approach with six thousand horse. The allies, inspired with fresh courage by this success, spread fire and slaughter through the country to the environs of Beejapore; and Ibrahim Adil Shaw not thinking himself able to oppose in the field, retired with his family to Koolburga. A.D. 1542.

Assud Khan, still earnest to serve his prince, though abandoned by him, privately dispatched Ali Mahummud Budukhshi, one of his faithful servants, to Elichpore, the capital of Berar, representing to Ummad Shaw, that from the strange turns of inconstant fortune, and the vicissitudes of chance, an astonishing event had taken place, by which he was confounded in a labyrinth of distress; but that if he would march to the aid of Ibrahim Adil Shaw, he would join him immediately when he should reach the borders of his country. Ummad-Shaw, in compliance with his request, moved without delay towards Koolburga; and Boorahan Nizam Shaw and Ameer Bereed, who were then before the citadel of Beejapore, upon intelligence of his march, raised the siege, after burning the suburbs of the city and laying waste the environs, intending to prevent a junction with Ibrahim

him Adil Shaw. Affud Khan on the route quitted the allies, and
with all his followers joined Ummad Shaw, to whom he reprefented,
that the traitor Eufuff, having filled the mind of his prince with
fufpicions of his loyalty, and Ibrahim liftening implicitly to every
report to his difhonour, the minifters of Boorahan Nizam Shaw had
from political views openly declared, that he had offered to join
their mafter if he would invade Beejapore. Sultan Ibrahim, believing
this, had entertained the higheft difpleafure againft him, removed
him from office, and attempted to deftroy his life by feveral methods.
The enemy, feeing their arts fuccefsful, had invaded the country;
and, neglected by his mifguided fovereign, he was out of felf-pre-
fervation obliged to join them for a time; but that as Ummad Shaw
had come to his affiftance, he threw himfelf on his protection, to
clear him if poffible from the accufations of his enemies in the eyes of
fultan Ibrahim : but if that could not be effected, he declared he
would refignedly fubmit to any punifhment he fhould decree for his
involuntary offences.

Ummad Shaw, convinced of the integrity of Affud Khan, conducted him the fame day to fultan Ibrahim ; to whom he foon made
clear the error he had been guilty of in liftening to the enemies of his
faithful minifter. Ibrahim Adil Shaw clafped Affud Khan in his
embrace, expreffing forrow for his ill-ufage ; and to convince him of
his fincerity, imprifoned Eufuff and his creatures, who had abufed
his confidence, beftowing the traitor's eftates on Ein al Moolk Canaanee, an officer of diftinction, whom Affud Khan had prevailed upon
to quit the fervice of Ameer Bereed. This reconciliation foon
changed the ftate of affairs. Ibrahim with Ummad Shaw marched
to give the allies battle, but they retreated with expedition towards
Dowlutabad and Ballagaut. The fultan followed them, and took
ample revenge for the depredations on his country, by burning and
deftroying the territories of his enemies. Ameer Bereed dying at
Ballagaut, Boorahan Nizam Shaw was reduced to beg for peace, and
the

the venerable Shaw Tahir was sent as his ambassador to obtain terms. It was agreed, that the five diſtricts ſhould be reſtored to Ibrahim Adil Shaw, and that Boorahan Nizam Shaw ſhould not again invade his dominions. The treaty being ſigned, and exchanges made, the ſovereigns returned to their ſeveral capitals.

The following year, 950, Ibrahim Adil Shaw married the daughter of Alla ad Dien Ummad Shaw, named Rabieh Sultana, and the nuptials were celebrated with royal magnificence. Boorahan Nizam Shaw, jealous of his military reputation, and vexed at his late defeat, could enjoy no repoſe till he recovered the pergunnahs he had been obliged to cede to Beejapore. On ſome diſguſts breaking out between Ibrahim Adil Shaw and Ummad Shaw, he found opportunity of executing his deſigns; and having formed alliances with Ramraaje and Jumſheed Koottub Shaw, marched with his own army and the troops of Ali Bereed and Khajeh Jehaun to the borders of Beejapore. He laid waſte many diſtricts, and ſeveral times defeated the army ſent to oppoſe his progreſs. Jumſheed Koottub Shaw entered the country by another road, and ſeized the diſtrict of Kaknee, in which he built a ſtrong fort, poſſeſſed himſelf of all the pergunnahs to the walls of Koolburga, and laid ſiege to the fortreſs of Angeer, near the city of Saugher. Ramraaje ſent his brother Negtaderee with a great army to reduce the fort of Roijore; ſo that Beejapore, attacked at the ſame time by three powerful princes in ſeparate quarters, was full of danger and diſorder.

A.D. 1543.

Ibrahim Adil Shaw was at a loſs how to act; and no opinion of his counſellors ſatisfying him, he at length called Aſſud Khan from Balgoan to his preſence, and demanded his advice on the alarming criſis of affairs. Aſſud Khan replied by obſerving, that Boorahan Nizam Shaw was the true enemy, who had prevailed on the reſt to commit hoſtilities, and if he could be removed, it would be eaſy to manage the others. He adviſed, that peace ſhould be made with him

by

by refigning the five diftricts dependant on Sholapore, and that ambaffadors fhould be fent to Ramraaje with letters and prefents to procure his friendfhip; obferving, that fmall conceffions would obtain his forbearance from war, as his own country, Carnatic, was not yet fully fettled, many roies being in a ftate of rebellion; that when free from the attacks of thefe two great powers, he would take the chaftifement of Koottub Shaw upon himfelf, and, by the royal aufpices, in a little time recover all the places he had taken from Beejapore fo unjuftly.

Ibrahim Adil Shaw, lending the ear of confent to this advice, acted according to it, and found every point turned out as the prudent minifter had foretold. When peace was concluded with Boorahan Nizam Shaw and Ramraaje, Affud Khan marched againft Jumfheed Koottub Shaw, took the newly erected fort of Kaknee in three months by ftorm, and levelled it with the ground. He then moved towards Angeer, but Koottub Shaw raifed the fiege on his approach; and, not thinking it prudent to hazard an engagement, retreated to his own dominions. Affud Khan followed him clofe to the walls of his capital, Golconda, when Jumfheed gave him battle, but was defeated in a very fevere action, himfelf receiving a wound in his cheek from Affud Khan as they fought, without being known to each other, hand to hand. Affud Khan after a glorious campaign returned triumphant to Beejapore, where he was received by the fultan, who regarded him as his deliverer, with the higheft honours.

Some little time after this, Boorahan Nizam Shaw, at the inftigation of Ramraaje, moved again to reduce Koolburga, and Ibrahim Adil Shaw marched from Beejapore to oppofe him. Upon his arrival near the town of Oorjaan, he found Nizam Shaw ftrongly pofted on the oppofite bank of the river Beemrah; and feeing it impoffible to crofs, the fultan encamped on this fide. Both armies lay inactive during three months of the rains, in fight of each other,

with

with the river between them. At length, Ibrahim Adil Shaw, tired of delay, found means to cross, and a general action ensued immediately, in which Nizam Shaw was totally routed with very great loss; leaving two hundred and fifty elephants, seventy pieces of cannon, and other appendages of royalty, to the victors. Ibrahim Adil Shaw in this battle fought personally with the greatest bravery, killing three antagonists with his own hand; but he attributed his victory to the conduct of Assud Khan, on whom he conferred several districts in addition to his jaghire.

The sultan, puffed up by vain glory, after this victory growing haughty and imperious, treated the ambassadors of Nizam Shaw in a contemptuous manner, and behaved tyrannically to his own subjects, putting to death many, and severely punishing others of his principal nobility, for slight offences, which occasioned disaffection to his government. Boorahan Nizam Shaw taking advantage of the dissentions, again invaded his dominions, and defeated him in two general engagements in the space of six months, taking many elephants, and committing such ravages as threatened the very existence of his government. Ibrahim, thinking his losses were occasioned by the disaffection of his amras and the bramins at the head of civil affairs, put to death forty Hindoos and seventy mussulmauns of rank, in the space of two months, on mere suspicion; so lighting up the flames of severity, that high and low about his court were terrified and dismayed, living in constant apprehension for their safety. At last, numbers reduced to despair, formed a conspiracy to dethrone the sultan, and place his brother Abdoolla in his room. One of the conspirators, in hopes of great rewards, betrayed the plot to Ibrahim, who put him to death, with most of those against whom he had informed. His brother, sultan Abdoolla, with much difficulty made his escape to Goa, where he was honourably received by the Portuguese, who afforded him protection. The sultan, enraged at his flight, punished all the bramin spies with various tortures, in the great square of Beejapore, till they expired in agony. Having again entertained suspicions of the fidelity of Assud Khan, he neglected him so much, that the old minister was seized with grief, and for self-protection took up his residence at Balgoan, from whence he sent a confidential friend, with an offering of nine elephants, nine horses, and many valuable curiosities, with the following letter to the sultan.

### VERSE.

"Why, Ah! why art thou thus estranged from me? What have
" I done, what hast thou heard, what hast thou seen of me?

" If I have committed a fault, to my head the sabre and the
" shroud! But to vex a friend is not generous.

" I know not the causes of this unkindness, nor what can have
" occasioned such great coldness.

" Whatever crimes interested persons may at the most glorious
" audience of the sultan have attributed to the charge of this loyal
" slave, I acknowledge an hundred in place of one; but I know not
" their accusations; and, like the * wolf of Eusuff unseen, am inno-
" cent of their forgeries. I never passed them from my tongue, nor
" conceived them in my mind; such ideas have no place in the
" conception of the slave.

" The reason of the delay of the humblest of slaves in his for-
" tress, and not coming to the court glorious as the sun, is to pre-
" vent the injuries of his enemies; who, in the august presence,
" represent the purity of his intentions and sincerity of attachment in
" the most unfaithful manner. Drawing the stains of disaffection
" over the face of his behaviour, they have made the peaceful recess
" of

---

* Alluding to the patriarch's falsely accusing the beast of destroying Joseph.

" of the king's heart a cell of forrow, nay, a mine of fire. Some-
" times accufing the faithful flave of treachery, they diminifh the
" purple glow of his chearfulnefs; and fometimes mixing the pure
" gold of his loyalty with fufpicious alloy, melt him in the torment-
" ing crucible of grief and forrow.

" If the unreftraining kindnefs of the king of kings compaffion-
" ates my fituation, and the aufpicious hint fhould be iffued for the
" difgrace and fhame of my enemies, I will at the end of a month,
" when the rains fhall be concluded, haften to kifs the feet of the
" throne of illuftrious royalty. In one month, with prefents and
" offerings, I will haften glad and rejoicing to the court."

Ibrahim Adil Shaw, moved by the above letter from Afiud Khan, having treated his family with many marks of favour, was going to fend them to Balgoan, when fuddenly the rebellion of the prince Abdoolla breaking out, his miftruft of the minifter was renewed, and his favourable intentions towards him laid afide.

Sultan Abdoolla, after his efcape to Goa from the cruelties of his brother, by the advice of many of the nobility of Beejapore, entered into a correfpondence with Boorahan Nizam Shaw and Jumfheed Koottub Shaw, in hopes of obtaining their fupport of his caufe. Thefe princes, feeing the confufed ftate of affairs at Beejapore, and the difguft of Affud Khan, joined in promifes to place him on the throne; and wrote the Portuguefe of Goa, that from the cruelties and tyranny of Ibrahim Adil Shaw fuch troubles muft foon break out in his government, as he could by no means overcome or extinguifh; therefore they wifhed the prince Abdoolla might be fent to them, as they intended feating him on the throne of Beejapore. The Portuguefe agreed to join in promoting their views, but obferved, they could only fucceed by the co-operation of Affud Khan.

Boorahan

Boorahan Nizam Shaw, on receipt of this anſwer, diſpatched one of his principal bramins to Aſſud Khan, to prevail on him to join in the plan; but that faithful miniſter, ſtarting with horror at the idea of diſloyalty, told the bramin indignantly, that but for the laws of nations which forbid the killing ambaſſadors, he would put him to death; commanding him, if he regarded his ſafety, to depart inſtantly from the reach of his authority, leſt reſentment ſhould get the better of his paſſions, and make him offend againſt the rules of policy. The bramin returned with haſte to Nizam Shaw, but the Portugueſe ſeeing that all the powers of Dekkan, excepting Aſſud Khan, were joined to ſupport Abdoolla, marched with him from Goa, and he aſſumed the royal titles. Almoſt all the nobility of Beejapore were preparing to deſert ſultan Ibrahim, and come over to him, when an accident changed the face of affairs. Aſſud Khan being taken very ill, Boorahan Nizam Shaw, ſuppoſing he might die, caſt the eye of avidity on the fort of Balgoan, and inſtead of marching to Beejapore with ſultan Abdoolla, which would have enſured him acceſſion to the throne, halted at Mirch, to carry on his own deſigns. He ſent his bramin again to Balgoan, with a vaſt ſum of money to corrupt the ſoldiers of the garriſon to give it up to him, in caſe Aſſud Khan ſhould die. The bramin had nearly ſucceeded in his commiſſion when the plot was diſcovered by Aſſud Khan, who put him to death, together with ſeventy of the ſoldiers whom he had bribed to give up the fort to his employer. The nobility of Beejapore upon this event, fully convinced that the old miniſter had no ſhare in the rebellion of Abdoolla, returned to their allegiance to Ibrahim Adil Shaw; and the other adherents of the rebel prince began to fall off daily.

The diſorder of Aſſud Khan continuing, and old age rendering nature too weak to ſtruggle againſt it, he prepared to meet death, and entreated ſultan Ibrahim to honour him with a farewell viſit in the following verſes:

" Haſte

"Hafte, like the morning breeze, to the garden of friendfhip;
"Come, like the fportive cyprefs, to the parterre."

Sultan Ibrahim thinking it advifeable to comply with his requeft, in the month of Mohirrim, 956, marched expeditioufly towards Balgoan; but when he had paffed Sikkree received accounts of his death. The fultan, arriving the fame night at Balgoan, comforted his mourning family with khelauts, and affurances of royal favour, but all his eftates and treafures he took for his own ufe. The Portuguefe marched back to Goa with fultan Abdoolla, and the other allies thought proper to retreat to their own dominions.

A.D. 1549.

Affud Khan was famed for his judgment and wifdom, and in his conduct of the important affairs of government during the reign of Ifmaeel Adil Shaw, he juftly exalted the ftandard of celebrity. For near forty years he was the patron and protector of the nobles and diftinguifhed of Dekkan. He lived in the higheft refpect and efteem, with a magnificence and grandeur furpaffing all his cotemporary nobility. The fovereigns of Beejanuggur and every country obferving a refpect to his great abilities, frequently honoured him with letters and valuable prefents. His houfehold fervants, Georgians, Circaffians, Hindoos, and Abyffinians, amounted to two hundred and fifty. He had fixty of the largeft elephants, and one hundred and fifty of a fmaller fize. In his ftables he had four hundred horfes of Arabia and Perfia, exclufive of thofe of mixed breed foaled in India. His treafures and effects were beyond amount. In his kitchen were every day expended [2] one hundred maunds of rice, Dekkan weight, fifty sheep, and one hundred fowls; from whence the expenditure of other articles may be judged. He invented a robe of cloth of gold, and a dagger, which have been ever fince worn by perfons of rank in Dekkan; and was the firft perfon who ufed the mode of riding elephants with a bridle, and managing them without

[2] Eight thoufand pounds weight.

without the kujjuk, or goad; but as thofe animals have frequently fudden ftarts of vice, this mode of guiding them has not been much followed. Ibrahim Adil Shaw, agreeably to his laft will, gave his daughter Mataab Bibi in marriage to Ali Bereed Shaw, with whom he fought an alliance.

Boorahan Nizam Shaw, foon after the death of Affud Khan, having fent ambaffadors to Ramraaje, prefents and profeffions of regard were interchanged between them; upon hearing of which, Ibrahim Adil Shaw treated the ambaffadors of the latter who were with him at Beejapore with great flight, and they returned abruptly without taking leave, to Beejanuggur, where they avowed to Ramraaje, that fultan Ibrahim, out of refentment to his alliance with Nizam Shaw, had they not made their efcape, would have put them to death. Ramraaje, enraged at this affront, wrote to Nizam Shaw, that as Ali Bereed had preferred to his alliance that of fultan Ibrahim, it would be prudent to take from him the fortrefs of Kallean in revenge for his defertion.

Boorahan Nizam Shaw without delay moved from Ahmednuggur with a great army, and, furrounding Kallean, effectually blocked up all communication from without. Ibrahim Adil Shaw marched to relieve it; and advancing within fight of the enemy, pitched his camp, round which he threw up a mud wall, not chufing to offer battle. As Nizam Shaw would not raife the fiege, he alfo fortified his camp. Sultan Ibrahim now ordered his [a] Bergee officers, who were very expert in predatory excurfions, to ftop up the roads, and prevent all fupplies of grain and forage from going to the enemy. His orders were fo well executed, that a famine foon prevailed in the camp of Boorahan Nizam Shaw, fo that in the month of [b] Ramazan, the king and his army, the believers and Hindoos, all fafted alike
from

---

[a] A term given to the Mharattas.
[b] The month of fafting among the muffulmauns.

from abfolute neceffity. Nizam Shaw in this diftrefs confulted his generals and nobility, fome of whom advifed raifing the fiege and retreating to Ahmednuggur, and others, making peace with Ibrahim Adil Shaw; but Shaw Jaffier and Cafim Beg gave their opinions for offering battle to the enemy, and Nizam Shaw approved their counfel. Accordingly, Syef ad Dien Ein al Moolk, with other amras, on the morning of the *Eeed al Fitter, at dawn of day, furprized the camp of Ibrahim Adil Shaw, whofe troops were off their guard, and employed in preparing for the feftival. The fultan, who was then in the warm bath, had fcarce time to make his efcape; and his troops fled in fuch confufion, that all the tents, baggage, and artillery, were left to the poffeffion of the victors. Nizam Shaw, elated by his fuccefs, affaulted the fort of Kallean, and the garrifon, alarmed at the defeat of their friends, laid down their arms, and furrendered without attempting any oppofition.

Ibrahim Adil Shaw after his defeat, in order to fave his own territories from devaftation, invaded the enemy's country; and coming fuddenly before Porundeh, finding the gates open, rufhed with a large body of troops into the fortrefs, which fubmitted, and was given in charge to one of his Dekkanee amras. He then laid wafte the country round, and having collected contributions, upon advice that Nizam Shaw was approaching, retreated towards Beejapore. Nizam Shaw marched to recover Porundeh; but before he had arrived within many miles, the cowardly governor, being alarmed, without acquainting any one of his defign, fled by night, and his followers the next morning imitated the example of their chief. The third day after, the empty fortrefs was taken poffeffion of by the former mafters.

Ibrahim Adil Shaw put the cowardly Dekkanee to death on his arrival at Beejapore, and began to make preparation to retake the fort

* Feftival of concluding the great faft.

fort of Kallean. Boorahan Nizam Shaw, upon advice of his defigns, fent ambafladors to Ramraaje, who agreed to meet him near Roijore, when they might form a plan for their mutual operations in the war. Ramraaje, agreeable to his promife in the year 959, moved with a confiderable force to the place appointed for an interview, and Nizam Shaw meeting him, it was refolved, that the former fhould have Mudkul and Roijore, and the latter the city and dependancies of Sholapore. The allies laid fiege to Roijore without delay; and upon its being taken, the garrifon of Mudkul furrendered the keys to Ramraaje, without making any oppofition; and he, having left his younger brother with an army to affift Nizam Shaw in the reduction of Sholapore, returned to Beejanuggur. Nizam Shaw took the place in a fhort time, and having ftrengthened it, returned to Ahmednuggur.

A.D. 1551.

Upon the death of Boorahan Nizam Shaw, a peace was eftablifhed between his fucceffor fultan Houffein and Ibrahim Adil Shaw, who had a friendly meeting on their borders, and parted much fatisfied with each other; but this good underftanding did not laft long, and agreement was changed to war. Khajeh Jehaun Dekkanee, who had fled to avoid the refentment of his fovereign Houffein Shaw, coming to Beejapore, infpired fultan Ibrahim with the defire of retaking Sholapore; and for this purpofe he concluded treaties of friendfhip with Ramraaje, and invited into his fervice Syef Ein al Moolk, commander in chief to the late Nizam Shaw, who had taken refuge in Berar from the oppreffions of his fucceffor. His offers were accepted by that general, and the fultan conferred upon him high titles, with confiderable jaghires, and an immediate prefent of money. By his advice he foon after fpread the umbrella of royalty over the head of Shaw Ali, fon of Boorahan Shaw, who had taken refuge at his court; intending, firft to feat him on the throne of Ahmednuggur, and then to poflefs himfelf of Kallean and Sholapore, in reparation of his former defeats and loffes. He firft fent Shaw Ali, with two thoufand thousand horse that had joined him from Ahmednuggur, to attempt drawing over the nobility of that kingdom to his cause, but with little success; and Houssein Nizam Shaw having put his army in motion, sultan Ibrahim marched from Beejapore, after distributing large sums among his forces by way of encouragement.

Both armies met in the plains of Sholapore, and drew up to engage. Ibrahim gave the command of his right wing to Syef al Moolk Canaanee and Ankufs Khan, and that of the left to Noor Khan and Immaam al Moolk; himself taking post with the household troops in the center. The herawul, or advanced line, was commanded by Syef Ein al Moolk, who began the action with great impetuosity; but sultan Ibrahim disapproving his separation so far from the main body, signified, that on the day of battle the herawul should remain nearer the army, in order sooner to receive support, if necessary. The general returned for answer, that his majesty's observation was very just; but that as he had advanced so far, to return would only give spirits to the enemy. When he had said this, he pushed on to the charge; and on the first onset seized the enemy's cannon, which he spiked up, and drove the enemy's herawul back on their main body: by this he was resolutely opposed, Houssein Shaw commanding in person. Many hundreds were slain, the army of Nizam Shaw began to give way, and must have been inevitably defeated, had the gallantry of Syef Ein al Moolk met with the smallest support. At this crisis, several amras who had been repulsed from the left of Ibrahim Adil Shaw advanced to the assistance of their sovereign, and almost surrounded Syef Ein al Moolk; who now in his turn began to be confused; but seeing the umbrella and standards of sultan Ibrahim, he, as was always his custom on desperate occasions, dismounted from his horse, resolved to conquer or die. Some weak people who saw him dismount, told the sultan, that Syef Ein al Moolk, having gone over to the enemy for a bribe, had just alighted to pay his compliments to Houssein Nizam Shaw. Ibrahim Adil Shaw, who

who upon his firſt advancing had entertained ſuſpicions of the general's fidelity, was now convinced of their truth, and without an inſtant's delay fled from the field, and did not ſtop till he reached Beejapore. Syef Ein al Moolk, ſeeing the rout of the king, nobly fought his way through the enemy with great loſs, and, upon his arrival near the city, ſent word reſpectfully to the ſultan, that he had loſt all his baggage, and was without tents or any covering for himſelf or miſerable followers; therefore he begged an advance of money from the treaſury, to enable him to repair his loſſes and come to the preſence in a proper manner. The ſultan, who regarded his defeat as owing to his firſt diſobedience of orders, replied, that he wanted not ſuch inattentive and obſtinate ſervants as himſelf, and that he might provide for himſelf wherever he could. Syef Ein al Moolk, who could not accuſe himſelf of any crime, was overwhelmed with aſtoniſhment, and ſent back his meſſenger to repreſent to the ſultan, that he had ſerved him to the danger of his life with unſhaken fidelity, and ſacrificed five hundred brave relations and friends in the battle for his majeſty; that in his preſent miſerable ſituation he could not move, had no other refuge but his threſhold, and no other place where to lay his head; that he was his ſlave, and could not move to any other court. The ſultan imagining there was ſomewhat of inſolence in the latter part of the meſſage, ordered the bearer of it to be beaten and turned out of the preſence.

Syef Ein al Moolk now deſpairing of aſſiſtance from the ſultan, had recourſe to the advice of his friends how to proceed. They propoſed his going to his jaghire, and raiſing the collections of the autumn harveſt, then juſt ripe; after which, ſhould the ſultan ſend a force to expel him, he might retire wherever he ſhould ſee beſt. Ein al Moolk, approving the plan, marched from Beejapore to the diſtricts of Maan, and collecting the revenues, divided them among his followers. Ibrahim Adil Shaw ſoon after ſent one of his amras with five thouſand horſe to expel him from the country; but the

royaliſts

royalists were defeated; and Ein al Moolk from this success being grown bolder, collected the revenues of many districts, as Malweh, Mirch, and some others. The sultan upon this, detached against him ten thousand horse and foot, under command of Beafs Koolli and Dillawer Khan Hubshee, who were also defeated; and so many elephants and horses, with such a quantity of valuable baggage, fell into the hands of the rebels, that Ein al Moolk, becoming formidable, extended his views to establish himself in the country as an independant chief, for which purpose he began to levy additional troops.

Ibrahim Adil Shaw thought proper now to march against the rebel in person, at the head of five thousand chosen horse, three thousand foot, and a great train of artillery. Ein al Moolk encamped on the river of Maan; and the sultan arriving, remained some days on the opposite bank without attacking him; which encouraged the rebel, who now resolved not to leave the country without fighting, and for three days together advanced towards the sultan's camp, as if to engage, but as often retreating; and the royal army remained under arms each day from dawn till sunset, expecting the attack. On the fourth day, Syef Ein al Moolk also put his troops in motion; but the royal army, supposing that his design was only to parade, as on the preceding days, neglected to make preparations, only keeping up the common guards of the camp. At length, the enemy's standard appearing in sight, Ibrahim Adil Shaw drawing up his troops in great haste and irregularity, moved out of the camp to give battle. Ein al Moolk, averse from engaging the sultan in person, consulted with his friends; observing, that it was treacherous to fight against the royal umbrella; to which all assented, except Mortiza Khan Anjoo, who remarked, that the umbrella did not fight, therefore there was no danger of shedding royal blood. Ein al Moolk, pleased with this casuistry, altered his mind, and without delay charged the royal army; and attacking the center, where sultan Ibrahim was posted.

posted, pressed so vigorously that it was soon disordered, and the sultan fled; upon which his whole line broke, and the victory was decided in favour of Ein al Moolk, who seized the royal umbrella, elephants, artillery, and other insignia of empire, besides all the tents and baggage. The sultan shut himself up in the citadel of Beejapore; and so great was the alarm of the people on this defeat, that the ruin of the royal family was pronounced to be inevitable. Syef Ein al Moolk followed his success, and came before Beejapore, where he for several days assaulted various parts of the city, and endeavoured to cut off all supplies of provisions from the inhabitants.

In this exigence, Ibrahim Adil Shaw applied to Ramraaje for assistance against the rebels, sending him a present of a large sum; upon which, that roy dispatched his brother Negtaderee with a great force to expel the enemy. Syef Ein al Moolk, imitating Assud Khan, resolved to surprize the infidels; but Negtaderee having intelligence of his designs, ordered his troops to be on their guard; and having procured long faggots, with cloth steeped in oil bound round one end of each, commanded his followers upon the alarm being given to light them, and, holding them up as high as possible, give the troops a full sight of the enemy. Ein al Moolk, agreeably to his intentions, having one night chosen two thousand men for the purpose, marched with Sullabut Khan to the enemy's camp, which he was allowed to enter unmolested; but upon a signal given, all the brands were instantly lighted up, and Negtaderee, who was prepared with his troops, rushed upon the surprizers, who expected no resistance, with such success, that above five hundred of them were killed before the detachment could clear the camp. Ein al Moolk and Sullabut with the greatest difficulty made their escape; but losing the road through the darkness of the night, a report spread in his camp on the return of some of the fugitives, that he was killed; and his troops being immediately struck with a panic, separated, and fled to different quarters. Ein al Moolk and Sullabut Khan, with two hundred

dred horfe, about daylight arriving at their ground, and feeing it deferted, fled in confufion by the route of Maan to the dominions of Nizam Shaw, where they fought protection, but were bafely affaffinated by his treachery; the particulars of which will appear in their proper place, in the hiftory of that dynafty.

Ibrahim Adil Shaw, foon after the reftoration of his affairs, from hard drinking and promifcuous amours with women of pleafure, was afflicted with a complication of diforders. During his illnefs he put to death feveral phyficians who had failed in cure, beheading fome, and treading others to death by elephants; fo that all the furviving medical practitioners, alarmed, fled from his dominions. At length, he departed this life, in the year 965, and was buried at Kookee, A.D. 1557, near his father and grandfather, after a reign of twenty four years and fome months. He left behind him two fons and two daughters.

SULTAN

# SULTAN

# ABOU AL MUZZUFFIR ALI

# ADIL SHAW BEEJAPOREE.

SULTAN Ali Adil Shaw, from his childhood, was remarkable for his ready wit and various accomplifhments. When he had but juft entered into youth, his father, fultan Ibrahim, one day in his prefence praifed God who had given him grace to quit the heretical opinions of his father and grandfather, and embrace the orthodox religion. The prince humouroufly remarked, that as the fultan had thought it proper to quit the faith of his parents, it was incumbent upon all children to follow fo excellent an example. The fultan, being difpleafed at this repartee, afked his fon what fect he followed; to which the prince replied, that at prefent he was of the fame opinion with his majefty, but hereafter God muft direct him. Sultan Ibrahim from this anfwer guefling him inclined to the fheea faith, difgraced his preceptor, Khajeh Einaiut Oolla Sheerazee, and in a few days after put him to death by the fentence of the divines of the fooni; and appointed Moolla Fatteh Oolla Sheerazee preceptor to his fon. This learned man was fecretly a fheea, though for his own fafety he outwardly profeffed the doctrines of Hunnefi; fo that he was much efteemed by his pupil. Not long after this, a party of the nobility having entered into the fchemes of Boorahan Nizam Shaw, propofed bribing the clerk of the kitchen to poifon fultan Ibrahim, to feat his

brother

brother Abdoolla on the throne, and reftore the publick exercife of the fheea faith. The clerk of the kitchen, who had at firft favoured the defign, no fooner heard the intention of changing the religion eftablifhed, of which he was a ftrict follower, than he revealed the plot to the fultan, who put all the confpirators to death, but his brother efcaped to the port of Goa. Ibrahim now became fufpicious of his fon, and fent him with his tutor to the fortrefs of Mirch, giving ftrict orders to the governor Secunder Khan to watch him clofely, and prevent any perfons of the fheea fect from approaching his perfon, or their doctrines to be mentioned in his prefence. It happened, however, that the governor and his fon in law, Kamil Khan Dekkanee, were privately fheeas; fo that inftead of obferving the orders of the fultan, they attached themfelves firmly to the prince, endeavouring to acquire his good opinion by indulgence. When the fultan was taken ill, and his end appeared nigh, the prince frequently afcending the pulpit in a mofque, read the prayers after the ritual of the fheeas, and fometimes Kamil Khan officiated. This behaviour coming to the knowledge of the fultan, he refolved to appoint his younger fon, Thamafp, to the fucceffion; but learning that he was by far a more zealous fheea than his brother, he was enraged againft him, and committed him to confinement in the fortrefs of Balgoan. He then faid he fhould leave the fucceffion to be determined by the decrees of providence, and the minifters of government to elect either of the princes they might chufe for their fovereign.

When the life of Ibrahim Adil Shaw was defpaired of, Mahummud Kifhwer Khan, governor of the diftricts of Bikree, Balgoan, and Roibaugh, of great wealth and influence, moved towards the fort of Mirch, reprefenting to Secunder Khan, who commanded that garrifon, that as the fultan's end was approaching, it was probable that many officers of the court and jaghiredaurs would embrace the caufe of fultan Thamafp, and raife diffentions in the ftate; therefore it would be prudent to fpread the umbrella of royalty over the

head

head of prince Ali immediately, and let him encamp under the walls of Mirch, that the people might join his ſtandard, and he be able to move to Beejapore without delay on the death of his father. Secunder Khan, approving this precaution, inveſted ſultan Ali with the inſignia of royalty, and ſent his ſon in law, Kamil Khan, to attend him out of the fort. He was immediately joined by Kiſhwer Khan, who preſented him with a large ſum of money, and was honoured with the khelaut of commander in chief, and Kamil Khan Dekkanee was alſo raiſed to the rank of nobility. The news of the prince's operations ſpreading abroad, the troops repaired to his ſtandard from various quarters, and many of the nobility of the court, with the body guards, quitted Beejapore, and haſtened to pay their compliments. Upon the death of Ibrahim Adil Shaw, ſultan Ali without delay moved towards the capital, and was met on the route by all the officers of the court, with the inſignia of royalty belonging to his father, which they laid at the feet of their ſovereign. On his arrival within two miles of the city, he aſcended the throne in the garden of Kiſhwer Khan. All the ſyeds and learned men pronounced prayers for his ſucceſs, and the nobility and officers, raiſing their voices in congratulation, preſented offerings. The ſultan gave orders for a town to be erected near the place, to commemorate his acceſſion; which was ſoon built, and called Shawpore. His attention to the flouriſhing ſtate of religion he gave immediate proofs of, by iſſuing orders for the khootbah to be read through all his dominions in the name of the Imaums, as during the reign of his grandfather. He ordered forty perſons to be employed in his train as criers, to utter curſes againſt and abuſe the Sahabeh, agreeably to the ceremonies of the ſheea ſect; which was accordingly done in the moſques, at the publick audiences, and whenever the ſultan appeared abroad. As juſtice is a treaſure, which encreaſes by expenditure, and a building which fire cannot burn, nor the engines of viciſſitude deſtroy, the ſultan, by his attention to equity, became enrolled among the juſt monarchs; paying ſuch regard to the caſe and rights of the ſubject,

that

that the revenues of his dominions were encreafed, and the circle of his kingdom greatly extended.

In the firft year of his reign, as he was eager to recover the forts of Kallean and Sholapore, which had fallen into the poffeffion of Nizam Shaw, without waiting for the cuftomary compliment of ambaffadors from the furrounding powers to congratulate his acceffion, he difpatched Kifhwer Khan and Shaw Abou Teraab Sheerazee to negotiate a treaty of alliance at Beejanuggur; at the fame time fending Mahummud Houffein Suddeekee for the fame purpofe to Ahmednuggur. Ramraaje received the ambaffadors with proper honours, and fent back one of his confidential officers with Kifhwer Khan, to congratulate the fultan's acceffion; but Nizam Shaw, who was jealous of the defigns of Ali Adil Shaw, did not fhew the proper compliments to his embaffy, nor fend any in return, but gave ftrong marks of difguft and enmity. Ali Adil Shaw, who was intent on extricating his dominions from the loffes of his father by alliance with Ramraaje, on the death of a fon of that monarch, with uncommon prudence and refolution went, attended by one hundred horfe, to Beejanuggur, to offer his condolance on the melancholy occafion. Ramraaje received him with the greateft refpect, and the fultan with the kindeft perfuafions prevailed upon him to lay afide his mourning. The wife of Ramraaje adopted the fultan as her fon, and at the end of three days, which were fpent in interchanges of friendly profeffions, he took his leave; but as Ramraaje did not attend him out of the city, he was difgufted, and treafured up the affront in his mind, though too prudent to fhew any figns of difpleafure for the prefent.

Ali Adil Shaw, on his return from Beejanuggur finding that the enmity of Houffein Nizam Shaw was daily encreafing, intimated to him that it was clear to the whole world, that the forts of Kallean and Sholapore belonged to his family by ancient right, though, owing to the misfortunes of his father, they had paffed into that of

Nizam Shaw; but that now he hoped they would be restored, or at least the former, from considerations of regard. Shaw Houssein Anjoo, though he used every argument, could not prevail on Nizam Shaw to give up either place to remove the causes of contention; so that the flames of enmity every day blazed higher. At length Ali Adil Shaw sent another ambassador to Ahmednuggur, representing, that passion and neglect in matters of such importance did not become great kings; therefore, to prevent ill consequences, Nizam Shaw must give up the forts, when agreement and friendship would encrease between their states; but if not, he might expect the march of an army into his dominions, which should be laid waste without mercy.

Houssein Nizam Shaw, inflamed by this message, sent back a reply so indecent in expression as to be unfit to relate; which encreased the anger of Ali Adil Shaw, who without delay changing the colour of his umbrella and standard from yellow to green, the colour of Nizam Shaw, by way of defiance, according to the custom of Dekkan, challenged him to come and reclaim his honour.

A. D. 1558.    In the year 966, Ali Adil Shaw having called Ramraaje to his assistance, they in concert invaded the dominions of Houssein Nizam Shaw, and laid them waste in such a manner, that from Porundeh to Khiber, and from Ahmednuggur to Dowlutabad, not a mark of population was to be seen. The infidels of Beejanuggur, who for many years had been wishing for such an event, left no cruelty unpractised. They insulted the honour of the mussulmaun women, destroyed the mosques, and did not respect even the sacred koraun. Houssein Nizam Shaw, by the advice of Casim Beg Hakeem, Shaw Jaffier, and other ministers, declining any opposition in the field, retired to Puttan, and after some time purchased his peace by giving up Kallean to Ali Adil Shaw; but the enemy had no sooner retired from his dominions, than he entered into alliance with Ibrahim

Koottub

Koottub Shaw, and marched in conjunction with him to retake the fort he had juſt ſurrendered. Ali Adil Shaw, upon receiving intelligence of the league againſt him, diſpatched Kiſhwer Khan and Abou Teraab to Beejanuggur, to demand aid from Ramraaje; and alſo invited Ali Bereed to enter into alliance. Ramraaje, who knew the abilities of the ſultan, judging that ſhould he refuſe his aſſiſtance, he would make peace with the muſſulmaun powers, and attempt the recovery of Mudkul and Roijore, marched to join him with fifty thouſand horſe and a great army of foot. The allies met on the banks of the Kiſtnah, and moved immediately towards Kallean, which was then beſieged by the united armies of Nizam Shaw and Koottub Shawee.

Ibrahim Koottub Shaw, according to his uſual mode of embracing the ſtrongeſt party, quitted his ally, and came over ſuddenly to Ali Adil Shaw; upon which Nizam Shaw without delay retreated to Ahmednuggur; but as the allies followed him with the utmoſt expedition to that city, he did not think proper to remain; and having thrown a reinforcement and ſupplies into the citadel, retired to the town of Khiber. The three ſovereigns laid ſiege to Ahmednuggur, and diſpatched detachments various ways to lay waſte the country round. The Hindoos of Beejanuggur committed the moſt outrageous devaſtations, burning and razing the buildings, putting up their horſes in the moſques, and performing their idolatrous worſhip in the holy places; but, notwithſtanding the ſiege was puſhed with the greateſt vigour, the garriſon held out with reſolution, hoping, that at the approach of the rainy ſeaſon, the enemy would be neceſſitated to raiſe the ſiege.

When the rains had ſet in, from the floods, damp, and want of proviſions, diſtreſs began to prevail in the camp of the allies, and Koottub Shaw alſo ſecretly correſponded with the beſieged, to whom he privately ſent in grain. Ali Adil Shaw, ſuſpecting the cauſes of the obftinancy of the befieged, and, probably, jealous of the behaviour of his Hindoo allies, perfuaded Ramraaje to raife the fiege, and march againft Sholapore. Upon their arrival within fome miles of that fortrefs, Kiſhwer Khan, feeing the danger of the aggrandizement of the Hindoo prince, reprefented to Ali Adil Shaw, that fhould the fort of Sholapore fall, Ramraaje would moft probably keep it for himfelf, and extend his views to the neighbouring countries; that, therefore, it would be more advifeable to endeavour at acquiring the fort of Nuldirruk by his aid, and leave the reduction of Sholapore to a more convenient time, when there would be no fear of rivalry in the poffeffion. Ali Adil Shaw, approving this advice, perfuaded Ramraaje to alter his views, and move to the place where raja Nul had formerly erected a ftrong fortrefs. Here, after throwing up an extenfive work of ftone, the allies took leave of each other, and returned to their feveral dominions.

In the firft expedition, on which Ali Adil Shaw preffed by the behaviour of Houffein Nizam Shaw, had called Ramraaje to his affiftance, the Hindoos at Ahmednuggur committed great outrages, and omitted no mark of difrefpect to the holy religion of the faithful, finging and performing their fuperftitious worfhip in the mofques. The fultan was much hurt at this infult to the faith; but, as he had not the ability to prevent it, he did not feem to obferve it. Ramraaje alfo, at the conclufion of this expedition, looking on the Iflaam fultans as of little confequence, refufed proper honours to their ambaffadors. When he admitted them to his prefence, he did not defire them to fit, and treated them with the moft contemptuous referve and haughtinefs. He made them attend when in publick in his train on foot, not allowing them to mount till he gave orders. On the return from the laft expedition to Nuldirruk, the officers and foldiers of his army in general, treated the muffulmauns with infolence, fcoffing, and contemptuous language; and Ramraaje, after taking leave, cafting an eye of avidity on the countries of Koottub

Shaw

Shaw and Adil Shaw, difpatched armies to the frontiers of each. Ali Adil Shaw, to purchafe peace, and preferve the reft of his dominions, gave up the diftricts of Outungpore and Bakreekobe; and Ibrahim Koottub Shaw, for the fame end, refigned Kowilcon-dah, Bankul, and Kunbore.

Ramraaje daily continuing to encroach on the dominions of the muffulmauns, Adil Shaw at length refolved, if poffible, to punifh his infolence and curtail his power, by a general league of the faithful againft him; for which purpofe, he convened an affembly of his friends and confidential advifers. Kifhwer Khan Laaree and Shaw Abou Teraab Sheerazee, whofe abilities had often been experienced, reprefented, that the fultan's defire to humble the pride of the roy of Beejanuggur was undoubtedly meritorious, and highly politic, but could never be effected, unlefs by a general alliance of the fultans of Dekkan, as the revenues of his country, collected from fixty feaports, and numerous flourifhing cities and diftricts, amounted to an immenfe fum; which enabled him to maintain a vaft force, againft which no fingle fultan of the muffulmauns could ftand with the fmalleft profpect of fuccefs. Ali Adil Shaw, approving thefe remarks, commanded Kifhwer Khan to take meafures to effect a general alliance; and an ambaffador was difpatched without delay to found the wifhes of Ibrahim Koottub Shaw, and open to him, if prudent, the defigned plan.

Ibrahim Koottub Shaw, who had long been inwardly ftung with indignation at the haughtinefs, infolence, and ufurpations of Ramraaje, eagerly agreed to the propofed alliance, and offered himfelf as mediator to effect a union of friendfhip between Ali Adil Shaw and Nizam Shaw, promifing to obtain for the former the fort of Sholapore, which had been the caufe of all their difagreement. With this view, fultan Ibrahim immediately difpatched Muftafa Khan Ardiftaance, the moft intelligent nobleman of his court, to Ali Adil

Shaw,

Shaw, with orders, if he should find him sincere in his intentions, to proceed to Ahmednuggur without delay, and conclude the alliance. Muftafa Khan, on his arrival at Beejapore, seeing every reason to believe that the sultan was resolved on the design of alliance, and war against the infidels, departed for Ahmednuggur without delay, and laid his commission in a private audience before Houssein Nizam Shaw. He represented to him, that during the times of the Bhamenee princes, when the whole strength of the muffulmaun power was in one hand, the balance between it and the force of the roies of Beejanuggur was nearly equal; that now the muffulmaun authority was divided, policy demanded that all the faithful princes should unite as one, and observe the strictest friendship, that they might continue secure from the attacks of their powerful common enemy, and the authority of the roies of Beejanuggur, who had reduced all the rajas of Carnatic to their yoke, be diminished, and removed far from the countries of Islaam; that the people of their several dominions, who ought to be confidered as the charge of the Almighty committed to their care, might repose free from the oppressions of the unbelievers, and their mosques and holy places be made no longer the dwellings of infidels.

These remarks had a full effect upon the mind of Houssein Nizam Shaw, who was pleased at the sincerity of Muftafa Khan, and treated him with the most honourable attentions, so that the minister had every opportunity he could desire of promoting his views, and which he did not neglect. After a negotiation of some days, it was determined, that Houssein Nizam Shaw should give his daughter Chaund Bibi in marriage to Ali Adil Shaw, with the fortress of Sholapore as a portion; and that he should receive the sister of that prince, named Huddeeah sultan, as a consort for his eldest son sultan Mortiza; that a firm friendship should for the future subsist between both states, and that they should unite sincerely to reduce the power of Ramraaje, and march against him in conjunction without delay. When these
points

points were fettled, Moolla Einaut Oolla came with Muftafa Khan as ambaffador to Beejapore; the proper treaties and agreements were drawn up, and confirmed by the moft folemn oaths. On the fame day, nuptial rejoicings and feftivals were held at Beejapore and Ahmednuggur, and the two princeffes fent in great pomp and magnificence to their feparate courts; after which, Houffein Nizam Shaw, Ali Adil Shaw, and Ibrahim Koottub Shaw, as alfo Bereed Shaw, began with great vigour preparations for the war againft Ramraaje.

Ali Adil Shaw, preparatory to the war, and to afford himfelf a pretence for breaking with his ally, difpatched an ambaffador to Ramraaje, demanding reftitution of fome diftricts that had been wrefted from him. As he expected, Ramraaje expelled the ambaffador in a very difgraceful manner from his court; and the united fultans now haftened the preparations to crufh the common enemy of the Iflaam faith. In the year 972, the four princes met with their armies, on the plains of Beejapore, and on the twentieth of Jummad al Awul the fame year, marched in conjunction from that neighbourhood. After fome days, they arrived near the banks of the Kiftnah, at Talicote; where, as that place belonged to Ali Adil Shaw, he entertained his allies with great fplendour, and fent ftrict orders to all the governors of his dominions, to forward fupplies of provifions from their diftricts regularly to the camp.

A.D. 1564.

Ramraaje, though he faw the union of the muffulmauns againft him, did not defcend in the leaft from his former haughtinefs, but treated their ambaffadors with fcornful language, and regarded their enmity as of little moment. He firft difpatched his youngeft brother Eeltumraaje, with twenty thoufand horfe, five hundred elephants, and one hundred thoufand foot, to remain on the bank of the Kiftnah, and block up all the paffages of that river. After this force, he fent his brother Negtaderee with a great army, and followed ed himself, by slow marches, with the whole power of his dominions. The allied princes, finding that all the known ferries and fords were blocked up by the enemy, dispatched their spies to explore the river, in hopes of finding some place at which they might be able to cross their troops; but, after much search, it was found that the only safe ford for an army was directly in their front, and in possession of the enemy, who had thrown up works fortified with cannon and fireworks on the opposite bank. The allies upon this information held a council, at which it was determined that they should march expeditiously to another part of the river, as if to cross, in hope that the enemy might quit their station to follow, when they might return suddenly, and gain the desired ford without interruption. The army of Islaam, agreeably to this plan, moved the next morning, and continued to do so for three days successively, which deceived the enemy, who quitted their stations, and followed their course along the opposite bank of the river. The sultans on the third night suddenly decamped, and moved with so much rapidity, that the next day they gained the ford which the enemy had deserted, and crossed the river without opposition. In the morning they moved to within ten miles of the camp of Ramraaje; who, though surprized at their activity, was not alarmed, commanded his brothers to join him, and kept strict watch during night round his camp, apprehending a surprize. The day following the allies arranged their army in order of battle. The right was entrusted to Ali Adil Shaw, the left to Ali Bereed Shaw and Ibrahim Koottub Shaw, and the center to Houssein Nizam Shaw. The artillery, fastened together by strong chains and ropes, was drawn up in front of the line, and the war elephants placed in various positions, agreeable to custom. Each prince exalted his particular standard in the center of his own army, and the allies moved in close order against the enemy.

Ramraaje entrusted his left to his brother Eeltumraaje, to oppose Koottub Shaw, and his right to his other brother Negtaderee, against
Ali

Ali Adil Shaw; while he himſelf commanded in his center. Two thouſand war elephants and one thouſand pieces of cannon were placed at different intervals of his line. About twelve o'clock in the day, Ramraaje mounted a \*ſinghauſin, in ſpite of the remonſtrances of his officers, who wiſhed him to be on horſeback, as much ſafer; but he ſaid, there was no occaſion for taking precaution againſt children, who would certainly fly on the firſt charge. Both armies being in motion, ſoon came to battle, and the infidels begun the attack by vaſt flights of rockets and rapid diſcharges of artillery, which did not diſcourage the allies. A general action took place, and many were ſlain on both ſides. Ramraaje finding a different behaviour in the enemy from what he had expected, deſcended from his ſinghauſin, and ſeating himſelf on a rich throne ſet with jewels, under a canopy of crimſon velvet, embroidered with gold and adorned with fringes of pearls, ordered his treaſurer to place heaps of money all round him, that he might confer rewards on ſuch of his followers as deſerved his attention. There were alſo rich ornaments of gold and jewels placed for the ſame purpoſe. The infidels, inſpired with the generoſity of their prince, charged the right and left of the allies with ſuch vigour, that they were thrown into diſorder; and Ali Adil Shaw and Koottub Shaw began to deſpair of victory, and prepare for retreat. Houſſein Nizam Shaw remained firm in the center, and puſhed ſo vigorouſly that of Ramraaje, that it began to be confuſed; upon which the roy again mounted his ſinghauſin, which was ſoon after let fall by the bearers on the approach of a furious elephant belonging to Nizam Shaw; and before he had time to recover himſelf and mount a horſe, a body of the allies took him priſoner, and conducted him to Chela Roomi, who commanded the artillery. He carried him to Nizam Shaw, who ordered inſtantly his head to be ſtruck off, and placed upon the point of a long ſpear, that his death might be proclaimed to the enemy. The Hindoos, according to cuſtom, when they ſaw their chief deſtroyed, fled in the utmoſt confuſion and diſorder from the field of battle, and were purſued by the allies with ſuch ſucceſsful

\* A ſort of litter.

succefsful flaughter, that the river which ran near the field was dyed red with their blood. It is computed, on the beft authorities, that above one hundred thoufand infidels were flain in fight and during the purfuit. The plunder was fo great, that every private man in the allied army became rich in gold, jewels, effects, tents, arms, horfes and flaves, as the fultans left every perfon in poffeffion of what he had acquired, only taking elephants for their own ufe. Firmauns with accounts of this very important victory were difpatched to their feveral dominions, and the fultans, a few days after the battle, marched onwards into the country of Ramraaje as far as Anicondeh, and the advanced troops penetrated to Beejanuggur, which they plundered, razed the chief buildings, and committed all manner of excefs. When the depredations of the allies had deftroyed all the country round, Negtaderee, who had efcaped from the battle to a diftant fortrefs, fent humble entreaties of peace to the fultans, to whom he gave up all the places which his brother had wrefted from them; and the victors being fatisfied, took leave of each other at Roijore, and returned to their feveral dominions. The raaje of Beejanuggur fince this battle has never recovered its ancient fplendour; and the city itfelf has been fo deftroyed, that it is now totally in ruins and uninhabited; while the country has been feized by the zemindars, each of whom hath affumed an independant power in his own diftrict.

Houffein Nizam Shaw dying not long after this event, was fucceeded by his fon Mortiza, then a minor; and Ali Adil Shaw thinking this a proper opportunity to execute his defigns, moved with an army to Anicondeh, in order to place Timraaje, the fon of Ramraaje, on the mufnud of Bilcondah, and depofe Negtaderee, hoping by degrees to acquire for himfelf Anicondeh and Beejanuggur. Negtaderee, being informed of his defigns, wrote to Mortiza Nizam Shaw and his mother Khoonzeh fultana, who directed his affairs, for affiftance, as he regarded himfelf as their dependant. The fultana, by by the advice of Moolla Einaiut Oolla, taking her son with her, marched at the head of an army to Beejapore; upon which Ali Adil Shaw retreated expeditiously from Anicondeh, and returned to his capital; before which frequent skirmishes happened between the two armies, but at length the sultana thought it advifeable to return with her son to Ahmednuggur.

The next year, at the requeft of the sultana regent, Ali Adil Shaw, accompanied the army of Nizam Shaw to Berar, which was laid wafte; but the sultan returned on the approach of the rains to Beejapore. This year the ftone wall round that city was completed. As, on account of the ill management of the relations of Khoonzeh fultana, the government of Nizam Shaw was much weakened, Ali Adil Shaw formed views of reducing fome parts of the country to his authority. He prefented Kummaul Kifhwer Khan with the ftandard of Affud Khan Balgoaanee; on which was embroidered an angry lion; and in the beginning of the year 975 fent him, with twenty thoufand horfe, to invade the territories of Nizam Shaw. The general poffeff- ed himfelf of fome pergunnahs with little oppofition, and in a fhort time erected a fort for their defence, which he named Darwer. Mortiza Nizam Shaw, having at length wrefted his power from the hands of his mother, marched to recover his poffeffions; upon which Kifhwer Khan fhut himfelf up in the fort, which he had well ftock- ed with ftores and provifions, to fuftain a fiege. Ankufs Khan, and other amras who had been fent to his fupport by Ali Adil Shaw, either out of hatred to him, difhonefty, or folly, chofe to quit him, under pretence of drawing off the enemy's attention by plundering and laying wafte the environs of Ahmednuggur. Nizam Shaw, un- intimidated by this feint, as he had taken an oath not to retire with- out reducing the fortrefs, made an immediate affault upon it, without any regular approaches, and fucceeded, contrary to the expectations of his own troops, by the lucky accident of Kifhwer Khan's being killed by an arrow, as he was conducting the defence; after which his fol- lowers

A. D. 1567.

lowers fled through a wicket out of the place, which fell into the hands of Nizam Shaw, with all the diſtricts that had been wreſted from his territories by the army of Ali Adil Shaw. Khajeh Meeruk and Peer Iſpahanee were immediately detached with a large force after Ein al Moolk, who had moved towards Ahmednuggur; and overtaking him, a deſperate action enſued, in which that chief was killed, Noor Khan taken priſoner, and the ſhattered remains of Adil Shaw's army returned to Beejapore with great difficulty and much loſs.

In theſe years, Ali Adil Shaw marched againſt Goa to reduce the Europeans, but retreated without effecting any thing, after the loſs of a great number of men. He then moved againſt the fortreſs of Oodnee, then in poſſeſſion of one of the principal amras of Ramraaje, who on the death of his maſter had aſſumed independance. Ankuſs Khan was diſpatched on this ſervice, with eight thouſand horſe, infantry, and a conſiderable train of artillery. Several actions were fought on the plain; and at length the chief ſhut himſelf up in the fortreſs, which was well ſupplied with ſtores and proviſions; but Ankuſs Khan carried on the ſiege with ſuch vigour, that at length it ſubmitted to his arms. Oodnee was ſituated upon the ſummit of a very high hill, and contained many ponds and fountains of clear and ſweet water, with numerous princely ſtructures. The roies of Beejanuggur regarding it as impregnable to the arms of Iſlaam, had all contributed to make it a convenient aſylum for their families; and it was fortified with eleven walls, one within another, ſo that it appeared impoſſible to reduce it by force, and nothing but the cloſe and long blockade of Ankuſs Khan could have reduced it to the arms of Beejapore.

This acquiſition having given great reputation to the arms of Ali Adil Shaw, he reſolved on other conqueſts; prior to entering upon which, he judged it proper to have a meeting with Mortiza Nizam Shaw,

Shaw, who, at his requeſt, came to an interview on his borders, at which it was agreed, that he ſhould poſſeſs himſelf of Berar, and that Ali Adil Shaw might conquer as much of the dependancies on Beejanuggur as he thought proper, without any interference from Nizam Shaw to interrupt his plans.

In the year 981, Ali Adil Shaw marched againſt the fortreſs of Toorkul, which he had loſt during the invaſions of Ramraaje, after whoſe death it had fallen into the hands of Vingti and Buſſabie, who after a ſiege of ſeven months ſurrendered themſelves priſoners, and were put to death by painful tortures. The ſultan then moved to reduce Darwer, one of the ſtrongeſt forts in Carnatic, and at that time poſſeſſed by one of the nobility of Ramraaje, who paid annually a ſmall acknowledgment to Eeltumraaje, and had acquired great power. By the good conduct of Muſtafa Khan Ardiſtaanee, who had been appointed prime miniſter, the fort was taken in ſix months; and when the ſurrounding country was perfectly reduced to order, Ali Adil Shaw, at the perſuaſions of his vizier, carried his arms againſt Binkapore, the principal reſidence of Velub Roy, who had been betel-bearer to Ramraaje, after whoſe death he had aſſumed independance, and had reduced the roies of Jerreh, Chundercote, and Caroore to become his tributaries. Upon the approach of the royal army he ſhut himſelf up in the fort, and detached his ſon, with a thouſand horſe and ten thouſand foot, to line the woods and paſſes, in order to haraſs the enemy as opportunity offered, and endeavour to cut off ſupplies of proviſions. At the ſame time, he ſent letters to Negtaderee, grandſon of Ramraaje, confeſſing great penitence and ſorrow for his diſaffection to him as his legal ſovereign, and begging for aſſiſtance againſt the ſultan; in conſideration of which he promiſed to pay an annual tribute, and in future continue firm to his allegiance. Negtaderee in reply wrote him, that by his wickedneſs and evil example, moſt of the dependants on his houſe had become rebels, and departed from their duty, ſo that it was with difficulty he
could

A.D. 1573.

could fupport himfelf at Bilcondah and Chundageereh, which the fultans of Iflaam had left him; therefore he would advife him, if money or jewels could purchafe peace, to lay afide his avarice, and procure it at any price; but if he fhould find that impoffible, he muft by all means in his power bring over the neighbouring roies to his caufe, and prevail upon them to join his fon with their followers, and harafs the muffulmauns by cutting off provifions, and by night robberies. He promifed to iffue his firmauns to all his vaffals to affift him, though he could not rely on their obedience.

Though Velub by this anfwer was reduced to defpair, yet agreeably to the advice of his prince, he prevailed on fome chiefs to join his fon; who acted with fuch vigour, that grain became very fcarce in the royal camp, which he molefted at night by parties of robbers, who did much execution. The footmen of the Carnatic, who valued their lives but little, quite naked, and their bodies anointed with oil, to prevent their being eafily feized, entered tents at night, and ftabbed the fleeping inhabitants without mercy. Every night numbers were killed by them in this treacherous manner; and fo great a dread and difcontent prevailed among the foldiers, that they were near forcing the fultan to raife the fiege. At length Muftafa Khan provided a remedy, both to prevent famine and the nightly murders. He detached the Bergee chiefs, with fix thoufand horfe, againft the enemy in the field, and ftationed a chain of eight thoufand foot round the camp every night. By this precaution the robbers were foon tired of attempts, as they found it impoffible to efcape with impunity. The Bergee chiefs performed their orders fo well, that the communication was kept open, and plenty reftored to the camp. The fiege however continued for one year and three months, when provifions in the garrifon began to fail, and the fon of Velub dying, all the vaffal roies who had attended him retired home. Velub, defpairing of relief, at length fent offers for furrendering the fort to the fultan, on condition of being allowed to march away with his family and effects,

which

which Ali Adil Shaw thought proper to grant, and the place was evacuated accordingly. The fultan ordered a fuperb temple within it to be deftroyed, and he himfelf laid the firft ftone of a mofque, which was built on the foundation, offering up praifes for his victory. Muftafa Khan by this fuccefs acquired new credit, was honoured with a royal drefs, and had many towns and diftricts of the conquered country conferred upon him in jaghire. The fultan, who was much given to pleafure, entrufted to his fole management all affairs of ftate, and refigned to him his feal, with orders to ufe it as he pleafed, without waiting for particular inftructions.

Four months after the reduction of Binkapore, when the country was properly fettled by the royal officers, and the different chiefs had fubmitted to pay tribute, Ali Adil Shaw took up his refidence in the fort, where he fpent his time in a round of amufements, and detached Muftafa Khan, with twenty thoufand horfe and a great body of infantry with artillery, to reduce the forts of Jerreh and Chundercote. On the arrival of the minifter near the former, the roy made offers of fubmiffion and tribute, which were accepted; and the army moved on, without molefting him, to Chundercote, the roy of which prepared for refiftance. Muftafa Khan laid fiege to the place, and detached the Bergee chiefs to employ the roies who had come to his affiftance. At the end of fourteen months the fort was carried by ftorm, in the year 983, and Ali Adil Shaw came from A.D. 1575. Binkapore to vifit it; and having continued at it three months, returned in triumph to Beejapore, after an abfence of fomewhat more than three years. Muftafa Khan remained at Chundercote to regulate the country, and the royal feal was left in his poffeffion; while orders were given to the heads of offices for all firmauns to be expedited by them from Beejapore for his approval.

The following year a petition came from Muftafa Khan, reprefenting, that the ancient fortrefs of Chundercote was fituated upon a
lofty

lofty hill, and better calculated for defence than that now ſtanding on the plain; ſo that he wiſhed the ſultan would come and view the old ſite, that, if he approved, it might be refortified without delay. Ali Adil Shaw, in compliance with his requeſt, went with a ſmall train; and approving the deſign of his miniſter, ordered a fort to be erected. It was finiſhed in the ſpace of one year, and the ſultan came again from Beejapore to view it. Subgeer Naik having come to viſit the ſultan, invited him to make the tour of his country; and Ali Adil Shaw accepting the offer, left his army at Chundercote, and with Muſtafa Khan and four or five thouſand men, proceeded to the fortreſs of Caroore. This place was ſituated in a mountainous country, full of foreſts, and ſo difficult of acceſs, that in moſt paſſages only one horſeman could enter at a time. The ſultan diſliking the appearance of the country, returned to Chundercote, leaving the Naik all his poſſeſſions; but Muſtafa Khan, in order to make a merit of his maſter's generoſity, told the Naik, that it was with difficulty he had perſuaded him from reducing the territory; therefore, if he wiſhed his own ſafety, he had better ſubmit to pay tribute, and draw over the ſurrounding roies to do the ſame. Subgeer Naik, by his repreſentations, prevailed on Seeb Naik of Jerreh, the rannee of Barcelore, and ſeveral other chiefs, to pay their reſpects to the ſultan; to whom they preſented an offering of conſiderable ſums, and agreed to pay an annual tribute. On the day on which theſe chiefs received their dreſſes of diſmiſſion from the ſultan, women's habits were prepared for Baradeo, the rannee of Barcelore, and another rannee, which they declined accepting, ſaying, that though women in ſex, they held their dominions by maſculine ſtrength: upon which the ſultan gave them men's dreſſes, and praiſed their valour. Theſe countries have been long governed by women, the daughters always ſucceeding to the raaje, and the men ſerving under them as officers, the huſbands of the rannees having no power in the ſtate.

Ali

Ali Adil Shaw having settled his new conquests, appointed a bramin governor, and Muſtafa Khan commander in chief of the whole, conferring the office of vaqueel upon Afzul Khan Sheerazee; after which regulations, he returned to Beejapore. Muſtafa Khan, who was a faithful ſervant, and anxious to extend the power of his ſovereign, ſent, not long after, one of his confidential friends to court, propoſing to his majeſty to march againſt Bilcondah. Ali Adil Shaw approving the plan, ordered his forces to aſſemble, and moved in great pomp to Oodnee; from whence, on the junction of Muſtafa Khan with the troops of Carnatic, he proceeded towards Bilcondah, and Negtaderee, on his approach, committing the place to the care of one of his nobility, retired with his treaſures and effects to the fortreſs of Chundageereh. The ſultan ſurrounded the city, blocking it up cloſely for three months; at the end of which the garriſon were near ſubmitting for want of proviſions, when Negtaderee bribed Hundeattum Naik, the chief of the Bergees, with * twenty four lacks of rupees and five elephants, to deſert from the ſultan with his followers and haraſs the camp; which he did ſo effectually, that Ali Adil Shaw thought proper to raiſe the ſiege, and retire to the neighbourhood of Binkapore; from whence he ſhortly after marched back to Beejapore, leaving Muſtafa Khan to protect the frontiers.

In the year 986, the Bergees committing exceſſes in their jaghires about Beejanuggur, the ſultan ſent againſt them Mortiza Khan Anjoo, with three thouſand foreign archers, and a number of Dekkanees and Abyſſinians, with whom they carried on ſkirmiſhes for near one year, without being at all weakened. Muſtafa Khan then repreſented to the ſultan, that it was uſeleſs ſending troops againſt them, and he had better prevail upon them by ſtratagem to come to Beejapore, when he might puniſh them in a manner worthy of their treachery. Ali Adil Shaw approving this advice, diſpatched Vaſoo Pundit, and others of their friends, to invite them to return. Hand-eattum

A.D. 1578.

* Two hundred and forty thouſand pounds.

eattum Naik in vain reprefented to them, that it was not poffible the fultan could forgive a treachery which had difappointed him of the conqueft of Bilcondah, but had invited them back to effect their deftruction. Moft of the chiefs and their followers however returned; but Handeattum Naik retired to Bilcondah, where he took fervice with Negtaderee. For fome time the fultan treated the Bergees with kindnefs, but at length put moft of them to death by treachery.

A. D. 1579.   In the year 987, as the fultan had no fon, he appointed his nephew Ibrahim, fon of his brother Shaw Thamafp, his fucceffor; and the following year he was affaffinated by a eunuch, whom he had forced againft his inclination to come to his court from Ahmednuggur.

SULTAN

# SULTAN

# ABOU AL MUZZUFFIR IBRAHIM

# ADIL SHAW 2ᵈ BEEJAPOREE.

IBRAHIM Adil Shaw upon his acceffion to the throne, being only in his ninth year, the management of publick affairs was given to Kamil Khan Dekkanee, and Chaund Bibi Sultana, wife to the late king, was entrufted with the care of the education of the minor monarch. Every day, excepting Wednefdays and Fridays, publick audience was given, at which fultan Ibrahim appeared feated on the throne, when publick affairs were tranfacted in his prefence. For fome time Kamil Khan behaved with due moderation in his high office; but, at length, intoxicated with power, he was guilty of fome infolence towards Chaund Sultana, who turned her thoughts to effect his deftruction. She fecretly fent a meffage to Hajee Kifhwer Khan, an officer of high rank, obferving, that as the regent was unfit for his important office, fhe wifhed to remove him, and beftow his honours upon himfelf, provided he would deftroy the minifter before his power fhould become fo great as to render his removal impoffible. Hajee Kifhwer Khan, inftigated by the hopes of advancement to the higheft honours of the ftate, formed a party with feveral chiefs, and one evening, when Kamil Khan was holding a durbar in the green palace, fuddenly entering the citadel with four hundred men, fhut the gates, confined the commanding officer of the garrifon, and proceeded to seize the regent. Kamil Khan, being alarmed, attempted to fly towards the haram, in hopes of protection from Chaund Sultana; when he was informed, by some eunuchs his friends, that the plot to seize his person was formed by her. Confounded at this intelligence, he ran out of the palace, and, as his only chance for escape, flung himself over the wall of the citadel into the ditch, then full of water. He swam over, and passed undiscovered to the Imaum gate of the city, which was however shut. By the help of his turban, sash, and other clothes tied together, and fixed to a battlement of the city wall, he descended, and hastened to his own house at no great distance, where he prepared for flight with his friends. Hajee Kishwer Khan not finding his intended victim, supposed he was concealed in the fort, and employed near an hour in searching all the private buildings and retired places; after which he dispatched a force to seek him without. Kamil Khan having provided himself with as many jewels and as much money as time would allow, fled with seven or eight friends towards Ahmednuggur; but had not gone above four miles before he was overtaken, and seized by the people of Kishwer Khan, who cut off his head, and carried it to their patron; but plundered all the jewels and treasure for their own use.

Hajee Kishwer Khan after this event, copying the example of Kamil Khan, by the patronage and support of Chaund Sultana, grasped the whole authority of the state, and ruled with uncontrouled sway. At this period, Behzaad al Moolk Turk, meer nobut to Mortiza Nizam Shaw, advanced from Ahmednuggur with fifteen thousand horse, to reduce some districts belonging to Beejapore; upon which the regent detached Ein al Moolk Canaanee with an army to repel the enemy on the frontiers. Behzaad al Moolk received a total defeat near Shawdirruk, and all his tents, baggage, elephants, and artillery, fell into the hands of the victors, who returned triumphant to Beejapore. The regent, by the advice of Chaund Sultana, ordered

ordered rejoicings for three days, and conferred rich gifts and honorary diſtinctions upon all the amras who had ſignalized themſelves during the expedition; but ſome time after, thought proper to iſſue firmauns demanding the elephants taken in battle from the captors, for the royal uſe. This order gave much diſguſt, and many of the nobility refuſing to comply, ſecretly combined together to remove him from the regency. Some adviſed addreſſing Chaund Sultana to call Muſtafa Khan from Binkapore, to take upon himſelf the adminiſtration of affairs; and others were for deferring any reſolution for the preſent, as Syed Mortiza, governor of Berar, was upon his march from Ahmednuggur to revenge the defeat of Behzaad al Moolk; therefore it would be dangerous to attempt a change till the enemy was driven away from the frontiers; but that being effected, they might then retire to Beejanuggur, and take meaſures, by the approbation of Chaund Sultana, to accompliſh their wiſhes for a new regent.

Kiſhwer Khan being informed of the deſigns forming againſt his power, took meaſures to prevent them. He ſent an order under the royal ſeal to Meer Noor ad Dien, a jaghiredaar near Binkapore, to aſſaſſinate Muſtafa Khan, promiſing to reward him for the deed with the eſtates and honours of that nobleman. Noor ad Dien, though he had been patronized by him, and was obliged to him for his preſent ſtation, undertook the action. He ſent the bearer of the firmaun into the fort, and at the ſame time a private meſſage to the principal officers of the garriſon, informing them, that Muſtafa Khan meditated to put them to death, and deliver the fort up to the raja of Carnatic, with whom he had entered into deſigns againſt the royal authority; therefore they would do well to obſerve the contents of the firmaun in the hands of Mahummud Ameen the bearer, and rid themſelves of their treacherous governor, for which they would be amply rewarded by the ſultan. Mahummud Ameen, upon his arrival at the gates of Binkapore, ſent word to Muſtafa Khan, that he

had

had brought a firmaun from the sultan: upon which he was admitted with great respect, and orders given for his accommodation. Pretending that it was late, he desired to be excused shewing the firmaun till the next morning; and Muftafa Khan, unsuspecting deceit, agreed to the delay. During the night, Mahummud Ameen shewed the paper to the officers of the garrison; who seeing the king's order for the death of Muftafa Khan, agreed to put it into execution. While he was at prayers the following morning, a number of them rushed upon him, and strangled him with a bow string.

When intelligence of this action arrived at Beejapore, Chaund Sultana was highly displeased, and uttered in bitter terms of reproach her disapprobation of the conduct of Kishwer Khan. The regent for the present concealed his resentment against her; but in a short time accused her of having secretly instigated her brother, Mortiza Nizam Shaw, to invade Beejapore, and obtained the sultan's orders to confine her for some time in the fortress of Sittara. She was accordingly forced out of the haram, with many indignities, and sent prisoner to that place. After this successful treachery, Kishwer Khan became self-secure, and conducted affairs with unbridled authority. He sent Mean Buddoo Dekkanee, on whose fidelity he had the greatest reliance, to command on the frontiers, with instructions to seize by treachery most of the Abyssinian nobility of the army, and confine them in Shawdirruk. This design by accident coming to the knowledge of the intended victims, they resolved to seize Mean Buddoo in his own snare, and then remove Kishwer Khan from the regency. With this view, Aklaafs Khan, the principal Abyssinian chief, pretending that he had received news from Beejapore of the birth of a son, made a grand entertainment, to which he invited Mean Buddoo; who, not suspecting his intentions, went to his tents, attended only by a select number of his friends, and was made prisoner by the very same stratagem he had designed to practise. Aklaafs Khan, with all the amras, and the whole army, moved the same day

towards

towards Beejapore; and Ein al Moolk and Ankufs Khan, with such of the nobility as were friends to Kishwer Khan, deserted on the route to their several jaghires.

Kishwer Khan on hearing of this league against him, gave over all thoughts of oppofition; but to preferve appearances, and prevent being feized by the inhabitants of the city, he invited the young fultan to a feaft at his own houfe; but as he attended him through the ftreets, the common people, and even women, uttered loud exclamations of abufe againft him, calling him the murderer of fyeds, and confiner of Chaund Sultana. The regent, feeing the minds of the publick enraged againft him, thought it high time to prepare for his efcape. When he heard that the army was arrived within a day's march of the city, he prevailed on the fultan to go with him, on pretence of hunting, to Koollabaugh, one of the royal gardens; where, on his arrival, he expreffed fears left the heat of the fun fhould hurt his majefty's health, and begged he would return to the palace, promifing to follow himfelf, as foon as he had taken a view of the gardens of Shawpore. The fultan returned, agreeably to his requeft; when Kifhwer Khan, who had a train of four hundred horfe, among whom he had diftributed his jewels and money, leaving his women and children behind in the city, took the road of Ahmednuggur. On his arrival, he found that court did not wifh to afford him protection; on which, he moved towards Golconda, the capital of Koottub Shaw, and he was fhortly after affaffinated in that city, by one of the friends of Muftafa Khan, in revenge for his treachery to that nobleman.

The Abyffinian amras entered Beejapore without oppofition, and were honoured by the young fultan with khelauts and other marks of approbation. Aklaafs Khan affumed the regency, and Chaund Sultana being conducted from her confinement in Sittara to the capital, was again entrufted with the care of the young fultan's perfon. At her requeft, Afzul Khan Sheerazee was appointed pefhwa, and Vafoo
Pundit

Pundit muftofee of the kingdom; but the new regent not long after put them both to death, on fufpicion of their entertaining defigns prejudicial to his intereft in concert with the fultana. He banifhed many principal noblemen from Beejapore; and, in conjunction with Hummeed Khan and Dillawer Khan, ruled the ftate as his caprice directed. He invited Ein al Moolk from his jaghire to court, and on his arrival near the city, with his companions, went out to meet him, in order to fhew their refpect for his dignity. Ein al Moolk, feeing the three minifters with but few attendants, treacheroufly feized them, put them all into heavy fetters, and the next morning prepared to enter the city with his prifoners upon elephants, in order to feize the regency. Upon his entering the city, he was told that the garrifon had fhut the gates of the citadel, and meant to oppofe him; upon which, without regarding his captives, he withdrew with expedition, and retired to his jaghire. Aklaafs Khan and his companions being thus unexpectedly releafed, reaffumed their authority; but fome of the nobility at court oppofing them, great diffentions prevailed at Beejapore, which gave encouragement to enemies to invade the kingdom.

Behzaad al Moolk, who after his defeat had retreated, returned with Syed Mortiza, the ameer al amra of Berar. Mahummud Koolli Koottub Shaw alfo, having entered into alliance with Nizam Shaw, and marching from Golconda, joined his generals before Shawdirruk; which place was laid clofe fiege to by the allies; but the commanding officer, notwithftanding the confufed ftate of affairs at Beejapore, made a firm refiftance, and refufed fplendid offers made him by the enemy to give up his charge; obferving, in anfwer to their promifes and temptations, that he would not forfeit his honour, the lofs of which nothing could reftore, as he muft give up with it the efteem of the world. The allies finding all their attempts fruitlefs, refolved to raife the fiege, and march againft Beejapore; where the diffentions prevailing among the minifters, would probably favour their caufe, and if they fucceeded in taking the capital, the dependancies

ancies muft foon fall. The allies accordingly broke up their camp before Shawdirruk, and, after laying wafte the country in their route, appeared before Beejapore with forty thoufand horfe.

As there were not then at the capital more than two or three thoufand horfe, the Abyffinians kept themfelves clofe in the city till the arrival of Ein al Moolk and Ankufs Khan, with eight thoufand horfe; after which they encamped near the gate of Allapore, and had repeated fkirmifhes with the enemy, whofe fuperiority of numbers gave them the advantage. About twenty yards of the wall of the city falling down, owing to heavy rain, and Ein al Moolk and Ankufs Khan going over in difguft at the Hubfheh chiefs to the enemy the fame night, the allies meditated an affault on the place in the morning; but Syed Mortiza, who was difpleafed at being fuperfeded by Behzaad al Moolk, prevented the execution of that defign, and the Beejaporees found time to repair the breach. At length, the Abyffinian chiefs feeing that the principal nobility and officers difliked their authority, and on that account declined coming to the fultan's affiftance, in confideration of the ftate of affairs, reprefented to the fultana, that they were willing to give up their power to whoever fhe fhould appoint, as they were loyal, and wifhed to fee the government rendered flourifhing, though they could not conduct it themfelves, owing to the refufal of the nobility to obey their orders.

Chaund Sultana believing their declarations, at their defire conferred the khelaut of ameer Jumlegee on Shaw Abou al Houffun, fon of Shaw Tahir, who immediately fent off expreffes with firmauns of encouragement to the Bergee chiefs of Carnatic, inviting them to return to their duty. He alfo wrote to Syed Mortiza, who had a profound veneration for the family of Shaw Tahir, advifing him to prevail upon the allies to quit the territories of Beejapore; threatening, if they did not, that when the amras joined the fultan, which would fhortly happen, their retreat fhould be cut off. Syed Mortiza,

FERISHTA's HISTORY OF DEKKAN.

who did not wifh that Koottub Shaw or Behzaad al Moolk fhould fucceed, immediately began his meafures to oblige them to retreat. He fent to Ein al Moolk and Ankufs Khan, who had deferted to him from Beejapore, defiring them to return; obferving, that at a time of fuch danger to quit the fervice of their fovereign, on pretence of diflike to his minifters, was acting unworthy the characters of noblemen. They took his advice, and returned the fame evening to Beejapore, where they renewed their allegiance to Ibrahim Adil Shaw. Moft of the nobility and the Bergees hearing of the change of affairs, haftened to court with their followers, and by the loyal endeavours of Abou al Houffun, in lefs than a month an army of above twenty thoufand men was collected at the capital, where affairs once more affumed a promifing appearance. The Bergee chiefs were detached to harafs the environs of the enemy's camp, and fucceeded fo well, that in a fhort time famine prevailed, and the allies repented of their expedition to Beejapore.

As the diftrefs of the allies encreafed, they held councils what meafures to purfue; and it was at laft determined that they fhould divide their armies, that Koottub Shaw fhould proceed againft Koolburga, and Behzaad al Moolk and Syed Mortiza recommence the fiege of Shawdirruk. They accordingly moved fuddenly from before Beejapore; but the Nizam Shawee army, on account of fome events which will be mentioned, proceeded immediately to Ahmednuggur, plundering the diftricts of Mirch and Kulhir on their route; and Mahummud Koolli Koottub Shaw, having left a detachment under Muftafa Khan to reduce fome diftricts of Adil Shaw, returned to his capital of Golconda. Muftafa Khan at the end of three months was totally defeated, by an army fent from Beejapore under the command of Dillawer Khan, who, after the victory, afpired to the office of prime minifter; for which purpofe he entered into a plot againft Aklaafs Khan with Hyder Khan, commanding officer in the citadel of Beejapore, to whom he made great promifes for his fupport.

When

When every thing was fixed for the execution of his defign, he marched expeditioufly to the capital, and encamping near the gate of Allapore, fent in fuch flattering meffages and declarations of attachment to Aklaafs Khan, as threw him off his guard, and made him neglectful of the fecurity of the city and palace. One day, when Aklaafs Khan was repofing in his own houfe without the citadel, Dillawer Khan with his fons, feven hundred horfe, and fifteen elephants fuddenly entering the city, proceeded to the palace, into which he was admitted according to promife by Hyder Khan; and after paying his compliments to the fultan, ftationed his followers in every part. Aklaafs Khan foon after advanced towards the gates with four thoufand men; but the cannon from the walls obliged him to retire to a diftance. He blocked up the citadel for near four months, but being then deferted by Bulleel Khan, his principal chief, with the greateft part of his followers, and difdaining to fly, he was taken in his houfe by Dillawer Khan; who, forgetting all his favours and kindnefs, ungratefully put out his eyes, and confined him. During this difpute, the inhabitants of Beejapore fuffered many injuries from both parties, and many fine edifices were deftroyed by the cannon.

Dillawer Khan, on his acceffion to the regency, endeavoured to attach the nobility to his intereft, by courting their alliance with his family and placing his relations in the higheft offices, particularly his fons, who had thofe immediately about the fultan's perfon. Bulleel Khan, who had by his coming over to him from Aklaafs Khan contributed greatly to his exaltation, he adopted for his fon; and chufing about one hundred foreigners and fixty Abyflinians, banifhed all the reft from the dominions of Ibrahim Adil Shaw. Shaw Abou al Houffun, who had been made prifoner in one of the forts by Aklaafs Khan, he firft blinded, and then put to death; as alfo Hajee Pofeer, a favourite of the late fultan; and circumfcribed the influence of Chaund Sultana in fuch a manner, that none of the court any longer attended

attended to her pleasure. He by stratagem got into his power Ghalib Khan, governor of the fortress of Oodnee, who had rebelled, and, to deter others, pulled out his eyes. He established the soonni ceremonies of religion in Beejapore, and ruled with absolute sway and authority in every department for eight years; during which period he restored the affairs of the kingdom to a flourishing situation.

The first act of his power, after he found himself secure, was, to detach Bulleel Khan with an army to collect the arrears of tribute from the roies of Malabar. Bulleel Khan, after being joined by Arsub Naik, roy of Jerreh, marched against Sunkir Naik, roy of Koorg, who refused to comply with his demands. One night, after he had begun the siege, as he was visiting the batteries, he had the ill fortune to be taken prisoner by a body of the enemy, and was carried into the fort, where he was put into heavy chains and confined. His troops, missing their chief, raised the siege, and separated to various quarters. Bulleel Khan after some time, by promises of great rewards, prevailed upon his keepers and a seller of grass to assist his escape; and he was carried out by the latter upon his shoulders, concealed in a bundle of forage. When he had got to a convenient spot, he contrived to pull off his chains, and hastened with all expedition towards the frontiers of Adil Shaw; where arriving in safety, he procured a horse, and proceeded to Binkapore, from whence he informed Dillawer Khan of his situation, and requested another army to take revenge on Sunkir Naik; but the regent chose for the present to lay aside farther attempts.

A.D. 1584.
Dillawer Khan, the same year, in order to settle a treaty of alliance with Mortiza Nizam Shaw, sent ambassadors in the name of the sultan to Ahmednuggur, by whom it was effected; and in the year 992, Nizam Shaw requested of Ibrahim Shaw his sister Khadijeh Sultana in marriage for his son sultan Houssein; which being agreed to, Casim Beg came with a train of four hundred horse to

Beejapore

Beejapore to receive the princefs, and efcort her to Ahmednuggur. She departed in great pomp at the end of four months, and was accompanied by Chaund Sultana, who defired to vifit her brother Mortiza Nizam Shaw.

In the year 995, as Mahummud Koolli Koottub Shaw neglected A.D. 1586. complying with the requeft of Ibrahim Shaw to fend his fifter Chaund Sultana, to whom he was betrothed, to Beejapore, Dillawer Khan marched with the fultan towards the frontiers of Nizam Shaw, at the inftigation of whofe minifters the princefs had been detained. On his arrival at the fort of Oofeh, Mortiza Nizam Shaw, who had long retired from publick affairs, judging that the conduct of his minifters had occafioned the invafion, confined Sullabut Khan, and gave the office of premier to Cafim Beg; who by his entreaties prevailed upon Dillawer Khan to quit the country. The regent then moved towards the dominions of Mahummud Koolli Koottub Shaw, who, to procure peace, fent his fifter in great pomp and fplendour to Ibrahim Shaw, without delay, and the nuptials were concluded with royal magnificence at Shawdirruk; after which the fultan returned to Beejapore.

In the year 996, Mortiza Nizam Shaw, who was become diftract- A.D. 1587. ed, endeavoured to take the life of his fon fultan Meeran Houffein; upon which the minifter, Mirza Khan, thought it beft to join the prince, and dethrone Nizam Shaw; to effect which, he requefted affiftance of Dillawer Khan, who marched with his fovereign from Beejapore in confequence of his application, but before he arrived at Ahmednuggur, fultan Houffein had dethroned his father. Ibrahim Adil Shaw fent congratulations to him upon his acceffion, and intended to have had an interview with him and the fultana his fifter, for which purpofe he remained encamped fome miles from Ahmednuggur; but upon hearing that Houffein Shaw had atrocioufly put his father to death, he was ftruck with horror at the parricide, and

refolved

resolved not to see him. He sent Meer Houssein Koord, who was remarkable for his free manner of speaking, to Houssein Shaw with a message, that he had marched from Beejapore solely with the desire of placing him on the throne, and obliging his father to retire to some fort where he might pass his time in religious exercises; but as he had wickedly put him to death, he would not see him; yet, lest the world should suppose that he acted from views of conquest, he should leave him to the vengeance of the Almighty, and return to his own dominions. The sultan, after sending this message, returned to Beejapore; from whence Bulleel Khan was again detached with twelve thousand horse to collect the arrears of tribute from the roies of Malabar, and, in case they refused payment, to reduce their forts.

A. D. 1588.
A year had scarce elapsed, when Houssein Nizam Shaw was assassinated, and Jemmal Khan became all-powerful in the government; upon which, Dillawer Khan advised Ibrahim Adil Shaw to move towards Ahmednuggur, to take advantage of the dissentions; and firmauns were dispatched to Bulleel Khan, commanding him to return from Malabar without delay. The sultan in 997 marched from Beejapore, and Dillawer Khan made the army halt near Shaw-dirruk above a month, in hopes of the junction of Bulleel Khan; but he not appearing, the regent judged farther delay dangerous, and moved on towards Ahmednuggur. Jemmal Khan, with Ismaeel Nizam Shaw, attended by fifteen thousand horse, a great body of foot, and artillery, advanced to meet him, and both armies lay near each other for many days without engaging. At length, Jemmal Khan thought proper to beg peace, and Dillawer Khan consented to grant it, on condition, that the princess Khadijeh, sister to Ibrahim and widow to the late Shaw Houssein, should be sent back to her brother; also that he should pay a sum of money. Jemmal Khan without delay sent the princess, with all her effects and a large sum of money; upon which Dillawer Khan retreated; and upon the same day Bulleel Khan joined the army, where his services were not now wanted,

wanted, and his departure from Malabar regretted, as he had nearly brought affairs in that quarter to a proper adjuftment, which was difturbed by his recall.

Dillawer Khan, who was difpleafed at his delay, which he fuppofed to be defigned, undervalued the effects which Bulleel Khan had brought as part of the tributes, and demanded the balances from the roies who had acccompanied him to pay their compliments to the fultan. In order to affront him ftill more, he accufed him, in prefence of the fultan, of difobeying the royal orders in not haftening sooner to the royal camp; but Bulleel Khan, knowing the fultan was well inclined towards him, boldly replied, that he had been guilty of no fault, nor delayed longer than he could well avoid. He obferved, that he was juft on the point of receiving a large fum in part of the arrears of tribute, which would have been loft to the treafury had he made publick immediately his orders of recall, and the troops would alfo have met with great difficulties. He obferved, that the regent, rather than he, was to blame for having led the fultan precipitately againft an enemy; whereas if he had remained fifteen days longer at Shawdirruk, the Malabar troops would have joined, and the country of Nizam Shaw might have been fuccefsfully invaded. Yet he was ready to confefs his own errors, and threw himfelf on the fultan's mercy for the crimes he might have committed. Dillawer Khan, though much enraged at this boldnefs; apprehending that his notice of it might occafion difturbances, thought it beft to conceal his difpleafure. Affuming then an air of approbation, he addreffed the fultan, faying, that Bulleel Khan was a loyal fubject, and had performed great fervices; fo that fince his excufes for delay had reafonable foundation, he requefted his majefty to forgive his errors, and confer upon him marks of the royal favour. The fultan, readily complying with this requeft, honoured Bulleel Khan with a rich khelaut; and after the breaking up of the court Dillawer Khan took him with him to his tents, where he entertained

him

him with much magnificence; and in order to apologife for his late ufage, faid, that as it was known by the publick that he had adopted him as his fon, if in the affairs of government he did not behave to him with the fame ftrictnefs as to others, it would be faid that he was partial to his own children. Shortly after, a khelaut was conferred on the fon of Arfub Naik, who had attended Bulleel to pay his compliments to the fultan, as well as many others of the roies of Malabar, who were all honourably difmiffed to their own country. The regent having by his hypocritical behaviour thrown the gallant general off his guard, a few months after the return of the army to Beejapore, forgetting all his great fervices to himfelf in the time of Aklaafs Khan, had him treacheroufly feized and deprived of fight, without the knowledge of the fultan; who, though much difpleafed, was too much in the power of Dillawer Khan to be able to exprefs his diffatisfaction; but opportunity fhortly offered of freeing himfelf from his intolerable influence.

A. D. 1589.   In the year 998, Ibrahim Adil Shaw, at the requeft of Dillawer Khan, marched from Beejapore to affift Boorahan Nizam Shaw in the recovery of the throne of Ahmednuggur from Jemmal Khan, who had fet up the fon in oppofition to the father. Jemmal Khan having raifed a confiderable army, advanced with his fovereign, Ifmaeel Nizam Shaw, to within fixteen miles of the fultan's camp, but without any intention to engage. He fent ambaffadors with great offers to Dillawer Khan if he would grant him peace; but the regent refufing to liften to any terms, and many officers deferting from Jemmal Khan, that general, to fecure himfelf from fudden attacks, retired to a ftrong poft furrounded by declivities and broken ground, at fome diftance from his former camp. Dillawer Khan thinking his enemy weak, and felf-fecure of victory, againft the exprefs requeft of the fultan marched after him, with thirty thoufand horfe, in hopes of taking him prifoner. Upon his arrival at the fpot where Jemmal Khan, contrary to his expectations, was ftrongly encamped, he

repented

repented of his rafhnefs; but, afhamed to retire, halted, in hopes that all his troops would foon join. At this inftant an officer from Ibrahim Adil Shaw arriving, reprefented, that as the army was not warned for action, the fultan defired he would put it off for the prefent, and ftay till the troops were properly arranged. Dillawer Khan returning for anfwer that he would fhortly bring Jemmal Khan bound to the prefence of the fultan, advanced towards the enemy. Having with great difficulty paffed over much marfhy ground, full of hollows, he at length, without proper order or difpofition, reached the enemy's front, and detached the Bergee amras with their cavalry to fall upon the rear, to prevent any of their baggage efcaping. Jemmal Khan, feeing no chance of efcape but by the fword, drew out his troops, and prepared for a defperate refiftance. In the very beginning of the action, Ein al Moolk Canaanee, Ankufs Khan and Aulum Khan, who knew that Ibrahim Adil Shaw was much difpleafed with the regent, deferted him with their troops, and leaving him in the gulph of deftruction, haftened to the royal camp at Darafung. Dillawer Khan, notwithftanding this, fought fo valiantly with his own troops, that he put the enemy into diforder; upon which his followers feparated to feize the plunder of the camp, according to the loofe cuftom of Hindooftan, leaving him with not more than two hundred horfe. A party of the enemy, who had retired in good order with their prince, Ifmaeel Nizam Shaw, feeing this, returned to attack him; and Dillawer Khan, after much gallant ftruggle, preferring fafety to deftruction, fled with feven perfons, among whom was the author of this hiftory, from the field of battle. On his way, fpies brought intelligence that Ein al Moolk, with the other amras who had deferted him, were haftening to the fultan, in hopes of deftroying his influence; upon which he redoubled his expedition, and reached Darafung before them, with three thoufand of his defeated troops, who joined him by parties on his route. Left the victors fhould purfue, he marched with the fultan all night towards Shawdirruk, where he arrived the next morning. Jemmal Khan

Khan, after this very unexpected succefs, having taken above one hundred elephants, advanced to Darafung; where the author of this hiftory, who had received fome wounds, and could not travel from weaknefs, fell into his hands, but made his efcape from him by a ftratagem. Jemmal Khan, learning that Boorahan Shaw, with his allies, Khajeh Ali Khan, and the amras of Berar, was advancing againft him, moved immediately from Darafung; upon which the Beejapore army returned again, and purfued him for near one hundred and fixty miles. The fultan then thought proper to halt with the main body, and detach on the purfuit the Bergee amras; but Dillawer Khan difrefpectfully infifted that the fultan fhould march on, without delay, to Kaat Rohngur. This infolence gave great diffatisfaction, and Ibrahim Adil Shaw, now of an age to act for himfelf, tired of being led in the trammels of a regent, refolved to free himfelf by effecting his deftruction.

As all the officers of the royal houfehold and the body guards were attached to Dillawer Khan, the fultan was fearful of communicating his wifhes to them, left they fhould betray him. After much precaution, he fixed upon two Hindoos, common fervants of no note, to be his confidants on this important occafion. Thefe he fent privately to Ein al Moolk, the ameer al amra, to complain of the unreafonable power of his minifter; and received in anfwer facred promifes of affiftance, if he chofe to engage in depofing him from authority. After much negotiation by the two Hindoos, it was fettled that the fultan fhould, on a certain night, when Dillawer Khan was afleep, repair fuddenly to the camp of Ein al Moolk, which was only at a mile's diftance, where he fhould be joined by him, Ali Khan and Ankufs Khan, who would faithfully obey his commands. Ibrahim Adil Shaw, relying upon thefe declarations,

A. D. 1589. on the night of the fourteenth of Rejib, 998, came out of his private apartments, and commanded Kufhfdaar Khan to bring him a horfe. The keeper of the ftables refufed obedience, faying, that

without

without the orders of Dillawer Khan he dared not comply. Kuſhf-
daar Khan, provoked at this infolence, gave him feveral blows;
upon which the grooms of the ſtables were terrified, and brought
horfes immediately. The fultan mounting, iſſued, attended by his
flaves from his tents; and on the way Elias Khan, his nurfe's fon,
who was upon guard, running up to him, aſked the cauſe of his
motion, and received for anfwer, that the prefent was not a time for
explanation, but he ſhould know the caufe if he chofe to attend him;
which he did immediately, with rather lefs than an hundred horfe.
When he arrived within a ſhort diftance of the camp of Ein al
Moolk, he halted, till that nobleman, with Ali Khan and Ankufs
Khan, joined him. As foon as the fultan's march was known,
feveral officers, among whom was the author of this hiftory, with
about three thoufand foldiers, haftened to join him during the night.

Dillawer Khan, though above eighty years of age, had that
night dedicated his hours to pleafure with a beautiful virgin of Dekkan, whom he had long fought after, and juft obtained; fo that,
though feveral fpies often requefted admittance to his prefence, to
inform him of the fultan's flight, his attendants, who had received
orders not to difturb him, refufed to acquaint him with their coming;
which neglect gave full time to Ibrahim Adil Shaw to complete his
defigns. Towards funrife, the regent was roufed from his dream of
pleafure, and with his fons and fix thoufand horfe, with many elephants, followed his fovereign, in hopes that on his arrival he would
be deferted by his friends, and again be obliged to throw himfelf into
his hands. When he came in fight of the royal army, the fultan
ordered Ein al Moolk to prepare to oppofe him; but that nobleman
fent privately a meſſenger to the regent, offering to ftand neuter
while he might attempt to carry off the king. Dillawer Khan, encouraged by this aſſurance, ſtopped his followers at a little diftance,
and coming on with an hundred horfe and four elephants clofe to the
fultan, addreſſed him, faying, that marching at night was improper,

but he hoped he would now return to his encampment. The sultan, enraged at this insolence, exclaimed, Will no one punish this traitor? Upon which an inferior officer of the body guard, named Awut Khan, spurring his horse up to the regent, gave him a wound with his sabre, and was preparing to inflict another stroke, when the regent's horse rearing at the flashing brightness of the weapon, threw him; and his elephant drivers rushing between him and Awut Khan, he had time to escape to his own troops, whom he endeavoured to lead on against the sultan; but they were alarmed at the enormity of assaulting their sovereign, and refused, many of them deserting him immediately. Dillawer Khan, overwhelmed with confusion and dismay, fled towards Ahmednuggur; but his son Kummaul Khan was overtaken at Darasung by the royalists, and put to death.

When the hand of providence had removed the thorns of the regent's usurpations from the skirts of Ibrahim Adil Shaw, and the veil of obscurity was taken from the lustre of his majesty, he gave khelauts of encouragement to Ein al Moolk, Ali Khan, and Ankufs Khan, notwithstanding their failure of promise, and, encamping, ascended the throne to give publick audience. Such as had distinguished themselves by their loyalty during the night, he rewarded with a generosity beyond their expectations, and gratified the nobility and army by his liberal behaviour. Upon his retiring into his private apartments to take repose, a circumstance happened worthy of remark. As Dillawer Khan, being of the disciples of Hunefi, had established the sooni ceremonies during his regency, many of the nobility, among whom were some strict soonites, judging that the sultan, copying his father and uncle, must be a sheeah, to please him gave orders to the criers to proclaim evening prayer in the manner of the latter sect. The sultan, who however had by education become a disciple of Hunefi, on hearing the call to prayer, was offended at the change, and gave orders for the criers to be confined; but upon being informed of the cause of the alteration, he smiled at the sudden

conversion

converfion of the foonite nobility, and would frequently rally them upon it, calling them political fheeahs. He however left every one to follow their own opinions in matters of faith, and both fects were publickly allowed to practife their religious ceremonies, as in the time of Eufuff Adil Shaw.

As, foon after the expulfion of the regent, intelligence arrived of the defeat of Jemmal Khan, and the acceffion of Boorahan Nizam Shaw, the fultan fent letters of congratulation to him on the occafion; and, as there now remained no caufe for continuing in the field, returned expeditioufly to Beejapore, where he employed himfelf in regulating the affairs of his government, which he did with fo much juftice, clemency, and prudence, that his people foon forgot their late troubles, and had reafon to congratulate each other on the happy deliverance of their fovereign from the thraldom of his minifters.

When Dillawer Khan fled to Ahmednuggur, he was received by Boorahan Nizam Shaw among his nobility, and appointed to reduce the forts of Sholapore and Shawdirruk; which coming to the knowledge of Ibrahim Adil Shaw, he fent ambaffadors to requeft that he might be fent to him, together with the elephants which had been taken from him by Jemmal Khan. Boorahan Nizam Shaw, inftead of granting this demand, forgetting every former obligation, prepared for war; and at the inftigation of Dillawer Khan, in the month of Jemmad al Sani, 1000, marched towards the territories of A.D. 1591. Beejapore with a great army; and, having paffed the frontiers, laid wafte the country as he advanced. Upon his arrival at Munglerreh, feeing that no army was fent into the field to oppofe him, he became fufpicious of ftratagem to draw him into the heart of the kingdom, and on that account would have retreated, but was prevailed upon by Dillawer Khan to remain, and advance as far as the river Beemrah, where he halted, and there finding a ruined fortrefs, ordered it to be repaired. Ibrahim Adil Shaw, who all this time had given no orders to aſſemble his nobility, or taken meaſures to defend his country, on hearing this, ſaid, that Boorahan Nizam Shaw would ſhortly act like the child, who builds walls of clay, and then deſtroys them with his own hands. He ſeemed to be unmindful that an enemy was in his country; and contenting himſelf with diſpatching a few horſe to obſerve their motions, appeared to give himſelf totally up to amuſements; which mode of conduct became the wonder of all, and every man formed his own conjectures upon it, both in his own dominions and the enemy's camp, without being able to account for his intentions. Boorahan Nizam Shaw conſulted upon it with his own officers and Dillawer Khan, when ſome ſaid that Ibrahim Adil Shaw, being a youth, was immerſed in pleaſures, and unmindful of the affairs of his kingdom; others, that, as he was jealous of the fidelity of his nobility, he was afraid of calling them together. The ſultan's ſpies brought him regular information of all that paſſed, and gave alarming accounts of the confidence of the enemy at his very extraordinary ſupineneſs.

Ibrahim Adil Shaw, at length, finding matters ripe for the execution of his intentions, ſent a meſſenger to Dillawer Khan, requeſting him to return, and once more take the charge of affairs upon himſelf; obſerving, that he ſaw, though late, the folly of his own conduct, in having liſtened to the repreſentations of deſigning men againſt ſo worthy a ſervant; but if he would once more accept of his office, he might depend on the utmoſt encouragement. Dillawer Khan, overjoyed at this invitation, returned for anſwer, that if his majeſty would aſſure him he ſhould not ſuffer any injury in his life or property, he would haſten to throw himſelf at his feet. All ſecurities he required being granted, the regent, in the hopes of once more attaining abſolute power and confining the ſultan as formerly, obtained his diſmiſſion from Boorahan Nizam Shaw; who in vain repreſented to him that he was haſtening to his own deſtruction, as behaviour like his to his ſovereign could never ſincerely be forgiven.

The

The regent haftened to Beejapore, where he arrived in the evening, as the fultan was returning in great ftate from the garden of the twelve Imaums towards the palace, and, having paid his refpects, proceeded on foot in the train. When he had paffed on a little, the fultan calling to Elias Khan, ordered him to fhew the regent a fpecimen of his own favourite punifhment in pulling out eyes. Dillawer Khan in vain reprefented that he had come to court on his majefty's affurances of pardon and fafety. The fultan told him, that he had only promifed not to injure his life or property, and that depriving him of fight could effect neither. He was accordingly blinded, and fent to the fortrefs of Sittareh, where he remained a prifoner till he died.

The fultan having fuccefsfully rid himfelf of his dangerous minifter, fent orders to all his nobility to haften from their jaghires without delay, and made preparations to march againft the enemy. He firft fent the Bergee amras, with fix thoufand horfe, to cut off all communication of fupplies from the enemy's camp; and in the month of Shaaban, having appointed Roomi Khan Dekkanee commander of his armies, difpatched him at the head of ten thoufand horfe, and, foon after, fent Elias Khan to reinforce him with three thoufand of the houfehold troops. The Bergee amras greatly diftreffed the enemy, and defeated feveral detachments fent againft them; till at laft, Boorahan Shaw marched in perfon; upon which, unable to oppofe, they recroffed the Beemrah, which was then fordable; and a lucky flood of the torrents from the mountains fwelled the river fo much immediately after, as to prevent their being purfued; upon which Boorahan Shaw returned to his camp. A famine and peftilential diforder growing to a great height, and carrying off great numbers of men and animals, obliged him to retire fome marches back towards his own country, to obtain relief. When he had received fupplies of provifions, and the plague had fomewhat ceafed, he moved again, with a defign to lay fiege to the fortrefs of Sholapore; but was oppofed on his march by Roomi Khan and Elias Khan, who
defeated

defeated a principal part of his army under Noor Khan, ameer al amra of Berar, and took an hundred elephants and four hundred horses.

After this loss, the affairs of Boorahan Nizam Shaw declined daily, and numbers of his troops, tired of long service and fatigue, deserted from his camp. A conspiracy was formed against his life by several of the nobility, who wished to place his son Ismaeel upon the throne in his room. Discovering the plot, and growing suspicious of all around him, he began his retreat towards Ahmednuggur; but was so harassed on his first march, that he thought it imprudent to attempt moving further till he could make peace with Ibrahim Adil Shaw, to whom he sent ambassadors for the purpose. The sultan for near a month refused listening to any terms; but was at last prevailed upon to cease enmity, on the condition that Boorahan Nizam Shaw should destroy the fort he had erected upon the bank of the Beemrah, which he did accordingly, throwing down the first stone with his own hands; after which his troops demolished the whole fabric, which had cost much trouble and expense. He then marched expeditiously back to Ahmednuggur, heartily repenting of his unprovoked invasion of the territories of Ibrahim Adil Shaw.

A.D. 1593. As affairs were now restored to order, the sultan resolved to humble the roies of Malabar, who, since the recall of Bulleel Khan, had neglected paying their tribute; and for this purpose dispatched Munjun Khan with a considerable army. This general upon his arrival at Binkapore halted, and summoned all the roies to meet him with their tributes, promising those who obeyed, protection and encouragement, but threatening the refractory with certain destruction. Most of them prepared to comply with his demands, and intended coming in a body to visit him; but as Gung Naik, who was one of the principal roies of Malabar, and had eight or ten thousand horse and foot in his pay, went first to pay his respects, the rest, jealous of of his power, and suspecting that he had gone to form some plan against them with Munjun Khan, broke off their engagements, and withdrew to the mountains. Munjun Khan not thinking it prudent to follow them into an unknown country, marched with Gung Naik against Jerrch, which belonged to Arfub Naik; who with his allies, to the number of twenty thousand men endeavoured to interrupt the siege. For three days bloody skirmishes were kept up, and, as the Beejaporeans could not use their cavalry, owing to bad ground, the success was frequently doubtful; but at length the good fortune of the sultan's arms prevailed, and Arfub, seeing further resistance vain, consented to pay a tribute, and made a present of two fine elephants to Munjun Khan, with many curious and valuable effects for the sultan. He also joined the army, and assisted at the siege of Mysore, belonging to Negtaderee Naik, which was reduced in three months, and twenty fine elephants were taken with it. Munjun Khan was proceeding rapidly in his conquests, when the rebellion of the sultan's brother in Balgoan occasioned his recall, and left the affairs of Malabar once more in an unsettled situation.

Sultan Thamasp had two sons, Ibrahim Adil Shaw and Sultan Ismaeel, who was brought up with his brother till the age of puberty, when Dillawer Khan sent him to be kept prisoner in the fortress of Balgoan, according to the usual policy of government. After the expulsion of the regent, Ibrahim Adil Shaw sent immediately one of his confidential servants to his brother, to express his concern that reasons of state would not permit him to satisfy the desire he had that they should live in the same place together, and to assure him of every indulgence and mark of affection that could be allowed. At the same time he sent orders to the governor of Balgoan, to give sultan Ismaeel the full liberty of the fort, and to provide every convenience and amusement that could make captivity less irksome. He also allowed him a monthly income of [a] one thousand oons, for his private

---

[a] Three hundred pounds.

private expenfes. The prince for fome time feemed fatisfied with his condition; but fuddenly lofing all fenfe of the generofity of his brother, confpired againft him, and by degrees bringing over the governor and garrifon of Balgoan to his intereft, and fecretly cor-' rupting many of the officers of the court, on the ninth of Ramazan, A.D. 1593. 1002, took poffeffion of the fort, and openly exalted the ftandard of rebellion.

Ibrahim Adil Shaw, regarding this behaviour as proceeding chiefly from the treachery of fome of his ungrateful nobility, and unwilling to proceed to extremities againft a brother, thought proper to try firft upon his mind the effects of admonition; for which purpofe he fent to him the venerable Shaw Noor Aalum, with folemn affurances, that if he laid afide his extravagant defigns, he fhould receive pardon, and be treated with every refpect and mark of affection due to a brother. The prince, inftead of liftening to the remonftrances of the Shaw, put him into confinement, and quickened his preparations to take the field; at the fame time fending ambaffadors to demand the affiftance of Boorahan Nizam Shaw, who promifed to fupport him with a confiderable army. Sultan Ifmaeel alfo brought over to his intereft Ein al Moolk, ameer al amra, and the adopted fon of Ankufs Khan. The former wifhing, for his own intereft, that the difputes for the throne might not foon be fettled, would not break out all at once, fo that Ifmaeel was obliged to content himfelf for the prefent with the fortrefs of Balgoan and its environs, where the khootbah was read in his name. Ein al Moolk, to deceive Ibrahim Adil Shaw, redoubled his fhew of loyalty, till matters fhould be ripe for the execution of his defigns in favour of the prince. The fultan on learning the behaviour of his brother to Shaw Noor Aalum, was much enraged, and immediately difpatched Elias Khan, his meer nobut, with an army to quell the rebellion and befiege Balgoan.

Elias

Elias Khan, with six thousand men, soon arrived before Balgoan; and as sultan Ismaeel had not yet been joined by his adherents, he shut himself up in the fort, which was closely besieged by the royalists. Ein al Moolk also, agreeable to the sultan's firmaun, joined the besiegers to preserve appearances; but, secretly attached to the rebel prince, kept up a constant correspondence with the enemy, and supplied them at night from his camp with grain and other necessaries. Intelligence of this treachery reaching the sultan, he, in order to try his fidelity, dispatched a firmaun, summoning him to court, on pretence that he wished to have advice from him on some affairs of importance, which could not be communicated to any other than himself. Ein al Moolk, in order to destroy suspicion, set out with many of his friends immediately on receipt of the firmaun to Beejapore, where he acted with so much art, as left the sultan in doubt of the truth of the accusations against him; and Ibrahim Adil Shaw, unwilling to destroy an old servant on suspicion only, hoped that, should it have any foundation in reality, the favours he received at his hands would impress his mind in such a manner, as to make him lay aside treacherous designs, and revive his loyalty. With this view, to do him honour, he received him with the greatest marks of attention in a full court. Ein al Moolk, according to custom, kissing the ground three times, advanced to the throne, the feet of which he also kissed; but his own guilt at this time struck him so forcibly, that he was seized with a trembling, which was observed by the sultan, who, desiring him to sit down, turned his face another way, that he might give him time to recover. He afterwards permitted him to eat with him, and after every mark of kindness and distinction, having conferred upon him a khelaut of great value, a dagger set with jewels, fine horses, and a bracelet of diamonds, gave him leave to return to the army without delay. The traitor departed from the capital the next day to his jaghire; and, forgetting his majesty's clemency, renewed his correspondence with sultan Ismaeel, and afforded him every aid of provisions as before; which conduct soon became

became the topic of common converfation throughout the royal camp. Not long after this, Hyaut Khan, cutwal of Beejapore, who had been to efcort ammunition and ftores, paffed on his return from camp near the refidence of Ein al Moolk, who invited him to an entertainment. Hyaut Khan, in hopes of obtaining a fum of money from him, upbraided him with his treachery, of which he had received full proofs in the camp; at the fame time threatening to difclofe all he knew to the fultan. Ein al Moolk, gueffing that his conduct was now beyond the power of hypocrify or prevarication to conceal, put Hyaut Khan into fetters for his rafh infolence, and openly avowed his defection, writing letters without delay to the governors of garrifons to join him in favour of the prince. Moft of them fent fair promifes, but waited to fee the turn of affairs, before they would dare to act openly; but the foldiers of the garrifon of Mirch inftantly confined their governor, and proclaimed fultan Ifmaeel. Ein al Moolk then fent expreffes to Boorahan Nizam Shaw, defiring him to expedite his march from Ahmednuggur, as the affairs of fultan Ifmaeel were in a profperous train, and, with his aid, would eafily attain an happy iffue, for which the forts of Sholapore and Shawdirruk, with their dependant diftricts, fhould be given up without delay. Boorahan Nizam Shaw, allured by this offer, began his march, and Ein al Moolk, encouraged by this fupport, withdrew his troops from Elias Khan before Balgoan; upon which great confufion prevailed through all the territories of Beejapore. The Hindoos of Malabar feizing the opportunity, invaded the diftricts of Binkapore; and Elias Khan, either through fear or treachery, raifed the fiege of Balgoan, and without orders returned to Beejapore, where his arrival threw the court and inhabitants into great difmay and terror. Dangerous infurrections enfued, and many courtiers formed defigns of taking poffeffion of the palace for the rebel prince, to gain his favour; but the firmnefs of mind of Ibrahim Adil Shaw on this trying occafion, at length prevailed over the fchemes of the feditious. He difplaced Elias Khan, Hajee Mahummud, and Roomi Khan,

Khan, and put them into strict confinement, to deter others from treachery, of which he had strong presumptions of their being guilty, at the same time issuing firmauns to all the amras to repair from their jaghires to court.

Ein al Moolk, seeing no army to oppose him in the field, marched without delay, with ten thousand horse and twenty thousand foot, to Balgoan, where he prevailed upon sultan Ismaeel to quit the fort; and without waiting for the junction of Boorahan Nizam Shaw, who had began his march from his capital of Ahmednuggur, resolved to move against the sultan at Beejapore. Ibrahim Adil Shaw, upon intelligence of this design, having appointed Hummeed Khan to the command of his army, sent him against the rebels; who, upon his arrival at Eesapore, sent some confidential persons to make him great offers of reward if he would come over to them. Hummeed Khan, by the instructions of his sovereign, received the messengers with much kindness, assuring them that he had no designs of opposition, and meant to join sultan Ismaeel; who, if he would quit the fort and take command of the army, might gain possession of the throne without trouble, or putting himself under any obligations for the assistance of Boorahan Nizam Shaw. Ein al Moolk, deceived by this promise, forgot his usual caution, and imprudently moved with sultan Ismaeel to an extensive plain at some distance from Balgoan, where, secure in his own mind, he was intent only on making magnificent preparations for the reception of Hummeed Khan and the other chiefs of the royal army. His son, Ghalib Khan, who had remonstrated to him without effect on his ingratitude to Ibrahim Adil Shaw, now warned him against the treachery of Hummeed Khan, and begged him at all events to be upon his guard against surprize, but all in vain. Hummeed Khan advanced in great order towards the camp of the rebels, where the prince and Ein al Moolk waited, with their principal adherents, in a magnificent tent to receive him; so that he was allowed to approach close to their lines without apprehension.

A.D. 1594.

He

He then, suddenly throwing off the mask, made a vigorous charge, which threw the camp into confusion and diforder. The prince and Ein al Moolk, upon being undeceived, mounted their horfes, and endeavoured to collect their troops for oppofition, but in vain. Ein al Moolk received a wound from a fabre, and, falling from his horfe, his head was immediately cut off by Soheil Khan. Sultan Ifmaeel was taken prifoner in trying to make his efcape to Ankufs Khan, with whofe affiftance he intended to join Boorahan Nizam Shaw. The rebel army difperfed to different quarters, and Hummeed Khan fent the head of Ein al Moolk, with congratulatory accounts of his victory to Beejapore. Ibrahim Adil Shaw ordered the head of the traitor to be placed on a high pole, before the principal gate of his palace, where it remained near a week; and Shujahut Khan Koord was fent to the camp, where, to prevent frefh rebellions, he by the fultan's orders put an end to the exiftence of fultan Ifmaeel. Hummeed Khan returned to Beejapore, and with many other amras was highly diftinguifhed by the royal favour. The head of Ein al Moolk being put into a great gun was blown into the air, that no traces might remain of him; and feventeeen perfons of the garrifon of Mirch, who had confined their chief and declared for the rebels, were put to death, after being brought in chains to Beejapore, by way of example. Boorahan Nizam Shaw, who had advanced as far as the fort of Porundch to affift the rebellion, on hearing that it was quelled, and the order of government reftored, retreated with expedition towards Ahmednuggur.

The great Author of events, and the Former of the world by words only, in order to difplay the fulnefs of his power, at frequent periods effects revolutions furprizing to human imagination, of which there could not be a greater proof than this victory, which was unexpected by all, as moft of the nobility favoured fultan Ifmaeel, and the zemindars were throughout the kingdom of Beejapore ripe for revolt.

Not

FERISHTA's HISTORY OF DEKKAN.

Not long after this, Boorahan Nizam Shaw entering into alliance with the roy of Bilcondah, refolved again to invade the territories of Ibrahim Adil Shaw; and accordingly difpatched Mortiza Khan Anjoo, at the head of ten thoufand horfe, with intentions to reduce Shawdirruk and Sholapore, while his ally laid fiege to fome of the forts on the frontiers of Carnatic. Mortiza Khan, when he had advanced as far as Porundeh, finding that the roy of Bilcondah had not yet begun his march, thought proper to halt; but fent out detachments to lay wafte and plunder the adjacent country. Thefe received a fevere defeat from the troops of Ibrahim Adil Shaw, and their commander, Uzbak Khan, was killed in the action, which ftruck the reft of the army with terror, and ftopped their operations. In the month of Rejib, Boorahan Nizam Shaw was taken dangeroufly ill of a bloody dyfentery; the news of which occafioned great commotions in the army at Porundeh, where diffentions arofe among the amras, and Mortiza Khan, with many of his friends, fearing affaffination from the mutinous chiefs, left his command, and retired to Ahmednuggur; at the fame time Khalifah Arab and Kuzzlbafh Khan fled for refuge to Ibrahim Adil Shaw. Boorahan Shaw, wafted by illnefs and the diffentions of his government, dying, was fucceeded by his fon Ibrahim, and Mean Munjoo Dekkanee became regent of the kingdom; but the young fultan's mother, who was an Abyffinian, gave fo much encouragement to the chiefs of her own nation, that the power of his office was withheld from him, and the upftart Abyffinians behaved fo difrefpectfully to the ambaffadors from Beejapore, as to make them quit Ahmednuggur in difguft.

Ibrahim Adil Shaw was fo much offended at the affront offered to his throne, that he refolved to be revenged on Nizam Shaw; for which purpofe, he on the twentieth of Shaaban having marched from his capital, encamped at Bhamenalee, and moved from thence towards Shawdirruk. Being however not fond of unneceffary war, he had determined in his own mind, if ambaffadors fhould be fent from

A.D. 1594.

from Ahmednuggur with apologies for the conduct of the ministers and desires of peace, to lay aside his expedition; and in this hope made designedly but very slow marches to Shawdirruk, where he fixed his head quarters.

Aklaafs Khan and the Abyssinian amras of Ahmednuggur, instead of endeavouring to make peace, marched with the sultan Ibrahim Shaw, at the head of thirty thousand men and a great train of artillery, to their borders; upon which Ibrahim Adil Shaw, thinking delay no longer adviseable, dispatched Hummeed Khan with other amras of distinction against them; at the same time giving instructions, that if Ibrahim Nizam Shaw did not attempt marching into his country, they should refrain from hostilities. The Nizam Shawee army passed the boundaries of Beejapore; upon which Hummeed Khan without delay marched to attack their camp, and a severe action ensued, in which he was near being defeated, his left wing giving way and flying from the field, closely pursued by the right of the enemy. Hummeed Khan however resolutely continued the battle with his center and right wing. Ibrahim Nizam Shaw, who had at first remained in the rear, to be out of danger, seeing the flight of part of the enemy's line, advanced with his household attendants; which being perceived by Soheil Khan, a eunuch, who commanded the right wing of the Adil Shawee army, he charged him; upon which the sultan's attendants begged him to retire, but he would not consent, exclaiming, that as his brother Ismaeel had disdained to fly from Dillawer Khan, it would be dishonourable in him to give way before a eunuch. Having said this, he drew his sabre, and with the elephants rushed towards Soheil Khan; but, after a short struggle, he received a mortal wound from an arrow, and died immediately. His attendants took up the body, and fled towards Ahmednuggur; and the other part of the army engaged with Hummeed Khan, learning the death of their king, were seized with a panic, and hastened from the field, of which they had nearly been the victors, leaving all

their

their baggage and artillery, with moſt of the royal elephants, to the plunder of the fortunate conquerors, who found themſelves ſuch, when they leaſt expected. While Hummeed Khan was enjoying the fruits of his victory, Ibrahim Adil Shaw received intelligence at Shawdirruk that his army was defeated, as many of the fugitives of the left wing, which had broken and diſperſed at the beginning of the action, had fled as far as the royal camp, which was thrown into great conſternation by their alarming accounts. Some ſaid, moſt of the nobility had been ſlain, and that all the elephants except one had fallen into the hands of the enemy. For three days, uncertain intelligence and frequent alarms were received; but on the fourth, full accounts were brought of the unexpected victory, and the death of Ibrahim Nizam Shaw, which changed the terrors of the multitude to the extravagance of joy. The ſultan, notwithſtanding this ſignal advantage, and the confuſed ſtate of the enemy's government, would not conſent to invade their territories, but recalled Hummeed Khan from the borders; and in the latter part of the month marched back towards Beejapore, but did not enter that capital till 1004. He A.D. 1595. halted on the banks of the Beemrah, from whence he diſpatched a force againſt one of the zemindars of the Carnatic, who, taking advantage of the war, had beſieged the fortreſs of Oodnee, which was in danger of falling from want of proviſions. On the thirteenth of Mohirrum, the ſultan made a triumphant entry into Beejapore, amid the acclamations of his people; who on this occaſion had adorned the ſtreets with tiſſues, velvets, brocades, other rich cloths, and coſtly ornaments. Soon after this, intelligence arrived that the infidels of Carnatic had, on the approach of the royal troops, raiſed the ſiege of Oodnee, and fled to their own country; but that many of them were cut to pieces in the purſuit. Meer Mahummud Saleh Hummadanee, a venerable ſyed, arriving near Beejapore, and bringing with him ſome hairs of the prophet, the ſultan, eager to pay his reſpects to ſuch valuable relics, went out to meet him; and having conducted him into the city, entertained him with royal magnificence for many

many days. He endeavoured to prevail upon him to fix his residence at his court, but the holy man was earnest to perform the pilgrimage to Mecca; and at his departure the sultan conferred upon him many rich presents, and received from him two of the sacred hairs, which he placed with care in a golden shrine set with jewels, and constantly visited it every Friday night, and upon all holidays.

Disputes growing to a great height in the government of Ahmednuggur, sultan Moraud, son of the emperor Akber, was invited into Dekkan by one of the parties; and, eager to take advantage of dissention to spread the authority of the Moguls in that country, marched from Guzarat to Ahmednuggur with an army of thirty thousand men, and laid siege to that city, which he was after many months obliged to raise, as Ibrahim Adil Shaw dispatched Soheil Khan with a great army to the relief of the besieged Nizam Shawceans, and, before his arrival, the Moguls retired.

A. D. 1596. FERISHTA concludes his history of the Beejapore sultans in the year 1005. What follows relative to them, is translated from a work called Lub al Towareekh, a summary history of Hindoostan, by Binderabun, a Hindoo, in the reign of Aurungzebe, as I could not obtain any fuller authority.

Binderabun writes, " I know not of any history, after Ferishta's, " of the sovereigns of Dekkan; but as the conclusion of his was at " the close of the reign of the emperor Akber, I have selected some " information from his history, some from that of the succeeding " emperors, and the rest from the conversation of well-informed, " credible persons, and partly I write from my own knowledge."

In

In the reign of Jehaungeer, Ibrahim Adil Shaw, in concert with the fultan of Ahmednuggur, difpatched an army againft Abd al Raheem Khankhaanan, the Mogul foubahdar of Khandefhe and Berar. The foubahdar, unable to oppofe the allies, was blocked up in the city of Boorahanpore. The Dekkanees poffeffed themfelves of feveral diftricts in both provinces; and carrying their depredations into Malwa, laid wafte the country as far north as the fortrefs of ᵃ Mandou. At length, the prince fultan ᵇ Khoorrum advancing with an army from Dhely, an engagement took place near Boorahanpore, when the Dekkanees were defeated with great flaughter, and fled. The imperial diftricts in Dekkan were recovered, and a very confiderable part of the Ahmednuggur fovereignty reduced to the Mogul government by the prince;. who, at length, confented to a peace, on the allied fultans paying him a fum of ᶜ fifty lacks of rupees.

Of the above fum, ᵈ twenty lacks were contributed by Ibrahim Adil Shaw, who in the year 1036 departed this life, after a reign of A.D. 1626. forty feven years and fome months.

ᵃ The ancient capital of Malwa.
ᵇ Afterwards Shaw Jehaun.
ᶜ Five hundred thoufand pounds.
ᵈ Two hundred thoufand pounds.

# SULTAN MAHUMMUD ADIL SHAW.

SULTAN Mahummud Adil Shaw on the death of his father acceded to the throne of Beejapore. As the Moguls were daily extending their conquests in Dekkan, and he knew that should the country of Ahmednuggur be reduced, his own would become the object of attack, he assisted Nizam Shaw against the imperial arms; and more than once suffered for his conduct, being obliged to purchase peace by large contributions. In the year 1044, the armies of the emperor Shaw Jehaun, under Khan Dowraun, Khan Zummaun, and Syed Jehaun Khan, invaded Dekkan on three quarters, and laid waste the country of Beejapore without mercy. After the reduction of Dowlutabad and other forts, with most part of the kingdom of Nizam Shaw, Mahummud Adil Shaw agreed to pay a considerable tribute to the emperor Shaw Jehaun. Though the government of Dekkan was entrusted to the prince Aurungzebe, he courted the patronage of Dara Shekkoh, and by his influence obtained royal titles from Shaw Jehaun, to whom he presented [a] forty lacks of rupees and forty elephants, with housings of gold and silver. He gave also [b] five lacks and some elephants to the princess Jehaunara Begum; and [c] fifteen lacks of rupees, as many elephants, and some valuable jewels, to the prince Dara Shekkoh. Afterwards, having displeased Aurungzebe,

A. D. 1634.

[a] Four hundred thousand pounds.
[b] Fifty thousand pounds.
[c] One hundred and fifty thousand pounds.

Aurungzebe, that prince obtained permiffion to invade Beejapore; which he entered, and took the fortrefs of Kallean and other places; but at this juncture intelligence arriving of the illnefs of Shaw Jehaun, and the confufion confequent at court, he moved from Dekkan. Mahummud Adil Shaw for the prefent faved his country. In the latter part of his reign, his vaffal Sewajee, the fon of Sahoo Bhofileh, by ftratagem and treachery obtained great power, and the foundations of the Beejapore monarchy became weakened, as will be accounted for in the hiftory of the reign of Aurungzebe. Mahummud Adil Shaw died in the year 1071.

A.D. 1660.

SULTAN

# SULTAN

## ALEE ADIL SHAW 2d.

THIS prince succeeding his father in his childhood, was unable to remedy the disorders which had occurred in his kingdom by the rebellion of Sewajee. This chief had possessed himself of all the strong holds in the Kokun country, and erected several new forts. Under pretence of making his submissions to the sultan, he begged an interview with the Beejapore general, Afzul Khan, whom he treacherously stabbed in an embrace. Rustum Khan was afterwards sent against him, and defeated. Alee Adil Shaw died in the year 1083, after a turbulent reign of between eleven and twelve years; during which he enjoyed little of royalty but the name, his country being usurped by Sewajee and other vassals. He was succeeded by his son Secunder Adil Shaw, an infant, who never acquired any real power, being the tool of his nobility; and in the year 1097, Beejapore, with its remaining dependancies, was reduced to the Mogul yoke by the emperor Aulumgeer.

A. D. 1672.

A. D. 1685.

END OF ADIL SHAWEE HISTORY.

☞ The history of the reigns subsequent to that of Ibrahim Adil Shaw 2d. the translator laments being too concise; but more detailed accounts were not to be obtained, though no enquiries have been spared in the search for them. The chasm however will be found in some measure filled up to the reader, by the account of the operations of the Mogul emperors in Dekkan, in another part of this work.

## FERISHTA's HISTORY

OF

## THE AHMEDNUGGUR SULTANS,

OR

## NIZAM SHAWEE DYNASTY.

# SULTAN

# AHMED NIZAM SHAW BEHEREE.

AHMED Nizam Shaw was the fon of Mallek Naib Nizam al Moolk Beheree, originally a bramin of Beejanuggur, but being taken prifoner in his infancy by the army of fultan Ahmed Shaw Bhamenee, was made a muffulmaun, received the name of Mallek Houffun, and was educated as one of the royal flaves. The fultan, feeing him a youth of abilities, gave him to his eldeft fon Mahummud fultan, with whom he finifhed his education, under the fame tutor, and became eminently learned in Perfic and Arabic literature. On fultan Mahummud's acceffion to the throne, he was raifed by that prince to the rank of a thoufand, and the charge of the royal falconry was entrufted to him, from which he acquired the appellation of a Beheree. By degrees he rofe to the higheft honours, received the titles of Afhruff Humaioon Nizam al Moolk Beheree, and by the patronage of Khajeh Jehaun Gawan, being appointed governor of Telingana, had Raajmundree and Cundapul, with their dependancies, conferred upon him in jaghire. Upon the death of Khajeh Jehaun, he fucceeded him in office, and was honoured with the title of Mallek Naib. Upon the death of Mahummud Shaw, he by his will became firft minifter to his fon fultan Mhamood, who added Beer and other diftricts to his jaghire; which he committed to the charge of his fon Mallek Ahmed, who took up his refidence at Khiber, and employed

---

a Beher is a fpecies of hawk.

employed himself diligently in the affairs of his government. As some of the forts granted to him were garrisoned by Mharattas, who refused to evacuate them, on pretence that sultan Mhamood, being an infant, was not capable of conducting affairs, Mallek Ahmed proceeded to reduce them by force; and first marched against the fortress of Seer, which was very strong, built round the summit of a high hill. The garrison, after a long siege, being in great distress, and seeing no hopes of relief, threw their weapons and shrouds on their necks, and came out to him with the keys of the place; at the same time laying at his feet five years tribute of the Kokun, which had been laid up there. This amounting to a very great sum enabled him to confer ample rewards upon his followers, and gave credit to his name. He successively reduced the forts of Johnde, Labgur, Sukkee, Terronee, Nuggoreh, Kundaneh, Perrub, Hussodun, Goherderruk, Meerunje, Maholee, and Palee, by which conquests all the country of Kokun fell into his hands. He was besieging the fort of Dundaraajepore when he received intelligence of the assassination of his father, Nizam al Moolk, and immediately returned to Khiber; where he assumed the titles of the deceased, and was generally known by those of Ahmed Nizam al Moolk Beheree, to which the people of Dekkan, though he did not affect it, added the name of Shaw, which we shall also use in mentioning him hereafter.

Ahmed Nizam Shaw, on his return to Khiber, after he had spent the usual time in mourning for his father, turned his attention to the welfare of his people; and so justly settled his country, that the loadstone dared not attract iron, and the ᵃ karooba refrained from molesting grass. As he had distinguished himself repeatedly as a general in the field, though sultan Mhamood wished to remove him from power, none of his nobility would accept the task of reducing him

---

ᵃ A plant, the leaf of which has the same effect on small bits of grass, as the loadstone on iron.

him. By the inftigation of Cafim Bereed, the fultan fent repeatedly firmauns to Eufuff Adil Khan, commanding him, in conjunction with Khajeh Jehaun Dekkanee and Zien ad Dien Ali Talifs, to march againft Khiber; but Adil Khan excufed himfelf, and even fent an envoy to warn Ahmed of his dangerous fituation, and to prepare for the defence of his dominions; at the fame time ordering his troops to evacuate to him the fortrefs of Indapore, and promifing him affiftance, fhould he require it.

Ahmed Nizam Shaw, having appointed Zerreef al Moolk Afghaun his ameer al amra, and Nufleer al Moolk Guzaratee his meer jumleh, fent a meffage to Zien ad Dien Ali Talifs, that as the rights of neighbourhood deferved the tokens of regard and generofity, and he efteemed him as endowed with valour and magnanimity, he wifhed that, erafing the characters of ftrangenefs from his mind, and forgetting the paft, he would look upon himfelf as the partner of his rifing fortunes. Zien ad Dien meeting his advances, made profeffions of duty and fubmiffion, but on Nadir al Zumman's marching to reduce Ahmed Shaw, with twelve thoufand horfe, wavered in his friendfhip, and refolved to join that nobleman. Ahmed Shaw on the approach of Nadir, having fent his family for fafety to the fort of Seer, marched with intentions to harafs the enemy; but as he was greatly fuperior in numbers, to avoid coming to an engagement. With this view he kept from them at the diftance of eight or ten miles, taking precautions to prevent a furprize. Finding that Zien ad Dien Ali Talifs waited only for an opportunity to join Nadir, he left his main body to the charge of Nufleer al Moolk, and with a felect party, under pretence of hunting, moved fuddenly towards Jagneh, the refidence of Zien ad Dien, who had no fufpicion, and kept but a loofe difcipline in the garrifon. He arrived at night, and applying ladders to the walls, mounted firft himfelf, followed by feventeen perfons, while others efcaladed at various quarters. Having got into the fort without oppofition from the drowfy and unfufpecting guards,

guards, he made a general flaughter of the garrifon, and Zien ad Dien with about feven hundred followers were put to death. Nufieer al Moolk upon hearing of the fall of Jagneh, became ambitious of diftinguifhing himfelf by fome important fervice, before the return of his fovereign, and with only three thoufand horfe marched againft the enemy, of whom he defeated two confiderable detachments; which encouraging him, he imprudently with his fatigued party gave battle to Nadir, but was defeated with great lofs. Ahmed Shaw, on his return from Jagneh, went to vifit him, and ufed every means to encourage him in his difagreeable fituation. Some nights after, having left his camp ftanding, he furprized the enemy fo effectually, that Nadir, with many of his principal officers, were killed, and his army totally difperfed, leaving all their baggage and tents to the fortunate Ahmed Shaw; who after his victory returned to Khiber, and, as before, turned all his attention to the flourifhing ftate of his people.

Sultan Mhamood Bhamenee, enraged at the defeat of his general, fent towards Khiber Uzmut al Moolk Dobeer, with eighteen amras of diftinction and a great army; upon which Ahmed Shaw, quitting the fortrefs, moved with his army into the mountainous country of Kadabad; and when the royal army had reached the pafs of Meeree, he with three thoufand horfe marched expeditioufly to Ahmedabad Bieder, and arriving during the night, was admitted by the guards, whom he had previoufly bribed to his interefts. He proceeded immediately to the palace, and having taken all the family of his father into his protection, fent them off immediately towards Khiber; then, having fecured the women and children of all the amras who were with the army fent againft him, left the capital in the morning, and carried them with him towards the fortrefs of Porundeh, but took the greateft care that no infults fhould be offered to the honour of the women.

The

The amras at the pafs of Meeree, upon hearing of this bold enterprize, and the fuccefs with which it had been attended, returned, in hopes of intercepting him; and arriving near, fent him a meffage, that as he had acted towards their wives and children as his own, they all were obliged, and bound by gratitude not to attack him; but that it was unbecoming his magnanimity to fly from them like robbers or banditti and diftrefs women; a behaviour not allowable among Koords or Fringes. Ahmed Shaw, hurt at this remark, immediately fent back to them the women and children, and marched to Porundeh. Juft then a firmaun full of reprimand and difpleafure came from fultan Mhamood to his amras, fetting forth, that Ahmed the fon of Nizam al Moolk, the falconer, fpreading his pinions like the hawk, foared on high, while they, trembling in the nefts of their tents, could not preferve the innocent mates of their affections from his talons; that if, having taken the rebel prifoner, they fhould repair paft errors, it was well; otherwife, being feized by the royal anger and difpleafure, they would give the honour of themfelves and their anceftors to the winds. The amras upon receipt of this firmaun halted, and fent off reprefentations to the fultan, that they were foldiers, whofe bufinefs it was only to fight the enemy, of whofe motions if the proper intelligence had been neglected, they were not to blame, but Uzmut Dobeer, who commanded the army; that if another chief fhould be fent them in his room, by the aufpices of the royal fortune, the expulfion of the enemy would be effected. Sultan Mhamood immediately recalled Uzmut, and fent Jehaungeer Khan, governor of Telingana, with three thoufand horfe as a reinforcement, to command the army in his room. This general, who was one of the firft minifters of the court, had performed many great exploits, and in courage and conduct was unequalled in Dekkan, upon his junction with the army, encouraged all the amras, and without delay advanced by continued marches to Porundeh.

Ahmed

Ahmed Shaw, not thing it prudent to engage, applied to Ummad al Moolk for affiftance; but feeing no hopes of obtaining it, and Jehaungeer Khan arriving near Puttun, he moved towards Khiber, and entering the hilly country by the pafs of Jeypore, was joined the fame day by Nuffeer al Moolk Guzaratee, with his army from Kadirubad, and a great fupply of treafure and provifions; upon which he placed guards in the paffes, and halted in the mountains. Jehaungeer Khan at length entered the hills by the pafs of Biefganou, and encamped near the town of Binkar. Both armies remained near a month inactive, within eighteen miles of each other; when Jehaungeer Khan on the fetting in of the rains, fuppofing that Ahmed Shaw muft perifh blocked up in the hills, or furrender to his fuperior army, became incautious, and gave himfelf up to his pleafures; and his example was followed by the officers and foldiers of his camp, who became negligent of duty.

A. D. 1489. Ahmed Shaw, who had good intelligence of the forgetfulnefs and felf-fecurity of the enemy, on the night of the third of Rejib, 895, moved from his camp with Azim Khan, and marched fo rapidly, that juft at daybreak he reached the enemy's camp, and rufhing upon them, like a fudden calamity of fortune, gave not a man time to oppofe him. Some, in the fleep of intoxication, took the road of futurity; and others, on opening their eyes, feeing death before them, gave themfelves up a prey to annihilation. Jehaungeer Khan and many officers of rank were killed in the confufion, and thofe who furvived were taken prifoners by Ahmed Shaw; who, after putting them on buffaloes, with their vefts torn in flips down to their waifts, and leading them round his camp for the fport of his foldiers, gave them leave to return to the capital with the accounts of their difgrace. This victory was called the victory of the garden, as Ahmed Shaw laid out on the fpot a magnificent garden, in which he built a fplendid palace, which was added to by all his fucceffors, who fortified and made it their general refidence, by the name of Baugh

Baugh Nizam. Ahmed Shaw, after returning thanks to God for his victory, and giving a town near his camp as a charitable foundation for holy men, returned to Khiber; where he now sat without an opposer on the mufnud of royalty; and, by the advice of Eufuff Adil Shaw, having difcontinued reading the khootbah in the name of Mhamood Shaw, put in his own, and fpread a white umbrella over his head. Khajeh Jehaun and feveral amras, however, reprefenting to him that his doing this while the Bhamenee fultan lived was ungrateful, he, to retain their attachments, left his own name out of the khootbah, and faid, that he ufed an umbrella only to fhelter himfelf from the fun, and not as a fign of royalty. The amras obferved to him, that as that was the cafe, they had no objections, provided he gave general leave to them and all his fubjects to ufe the umbrella. As he could not well refufe, permiffion was given; and from that time to this in his country, the king and the beggar carry it over their heads; but to diftinguifh the fultan from his fubjects, the royal umbrella has a piece of red upon it, while the others are all white. This cuftom fpread throughout all Dekkan, contrary to that in the Mogul empire, [a] where no one but the fovereign dare ufe an umbrella. A few days after, Khajeh Jehaun repented of his boldnefs, and, with all the amras, requefted him to replace his name in the khootbah, which at their earneft entreaties he agreed to; at the fame time pretending, it was only in compliance with their wifhes, and not from any ambition of his own. Soon after this he marched to reduce the fortrefs of Dundaraajepore, a ftrong place near the feaport of Choul; and having taken it after a long fiege, and by this means fecured quiet poffeffion of the country of Kokun, he turned his thoughts to the acquifition of Dowlutabad; for which purpofe he formed connections of friendfhip with the governors, on whom he hoped to prevail to deliver it up.

Mallek

[a] This is the cafe at prefent, except in the Englifh dominions.

Mallek Wojeh and Mallek Afhruff were brothers, and originally fervants of Khajeh Jehaun Gawan, after whofe death they became enrolled among the corps of fillehdaars of fultan Mhamood, and were at length raifed to the rank of nobility, by the patronage of Mallek Naib Nizam al Moolk Beheree, when Mallek Wojeh was appointed governer of the garrifon of Dowlutabad, and Mallek Afhruff of the diftricts dependant upon that fortrefs. They conducted affairs fo well, that the banditti of Dowlutabad, long famous for their daring robberies, were expelled, and the roads to the frontiers of Sultanpore, Nuddirbar, Buggellana and Guzarat became fo fecure, that merchants and travellers paffed without guards; and the inhabitants being happy under their government, the country became populous and flourifhing. Both the brothers, in gratitude for the patronage of Nizam al Moolk, kept on terms of the ftricteft friendfhip with his fon Ahmed Shaw; who, to cement their alliance ftill ftronger, after the victory of Baugh Nizam, gave his fifter Bibi Zeenut in marriage to Mallek Wojeh. A fon being born from this union, the younger brother, Mallek Afhruff, who had entertained ambitious views of fucceeding Mallek Wojeh and founding a kingdom for himfelf, was alarmed at it, and atrocioufly contrived to affaffinate both father and fon; after which crime he affumed independance at Dowlutabad, and endeavoured to form alliances with the fovereigns of Boorahanpore, Berar, and Guzarat. Bibi Zeenut, after the murder of her hufband and fon, having made her efcape to Khiber, demanded protection of her brother Ahmed

A.D. 1493. Nizam Shaw; who, in confequence, moved in the year 899, with intention to reduce Dowlutabad. Upon his arrival at the garden of Nizam, ambaffadors came to him from Cafim Bereed, requefting his affiftance againft Eufuff Adil Khan, who had laid fiege to the capital of Ahmedabad Bieder, and promifing, if he would comply, to afford him aid in the reduction of Dowlutabad. Ahmed Shaw confenting to the requeft, marched to Bieder, which he relieved in the manner we have related in the hiftory of Eufuff Adil Shaw; and then returning by the fame route, proceeded to execute his

original

original defign; but finding, after a fiege of two months, that Dowlutabad was too ftrong to be taken by force, he retreated towards Khiber. On his arrival at the town of Binkar, fituated nearly at an equal diftance from both places, he formed the defign of raifing a city for the capital of his dominions; from whence he refolved, every year at the harveft feafons, to difpatch an army to lay wafte the territories dependant upon Dowlutabad, hoping that the garrifon, being deprived of refources and diftreffed for provifions, would in procefs of time defert their chief, and give up that important fortrefs. With this view, in the year 900, at an inftant fixed upon by the aftrologers as aufpicious, he began the foundations of a city near the garden of Nizam, upon the bank of the river Seen, to which he gave the name of Ahmednuggur. Such diligence was ufed in erecting buildings, by the fultan and all his dependants, that in the fhort fpace of two years the new city rivalled in fplendour Bagdad and Cairo. His army every year marching into the territories of Dowlutabad, left nothing undone in ruining cultivation, wafting grain, and fetting fire to the habitations of the farmers at both the harvefts. In the year 905, fultan Mhamood of Guzarat, at the requeft of Mallek Afhruff, marched towards Dekkan; refolving firft to humble Adil Khan Farooki, fovereign of Khandefhe, and then proceed to Dowlutabad, which was befieged as ufual by Ahmed Nizam Shaw. Upon his arrival at Sultanpore, Adil Khan being alarmed, requefted the affiftance of Ummad al Moolk and Ahmed Shaw; upon which the latter immediately evacuated the vicinity of Dowlutabad, and haftened with fifteen thoufand horfe to Boorahanpore, fultan Mhamood being then encamped with a great army near Afere. Nuffeer al Moolk, by the advice of Ahmed Shaw, by means of a large fum of money, prevailed upon the keeper of the fultan's elephants to let loofe from his chains one of thofe animals, who was remarkably vicious. On the night appointed, Ahmed Shaw, with five thoufand men, marched towards the Guzaratee camp; and at twelve o'clock, when, by a fignal agreed upon, the elephant was let loofe and occafioned great confufion, he fuddenly

A. D. 1493.

A. D. 1494.

suddenly poured in upon the line showers of rockets and musquetry. Sultan Mhamood and his officers, who apprehended nothing less than an attack from so inferior an enemy, and were sleeping quietly in their tents, alarmed at the uproar, rose from their beds with hasty confusion. At this instant, the elephant ran towards the tents of the royal haram, the ladies of which, frightened, made dreadful shrieks; upon this the sultan, supposing the enemy had penetrated his camp and were beginning a slaughter of his family, made his way out of his tents, and fled with a few attendants to the distance of six miles. The Dekkanees continued at the limits of the camp firing rockets, till the Guzarat amras had turned out their troops, and then retreated; upon which, the latter hastened in a body to the royal tents, to congratulate the sultan on the repulse of the enemy; but not finding him, they thought proper to follow with the whole army; and Ahmed Shaw in the morning took up the ground they had left, with his allies, Adil Khan and Ummad al Moolk. A peace being concluded with sultan Mhamood shortly after, Ahmed Shaw returned towards Dowlutabad, and encamping on Ballaghaut, relaxed from his cares in a variety of amusements. While here, some gardeners brought him several baskets of mangoes, which they said had grown from kernels that had fallen on the ground he was encamped upon, when besieging Dowlutabad seven years before, which the sultan regarded as a lucky omen, that presaged his speedy acquisition of the fortress. Ashruff Khan being reduced to great distress, applied once more for assistance to sultan Mhamood of Guzarat, promising, if he would relieve him from the power of Ahmed Shaw, to read the khootbah at Dowlutabad in his name, and pay an annual tribute. The sultan, tempted by these offers, returned with a great army to the bank of the Tapti; upon which Ahmed Shaw raised the siege, and retired to his capital. Ashruff, agreeable to promise, read the khootbah in the name of sultan Mhamood, and going to his camp, made him valuable presents, which he agreed to renew every year as his vassal. The sultan, after collecting the arrears

of

of tribute from Adil Khan of Boorahanpore, returned to Guzarat; which was no sooner made known to Ahmed Shaw, than he again marched towards Dowlutabad, the garrison of which, disgusted at their chief for reading the khootbah in the name of Mhamood, sent him assurances that they were his servants, and would, if he arrived expeditiously, give him a convincing proof of their attachment. Ahmed Shaw, who received these letters on the banks of the Gung, set out instantly, with three thousand chosen men, and reaching Dowlutabad the same night surrounded the place. Mallek Ashruff discovering the defection of his followers, who were mostly Mharattas, was taken ill with vexation, and died five or six days after; upon which the garrison immediately delivered up the place to Ahmed Shaw, sending a deputation to him with the keys. He immediately went to view the fort, and gave orders for necessary repairs, settling in it a garrison of his own faithful troops; after which, he returned triumphant to Ahmednuggur, and built a citadel round the garden of Nizam, in which he had erected a palace of red and green stone. He also reduced Ashwer and other forts, and made the rajas of Kalneh and Buggellana become his tributaries.

In the year 913, Daood Shaw Farooki dying, disputes happened about the succession to the throne of Boorahanpore, and Mallek Hisham ad Dien Mogul, one of the principal amras of the government, requested assistance of Ahmed Shaw to favour the cause of Aalum Khan, a descendant of the ancient possessors of Asere. Sultan Mhamood at the same time resolving to place on the throne Adil Khan, the son of Houssun Khan Farooki, his sister's son, marched towards Khandeshe with a considerable army; upon which, Mallek Hisham ad Dien calling for the aid of Ahmed Shaw and Ummad al Moolk of Berar, they marched to Boorahanpore; but the former, finding disputes grow high, returned shortly to Dowlutabad, where Aalum Khan came to seek his protection. Upon the return of sultan Mhamood to Guzarat, Ahmed Shaw advanced with an army to his frontiers, A.D. 1507.

frontiers, and sent an ambassador, with a letter to the sultan, desiring that as Aalum Khan had taken protection with him, he would give him part of the territory of Afere and Boorahanpore: but Mhamood behaved roughly to the ambassadors, exclaiming, What right had the son of a slave to the sultans of Bhamenee to write to him, and extend his feet beyond his covering! that if he did not shortly change his behaviour, and repent, he should meet punishment! Ahmed Shaw, thinking it rash to proceed to extremities, upon this returned with Aalum Khan to Ahmednuggur, without delay, by continued marches.

A. D. 1508. In the year 914, Nusseer al Moolk dying, his office was conferred on Mukkummul Khan Dekkanee; and two or three months after, Ahmed Shaw was taken dangerously ill. He appointed his son Boorahan, an infant of only seven years, his successor; and conjuring all the nobility to obey him faithfully, took their oaths of allegiance, and shortly after paid the debt of nature.

Though the virtues of this prince exceeded all that can be comprized in the bounds of description, yet, in compliance with the custom of historians, the author attempts to relate a few. Among his great qualities, were continence and modesty. When he rode through the streets of the city, he never looked aside to the right or left, lest his eyes might fall upon another's wife. When he was a young man, and marched to reduce the fortress of Kaweel, there was taken among the captives a young lady of exquisite beauty, who was presented as an acceptable gift to the sultan by his first minister. Ahmed Shaw was charmed with her person, but being told by her that she had a husband, who, with all her family, was among the prisoners, he bridled his desire, and restored her uncontaminated to her friends, with presents to a great amount.

It

It was the cuftom of Ahmed Shaw, if any of his officers in the day of battle neglected difplaying a proper fpirit, that, inftead of reproaching, he rewarded them among the firft who had diftinguifh-ed themfelves by their gallantry. One of his courtiers once taking the liberty of enquiring the caufe of this unufual conduct, he replied, that he fhould have an explanation of it another time. Nor was it long before an officer, who had been backward in his duty and had been noticed by the fultan, diftinguifhed himfelf very particularly; and the fultan having honoured him with marks of approbation, faid to his courtier, Princes are mafters of the hunt, and fhould thus prepare young warriors for the game of war.

The cuftom of yulleek, or fingle combat, in Dekkan, is alfo a memorial of this prince, who was well fkilled in the fword, and delighted much in the fcience. Accordingly, as is ever the cuftom, the people being eager to copy the prince, both high and low devoted themfelves to it; and inftead of colleges, cuftomary in the cities of Iflaam, fchools for fword-playing were eftablifhed in all quarters of Ahmednuggur, and nothing was talked of but defence in every affembly. As is the effect of the ftrife-breeding climate of Dekkan, every perfon opened his mouth in vaunting over his fellow, and many contentions occurred between rafh young men, who brought them for decifion before the fultan. He gave orders for them to fight with fabres in his own prefence, deciding in favour of him who firft wounded his adverfary. In confequence of this encouragement, a crowd of young men every day attended in the hall of audience, to contend before the king; and, by degrees, this extravagance rofe to fuch a height, that every day two or three of the combatants were killed. At length, the fultan taking a difguft at fuch tragedies, commanded that no trials of fkill fhould be made in his prefence; but on the plain before the fort claimants might decide their pretenfions, and that their friends fhould not interfere. He alfo commanded, that if either of the duellifts was flain in conflict, retaliation, or
punifhment

punishment for his death, should not be demanded. This evil custom proving agreeable to the mussulmauns of Dekkan, spread from Ahmednuggur into every city; and its abomination was so far forgotten, that to this day even the learned and venerable sages, and the princes and the nobles of the land, practise duelling, and esteem it a great accomplishment; so that if their children do not court it, they do not number them among the valiant, but reprove them. The writer of these sheets, Mahummud Casim Ferishta, saw the following occurrence in the streets of Beejapore. Syed Mortiza and Syed Houssun, two white-bearded brothers, who were in great esteem with Ibrahim Adil Shaw, and regarded by all as respectable in Dekkan, had a dispute about a very trifling matter with three Dekkanees, also brothers, white-haired, and known to the king. First, the son of Syed Mortiza, a youth of twenty, engaged a Dekkanee, and was killed; upon which his father singled out another, and, like the son, resigned himself to death. Syed Houssun next fought the third Dekkanee, and scattered the dust of annihilation upon his own countenance. The three bodies were not yet removed from the street, when the Dekkanees, who had received mortal wounds from the slaughtered, gave up their lives to the Keeper of souls: and thus, in an instant, without any former enmity to each other, six respectable persons were destroyed. The mussulmauns of Dekkan are certainly unequalled in the management of the sabre, and in single combat, and no one can face them, who has not learned the science; but as most of them practise on foot, and are ignorant of horsemanship and throwing the lance, before an army, especially of Dekkanee cavalry, they are much inferior; but for private quarrels and street contentions, they are as tearing lions.

Since the dynasty of Bhamenee, no princes of Dekkan have tried to discourage or abolish this abominable custom, but have rather endeavoured to promote it, except Ibrahim Adil Shaw 2d of Beejapore, in whofe reign it has been much difufed; and there is hope, that this deteftable practice, which never exifted in any other country, will, by the happy aufpices of wife and juft princes, be altogether done away; and this country, refembling paradife, be purified from fuch abomination.

SULTAN

# SULTAN

# BOORAHAN NIZAM SHAW.

BOORAHAN Nizam Shaw afcended the throne of his father, at Ahmednuggur, in the feventh year of his age. Mukkummul Khan Dekkanee, who was an able ftatefman and general, as in the lifetime of Ahmed Shaw, was honoured with the offices of [a] pefhwa and [b] meer jumla, and his fon Jummaul ad Dien became diftinguifhed by the title of Yezzeez al Moolk and poft of [c] fer nobut. The father and fon, having thus brought the royal houfehold under their controul, obtained full power over all the affairs of government. Near three years paffed in this manner, when the pride and want of moderation of Yezzeez al Moolk exceeded all bounds, and the other minifters and nobles, as Roomi Khan, Kerrum Khan, and Meer Khan, became jealous, and weary of his authority. But as much as they ftrove to remove him, they could not accomplifh their wifhes. At length, they gained over to their views one of the women of the haram, named Bibi Aiefha, who was nurfe to the mother of Boorahan Shaw, and enjoyed much of her confidence. It was agreed that fhe fhould contrive to deliver over to them Raja Jeou, the infant brother of the king, whom they would place on the throne, and thus, by depofing Boorahan Shaw, free themfelves from the tyranny of Yezzeez al Moolk and Mukkummul Khan. Bibi Aiefha accordingly,

one

[a] Prime minifter.
[b] Commander in chief.
[c] General of the body guards.

one day, having dreffed the young prince, who was only four years old, in girl's clothes, and put him in her own litter, took him from the palace towards the city. She was fcarce gone, when the mother called for her fon, and, upon his not being found, a great tumult arofe among the attendants within and without the palace. Some, guefling that he might have fallen into a canal or fountain, went to fearch; while others purfued Bibi Aiefha, towards the city, and over- taking her before fhe reached the houfe of Roomi Khan, brought her back with the child. As Bibi Aiefha was regarded as a grandmother to the princes, and now and then took them to her own houfe, where fhe kept them for two or three days at a time, fhe now pre- tended that fhe was carrying the young prince only on a vifit; but in a few days the fecret was difclofed, that fhe had done it in concert with the amras. Upon this, the minifters took greater caution than ever for the fafety of the princes. They ufed fo much attention in the education and inftruction of Boorahan Shaw, that in his tenth year he read verfe and wrote with elegance; and the writer of this hiftory has feen a treatife on the duties of kings, written by him, in the library of the Ahmednuggur fovereigns.

As the enmity between the minifters and the abovementioned three amras now exceeded all bounds, the latter fuddenly fled from Ahmednuggur, with near eight thoufand followers; and, taking the road of Berar, excited Shekh Alla ad Dien Ummad al Moolk to in- vade the dominions of Boorahan Shaw, by reprefenting the conqueft as eafy. The Berar chief, deceived, and tempted by their declara- tions, collected his forces, and, marching from Elichpore, moved to the frontiers of Nizam Shaw, and poffeffed himfelf of fome towns and diftricts. Mukkummul Khan, upon intelligence of this invafion, bent his whole attention to expel it, and marched with Boorahan Shaw, attended by Khajeh Jehaun Dekkanee, in great force againft the enemy. An engagement enfued near the town of Ranooree, in the year 916, in which the invaders received a total defeat; and Ummad al A.D. 1510.

FERISHTA's HISTORY OF DEKKAN.

al Moolk flying from the field, did not draw in his reins, till he reached his capital of Elichpore. His baggage, horfes, and elephants, fell into the hands of the Nizam Shaweeans, who laid wafte great part of Berar. In this battle, Boorahan Shaw, on account of his tender years, was carried on horfeback before Ardoo Khan, a confidential Turkifh flave. Ummad al Moolk, upon Mukkummul Khan's following him into Berar, feeing his fafety in flight, went to Boorahanpore, the chief of which fent learned and refpectable perfonages to the camp of Boorahan Shaw, who reprefented, from the authority of the koraun and the traditions of the prophet, the difgrace of the faithful making war on each other. A peace was concluded, and both parties retired into their own country.

It is faid, that the anceftors of the Nizam Shawee kings were natives of Paterree; but for fome caufe, one of them, quitting his birth place, removed to Beejanuggur, where he fettled. When the family arrived at royalty, all the relations came to Ahmednuggur, and expreffed a defire to recover their ancient home of Paterree; upon which Mukkummul Khan fent a meffage to Ummad al Moolk, as from Boorahan Shaw, requefting that he would, from regard, give up this tract with which he was fo connected, and receive in lieu of it a pergunnah yielding a richer revenue. Ummad al Moolk would not confent to the exchange; and forefeeing that a quarrel muft enfue on this point, began to build a fort for the protection of the pergunnah. Mukkummul Khan requefted him to defift, but in vain, and the work was completed. Mukkummul Khan, pretending to go to Dowlutabad, marched fuddenly againft this place, and carried it by ftorm; after which he left it in charge of Mean Gori, who had fhewn great fpirit in the attack, and conferred upon him the title of Kamil Khan.

Boorahan Nizam Shaw upon his approach to manhood, became enamoured of a dancing girl, named Ameena, whom he married,

and

and placed at the head of his haram. From her example he learned to drink wine; upon knowing which, Mukkummul Khan, who was a wife and virtuous perfon, bowing his head to the ground before the throne, and laying down the feals of his office, faid to the fultan, " While you were a child, I, the humbleft flave of the " throne, to the utmoft of my ability, carried on the affairs com- " mittted to my charge, under the royal aufpices; but now, that " your majefty is able perfonally to conduct the affairs of the ftate, " you will excufe your ancient flave from bufinefs." Boorahan Shaw complied with his requeft, and exalted his fons among the chief amras, but conferred the office of pefhwa on fhekh Jaffier Dekkanee. Mukkummul Khan lived retired in his own houfe; only now and then, at the earneft requefts of his relations, going to court on days of feftivals, but would not engage in any publick bufinefs; till at length he became united to the mercy of the Deity.

In the year 930, Boorahan Nizam Shaw and Ifmaeel Adil Shaw, A.D. 1523. by the endeavours of Shaw Tahir, had a meeting in the fort of Sholapore; and Bibi Mariem, fifter to the latter, was given in marriage to the former, and the nuptials celebrated with great pomp. As Affud Khan Balgoance had promifed to give Sholapore as a marriage portion, Boorahan Nizam Shaw demanded it; but Ifmaeel Adil Shaw denied having knowledge of the promife, and faid, if it had been made unknown to him, it was not binding upon him. Boorahan Nizam Shaw, by advice of Shaw Tahir, did not infift on the performance, but returned to Ahmednuggur. Ameena behaving very improperly to Bibi Mariem, fhe, after fome time, complained to her brother Ifmaeel Adil Shaw, who obferved to the ambaffadors of his brother in law, then at Beejapore, that placing a dancing girl over the head of the daughter of a king, was departing from true dignity: which fpeech being told to Boorahan Shaw, became the caufe of a long difpute. Boorahan Shaw inftantly difpatched embaffies to Ameer Bereed and Ummad al Moolk, courting both princes to his alliance.

A.D. 1524. In the year 931, in conjunction with them, he moved at the head of thirty thoufand horfe and a confiderable artillery, with intentions to befiege Sholapore.

Ifmaeel Adil Shaw advanced to meet the enemy with nine thoufand archers, and an engagement took place on the borders, fo bloody, that nature feels horror at the remembrance. Ummad al Moolk was broken by the attack of Affud Khan Balgoanee, and fled precipitately to Kaweel without halting; and Boorahan Nizam Shaw being overcome with heat and thirft, in the height of conflict, fainted away, and was borne off haftily in a pallanquin by his Turkifh flaves to Ahmednuggur, which he reached with great difficulty.

A.D. 1526. In the year 933, Ummad Shaw, at the inftigation of Ifmaeel Adil Shaw, in conjunction with Sultan Koolli Koottub Shaw, led an army againft the fort of Paterree, which he recovered from Boorahan Nizam Shaw; who, however, fhortly after retook it, razed the fortifications, and gave the diftrict dependant upon it to his relations the bramins; in whofe hands it continued for generations, till the reign of the emperor Akber. From thence, Boorahan Shaw, having marched to Mahore, took that fort, and then moved towards Elichpore. Ummad al Moolk, unable to withftand him, fled as formerly to Boorahanpore. Mahummud Shaw Farooki, chief of that country, affifting him with troops in perfon, they moved againft Boorahan Shaw, who defeated them; taking from them near three hundred elephants, their tents, infignia of royalty, and much baggage. Many places in Berar fell into his hands. Ummad al Moolk and Mahummud Shaw feeing affairs in this fituation, fent ambafladors with valuable prefents to fultan Bahadur Shaw of Guzarat, to requeft his affiftance. Sultan Bahadur regarding their requeft as fortunate to his
A.D. 1528. arms, in the year 935 entered Dekkan with a great army, by the route of Nudderbar and Sultanpore.

Boorahan

Boorahan Nizam Shaw being much alarmed, sent letters to Shaw Baber of Dhely, congratulating him on his acceſſion, profeſſing allegiance, and begging his protection. He at the ſame time requeſted aſſiſtance from Iſmacel Adil Shaw and ſultan Koolli Koottub Shaw. The former ſent Ameer Bereed with ſix thouſand foreign horſe to join him; but the latter excuſed himſelf, under pretence of being engaged in war in another quarter.

Bahadur Shaw having entered Berar with a view to retake Mahore and Paterree, and liking the country, remained ſome time in it; upon which Ummad al Moolk, dreading the waſte of his dominions, repreſented, that if he would move into Boorahan Shaw's country, and procure ſome parts of it for him, he would remove his family from Kaweel, and, reſigning that place up to him, attend conſtantly on his ſtirrup. Sultan Bahadur, complying with his requeſt, moved towards the army of Boorahan Shaw, which was encamped in the hilly country. Ameer Bereed, with the auxiliaries of Adil Shaw and about three thouſand horſe of his own, attacked part of the Guzarat army ſuddenly, on its march between the towns of Beer and Puttun, killed near three thouſand men, took much baggage, with ſeventy mules laden with treaſure. Sultan Bahadur, enraged, detached Khodawund Khan, his vizier, with eight thouſand horſe, to revenge the affront, and Ameer Bereed defeated them by an ambuſh. The ſultan then ſent twenty thouſand horſe to reinforce Khodawund Khan, under the command of Ummad al Moolk. Boorahan Shaw with his allies, finding it impoſſible to oppoſe ſo great a force, fled to Porundeh, and from thence, being purſued by the enemy, towards Joneer. Sultan Bahadur now proceeded to Ahmednuggur, where he took up his reſidence in the palace, and his amras choſe their quarters in the houſes of the citizens. The ſultan commanded a great terrace to be formed of lime and ſtone, that had been collected for buildings, which was raiſed in one night, and called the black terrace, the ſtone being of that colour. Upon this, the ſultan ſat for forty days ſucceſſively, succeffively, to receive the compliments of the people, and amufe himfelf with fights of elephants and other animals. Boorahan Shaw and his allies laid wafte the country round, and prevented fupplies from coming to his army; fo that famine prevailed. About this time, he dreamed one night, that a number of frightful dæmons and evil fpirits furrounded his bed, fome with brands of fire, and others with great ftones in their hands, which they threatened to caft upon him. He was affrighted from fleep, and immediately fummoned a confultation of his nobles, who informed him, that in that fpot Ahmed Nizam Shaw had fought a battle, in which great numbers of infidels and muffulmauns were flain when intoxicated, and that their fpirits, unable to afcend the upper regions of the air, now hovered about this fpot. Sultan Bahadur was alarmed at this account, flept in his tents the next night, and a few days afterwards moved from the city towards Dowlutabad; and leaving Ummad al Moolk with the Guzarat amras to befiege that fortrefs, encamped with Mahummud Shaw Farooki, on the mountains of Ballaghaut.

Boorahan Nizam Shaw now wrote to Ifmaeel Adil Shaw, that though he had fent him aid, as became a brother, unlefs he came to his affiftance in perfon, he fhould never be relieved from the prefent troubles. In anfwer to this, Ifmaeel Adil Shaw replied, that the infidels of Beejanuggur were encamped near Roijore, and, if he left his country, would inftantly invade it; but that he had fent him five hundred chofen horfe in additional aid, under the command of Hyder al Moolk Cafbeenie, and hoped that he would fhortly be gladdened by victory. Boorahan Shaw, difappointed, was at a lofs how to act. As the people and army were difpleafed at the adminiftration of Shekh Jaffier, he removed him from the office of pefhwa, which he beftowed on Kanwerfein, a bramin, who was endowed with wifdom, penetration, and integrity. By his advice he moved, with all the troops he could collect, from Joneer to his capital of Ahmednuggur. Soon after this, he marched with great caution, and fixed his camp

in

in the hills, within eight miles of the Guzarat army, which he haraffed by fkirmifhes for near three months. At length, finding that this had no effect upon the fortitude of the Guzaratees, he, by the advice of Kanwerfein, privately afked peace of Mahummud Shaw and Ummad al Moolk, promifing to return the forts and elephants he had taken from them; upon which they reprefented to Khodawund Khan, that they had called in fultan Bahadur only to recover Paterree and Mahore, for which they had engaged to read the khootbah of Berar and Ahmednuggur in his name, and make him annual prefents, but that the fultan had extended his views to the poffeffion of their country. The vizier in reply told them, that this was their own fault, for if the kings of Dekkan would agree with each other, all would be well. They underftood his meaning, and departed. Ummad al Moolk fuffered large fupplies of provifion to be conveyed to Dowlutabad through his lines, and at the commencement of the rains retired fuddenly towards Elichpore.

Sultan Bahadur and Meeran Mahummud Shaw now confulted whether to ftay, or retreat; and all the minifters obferved, that when the rivers fhould be full from the rainy feafon, it would be impoffible to obtain fupplies from Guzarat or Khandefhe, and it was poffible the princes of Dekkan might unite; therefore it would be prudent to leave their feveral countries in the poffeffion of Ummad al Moolk and Nizam Shaw, and be content with their acknowledgments of homage. Sultan Bahadur confenting to this, Boorahan Nizam Shaw and Ummad al Moolk fent their ambaffadors with prefents, and read the khootbah in the name of Bahadur Shaw; who afterwards returned to Guzarat. Boorahan Nizam Shaw on his arrival at Ahmednuggur received a demand from Meeran Mahummud Shaw for the elephants he had promifed him, and the forts for Ummad al Moolk. With the firft he complied in part, but refufed the latter; and as Mahummud Shaw obtained his own wifhes, he did not urge more on the fubject, but kept up a friendly connection with Boorahan Nizam Shaw.

Boorahan Shaw the following year fent Shaw Tahir with prefents of rich goods, elephants, and horfes, to fultan Bahadur of Guzarat, who delayed giving him an audience, and wrote to Meeran Mahummud Shaw, that he had heard, Ummad al Moolk had only once read his name in the khootbah. Meeran Mahummud Shaw in anfwer, affured him, that Boorahan Shaw was his loyal vaffal, and that if he had only read it once, it was to fave appearances with the other fultans of Dekkan; therefore he fhould forgive him, and receive his embaffy. Sultan Bahadur accordingly received Shaw Tahir, but did not for fome time fhew him much encouragement; till at length his great qualities and learning fo won upon him, that he altered his behaviour, and at the end of three months difmiffed him with honours and prefents.

A. D. 1530  In the year 937, when fultan Bahadur had fubdued Malwa, Boorahan Nizam Shaw, being alarmed, fent Shaw Tahir with Nerfoo Pundit to congratulate him upon his conquefts. They were introduced to the fultan at Boorahanpore, by Meeran Mahummud Shaw; who obferved, that as the empire of the chief provinces of Hindooftan had now devolved on the family of Timur, the ftar of whofe profperity was daily afcending, it was political to make a friend of Boorahan Nizam Shaw. Sultan Bahadur, who was a prince of much ambition, and fought an equality with the fovereigns of Dhely, liftened to the advice of Mahummud Shaw, and conferred many favours on Shaw Tahir; who was difmiffed with expedition to Ahmednuggur, in order to prevail on Boorahan Nizam Shaw to come to an interview with the fultan. Shaw Tahir on his arrival, at firft diffuaded the fultan from the meeting; but, being overcome by the arguments of Kanwerfein, confented. Boorahan Shaw having left his fon Shaw Houffein as his heir, and the direction of all affairs under

the

the care of Kanwerſein, moved towards Boorahanpore, with a force ſomewhat leſs than ſeven thouſand horſe, and diſpatched Khajeh Ibrahim and Sabajee as ambaſſadors before him, to ſettle the mode of interview, and the proper offerings. Upon Boorahan Shaw's arrival on the bank of the river Chattukdeo, near Boorahanpore, he was met by Meeran Mahummud Shaw, who informed him, that ſultan Bahadur would receive him on his throne, on each ſide of which holy men were permitted to ſit; but all perſons elſe, of whatever rank, ſtood with their arms croſſed before them in the front of the throne. Boorahan Shaw, underſtanding his reaſons for this remark, ſaid nothing in reply; but, when Mahummud Shaw took leave, called his confidants to him privately, and declared, that he would never ſubmit to the indignity of ſtanding before the throne of Bahadur Shaw, after having drawn his head from the yoke of the houſe of Bhamenee; that he would rather decline the meeting, and truſt his ſafety to the goodneſs of the Almighty. Shaw Tahir replied, that God was merciful, and would, he hoped, grant every thing agreeable to his deſire; but that he muſt not be haſty, nor repeat ſuch declarations, ſince policy demanded that he ſhould for one day agree to a humiliation, that he might paſs the remainder of his life in power and dignity. Boorahan Shaw, who was a perſon of judgment, ceaſed from violence, and agreed to the reaſoning of Shaw Tahir; who now obſerved, that he had in his mind a remedy againſt indignity. He ſaid he had in his poſſeſſion a koraun in the handwriting of the holy Ali, which Bahadur Shaw was very deſirous of ſeeing; that he would carry it with him, ſo that Bahadur Shaw might from neceſſity deſcend from his throne, and meet him. Boorahan Shaw was pleaſed with this, and the next morning ſet out to the place appointed for the interview, in company with Shaw Tahir and Meeran Mahummud Shaw. When they arrived near the royal tents, Shaw Tahir placed the koraun upon his head, and Bahadur Shaw ſeeing him at a diſtance, aſked his vizier, Khodawund Khan, what he was carrying. Upon being anſwered, a koraun in the hand of Ali; he

inſtantly

instantly descended from his throne out of respect, and having received it, kissed it three times, and rubbed it on his forehead; then received the compliments of Boorahan Shaw, and asked him, in the Guzarat language, after his health; to which Boorahan Shaw replied in Persic, that by the auspices of the sultan he was happy. Sultan Bahadur then reascended his throne, and Boorahan Shaw and Meeran Mahummud Shaw stood before it. Sultan Bahadur seeing Shaw Tahir standing, desired him to sit, which he declined; but being repeatedly pressed, he represented that he was ready to obey, but it did not become him to sit, while his master stood. The sultan then desired Boorahan Shaw to sit. Sultan Bahadur entered into conversation with Boorahan Nizam Shaw, in the Persian language, enquiring how he had passed the days of distressful vicissitude. Boorahan Shaw replied, that afflictions, which lead to prosperity, and absence bounded by enjoyment, make the approach to be forgotten in the conclusion; that the present moment was a sufficient recompense for what evils had happened to him for a series of years. When sultan Bahadur heard this answer, he turned to Meeran Mahummud Shaw, and said, " Heard you the answer of Boorahan al Moolk?" He replied, that he did not. Upon which sultan Bahadur repeated his question, and received the same reply. He then praised him in a voice loud enough to be heard by all present. Shaw Tahir then arose, and said, These are the marks of the royal bounty, which I hope will daily encrease towards us. Sultan Bahadur, taking a sword and dagger set with jewels from his own waist, girded them on Nizam Shaw; and as he had not till that time stiled him Shaw, said, May the title of Shaw prove auspicious to you! At the same time he presented him with the umbrella of royalty taken from the sultan of Malwa, and commanded Khodawund Khan, his vizier, and Meeran Mahummud Shaw to conduct him to the tents pitched for his reception, which had belonged to the same prince, sultan Mhamood Khiljee of Malwa. The following day, sultan Bahadur made a grand entertainment, and seated Boorahan Nizam Shaw and Meeran

Mahummud

Mahummud Shaw on chairs of gold before his throne. At the breaking up of the affembly, he prefented Boorahan Nizam Shaw with five horfes, two elephants, and twelve fighting deer. The two kings then played together at the * chowgaan. Nizam Shaw prefented fultan Bahadur his offerings, all of which he approved, but taking only a koraun, and a fcymetar, on which was engraved the name of one of the Abaffide caliphs, with four elephants, and two Arab horfes, faid to Nizam Shaw, " I give you back the remainder " of your prefents, with all the countries of Dekkan;" at the fame time difmiffing him, with permiffion to return to Ahmednuggur. Accordingly he took his departure; and going by the way of Dowlutabad and Ballaghaut, paid his devotions at the tombs of holy men at thofe places: after which he encamped for fome time at the refervoir of Kuttulloo, where he was met by his fon Houffein Shaw, Kanwerfein, and his other minifters, alfo the ambaffadors of Adil Shaw and Koottub Shaw, who came to congratulate him.

The difagreements between the fultan of Guzarat and Boorahan Shaw being now done away, the latter was at leifure to attend to the regulation of his dominions; and accordingly, by the wife policy of his minifter Kanwerfein, he took thirty forts from the rajas of the Mharattas, who had not paid obedience fince the death of Ahmed Nizam Shaw, and entertained thofe chiefs in his fervice, leaving them lands for their fupport. He honoured Khajeh Ibrahim with the title of Lutteef Khan, and Sabajee with that of Pertab Roy, admitting them among his confidential fervants. The gardens of Nizam, which had been injured by the Guzaratees, he repaired and improved.

In the year 938, Ifmaeel Adil Shaw having meditated the conqueft of the forts of Kallean and Candahar, Ameer Bereed fought the protection

A. D. 1531.

* A game fomewhat fimilar to that in Scotland called goff, only it is exercifed on horfeback.

protection of Boorahan Nizam Shaw, who wrote a haughty letter to Adil Shaw, commanding him to defift, which was anfwered by defiance. This brought on difputes about their borders. Ifmaeel Adil Shaw, in his anfwer to Nizam Shaw, afked if he had forgotten the former defolation of Ahmednuggur; remarking, if he prided himfelf on the tattered infignia of the Malwa princes, the boaft was ridiculous; nor had he fuperiority in the title of fultan, beftowed upon him only by the chief of Guzarat; whereas his royalty was given him by the kings of Perfia, defcendants of the prophet; that if he repented of fuch follies, it would be fortunate, but if not, he fhould quit the gardens of Nizam, where he would meet him and try the force of arms to humble his vanity.

Boorahan Nizam Shaw, though afhamed of his vaunting, yet marched immediately to Ameerapore, where he remained fome days to collect his forces, and then moved towards the borders of Adil Shaw, who gave him a total defeat, and obliged him to retreat to Ahmednuggur, with the lofs of all his baggage and near four thoufand men; which difgrace fully leffened his pride and vain glory.

A. D. 1532.   In the year 939, by the mediation of ambaffadors, a meeting was effected between Boorahan Nizam Shaw and Ifmaeel Adil Shaw; when it was agreed, that the former fhould undertake the conqueft of Berar, and the latter of Telingana; and that they fhould divide Dekkan in a brotherly manner between them: but this plan was deftroyed by the premature death of Ifmaeel Adil Shaw, and the difputes which took place between his fucceffor and Nizam Shaw.

A. D. 1537.   In the year 944, at the inftigation of Shaw Tahir, Boorahan Nizam Shaw rejected the names of the Sahabeh from the khootbah for thofe of the Imaums; and as the colour of their ftandards was green, and tradition relates, that at the refurrection thofe of the prophet will alfo be of that colour, he changed his umbrella and
ftandards

standards to it. He alſo (God forgive him) ſettled penſions on perſons to curſe and revile the three companions and their followers in the moſques and ſtreets; thus accompliſhing a wiſh which Euſuff Adil Shaw, through fear of his principal amras of the ſoonni ſect, was obliged to carry with him to the grave, uneffected. Boorahan Shaw however ran ſome hazard from his religious zeal. He was beſieged in his palace by a number of malecontents, headed by Moolla Peer Mahummud, a furious ſoonni, whom he took priſoner and confined; upon which the tumult ſubſided. The kings of Guzarat, Beejapore, and Khandeſhe, enraged at the inſult offered to the ſoonnites, entered into alliance with each other, and agreed to divide the dominions of Boorahan Nizam Shaw between them; upon which he ſent an embaſſy to the emperor Humaioon, offering his ſervices to aſſiſt in an invaſion of Guzarat; but the rebellion of Shere Shaw falling out, prevented its ſucceſs. Boorahan Shaw found means to ſatisfy the ſultans of Guzarat and Khandeſhe; and entertaining in his ſervice all the foreigners diſbanded by Ibrahim Adil Shaw, marched to invade Beejapore. Being ſucceſsful, he brought triumphantly to Ahmednuggur an hundred elephants and ſome pieces of cannon.

In the year 949, Boorahan Shaw again invaded Beejapore; but, though ſucceſsful in the beginning, was at laſt forced to retreat to the fortreſs of Dowlutabad, leaving his capital a prey to the Beejapore troops. He made his peace by giving up many places. The account of this expedition has been related in the hiſtory of the reign of Ibrahim Adil Shaw, as well as of ſeveral others, which compoſe the whole tranſactions of the reign of Boorahan Nizam Shaw, and would be tireſome in the repetition. He died in the year 961, and was buried in the ſame tomb with his father.

A.D. 1542.

A.D. 1553.

SULTAN

# SULTAN

# HOUSSEIN NIZAM SHAW.

HOUSSEIN Nizam Shaw fucceeded his father in the thirtieth year of his age. His brother Abdul Kader and the other princes efcaped from the palace the day of his acceffion, and two parties were formed in the ftate; the foreigners and Ethiopians embracing the caufe of Houffein, and the Dekkanees, both muffulmauns and Hindoos, that of Abdul Kader; who, however, was at length deferted, and fled into Berar for protection to Ummad al Moolk; his brothers, Shaw Ali and Meeran Mahummud Bahir, fought an afylum at Beejapore. Khajeh Jehaun, governor of Porundeh, refufed to come to court, and claimed the throne for his fon in law, Hyder Shaw, alfo fon to the late king. Houffein Shaw marched againft him, and Khan Jehaun fled with the prince to Beejapore. The fultan reduced the fort, and returned to Ahmednuggur. The king of Beejapore embraced the caufe of Shaw Hyder. Houffein entered into an alliance with Ummad al Moolk, who furnifhed him with feven thoufand horfe. He marched to relieve Sholapore, then befieged by Adil Shaw. An account of this expedition has been given in the hiftory of that prince. Syef Ein al Moolk, who had left his fervice, and gone over to Beejapore, being driven from that kingdom, afked leave to return to Ahmednuggur. Houffein Nizam Shaw affured him of a favourable reception, but upon his arrival cut him off by treachery. His women and effects were faved by the gallantry of his chief dependant, Kubbool Khan, who conducted them in fafety to Golconda, where he

was

was received into the service of Ibrahim Koottub Shaw. The grave of Syef Ein al Moolk is frequented by soldiers, who eat the turf near it, as a stimulus to valour. He was celebrated for the goodness of his troops, and living with them in a brotherly manner. Ibrahim Adil Shaw dying, Houssein Shaw invaded Beejapore in conjunction with Koottub Shaw, who after some time deserted him, and he was obliged to return to Ahmednuggur. Ali Adil Shaw formed an alliance against him with Ramraaje and Koottub Shaw, in revenge for the invasion; upon which he strengthened himself by treaty with Ummad al Moolk, and they met in the year 966. The daughter of A.D. 1558. the latter was married to the former. The same year Houssein Nizam Shaw detached Mahummud Aftad Neeshaporee and Cheleh Roomi against Reegdonda, a fort built by the Portuguese, on the coast of Malabar. They begged peace, and entered into a treaty not to molest the subjects of Nizam Shaw; who, upon this, ordered his army to retreat. In 967, Nizam Shaw subdued several forts A.D. 1559. belonging to Annee Roy. The allies invaded his territories. He was offered peace on condition of surrendering the fort of Kallean, but refused, and fled from Ahmednuggur, which was besieged by the allies. The city held out, owing to the treachery of Koottub Shaw, who privately conveyed provisions to the garrison, and at length deserted his allies. Houssein Nizam Shaw, assisted by the troops of Ummad al Moolk, cut off supplies from the enemy's camp, in which scarcity of provisions prevailed. They raised the siege on this account, and encamped at Ashtee.

Houssein Nizam Shaw, by the advice of Casim Beg, sent Moolla Einaiut Oolla to ask peace of Ramraaje; who offered to grant it on three conditions: first, that he should cede the fortress of Kallean to Ali Adil Shaw: secondly, that he should put to death Jehaungeer Khan, who commanded the auxiliary troops from Berar, as he had done much injury to his army by his attacks: and thirdly, that Nizam Shaw should submit to pay him a visit, and receive from him

him a betel of encouragement. The sultan, in order to preserve his kingdom, accepted the conditions; and opening the doors of injustice on his friends, sent assassins to the tents of his guest and faithful auxiliary, Jehaungeer Khan. After having thus, at the instigation of an infidel, murdered one of the faithful, and verified the remark, that " There is no confidence in princes," the sultan proceeded to the camp of Ramraaje, who rose on his entering his tents, and kissed his hand. The sultan, from foolish pride, called for a bason and ewer, and washed his hands, as if they had been polluted by the touch of Ramraaje; who, enraged at the affront, said in his own language, " If he was not my guest, he should repent this " insult;" then calling for water, he also washed. Houssein Nizam Shaw, giving the keys of Kallean to Ramraaje, said, " I give them " a present to you :" and Ramraaje immediately sent them to Ali Adil Shaw. Having received a betel from Ramraaje, he took his leave; and, without visiting Ali Adil Shaw, quitted the camp, and returned to his own capital, which he surrounded with a deep ditch, and strengthened by building the citadel of stone.

A. D. 1562.  In the year 970, the sultan had an interview with Koottub Shaw, and their alliance was cemented by intermarriages. They besieged the fort of Kallean, but were obliged to retreat by Ramraaje and Ali Adil Shaw, who gave them a total defeat, and Houssein Nizam Shaw, with difficulty, reached the fort of Ouseh, with the loss of all his artillery and baggage. In his flight he carried the umbrella of royalty over his own head, and, though attended only by a thousand horse, made his way good through six thousand of the enemy. Being remarkably strict in his observance of the stated prayers, one afternoon, when closely pursued, his friends represented the danger of dismounting to pray, but he regarded them not; and the enemy were so struck with his gallantry, that they stopped at some distance to admire it. After prayers, on observing that he had on a girdle interwoven with gold, he recollected that it was unlawful to pray in it, it, therefore casting it off, he repeated his devotions. The enemy agreed, that to succeed against him was impossible, and resolved on giving over their pursuit. The sultan having thrown supplies into Ahmednuggur, retired to the fortress of Joneer. The allies now besieged Ahmednuggur, and the Hindoos of Ramraaje committed every cruelty on the faithful, polluting the mosques, and dishonouring the women. Ali Adil Shaw, vexed at these indignities to religion, but unable to prevent them, advised Ramraaje to raise the siege and pursue Nizam Shaw; who, upon this, retired to the hills, and dispatched a force to lay waste all the country in the enemy's front, so as to distress and retard their march; but this detachment was defeated, and the general slain. At the approach of the rains, the allies returned to the siege of Ahmednuggur. A great rise of the waters drowning near twelve thousand horse, a great number of elephants and footmen, much baggage, and cattle innumerable, Ramraaje retired to his own country.

An alliance was now formed between the three sultans against Ramraaje, whose defeat and death has already been related in the history of the Adil Shawee sovereigns. Houssein Nizam Shaw died, eleven days after his return from this expedition, of a disorder occasioned by excess of venery and drinking. He left behind him four sons and four daughters.

# SULTAN MORTIZA NIZAM SHAW.

AS this prince acceded to the throne in his minority, his mother, Khoonzeh Sultana, became for six years chief manager of affairs. She raised her brothers, Ein al Moolk Taaje Khan and Etibar Khan, to the first rank of nobility. Having appointed Moolla Einaiut Oolla peshwa, she sat daily in court behind a curtain and transacted business. Mortiza Nizam Shaw was engaged in amusements becoming his age, and took no part in the affairs of government.

At this crisis, Ali Adil Shaw led an army against Anicondeh, hoping to reduce to his dominions all the territories of Beejanuggur. Vingtaderee, chief of Bilcondah, upon this applied to Khoonzeh Sultana for assistance, and she with her son led an army against Beejapore; upon which Ali Adil Shaw, giving over his expedition, returned to the defence of his own country. The two powers concluded peace at the representations of holy men, and the next year marched against Tuffal Khan, who had usurped Berar, which they plundered, and returned at the beginning of the rains. On the march Adil Shaw conspired to seize the person of Nizam Shaw; but Khoonzeh Sultana discovering his design, marched suddenly to Ahmednuggur, assisted by the sudden swelling of a river between the camps.

In the year 975, Adil Shaw invaded the country, and taking several places, defeated the Nizam Shawee army, by his general Kummaul

Kummaul Kishwer Khan. Khoonzeh Sultana disgusted all the amras by her partiality to her brethren, who expended the publick treasures on their own pleasures, without attending to the wants of the army. At length, Shaw Jemmal ad Dien Houssein Anjoo, Casim Beg, and others, the sultan's companions, became alarmed at the disordered state of the royal household, and complained to him in private of his mother's conduct. The sultan observed, that the whole ministry were attached to her, how then could he remove her usurped authority. They replied, that with his permission they would bring over the principal amras, and effect a cure for the present evils. Nizam Shaw having given his consent, they, with their friends, repaired to the palace; but as it happened, the queen at this instant having the sultan with her, his childish fears made him suppose the secret betrayed, and, to save himself, he told his mother that certain chiefs had conspired to seize her; upon which she confined the principal conspirator, and the rest escaped.

In the year 977, the sultana marched with her son to oppose the encroachments of Kishwer Khan, the Beejapore general. Mortiza Nizam Shaw, now able to judge for himself, resolved to be free from the usurpation of his mother. Having brought over the principal amras, he sent to her Hubsheh Khan, to inform her that it was his pleasure she should no longer engage in publick affairs, but live retired, like the other princesses. Enraged at this, she summoned her creatures; and, throwing a veil over her face, came from the palace on horseback, armed with a bow, sword, and dagger. She was, however, seized after a short resistance, and her attendants fled. The sultan now took affairs under his own management; and, having levied forces, marched against the fortress of Darwer, and to expel the invader Kishwer Khan.

A.D. 1569.

When the sultan arrived within a short distance of Darwer, a messenger from Kishwer Khan brought him a sealed paper, which, upon

upon opening, was found to contain such infolent expreffions, as enraged him to the higheft pitch. Mounting his horfe, he fwore that he would not difmount till he fhould enter Darwer. When he arrived near, he rode towards the gate; upon which his attendants reprefented, that fortreffes were not to be taken in this manner, and that expofing his perfon was improper. The fultan replied, that by the divine bleffing he would force the gate with his fword, and hew his paffage; that if victory was decreed him, no injury could occur; and that if his death was fixed, it was vain to avoid the danger. The officers, feeing that the royal determination was unalterable, begged that he would put on armour, which was allowed by the prophet. To this he confented, and then proceeded. By this time fhowers of fhot, arrows, and rockets, poured from the fort walls, and killed many perfons, elephants, and horfes. The fultan ftill went on, and efcaped unhurt. At length, the fire from the fort fuddenly ceafed. The fultan was aftonifhed. He fent perfons to enquire the caufe. They entered unoppofed, and found the fort evacuated. An arrow had pierced the heart of Kifhwer Khan, who lay dead on the ground. They cut off his head, and hung it over the battlements; when the fultan offered thankfgivings for his victory. The fultan now invaded Beejapore, in conjunction with Koottub Shaw; againft whom he fuddenly became incenfed by the artifice of Shaw Abou Houffun. Koottub Shaw efcaped, but his camp was plundered. Nizam Shaw concluded a treaty with Ali Adil Shaw, and returned to Ahmednuggur. He appointed Jemmal ad Dien Houffein his prime minifter, and marched againft the fort of Reegdondah, belonging to the Portuguefe; but was obliged to raife the fiege, after a blockade of fome months, as the enemy obtained provifions by fea, and from the treachery of the fultan's own amras, who were bribed by prefents, particularly of wine. The fultan, upon his return from this expedition to Ahmednuggur, difplaced feveral of his chief amras, and conferred the office of vaqueelut on Chungeeze Khan, a nobleman of great abilities, who by his attention reftored the publick affairs. He defeated

feated a propofed alliance between Ali Adil Shaw and Koottub Shaw, and effected one between the former and his mafter, who had an interview on their borders. It was agreed between the fultans, that Ali Adil Shaw fhould conquer as much of the Carnatic as would produce a revenue equal to Berar and Bieder; which countries Nizam Shaw fhould be at liberty to wreft from the hands of Tuffal Khan and Ali Bereed. Koottub Shaw was excluded from any fhare in this treaty. In the year 980, Nizam Shaw began his expedition to Berar; and fucceeded by the gallantry and conduct of Chungeeze Khan, who drove Tuffal Khan from Elichpore, forced him to feek fhelter in the woods, and brought over the inhabitants of the diftricts by his clemency. Tuffal Khan fled from place to place, and wood to wood, for fix months; at the end of which he was forced into a defile, which had no other paffage but what could be blocked up by the fultan's troops, and would have been taken, had not the fultan been ftopped by a religious fuperftition for fome time on his march. A mad devotee, Meer Moufeh Mazinderanee, met the fultan on his march, and conjured him for the love he bore the twelve Imaums, not to move farther till he had given him a large fum of money; and the fultan complied with his requeft, though the minifter entreated him to defer giving the money to the fanatic till the camp was pitched. He would not, and the opportunity of overtaking Tuffal Khan was loft by delaying the march. Tuffal Khan fled to Khandefhe, the fultan of which, at the threats of Nizam Shaw, refufed him protection. He returned into Berar, took refuge in the fort of Pernalleh, and applied for affiftance to the emperor Akber; who fent an ambaffador to Nizam Shaw, commanding him to defift from his invafion of Berar; but no attention was paid to the meffage. Pernalleh was taken, as alfo other fortreffes, with Tuffal Khan and Direa Ummad al Moolk, who were kept prifoners.

A.D. 1572.

Nizam Shaw next marched againft Bieder, when a pretender ftarted up in Berar, affifted by troops from Meeran Mahummud Shaw, and

and was joined by seven thousand of the inhabitants. The sultan's officers entreated him to come in person, and quell the rebellion. He marched with the greatest expedition, and commanded Chungeeze Khan to follow him with the main army. Syed Mortiza, who had gone on in front with a detachment of eight thousand horse, came up with the pretended Ummad al Moolk, obliged him to fly, and his adherents to disperse. Nizam Shaw entered the province of Khandeshe, where he did much damage, even to the neighbourhood of the capital Boorahanpore.

Chungeeze Khan having heard great praises of the fortress of Asere, where Mahummud Shaw had retired with his army, went with two or three thousand horse, by the sultan's permission, to view the country. Mahummud Shaw sent some of his nobility, with seven or eight thousand men, in the hope to intercept and cut him off; but Chungeeze Khan defeated this detachment, and took many chief men prisoners. Nizam Shaw then moved to the vicinity of Asere, from whence he sent out parties, who left not a vestige of population in the surrounding country. At length, Mahummud Shaw purchased the retreat of Nizam Shaw by a present of a large sum of money.

Mirza Ispahanee, who had come to pay the compliments of congratulation on his victories to Nizam Shaw from Ibrahim Koottub Shaw, judging that the attack of Bieder would be renewed, endeavoured to prevent the expedition. He offered Chungeeze Khan a great bribe with this view; but that minister refused it, observing, that he had the treasures of Nizam Shaw at his command, and wanted nothing. He said, it was his wish that, Bieder being reduced, Nizam Shaw, Koottub Shaw, and Adil Shaw, should join in brotherly alliance, and preserve themselves from the attack of the soonnite emperor of Dhely, Akber.

The

The ambaſſador, finding it vain to bribe the miniſter, endeavoured to effect his purpoſe by bringing over to his deſign Saheb Khan, a favourite minion of the ſultan's, who had been roughly treated by Chungeeze Khan. He inſinuated to him, that the miniſter had intentions of aſſuming the royal titles in Berar. Saheb Khan willingly believed the accuſation, and informed the ſultan; who at firſt would not believe it, and told his favourite, that he knew his ſtories to be the effect of malice, for the puniſhment he had received from the miniſter. Saheb Khan however would not give over the attempt, but pretended to weep; and deſired the ſultan, if he would not believe him, to ſend for Mirza Iſpahanee, who was of the ſame city with the miniſter, and hear what he had to ſay. The ſultan did ſo, and his declarations made ſome impreſſions on his mind, but he reſolved to wait for proof of his ſuſpicions. At length, for a trial, he one day ſent for Chungeeze Khan, and ſignified his wiſhes to return to Ahmednuggur, as he was tired of the field. The miniſter obſerved, that as this was a newly conquered province, it was more adviſeable for his majeſty to remain in it five or ſix months, in order to attach the inhabitants to his government; or, in caſe that was not agreeable, to leave him with an army for that purpoſe. Nizam Shaw, upon this anſwer, believed all the accuſers of the miniſter had ſaid, and immediately altered his behaviour towards him. Chungeeze Khan perceiving this, was alarmed, and, under pretence of illneſs, ſtayed ſome days from court. The ſultan, diſpleaſed at this, reſolved to diſpatch him, and ſent his phyſician to him with a poiſoned draught, under the pretence of medicine. Chungeeze Khan at firſt refuſed to take it; but, fortifying his mind, at laſt reſolved on ſacrificing himſelf to loyalty, and drank the poiſon. During his laſt moments he wrote the following addreſs to the ſultan.

" The faithful ſervant Meeruk, the ſun of whoſe age has paſſed
" through ſixty manſions, and was haſtening to the ſeventieth, hav-
" ing

"ing laid the head of submission on the threshold of your majesty, represents, that the draught mixed with the water of life he has knowingly, and with eager desire, drank. Having placed the treasures of duty and loyalty to the sultan, by whose bounty I was cherished, in the casket of my bosom, I shut my eyes from the observance of strangers. As lasting as the grave will be to me, so be the life of your majesty. I hope thus much from the sultan, that, esteeming me both in life and death among the number of loyal subjects, he will act according to the maxims I send written in my own hand; that he will send my body to Kerballa; that he will esteem certain amras, named in the petition, as worthy of distinction, and entertain my foreign servants among his own guards." This address, with some instructions, he committed to the care of Syed Mortiza; and then reclined upon his bed till the next day, when he departed from this borrowed, fading mansion.

Mortiza Nizam Shaw was shortly convinced of the uprightness and sincere attachment of his minister, whose death he regretted with unfeigned sorrow; and, upon his return to Ahmednuggur, resolved on retiring from the world. He called before him the principal inhabitants of Ahmednuggur, and said to them, "Know ye, that I have not abilities for empire, for I find not in myself the capacity of distinguishing justice from injustice; so that I frequently am guilty of oppression under the cloak of justice; and when the truth becomes known unto me, I am disgusted at my own dominion. Therefore I now take you to witness, and shall call upon you to testify at the day of resurrection, that I have appointed Cauzi Beg my vaqueel muttulluk, who is of the descendants of the prophet; that he may do unto every one agreeably to law and justice; and, not in the least giving a preference to the strong over the weak, may have no regard to private claims. Should any person take even the needle of a weak old woman, and it shall be questioned me concerning it at the day of judgment, that such oppres-
"sion

" fion occurred in my reign, and I was unmindful of it, I will make
" anfwer, that I had no bufinefs in fuch affairs, which depended on
" Cauzi Beg, the defcendant of the prophet." Then addreffing
himfelf to that minifter, he faid, " Affairs are now in your hands; if
" thou canft not direct them alone, let Ameer al Moolk, Mirza
" Mahummud Nukki, and Cafim Beg, be your partners in publick
" affairs; while I, who am fearful and apprehenfive of the anger
" and punifhment of the Almighty, and afhamed of my behaviour
" in the affair of Chungeeze Khan, feek retirement, and employ
" my days in repentance and prayer." The fultan, after this, retired
to an apartment in the palace of Ahmednuggur, called Bagdad,
where no one, male or female, was admitted to his prefence, but
Saheb Khan.

In the year 984, the emperor Akber advancing to the frontiers of A. D. 1576.
Dekkan to hunt, the fultan moved with a few troops, but in a covered litter, to obferve his motions, and be in readinefs to defend his
dominions. He would have marched to attack the emperor, had
he not been prevented by the entreaties of his nobility. At their
requeft he remained on his borders, till Akber returned to his own
dominions, when he retired again to his privacy in Ahmednuggur.
In the rains the fultan went to Dowlutabad, and vifited the tombs of
the faints. Being feized with a religious enthufiafm, he one day,
unknown even to Saheb Khan, withdrew from his apartment, and
was going alone on foot towards the tomb of Imaum Reza, when he
was known by a countryman, who gave information to the minifters.
It was with much entreaty that they could prevail upon him to return.
He haftened back to Ahmednuggur, and took up his quarters in the
garden of Hefht Behifht, or the eighth paradife.

At this time, his favourite, Saheb Khan, committed great excefies,
with his adherents, about three thoufand fcoundrel Dekkanees, frequently forcing children from their parents, for the worft of purpofes.

He seized the daughter of Meer Mhadie, who was killed in defending the honour of his family. These injuries gave great disgust, but the regent was afraid of the favourite's influence with the sultan. At length, Saheb Khan became so insolent, as to order a nobleman to change his name, because it happened to be the same as his own, and, upon his not consenting, resolved to destroy him, but was prevented by Sullabut Khan's informing the sultan of his behaviour. Saheb Khan, enraged, fled; but the sultan, distressed at the loss of his favourite, pursued him, and overtaking him at Ahmedabad, persuaded him to return by agreeing to his unreasonable requests of displacing Sullabut Khan, and taking for him the city of Ahmedabad from Ali Bereed, who, upon his besieging it, required and received assistance from Ali Adil Shaw.

At this time, Boorahan Shaw, the sultan's brother, escaped from prison, and raised a rebellion; which obliged the sultan to return suddenly to Ahmednuggur, and recall Sullabut Khan to his presence. Saheb Khan, disgusted at this, fled a second time. Boorahan Shaw was defeated and obliged to fly to Beejapore. The sultan endeavoured again to obtain Saheb Khan's return, but he was put to death by the amras, weary of his insolence, who persuaded Nizam Shaw, that he was killed in opposing the troops sent to conduct him to the presence. Upon his death, Sullabut Khan became minister without a rival, and continued in power for some years, to the satisfaction of the publick. The country of Mheerut was never so well governed as by him, since the reign of sultan Mhamood Bhamenee.

A. D. 1580.   In the year 988, Ali Adil Shaw dying, was succeeded by his brother Ibrahim, then only in his ninth year. Sullabut Khan, judging his minority favourable to conquest, persuaded Mortiza Nizam Shaw to invade his dominions. An army was accordingly sent, under Behzaad al Moolk, who was defeated, with the loss of all his elephants.

phants. The event of this war has been already related, in the hiftory of the Adil Shawee kings.

In the year 992, the fultan fent a fplendid embaffy to Beejapore, A.D. 1584. to demand in marriage the fifter of Ibrahim Adil Shaw for his fon Meeraun Houffein; and his requeft being complied with, the princefs was brought to Ahmednuggur in great pomp. Several nobles forming a combination to difplace the regent, Sullabut Khan, he perfuaded the fultan to take up his refidence in the citadel, and marched againft the rebels, who were defeated. Shortly after this, a difcontented faction having brought Boorahan Shaw, the fultan's brother, in the difguife of a religious to Ahmednuggur, confpired to fet him on the throne; but on the very day intended for the attempt, Sullabut Khan difcovered the plot. Boorahan Shaw made his efcape, and fled to the Kokun; but, not thinking himfelf fecure in that country, fought an afylum with the emperor Akber, from whom he obtained a force to invade Dekkan, but without fuccefs.

Fatteh Shaw, a dancer, who had fucceeded Saheb Khan in the fultan's affections, began to make an ill ufe of his power, by obtaining large grants of land, and gifts of the royal jewels, which were lavifhly beftowed upon him by his mafter. At length he afked for two rofaries, which had been brought into the treafury from the plunder of Ramraaje, compofed of moft valuable rubies, emeralds, and pearls. The fultan commanded them to be given to him; but Sullabut Khan, unwilling that fuch ineftimable curiofities fhould be loft to the royal family, fubftituted two ftrings of mock jewels in their place. After fome time, Fatteh Shaw, difcovering the impofition, complained to the fultan; who being enraged, commanded the regent to lay out in an apartment all his jewels for him to examine. Sullabut Khan, having concealed the moft precious, placed the reft as he was ordered; but the fultan miffing them, was fo angry, that he threw all before him into a large fire, and withdrew paffionately to his chamber. On his departure the regent haftened to fave them from the flames, and only the pearls had received any damage. From this time the fultan was confidered and treated as a madman.

The fultan having conceived that his fon Meeraun Houffein defigned to dethrone him, attempted to put him to death; but Sullabut Khan watched the fafety of the young prince. At this time, Ibrahim Adil Shaw demanded that the nuptials of his fifter fhould be celebrated with the fultan's fon, or the princefs be fent back to Beejapore; but Sullabut Khan refufed compliance with either demand, unlefs he would deliver up the fortrefs of Sholapore to Nizam Shaw. Ibrahim Adil Shaw, enraged at this, laid fiege to the fort of Oufeh. Nizam Shaw, difpleafed at the conduct of his minifter, upbraided him with treachery, and declared himfelf weary of his controul; on which the regent, to fhew his loyalty, begged the fultan to appoint any place for his confinement, and he would voluntarily put chains on his own feet and repair to it. Nizam Shaw named the fort of Dunda Raajepore, and Sullabut Khan, in fpite of the remonftrances of his friends and numerous dependants, immediately refigned himfelf to the fultan's guards, and was carried to his prifon.

Mortiza Nizam Shaw, on the imprifonment of Sullabut Khan, conferred the regency on Cafim Beg, and the vizarut on Mirza Mahummud, commanding them to conclude peace with Ibrahim Adil Shaw, which they did; and the nuptials of his fifter with the prince Houffein were celebrated with great pomp and feftivity. Not long after this, the fultan, jealous of his fon's fidelity, in a fit of madnefs refolved to deftroy him. He told his minifters that he longed for the company of his fon, and they, delighted at his returning kindnefs, fent the young prince into the fort to him. The fultan pretended great affection, and gave him a chamber near his own; but the next morning while the youth was fleeping, he fet fire to his bed clothes, and faftened the door upon him. The prince, awakened by by the smoke, and freeing himself from the clothes, hastened to the door. Finding it locked, he cried out for help, but was almost suffocated with smoke, when he was released by his father's favourite, Fatteh Shaw, and carried to the ministers, who conveyed him secretly to Dowlutabad. The sultan, after some time, going to the apartment to examine the ashes for the bones of his intended victim, and not finding them, was enraged. Fatteh Shaw told him the prince had been burned to ashes; but he would not believe him, and demanded him from the favourite, whom he suspected of saving him from the fire. At length, Fatteh Shaw disclosing the truth, the sultan sent for the ministers, and ordered them to be confined, appointing others; but they also refusing to kill his son, he, after nine days, displaced them, and gave the regency to Mirza Khan.

Mirza Khan seeing the distracted state of the sultan's intellects, pretended acquiescence with his commands, and courted the favour of Fatteh Shaw and his dependants by frequent gifts; but wrote privately to Beejapore, that as the sultan was mad and wanted to murder his son, if a detachment was sent to the borders, he would have a pretence to raise troops, and espouse the cause of the young prince. Dillawer Khan, regent of Beejapore, complied with his request; and Mirza Khan asked the sultan what steps he should take against the enemy. Nizam Shaw directed the regent to pursue what measures he might think proper; and Mirza Khan collecting the troops, they marched from Ahmednuggur, and encamped near the town of Rannowrd, where they halted by his orders. The sultan, surprized at their not moving onwards, sent the writer of this history to enquire the cause. As the regent knew my loyalty to be firm, he guessed, that having penetrated his treasonable designs, I would make them known to the sultan. He therefore bribed Fatteh Shaw to obtain the sultan's orders for him to repair to camp, and hasten the march of the army. I was in camp when he arrived, and had found out the real intention of the minister, who had given orders to prevent my return;
but

but having timely notice, I made my efcape in the night. On my arrival in the city, I related what I had feen and heard to Fatteh Shaw, who would not believe me. I obferved, that I had no intereft or hatred to gratify, that I fhould falfely accufe the minifter, and that the truth of my account would quickly appear. While we were talking, fome fpies brought intelligence, that Mirza Khan had marched to Dowlutabad, in order to bring the prince Meeraun Houflein, and feat him on the throne. The fultan now afked my advice how to avert the threatened ftorm. I replied, that there were two meafures which promifed fuccefs. Firft, that the fultan fhould leave his retirement, and march from the city at the head of his guards, when, probably, moft of the nobility would defert the regent, and join him. He replied, that he was too ill to mount a horfe. I then recommended that he fhould fend for Sullabut Khan from confinement, and put him at the head of affairs, as he was beloved and refpected by all ranks, who would flock to his ftandard; that his majefty fhould alfo fet out in a litter to meet him, as far as the fort of Khiber. The fultan approving of this advice, inftantly fent off exprefs orders to releafe Sullabut Khan, and prepared to move himfelf; when the cowardly Fatteh Shaw fell at his feet, and weeping, faid, that fhould his majefty quit the palace, the guards would immediately feize and fend him prifoner to the prince, in order to make their court to a new fovereign. The fultan, alarmed at this remark, altered his intention, and refolved to wait in the palace for the arrival of Sullabut Khan. The troops feeing the fultan's fears, now deferted in crowds to Dowlutabad; and Mirza Khan advanced from thence with the prince to the capital by forced marches, in order to prevent the arrival of Sullabut Khan. I had the guard of the palace, and wifhed to defend it; but being deferted by my people, and no one being left but the fultan, Fatteh Shaw, and a very few domeftic attendants, oppofition was vain. At length, the prince and Mirza Khan arrived, and entering the palace with forty armed men, put to death whomfoever they found. The prince fortunately knew me, and

and reflecting that we had been fchoolfellows, ordered my life to be fpared. Having reached the prefence of his father, the prince behaved to him, both in word and action, with every poffible infult and abufe. Nizam Shaw was filent, and only looked at him with contempt; till the prince, putting his naked fabre acrofs his breaft, faid, " I will put you to death." Nizam Shaw then breathing a deep figh, exclaimed, " O thou accurfed of God, it would be better " for thee to let thy father be his few remaining days thy gueft, and " treat him with refpect." The prince, relenting for a moment at this expreffion, ftopped his hand, and withdrew from his father's apartment. Not having patience, however, to wait for his death, though he was then in a mortal illnefs, he commanded him to be put into a warm bathing room, and fhutting faft the doors and windows to exclude all air, lighted a great fire under the bath, fo that the fultan was fpeedily fuffocated by the fteam and heat. This parricide was perpetrated in the year 996. The deceafed fultan was buried in A. D. 1587. great pomp, in the garden Rozeh; but his bones were afterwards taken up and carried to Kerballa, where they were depofited near thofe of his father and grandfather.

### VERSE.

Alas, that there is no ftability in fortune! for endlefs is the circle of her revolution. Expect not thou to be free from the encroachments of time, for there is quarter to no one from his cruel fword.

SULTAN

# SULTAN

# MEERAUN HOUSSEIN NIZAM SHAW.

MEERAUN, on his acceſſion to the throne of Ahmednuggur, being of an impetuous and cruel diſpoſition, began his reign by tyranny and oppreſſion. He appointed Mirza Khan prime miniſter, but paid little regard to his advice; diſappointing him of the hopes he had entertained of making a pageant of the prince, and keeping the real power in his own hands. Meeraun having promoted ſeveral young perſons of his own age to high rank, made them his companions in his pleaſures and exceſſes. It was frequently his cuſtom, in fits of intoxication, to ride through the city with his drunken aſſociates, and put perſons to death, though not guilty of any crime. It being reported to him, that Mirza Khan had privately brought from the fort of Sutteeza, Shaw Caſim, brother to Mortiza Nizam Shaw, and concealed him in his houſe, with a view to raiſe a rebellion in his favour, the ſultan was alarmed, and confined the miniſter. The next day, however, finding the accuſation falſe, he reſtored him to his employments, and gave him his full confidence; and Mirza Khan, to prevent future ſuſpicion, adviſed the ſultan to put to death the males of the royal family. Meeraun approved the meaſure, and fifteen princes were murdered in one day. Not long after this event, the power of Mirza Khan becoming irkſome to the ſultan's companions, they again accuſed him of treachery, and Meeraun believing them, in his drunken hours would exclaim at one time, that he would behead him with his own hand;

and

and at another, that he would have him trod to death by elephants. These declarations being carried to Mirza Khan, he at length resolved to secure his own safety by deposing the sultan; who, in his turn, tried every means to get the minister into his power. On the tenth of Jemmaud al Awul, 997, he repaired to the house of his favourite, Ankufs Khan, and sent for Mirza Khan to come and partake of a banquet, intending to have him assassinated; but the minister, being on his guard, excused himself under pretence of illness, sending his friend Agga Meer to make his apology. Agga Meer reached the house of Ankufs Khan just as the sultan had dined; but the master of the house had waited, and sat down to eat with him. When Agga Meer had eaten, he suddenly pretended violent pains, declared that he was poisoned, and left the house. Mirza Khan soon after sent a message, that the agga was dying, and entreated to see him. The sultan immediately repaired, with a few attendants, to the fort, where he was seized by the minister, and confined. Mirza Khan then sent off Meer Tahir Neeshaporee to bring the two sons of Boorahan Nizam Shaw from the fort of Bhaughur, that he might chuse one of them to place on the throne, concealing the imprisonment of the sultan till their arrival.

A.D. 1538.

On the third day, Meer Tahir returned with the princes; and the minister, summoning several of the principal nobility into the fort, declared to them the deposal of Houssein, and accession of Ismaeel Nizam Shaw, then only in his twelfth year. While the assembly was engaged in saluting the new sultan, a great tumult was heard at the gates of the fort, where Jemmal Khan, a munsubdar, with several other officers and a mob of soldiers, had assembled, demanding to see sultan Meeraun Houssein, their lawful sovereign. Mirza Khan sent them word, that Meeraun having no abilities to govern, he had deposed him, and inaugurated sultan Ismaeel, who should appear and receive their homage. Jemmal Khan became more clamorous, and sent persons to proclaim through the city, that

C c c the

the minifter, aided by his foreign mercenaries, having depofed their fovereign, had feated another prince on the throne; and if he was allowed in this manner to make kings, and act uncontrouled, the native nobles and inhabitants of the country would foon become flaves to foreign adventurers. The Dekkan troops and people, inflamed by this report, fled to arms, and in a fhort time about five thoufand horfe and foot, with a numerous mob, flocked to Jemmal Khan. They were alfo joined by all the Ethiopian troops.

Mirza Khan thinking to quell the tumult by the death of fultan Houffein, commanded his head to be ftruck off; which being done, it was ftuck upon a pole planted on a baftion of the citadel. At the fame time a perfon cried out to the multitude below, that, as they muft now be convinced of the death of the fultan, if they would retire quietly to their habitations, they fhould be rewarded by the favour of Ifmaeel Shaw, now their fovereign. Several of the principal amras were for retiring; but Jemmal Khan cried out, If Houffein was murdered, they ought to revenge his death on the foreigners, take into their own hands the adminiftration of fultan Ifmaeel, and not fuffer the country to be governed by ftrangers. Upon this, all refolved to ftorm the fort; and having heaped piles of wood and ftraw to the gates, fet them on fire. About funfet the gates were burned; but the quantity of hot afhes yet glowing prevented any one paffing in or out, till midnight, when Mirza Khan and his friends rufhed from the citadel, and tried to make their efcape from the city. Numbers were flain in the attempt by the mob; but Mirza Khan made his flight good towards the fort of Khiber. The Dekkanees, Ethiopians, and populace, having entered the fort, put to death every foreigner they found within, who amounted to nearly three hundred, and among them were feveral perfons of high rank and eminent characters. Their bodies were dragged out to the open plain, and orders given for them to lie unburied. Not contented with the paft flaughter, Jemmal Khan commanded his adherents to

murder

murder the foreigners of every rank and occupation in the city, and to plunder and burn their dwellings. The foldiers and their followers having extended the hand of rapine from the fleeve of cruelty, put to death indifcriminately the noble, the rich, the mafter and the fervant, the merchant, the pilgrim, and the travelling ftranger. Their houfes were fet on fire, and the heads of thofe lately exalted to the fkies, were brought low, and trampled in the duft. Virgins, who from modefty concealed their faces from the fun and moon, were dragged by the hair into the affemblies of the drunken. On the fourth day, Mirza Khan, who had been feized near Khiber, was brought to Jemmal Khan, and being firft carried through the city on an afs, his body was cut into pieces, which were affixed on different buildings. Several of his friends, taken with him, were alfo put to death; and their bodies being rammed into cannons, were blown into the air. In the fpace of feven days nearly a thoufand foreigners were murdered. Some few efcaped under the protection of Dekkanee and Ethiopian officers, their intimates and friends. The reign of Meeraun Houffein was only two months and three days. Among thofe princes recorded in hiftory as murderers of their fathers, we find none whofe reigns extended beyond one year: and a poet obferves, " Royalty befits not the deftroyer of a parent, nor will the " reign of fuch a wretch be long."

# SULTAN ISMAEEL NIZAM SHAW.

It has been already mentioned, in the hiftory of Mortiza Nizam Shaw, that Boorahan Shaw, his brother, having been defeated in an attempt to dethrone him, fled for protection to the court of the emperor Akber. On his departure he left behind him two fons, named Ibrahim and Ifmaeel, who were kept confined in the fortrefs of Lahaghur. The younger being raifed to the throne on the death of Meeraun Houffein Shaw, took the title of Ifmaeel Nizam Shaw, and was acknowledged by the victorious minifter, Jemmal Khan.

Jemmal Khan, being of the fect of Mhaudee, perfuaded the fultan to embrace his tenets, and commit the power of government into the hands of his followers. In the beginning of his adminiftration he obliged the few foreigners who had efcaped the maffacre in the laft reign, to leave Ahmednuggur, after feizing their effects, and they embraced the fervice of the fultan of Beejapore. Among them was the writer of this hiftory, who was exalted in the fervice of Ibrahim Adil Shaw.

Intelligence of the commotions of Ahmednuggur having reached the emperor Akber, he recalled Boorahan Shaw from his jaghire, and offered him a force to regain the throne of his anceftors, now his right, but ufurped by his own fon and a defpotic minifter. Boorahan Shaw

Shaw reprefented, that fhould he accept the aid of Mogul troops, the people of Dekkan would be alarmed, and object to his authority; but that if his majefty would allow him to repair to the borders of the country with his own dependants, he would try to draw his fubjects to allegiance by gentlenefs and conciliation. Akber approving his propofal permitted him to depart for Dekkan, and allotted the frontier diftrict of Handea for his fupport till he fhould regain his dominions; at the fame time commanding raja Alee Khan, prince of Khandefhe, to afford him affiftance to his utmoft ability. Boorahan Shaw having received offers of allegiance from many of the nobility, marched againft his fon, but was defeated. However, in a fhort time after this, he renewed his attempts; and, being joined by a great majority of the chiefs and people, attacked Jemmal Khan, who was killed in the action. Ifmaeel was taken prifoner, and confined by his father, who afcended in his room the throne of Ahmednuggur.

SULTAN

# SULTAN

# BOORAHAN SHAW.

BOORAHAN Shaw, during the reign of his brother Mortiza Nizam Shaw, was confined to the fort of Lahaghur, but had a large jaghire allowed him for his fupport, fo that he paffed his days with fatisfaction. When Saheb Khan behaved tyrannically, and the nobles were difgufted at Mortiza Shaw, who had left the capital to induce his favourite to return, a party of them befought Boorahan Shaw to rebel, on pretence that his brother was mad, and unfit to govern. Allured by promifes of fupport, he gained over the governor of the fort, and appeared in arms at the head of fix thoufand horfe, with which force he moved towards the capital. Mortiza Nizam Shaw, upon intelligence of this rebellion, haftened from Bieder to Ahmednuggur. Paffing through the ftreets to the palace, he ftopped his elephant at the fhop of an apothecary, and afked if he had any medicine that would cure madnefs, faying, that he did not know who required it moft, himfelf, who wifhed to live the life of a reclufe and yet rule a kingdom, or his brother, who, with the enjoyment of eafe, was plunging himfelf into publick cares. The apothecary replied, that his brother was the madman who could ungratefully offend fo kind a protector, and would not profper in his treafon. The next day Boorahan Shaw was defeated, and fled to Beejapore. Two years afterwards he made another attempt, with fimilar fuccefs, and fought protection with the emperor Akber, with
whom

whom he continued till the acceffion of his fon to the throne, which he difpoffeffed him of, as above related.

Boorahan Shaw was advanced in years when he afcended the throne; but, notwithftanding his age, gave himfelf up to pleafures unbecoming his dignity. His reign was marked by an unfuccefsful war with Beejapore, and a difgraceful defeat from the Portuguefe, who had feized the fea coafts of his dominions. He died in the year 1003, four years and fome months after his acceffion. He was A.D. 1594. fucceeded by his fon Ibrahim Shaw, who, after a reign of only four months, was flain in action againft the fultan of Beejapore.

On the death of Ibrahim Shaw, feveral factions arofe in Ahmednuggur, each fetting up a nominal fovereign. Mean Munjoo, who poffeffed the city, and acknowledged the title of Bahadur Shaw, infant fon to the late fultan, being befieged by his competitors, invited Moraud, fon of the emperor Akber, then governor of Guzarat, to his affiftance, for which he offered to become tributary to the Mogul power. Sultan Moraud embraced the propofal, and in the year 1004 arrived before Ahmednuggur with a confiderable army. A.D. 1595. Mean Munjoo by this time, having overcome his rivals, repented of his offers, and prepared to oppofe the fultan. Having committed the city to the charge of Nuffeer Khan his deputy, and the care of Chaund Beebee, great aunt to fultan Bahadur, he departed to raife levies and implore the affiftance of Koottub Shaw and Adil Shaw. Sultan Moraud befieged Ahmednuggur, which was gallantly defended. Breaches were made, but immediately repaired by the heroic conduct of Chaund Beebee; who, covering herfelf with a veil, headed the troops. At length, fupplies growing fcarce in the camp, and the allies of Beejapore and Golconda approaching, fultan Moraud thought proper to accept of fome offers of tribute from Chaund Beebee, and raife the fiege. Some money was paid, and the diftricts in Berar belonging to the Nizam Shawee government were ceded to the Moguls.

On the retreat of fultan Moraud, Chaund Beebee requefted the affiftance of Ibrahim Adil Shaw to reprefs the infolence of the Nizam Shawee nobles, and eftablifh the authority of the fovereign. Soheil Khan, a eunuch, celebrated for his valour, wifdom and juftice, was fent to her aid with eight thoufand horfe, and ftrict injunctions to pay implicit obedience to her orders. On his arrival, the refractory became fubmiffive. Affairs being fettled at Ahmednuggur, the auxiliaries departed; but intelligence arriving that the Dhely forces had taken poffeffion of fome diftricts not ceded by the late treaty to the emperor, Soheil Khan halted, and fent for frefh inftructions from Beejapore. Ibrahim Adil Shaw commanded him to oppofe the encroachments of the imperialifts, and affift Chaund Beebee. Soheil Khan being joined by her troops, and a force from the fultan of Golconda, marched towards Berar. The khankhanaun who was encamped at Jaulneh, hearing of the advance of the Dekkanees, retreated to the head quarters of the prince at Shawpore, from whence, having collected an army of twenty thoufand horfe, he advanced to meet the enemy on the banks of the Gung. A fevere action took place, in which the Dekkanees were defeated. Some time after this, the prince Moraud died of exceffive drinking, and Akber appointed his fon fultan Daniaul governor of Dekkan, with orders to reduce Ahmednuggur, while he himfelf was befieging the fortrefs of Afeerghur in the province of Khandefhe. At this juncture, the Dekkanees put to death the heroic Chaund Beebee, and confined the fultan Bahadur Nizam Shaw; not long after which Ahmednuggur was taken by the Moguls, and the captive fovereign fent to perpetual imprifonment in the fortrefs of Gualior.

On the fall of Ahmednuggur, Mallek Umber, an Abyffinian, who had rifen from the condition of a flave to great influence and
command,

command, and Rajoo Minnaun, a Dekkanee chief, divided the remaining territories between them. The former poffeffed from the Telingana frontier to within eight miles of Ahmednuggur and four of Dowlutabad; the latter, northward from that fortrefs to the borders of Guzarat, and fouthward to within twelve miles of Ahmednuggur, leaving to a nominal fultan, Mortiza 2$^{d.}$ whom they placed on the throne on the capture of Bahadur Nizam Shaw, only the fortrefs of Oufeh with a few villages for his fupport. As each of thefe chiefs coveted the territories of the other, there was conftant difagreement between them. In the year 1012 Mallek Umber, by the affiftance of the Mogul arms, defeated Rajoo, and, taking him prifoner, feized his country. At this period feveral commotions happening in the Dhely government, owing to the rebellion of fultan Seleem, the death of Akber, and revolt of fultan Khoferroo, fucceffively, Umber had leifure to regulate his county, levy great armies, and even dared to feize feveral of the imperial diftricts. When the authority of Jehaungeer was eftablifhed, he fent frequent armies to Dekkan; but Umber was not to be fubdued, and, though fometimes defeated, continued to oppofe the royal ftrength. At length he gave up the places taken from the Moguls to the prince Shaw Jehaun, to whofe intereft he became attached, and continued loyal. After this he remained unmolefted by the Dhely government, and conducted his affairs with much glory, often obliging the fultans of Golconda and Beejapore to pay him contributions. He died in the year 1035, in his eightieth year, and was buried in Dowlutabad, under a fplendid dome which he had erected: and fuch is the efteem in which his character has been held, that notwithftanding the various changes of property, the lands dedicated to the fupport of the attendants of his tomb are yet left unconfifcated, for that purpofe. He was the firft general, politician, and financier of his age, and his country was the beft cultivated, and his fubjects the happieft, of any in Dekkan. He founded Ghurkeh, five cofs from Dowlutabad, now called Aurungabad, and ornamented it with a magnificent palace, gardens, and noble pieces

A.D. 1603.

A.D. 1626.

D d d   of

of water lined with ſtone, which yet remain. His charities and juſtice are yet celebrated; and he was alſo eminent for his piety.

Futteh Khan, the ſon of Umber Hubſhee, ſucceeded to his authority; but Mortiza Nizam Shaw 2$^{d.}$ being weary of his controul, took him priſoner by treachery, and confined him in the fort of Chumber, or Khiber. Having made his eſcape, he rebelled, but was again taken, and confined in Dowlutabad. In time he was releaſed, and appointed generaliſſimo by the influence of his ſiſter, mother to Nizam Shaw. He ſhortly, to prevent another removal from office, confined the ſultan under pretence of inſanity, and put to death twenty five of the principal nobility in one day, writing to Shaw Jehaun, that he had thus acted, to prevent them from rebelling againſt him. The emperor in reply commended his attachment, and ordered him to put the captive prince to death; which he did, and placed his ſon Houſſein, an infant of ten years, on the throne; but Shaw Jehaun demanding the royal jewels, treaſures, and elephants, Futteh Khan delayed to obey. Upon this, an army was ſent againſt him; but he averted the wrath of the emperor, by offering a preſent to the amount of eight lacks of rupees, and agreed to pay tribute; on which he was allowed to keep what territory yet remained to the Nizam Shawee ſovereignty. Adil Shaw preparing to wreſt from him Dowlutabad, he offered it to Shaw Jehaun, ſaying, that his father had commanded him, rather to ſweep the courts of the Timur princes, than accept the higheſt office in that of Beejapore. The emperor ſent his general, Mahabut Khan, to receive the fort; but Futteh Khan, on his arrival before it, repented of his ſubmiſſion, and held out till diſtreſs for proviſions forced him to ſurrender. The fall of this place put a final period to the dynaſty of Nizam Shaw, which had ſwayed the ſceptre for one hundred and fifty years. Houſſein Nizam Shaw was confined for life in Gualior, but Futteh Khan was received into favour, and had all his property given up to him. He was upon the point of being promoted to a high rank of nobility,

when

when he became infane, from the effects of an old wound in his head; upon which the emperor allowed him to retire to Lahore, on a penfion of two lacks of rupees, which he enjoyed till his death, many years afterwards, in that city. His younger brother, Chungeeze Khan, had before accepted the imperial fervice, and was appointed an ameer of two thoufand, with the title of Munfoor Khan. Many of his relations and dependants alfo were promoted. From this period the Nizam Shawee kingdom funk into a province of the Mogul empire.

**END OF THE NIZAM SHAWEE DYNASTY.**

# HISTORY

OF

## THE SULTANS OF GOLCONDA,

OR

KOOTTUB SHAWEE DYNASTY.

# SULTAN

## KOOLLI KOOTTUB SHAW.

THIS prince, the founder of the fovereignty of Golconda, was originally a Turkifh adventurer, who came to try his fortune in Dekkan, and embraced the fervice of Mahummud Shaw Bhamenee. By degrees he was promoted to high rank; and in the reign of Mhamood Shaw obtained the title of Koottub al Moolk, and the territory of Golconda, part of Telingana, in jaghire. On the decline of the Bhamenee authority, when Adil Khan and others affumed royalty, Koottub al Moolk alfo, in the year 918, ftiled himfelf A.D. 1512. fultan of Telingana, under the title of Koottub Shaw. He was a chief of great abilities, and reigned thirty nine years; at the end of which he was affaffinated by a Turkifh flave, fuppofed to be bribed by his fon and fucceffor,

## JUMSHEED KOOTTUB SHAW.

He reigned feven years and fome months, and was fucceeded by his brother.

SULTAN

# SULTAN

# IBRAHIM KOOTTUB SHAW.

IBRAHIM Shaw was a wife and politic prince, but arbitrary and severe; punishing flight faults with death. He was fond of the pleasures of the table, but neglected not business for luxury. He so governed the country of Telingana, remarkable for the numbers of its thieves and banditti, that merchants and travellers could journey night and day, without going in caravans, in perfect security. In his reign the sovereignty of Koottub Shaw acquired weight and respect, from the able characters whom he encouraged at his court. No wars of any consequence occurred in his time. He died in the year
A.D. 1581. 989, after a prosperous reign of thirty two years.

## SULTAN MAHUMMUD KOOLLI KOOTTUB SHAW.

THIS prince, on the death of his father, afcended the throne of Golconda, in his twelfth year. In the beginning of his reign he was engaged in war with Adil Shaw, with whom he concluded peace in the year 995, giving him his fifter in marriage. The air of Golconda not agreeing with his conftitution, he founded a city at about eight miles diftance, which he called Bhaugnuggur, after his miftrefs Bhaug, a celebrated courtezan; but being afterwards afhamed of his amour, he changed it to Hyderabad. He entrufted his brothers with high offices, making them his friends and companions; and they in return were loyal and affectionate. Shaw Abbas, emperor of Perfia, courted his alliance, by afking his daughter in marriage for one of his fons; and Mahummud, efteeming connection with fo auguft a monarch as an honour, complied with the requeft.

A. D. 1586.

# SULTAN MAHUMMUD KOOTTUB SHAW.

MAHUMMUD Koolli, leaving no fon, was fucceeded by his brother Mahummud, who was fucceeded by Abdoolla Koottub Shaw. Abdoolla reigned many years under the protection of the emperor Shaw Jehaun, to whom he acknowledged himfelf tributary, and paid an annual fum; but in the year 1066 he difpleafed that monarch, and brought upon himfelf much trouble and diftrefs. The caufe of offence was this: Meer Mahummud Saad, prime minifter to Abdoolla Shaw, having acquired great wealth and power, became fufpected of difloyal intentions towards his fovereign, who wifhed to difplace him. Meer Mahummud, to avoid the difgrace of removal, and the probable confifcation of his treafures, offered his fervices to the prince Aurungzebe, then governor of the imperial territories in Dekkan. The prince recommended him to his father Shaw Jehaun, who immediately honoured him with the rank of five thoufand, his fon Mahummud Ameen with that of two, and commanded Abdoolla Koottub Shaw to permit them to repair with their effects to court. Koottub Shaw difobeyed the mandate, and confining Mahummud Ameen, then at Hyderabad, feized part of his wealth. Aurungzebe, enraged at this conduct, marched to Hyderabad, which he took and plundered. Koottub Shaw was obliged to purchafe pardon by a contribution of a \*corore of rupees, and the gift of his daughter in marriage to the fon of his enemy, the prince fultan Mahummud.

A. D. 1655.

\* One million fterling.

Mahummud. From this time Abdoolla Shaw, during the remainder of his life, was in fact a vassal of the empire. He died in the early part of the reign of Aurungzebe, and was succeeded by his son in law,

## ABOU HOUSSUN,

Who, after some years, was taken prisoner by the emperor Aulumgeer, and confined for life in the citadel of Dowlutabad. Golconda was then reduced to a province of the empire of Hindooftan.

Besides the sovereignties of Nizam Shawee, Adil Shawee, and Koottub Shawee, founded on the ruins of the Bhamenee princes of Dekkan, there were two others, composed of parts of their once extensive dominions. One was founded by Ameer Bereed, prime minister, or rather, confiner of the two last Bhamenee sultans, and called from him, Bereed Shawee. His dominions were small, consisting only of the capital of Bieder, and a few districts round that city; nor did the honours of royalty long remain in his family, his territories being wrested from his grandson by the other Dekkan princes, and the kingdom of Bieder destroyed.

The other sovereignty was stiled Ummad Shawee, and consisted of the southern part of Berar. It was so called from the founder, Ummad al Moolk, a chief of the Bhamenee sultans. This monarchy lasted through four generations. The last prince, Boorahan Ummad Shaw, was only nominal sovereign, the power being usurped by his minister Tuffal Khan. He was reduced by Mortiza Nizam Shaw, who added Berar to his own dominions in the year 982. A.D. 1574. With the dominions of Ahmednuggur, Berar also fell into the hands of the Mogul emperors.

END OF THE KOOTTUB SHAWEE DYNASTY.

www.ingramcontent.com/pod-product-compliance
Lightning Source LLC
Chambersburg PA
CBHW020545300426
44111CB00008B/804